GRAHAM GREENE

GRAHAM GREENE
Man of Paradox

Edited by A. F. Cassis
Foreword by Peter Wolfe

A Campion Book

Loyola University Press
Chicago

Loyola University Press
3441 North Ashland Avenue
Chicago, Illinois 60657

Cover and book design by Tammi Longsjo.
Cover photograph of Graham Greene from Archive Photos, New York.

Library of Congress Cataloging-in-Publication Data
Graham Greene: Man of paradox/edited by A. F. Cassis;
 foreword by Peter Wolfe.
    p.   cm.
Includes bibliographical references and index.
ISBN 0-8294-0781-2 (hardcover) ISBN 0-8294-0770-7 (paperback)
1. Graham Greene, 1904–1991—Interviews.   2. Novelists, English—20th
century—Interviews.   3. Fiction—Authorship.   I. Cassis, A. F.
PR6013.R44Z633462   1994
823' . 912—dc20   94-16131
                                                        CIP

To Hilda and the girls.

Contents

Foreword

Although Graham Greene disliked interviews, he comes forth, in the works reprinted by A. F. Cassis, as a conversationalist and raconteur of wit, control, and polish. These works, spanning some fifty years, disclose fresh insights into well-known concerns of Greene. Violence can hide behind the familiar, as he pointed out in the essay, "The Revolver in the Corner Cupboard" (1947). Yet the 1952 nonfiction work in which the essay was first collected, *The Lost Childhood and Other Essays*, turns out to be mistitled. Greene imparted an aura of timelessness to many of his interviewers because he never shed his childhood. This believer in the impact of early experience always enjoyed the adventure fiction he read as a boy; nor did he outgrow his early addiction to practical jokes. Yet also belonging to his childhood is the unhappiness symbolized in his work by the green baize door, the cracked bell, and the recurrence of villains named Carter or Davis.

Unhappiness always dogged him. *The Power and the Glory* (1940) describes the separating effects of success; in *A Burnt-Out Case* (1961), success looks like a form of divine punishment; the autobiographical *A Sort of Life* (1971) includes Greene's odd claim that he even failed at failure.

Yet superior technique brightens this gloom. The belief that tragedy resembles farce more than it does comedy helped hone his sense of the ridiculous. Major Jones, for instance, disguises himself as a woman to trick Papa Doc's border guards in *The Comedians* (1966). That he will later die because his feet give out during a march keeps him in the realm of the absurd without diminishing him. Greene believes that truth can be best approached through distortion, juxtaposition, and the mirror image (one thinks of the three nonbelievers in *The End of the Affair* [1951], all of whom, against stiff odds, come to love God). The truth is always human. Greene told Marie-Françoise Allain in 1983, "the existence of the Trinity is to me of no importance: it illustrates an attempt to explain the inexplicable." If such statements sound heretical, they don't frighten Greene. His journalist's respect for facts fuels his assertion, made several times in the following pages, that he was a novelist who was Catholic rather than a Catholic novelist.

As he claimed in *Brighton Rock* (1938), good and evil have supernatural weight absent in mere right and wrong. He also describes the clash of good and evil within people, a clash not completely one-sided, with reason and decency surrendering to inborn depravity. We can't be reduced to the Judas complexes we all harbor. A belief in the sovereignty of the individual feeds his preference for an active evil over a passive goodness. Whereas passiveness leads to authoritarianism, activity promotes confrontation. The confrontation may cause injustice and tyranny, as Monsignor Quixote and Sancho agreed in Greene's 1982 novel *Monsignor Quixote*. Yet all the mistakes of both the politburo and the Roman Curia have left a central core of idealism unsmirched. Greene remained a Catholic, albeit a flawed one, and he always kept the slim hope that socialism could wear a human face. Believing in something worthwhile can induce the desire to improve it; the ideologue, on the other hand, only wants to preserve the status quo. Greene's former chief in British security, Kim Philby, "lived out his belief" in Soviet Communism, even though the system ignored poverty and human rights in favor of advancing state capitalism.

The lesson he learned, and put into practice, resembles that implemented by Maurice Castle in *The Human Factor* (1978), that is, that we often have to defend the bad against the worst. And the worst is often vested authority, a body politic concerned chiefly with both solidifying and extending its power. If Greene was naive in his belief that any outcries against injustice coming from a Philby would have been welcome in the former USSR, he did perceive their value. His 1969 speech, "The Virtue of Disloyalty," given at the University of Hamburg, set forth the claim that we're most godlike when we defy vested authority. He's not favoring disloyalty to accepted norms in order to dodge the toil of judging things on their own merits. To challenge officialdom is to accept the burden of deciding for oneself. Accompanying this burden is a new clarity of vision. Greene's version of Joyce's epiphany, of Virginia Woolf's moment of sufficiency, and of William Gaddis's recognition declares itself in the relief felt by the outlaw, or sinner, who has hit rock bottom or reached the end of the line. Only in having exhausted all other forms of help, like governmental intervention, can the individual take an accurate spiritual self-inventory. Loss and gain switch places in Henry Scobie's insight into the life endured in swampy Freetown, Sierra Leone, in *The Heart of the Matter* (1948): "Here you could love human beings as God loved them, knowing the worst." An awareness of how suffering infuses ordinary life lends Greene's work power and drive. But it also calls forth a tenderness he's rarely credited with. We might have taken our cue from his statement in *Journey Without Maps* (1936), that, as a boy, whenever he looked at the unexplored continent of Africa on a globe, he saw "the shape of a human heart."

Both the heart and the frame it inhabits suffer when they belong to a dissenter, particularly in a police state. The outsider and the oppressed need someone to stand up for them. They're not villains in their own eyes; their opinions and their motives both seem valid to them. Perhaps their only sin consisted of offending those in power. Greene's attentiveness to their plight, as expressed to Philip Toynbee, is nearly godlike: "It's . . . the writer's job to try to engage people's sympathy for characters who are outside the official range of sympathy," he told Toynbee in 1957, adding, "one of the things which interests me most is discovering the humanity in the apparently inhuman character."

This view of life as a network of division and subdivision captures what Greene means by the human factor. It also validates his credentials as a wayfarer on life's lawless roads. His imagination dwells on "the dangerous edge of things," that frontier peopled by exiles, rebels, and foes of the establishment. If traversing this wild border has hurt him as a person, it has also strengthened his vision. Living out of a suitcase in a war zone like Indochina has helped him gain insight both to portray cowardice as bravery and to show the nobility sometimes lurking behind failure. And how can we define failure anyway? We probably lack the necessary information. Greene's attraction to the miracles in Christianity (borne out by the many references in the following pages to Padre Pio) rests on faith in God's mercy. One of the clearest statements of his faith comes, characteristically, in a little English proverb in *Brighton Rock*, a favorite of the tormented Pinkie (who only recites the proverb's first line): "Between the stirrup and the ground/ He mercy asked and mercy found."

Although inscrutable, God's grace lies within reach of all. Shockingly, the only ones Greene excludes from it are himself and, perhaps, his immediate circle. It would be good to know his thoughts when he named his son (born September 1936) Francis. Francis was the name of the unlucky main figure in his rejected second novel, *The Episode*; of the treacherous, guilt-racked hero of *The Man Within* (1929); and of the frightened lad who dies in "The End of the Party" (1931). Certainly, Greene wanted better for his new son than the woes suffered by his like-named characters. Perhaps a warped sentimentality addled his judgment. We needn't fault him. His books brim with self-blamers who insist that they're much worse than they are.

In his best moments, Greene was willing to suspend moral judgment in favor of trusting such matters to God. In his very best moments, this willingness gives his words a clarity and a depth that sound divine. He moves closest to God when, rather than affecting godlike poses, he discloses the mystery of unity swathing us all. Let our last recommendation for *Graham Greene: Man of Paradox* be Greene's, and let him make it with one of his best effects — a lyrical glimpse into the heart of things, lit by precise phrasing and made dramatic by a fine flat tone. The effect comes from his 1965 review of *Journal of a Soul: Diary of Pope John XXIII*, and it appears in his *Collected Essays* (1969). He's looking at a photograph:

> Pope John is caught by the camera talking to a little girl sick with leukemia — he speaks with extreme

gravity and she listens with the same seriousness. It is impossible to say which of them is the elder, which will be the first dead. He speaks to her as to an equal. (400–1)

This faith in our equality before God enriches the interviews and impressions that A. F. Cassis has reprinted in this collection. Greene may have miscued, such as when he said that he'd rather live in East Germany than in the United States, but he always kept faith with the idea that our deeds—and our selves—matter to God.

—Peter Wolfe
University of Missouri, St. Louis

Acknowledgments

I wish to express my gratitude to William B. Lambert, Dr. Raymond C. Huel, Dr. Gaston R. Renaud, Dr. Peter Wolfe, and Father Donald O'Gorman, C.S.B., for their help in editorial matters, information, and the translation of texts and to Pierre Joannon for his advice and the selection of articles and interviews he brought to my attention. I also wish to acknowledge the support and encouragement of my colleagues in the department of English at the University of Lethbridge and to Miss R. Ramtej for her assistance.

I have relied heavily on certain publications to retrieve information and sometimes to verify my own findings. I have tried to acknowledge these sources each time I drew from them; but if I have overlooked any, I wish to acknowledge my indebtedness for the immense help I received from them, especially the following publications: Norman Sherry, *The Life of Graham Greene Volume I: 1904–1939* (London: Jonathan Cape; New York: Penguin Books; Toronto: Lester and Orpen Dennys, 1989); R. A. Wobbe, *Graham Greene: A Bibliography and Guide to Research* (New York: Garland Publishing, 1979); Gene D. Phillips, S.J., *Graham Greene: The Films of His Fiction* (New

York: Teachers College Press, 1974); and to a more recent work that has come to my attention, Henry J. Donaghy's edition of *Conversations with Graham Greene* (Jackson, Miss.: University Press of Mississippi, 1992). The much anticipated publication of *The Life of Graham Greene Volume II* by Norman Sherry (New York: Viking Penguin) is scheduled for a March 1995 release.

I wish to thank the University of Lethbridge for granting me leave in 1992–93 to complete the project that I had begun in 1988; the University of Lethbridge Research Fund for support; and the library staff at the University of Lethbridge; Trinity College, University of Dublin; the British Library, London; and the Newspaper Library, Colindale, London.

The use of selections from copywritten material has been graciously granted by the following publishers and copyright holders:

Marie-Françoise Allain, Guido Waldman, translator, and Bodley Head, *The Other Man: Conversations with Graham Greene* (1983).

America Press, Inc., 106 West 56th Street, New York, NY 10019, "Graham Greene: Saint or Cynic?" by Richard McLaughlin. © 1948. All Rights Reserved.

The Estate of H. E. Bates and Michael Joseph, Ltd., publisher, *The Blossoming World* (1971).

Anthony Burgess, "God and Literature and so forth . . . "

Madeleine Chapsal, *Les Ecrivains en personne* (1960).

John Cornwell, "Why I Am Still a Catholic."

Louise Dennys and Eric Young, "The Greene Factor." © Louise Dennys, 1978.

Doubleday and Company, Inc., and Otto Preminger, *Preminger: An Autobiography*. © 1977 Otto Preminger.

Elizabeth Easton, "A Conversation with Graham Greene." Reprinted from *Book-of-the-Month Club News*, Fall 1973, by permission of the Book-of-the-Month Club, Inc. All rights reserved.

Le Figaro, "Je n'écrirai plus de romans policiers" by Jean Duché and the articles: "Graham Greene établit son panthéon des littératures anglaises et française" by George Adam and "Interview de Graham Greene" by Bernard Violet. © Copyright *Le Figaro* 1993 by Jean Duché, Bernard Violet, and George Adam.

Barbara Greene and Settle Press (10 Boyne Terrace Mews, London W11 3LR), *Too Late to Turn Back*, introduction by Paul Theroux (London: Settle Press, 1981; Penguin Books, 1990).

Alex Hamilton, "Graham Greene," *Guardian* (1971). Copyright © 1971 Alex Hamilton.

Pierre Joannon and *Etudes Irlandaises*, "Graham Greene's Other Island" (1981).

Frank Kermode, "The House of Fiction: Interviews with Seven English Novelists." First appeared in *Partisan Review* 30, no. 1 (1963). © Frank Kermode.

Karel Kyncl and *Index on Censorship*, "A Conversation with Graham Greene," 13, no. 3 (1984).

The Illustrated Weekly of India, "Graham Greene" by S. V. V. (1964).

Norman Lebrecht, "The Greene Factor," *Sunday Times* (1984). © Norman Lebrecht.

David Lewin, "Friendship, Sex . . . and a Sense of Doom." © David Lewin, 1966.

Little, Brown and Company, *The Diaries of Evelyn Waugh*. Copyright © 1976 by The Estate of Evelyn Waugh: Introduction and Compilation © 1976 by

Michael Davie. By permission of Little, Brown, and Company.

The Estate of J. Maclaren-Ross and *London Magazine*, "Excursions in Greene Land" (1964).

Michael Mewshaw and *London Magazine*, "Graham Greene in Antibes" (1977).

Malcolm Muggeridge and Collins Publishers, *Chronicles of Wasted Time. Chronicle 2: The Infernal Grove* (1974).

Malcolm Muggeridge and HarperCollins Publishers, *Like It Was: The Diaries of Malcolm Muggeridge*, selected and edited by John Bright-Holmes.

New York Herald Tribune, Inc., "The Real Africa: Heart Before Politics," by Martin Tucker, *New York Herald Tribune*. © 1962, New York Herald Tribune Inc. All rights reserved. Reprinted by permission.

New York Times, "Graham Greene at 66," by Israel Shenker. Copyright © 1971 by the New York Times Company. Reprinted by permission.

Observer, "Graham Greene on 'The Job of the Writer,'" by Philip Toynbee © 1957; "Graham Greene: A Brief Encounter," by Roy Perrot © 1969; and "On the Dangerous Edge," by John Heilpern © 1975.

Jay Parini, "Getting to Know Graham Greene" © Jay Parini, 1988.

Paulist Press, "Interview with Graham Greene" by Robert Ostermann (1950) and "Graham Greene: On the Screen—An Interview" by Gene D. Phillips, S.J. (1969) in *Catholic World*.

Penguin Books, Ltd., *The Land Unknown* by Kathleen Raine (Hamish Hamilton, 1975), pp. 78, 180–81, and 184. Copyright © Kathleen Raine, 1975. Reproduced by permission of Penguin Books, Ltd.

Peters, Fraser and Dunlop Group, Ltd., "Graham Greene into the Light" by V. S. Pritchett (1978) in the *Times*. Reprinted by permission of the Peters, Fraser and Dunlop Group, Ltd.

Peters, Fraser and Dunlop Group, Ltd., *Letters to a Friend, 1950–1952*, by Rose Macauley. Edited by Constance Babington Smith (1961). Reprinted by permission of the Peters, Fraser and Dunlop Group, Ltd.

The Marble Foot: An Autobiography 1905–1938 (1976) by Peter Quennell. Collins, an imprint of HarperCollins Publishers Limited. *The Sign of the Fish* (1960) by Peter Quennell. Collins, an imprint of HarperCollins Publishers Limited. Copyright Peter Quennell, reproduced by permission of Curtis Brown Group, Ltd., London.

Charles Rolo and the *Atlantic*, "Graham Greene: The Man and the Message."

A. L. Rowse and Methuen London, "Graham Greene: Perverse Genius." Copyright © A. L. Rowse, 1989. Reprinted by permission of Methuen London.

St. Martin's Press, Inc., *Graham Greene: On the Frontier* by Maria Couto. © Maria Couto, 1988. Reprinted by permission of St. Martin's Press, Inc.

Phillippe Séjourné, "Graham Greene: On the Short Story," *Cahiers de la Nouvelle* 4 (1985): 11–24.

Society of Authors as literary representative of the Estate of Cecil Roberts, *The Bright Twenties*. (1970).

Spectator, "Greene's Jests" by John Sutro (1984) and "I'm an Angry Old Man, You See" by John Mortimer (1986).

Straight Arrow Publishers, Inc. and Gloria Emerson, "Graham Greene: Our Man in Antibes," *Rolling Stone* (1978). © Straight Arrow Publishers, Inc. All Rights Reserved. Reprinted by permission.

Times Newspapers Limited, J. W. Lambert's "Graham Greene: The Next Move" and "The Private World of Graham Greene." © Times Newspapers, Ltd., 1966/70/78.

Auberon Waugh and the *Sunday Telegraph*, "Travels with the Complete Hero." © The Telegraph plc, 1982.

Introduction

Few writers have achieved Graham Greene's international recognition, fame, and even notoriety in their lifetimes. Greene is a prolific writer whose works, including his short stories, have been translated into no fewer than twenty-five languages. His novels, no less than his letters to the editor of the *Times* and other dailies and weeklies, have aroused endless controversy by the religious views and the social and political values they express and challenge. His choice of the genre of the "thriller" whose setting, more often than not, is one of the political hot spots of the world, his general interest in melodrama, and his sympathy for characters outside the accepted or general range of sympathy has helped account for his widespread popularity. Also instrumental in creating this popularity are the clarity and simplicity of his style and the incredible economy of his storytelling—Greene is an accomplished storyteller who has successfully combined the lesson he learned from Henry James regarding the importance of a firm point of view combined with the fluidity and motion of the modern camera.

One need not survey reported annual sales in Great Britain, the U. S., and Canada to determine Greene's popular appeal. Suffice it to say that his novels almost always made the bestseller lists or were included in the "Editor's Choice" list. They have been consistently reviewed by the popular as well as the more academic or "highbrow" weeklies and periodicals. Moreover, his works have been readily available for years in Penguin paperbacks, "the current gauge of academic respectability in the United States," as Lionel Stevenson once observed in his commentary on Thackeray.[1] Greene contributed much to the religious drama of the fifties, but his achievement as dramatist, often overlooked, remains minor and secondary to his achievement as writer of fiction. (It is worth noting, however, that no less a dramatist than Jean Anouilh thought fit to translate *The Complaisant Lover* into French.) Still wider recognition came through his involvement with the cinema. His five years as film critic for the *Spectator* in the thirties taught him to appreciate the popular appeal of film and its technique. Not by accident his twenty-two novels, with the exception of two as well as numerous short stories, have been adapted by him and others to film, albeit sometimes with disastrous consequences. Greene himself also wrote directly for the screen and never lost sight of the "proper popular use of the film," and he always advocated the acceptance of its popularity "as a virtue" rather than "a vice from which one turns away."[2]

Greene's widespread popularity may have had its drawbacks. It is this popularity that seems to have disqualified him from the Nobel Prize. Artur Lundkvist, an influential and senior member of the Literature Committee of the Swedish Academy, "sulkily" complained that "Greene is too popular."[3] And so it becomes, in the words of Per Wastberg, editor-in-chief of the Swedish *Dagens Nyheter*, "a matter of deep regret that he [Greene] has not been awarded the Nobel Prize—E. M. Forster, Virginia Woolf and W. H. Auden are to be joined by yet another genius."[4] But squeamishness in the face of success and popularity is not confined to members of the Swedish Academy. Academics—or is it orthodox academe only?—find it difficult to make the transition from a Virginia Woolf or a James Joyce—a "novelist's novelist"—to the popular genre of the thriller that Greene uses. And so while academics wonder about Greene's place in "the canon," whether he should be relegated to the company of Anthony Hope *et al.*, or be considered as a worthy successor of Henry James, the Greene industry has gone into top gear. Apart from the many doctoral dissertations written to date, there were, as far as one can ascertain, no less than fifteen monographs on Greene published in the eighties.

In spite of the abundance of this critical material, there is now only one full-length biography of Greene available, even though he has been a subject of public interest for the past fifty years. The first volume of the biography by Norman Sherry—the biographer whom Greene approved of and trusted—appeared in April 1989 and covers Greene's life through 1939. It is not clear when the second volume will be published.

Greene seems to have been genuinely dismayed at the sight of a camera or tape recorder and rarely submitted to being photographed or interviewed. He was uneasy at interviews and disliked talking about himself. He did not want to be treated like a public figure and maintained that a writer should be as unrecognizable as possible.

Faced with a dearth of material about Greene the man, scholars and literary critics, as well as interested and intelligent readers, are driven to create a "composite" or, in the

words of Richard Mayne of the *Listener*, an "identikit portrait"[5] of Greene by piecing together impressions and reminiscences of friends, biographical sketches, literary
profiles, and information from interviews and conversations, supplemented by Greene's highly selective account
in *A Sort of Life* (1971) and *Ways of Escape* (1980).

Though Greene had a strong sense of humor that never
seemed to have left him, his novels express a poignant and
deep sense of anguish; he was a "natural solitary"[6] who
enjoyed and cherished his solitude as a writer but publicized his manic depression and lifelong battle against boredom. Such apparent contradictions lend themselves easily
to the growing legend surrounding Greene as an "enigma,"
a figure surrounded by paradox and ambiguity with an
undefinable sense of mystery about him. The legend is
given further credence by Greene's creation of characters
who were themselves often riddled with contradictions.

Malcolm Muggeridge, who came to know Greene well
during the London blitz, and who was his colleague at
MI6 and later his publisher, describes Greene affectionately as a "difficult" but loveable character, a "sinner manqué"[7] who is "spiritually, even physically, . . . one of
nature's displaced persons."[8] There is little doubt that
Greene was a highly "complex"[9] personality not because
he was psychoanalyzed at the age of sixteen when psy-
choanalysis was still in its infancy or because he played
Russian roulette with his brother's revolver, but because
he possessed what Richard McLaughlin perceptively
described in 1948 as the "contradictory traits that make
up the thinking man."[10] These "contradictory traits," cou-
pled with his instinctive evasiveness make him, in the
words of Edward Sackville-West, "the electric hare whom
racing dogs are not meant to catch."[11]

Furthermore, as a novelist, Greene renounced all allegiances to creed and country. A believer primarily in the
"virtue of disloyalty," he was always ready "to change
sides at the drop of a hat."[12] Greene's conscious rejection
of a unified view of life or even loyalty to his own invented
ideology gave him that "extra dimension of sympathy"
that enabled him to write, as he once put it, "from the
point of view of the black square as well as the white."[13] It
becomes most fitting for him, as a novelist, even at the
height of the Cold War, to be the Marxist grist in a capitalist state, to the discomfort of Americans, or a capitalist
grist in a socialist state, to the discomfort of Marxists. It
should be noted that in his personal views, he seemed to
be left of center, with a pronounced antipathy for the
"chromium plated civilization" of America. He supported
the Sandanistas, donating half the royalties of the Spanish
translation of *Monsignor Quixote* to them and the other half
to the Trappist monastery at Osera, Spain. He never hesitated to speak his mind politically—he resigned from the
American Academy of Arts and Letters in protest over
Vietnam and challenged Reagan as a menace to peace and,
thus, provoked the ire of the extreme right—but he was
also not a political person involved in the ideology of politics; he seems to have voted only once in his life. He advocated liberal theology, admired Pope John XXIII, and
believed in the Assumption of the Virgin Mary but
defended himself as a "Catholic agnostic"[14] who found
Catholicism less interesting as it became more permissive.
He was not religious but was fascinated by the mystery of
religion and the distinction between faith (which he had
and which grew with age) and belief (which he found
more and more difficult); he "sometimes" believed in God
but said the Hail Mary every time he took off in a plane

and prayed frequently to Padre Pio, a Franciscan priest in southern Italy who bore the stigmata on his hands and whose photograph he kept in his wallet. At the height of his success as a novelist, he was beset by a sense of failure. He was frightened by violence but irresistibly drawn to the frontier and life in the raw. The list of natural and cultivated contradictory traits goes on and on.

Greene jealously guarded his privacy. In an age when writers and artists welcome, if not solicit, television publicity, Greene refused consistently to appear on French National TV or the BBC. He did, however, give two TV interviews, one in June 1982 to FRS (Côte d'Azur) and the other to the German ARD in November 1982, but these were mainly to explain his contention with Nice society and its underworld after his indictment of it in *J'Accuse* was banned by the French courts. He rarely spoke about his personal relationships. Even his trusted biographer, Norman Sherry, who had access to private letters and had numerous interviews with Greene and corresponded with him until the end, attests to the author's elusiveness. When plied with questions, some of Greene's answers were "furtive, others cunning, others informative but not going to the heart of his matter."[15] He resented journalists and academics "plundering" his private life for personal or commercial reasons. In fact, his dislike of journalists was legendary, almost irrational.[16]

In the face of such "rationed" information, a reader will find value in the seventy-five interviews or so that Greene did allow and that were published in a wide variety of periodicals over the past fifty years. Because Greene "so carefully disguises his life in fiction,"[17] the interviews he did grant and the conversations of people with him give a better understanding of Greene than a doubtful or even hazardous identification of Greene with his characters, especially those who are artists or novelists with identifiable traits traceable to him. Even the "autobiographies" tend to create a careful and measured response from the reader; Peter Wolfe raises the interesting issue of whether Greene in *Ways of Escape* "isn't planting road markers next to his tracks rather than covering them."[18]

But interviews by themselves do not go far enough. Greene is not the kind of writer whose character can be understood by an interviewer after an hour. His aloofness, detachment, and courtesy make it necessary to resort to personal impressions, diary entries, and recollections of this "natural solitary" by his friends and contemporaries. For his fascination with any insight into human absurdity and evil; his remarkable sense of humor; his "sharp, clear, and cruel brain" and care for detail; his highly organized business sense; his kindness, gentleness, and compassion; his lack of pretension and reluctance to pass moral judgments on anybody—for these and other personal qualities one has to go to the diaries and recollections of his contemporaries.

In this collection of interviews, together with excerpts from different works ranging from personal memoirs, recollections, and reminiscences to autobiographies and literary profiles in weeklies and monthlies, Greene speaks with varying degrees of restraint on a vast array of topics. These topics range from his conversion to Catholicism and his views on the Sacraments, Faith, and God to the job of the writer and what constitutes a novelist's material. His comments are often interspersed with his views on leading novelists and politicians. The picture that emerges is invaluable to our understanding of Greene and his varied career as dramatist, journalist, traveler, scriptwriter, and novelist.

For the reader's convenience, these excerpts are arranged to coincide with different stages in Greene's life. They have been selected because they throw light on many facets of his art and life; they are also hard to find, even for the most determined literary sleuth. Explanatory notes are reduced to a minimum and the original titles retained, unless otherwise indicated. Further, I have tried to preserve the original spelling and punctuation except when such adherence would be obtrusive to the reader. A chronological listing of Graham Greene's works, with full publishing details, is appended as is a supplementary reading list.

Notes

1. Robert A. Colby, "William Makepeace Thackeray," *Victorian Fiction: A Guide to Research*, ed. George H. Ford (New York: Modern Language Association, 1978), 114.
2. Graham Greene, "Subjects and Stories," *Footnotes to the Film*, ed. Charles Davey (London: Lovat Dickson, 1938), 64–65.
3. Peter Lennon, "Why Graham Greene Hasn't Won A Nobel Prize and Solzhenitsyn Has," *Book World*, 28 December 1980, 6.
4. Per Wastberg, "The Empire of Imagination," *Adam International Review* 46, nos. 446–48 (1984): 29.
5. Richard Mayne, "Collected Guilt," *Listener*, 2 April 1970, 455–56.
6. J. W. Lambert, "Knowing the Worst," *Adam International Review* 46, nos. 446–48 (1984): 17–19.
7. Malcolm Muggeridge, *Like It Was: The Diaries of Malcolm Muggeridge*, sel. and ed. John Bright-Holmes (London: Collins, 1981), 316–17.
8. _____, *Chronicles of Wasted Time. Chronicle 2. The Infernal Grove* (New York: William Morrow and Co., 1974), 78–79.
9. Unsigned, "Greeneland Aboriginal," *New Statesman*, 13 January 1961, 44–45.
10. Richard McLaughlin, "Graham Greene: Saint or Cynic?" *America*, 24 July 1948, 370–71.

11. Edward Sackville-West, "The Electric Hare: Some Aspects of Graham Greene," *Month*, September 1951, 141–47.

12. Graham Greene, "The Virtue of Disloyalty," *Observer*, 24 December 1972, 17.

13. *Why Do I Write? An Exchange of Views between Elizabeth Bowen, Graham Greene, and V. S. Pritchett* (London: Percival Marshall, 1948), 32. Greene is referring to lines 211–12 of Browning's celebrated but sardonic monologue "Bishop Blougram's Apology."

14. John Mortimer, "'I'm an Angry Old Man, You See,'" *Spectator*, 14 June 1986, 11.

15. "Memorial Preface," *Essays in Graham Greene. An Annual Review. Vol. III*, ed. Peter Wolfe (St. Louis, Mo.: Lucas Hall Press, 1992), 7.

16. Greene's dislike for journalists dates back to the fifties. An entry in his "Congo Journal" dated 6 March 1959 reads: "Usual trouble with a journalist. Made an appointment for tomorrow evening when I shall be gone." (*In Search of a Character*, 90). The dislike for journalists seems to have grown more acute with time. Michael Mewshaw notes that Greene had "learned the hard way to avoid idle conversation with journalists" and records Greene's words: "It's got so I hate to say who I am or what I believe." See Mewshaw excerpt, "Graham Greene in Antibes," on pp. 255–63.

17. Philip Stratford, "Unlocking the Potting Shed," *Kenyon Review* 24 (winter 1962): 129–43.

18. Peter Wolfe, "Ways of Escape," *Modern Fiction Studies* 27 (1981): 706–8.

Chronological Table

1904 Henry Graham Greene born 2 October; baptized at Berkhamsted School Chapel 13 November.

1910 Visits Brighton. Convalesces from jaundice. Hugh Greene born.

1911 Charles Henry Greene, Graham Greene's father, becomes headmaster at Berkhamsted School.

1914 Junior School.

1915 Senior School, a period of extreme unhappiness, also marred by poor health.

1918 Boarder at St. John's.

1921 Psychoanalysed by Kenneth Richmond. Spends six months in London.

1922 Balliol College, Oxford.

1923 Walking tour of Ireland; coeditor of *Oxford Outlook*.

1924 Tour in Germany with Claud Cockburn; experiments with Russian roulette; editor of *Oxford Outlook*.

1925 Visits Paris; meets Vivien Dayrell-Browning; joins the Communist Party (for four weeks); publishes *Babbling April*; first novel *Anthony Sant* turned down; journalist on probation at Nottingham.

1926 Converts to Catholicism; copy editor, the *Times*; hospitalized for appendicitis.

1927 Marries Vivien and lives in London; Charles Greene retires as headmaster of Berkhamsted School.

1929 *The Man Within*; Hellenic cruise; leaves the *Times*.

1930 *The Name of Action*; visits Oberammergau and travels to Burgundy with Raymond Greene.

1931 *Rumour at Nightfall*; moves to Chipping Camden; travels to Cologne on the Orient Express.

1932 *Stamboul Train*; begins to review for the *Spectator*.

1933 *Stamboul Train* bought by Twentieth-Century-Fox; moves to Oxford; travels to Sweden with Hugh Greene; birth of daughter, Lucy Caroline.

1934 *It's a Battlefield*.

1935 *England Made Me* and *The Basement Room and Other Stories*; goes on Liberian trek with his cousin, Barbara; becomes film critic for the *Spectator*; moves to Clapham Common, London.

1936 *Journey Without Maps* and *A Gun for Sale*; sells *A Gun for Sale* to Paramount; meets Alexander Korda; birth of son, Francis.

1937 Scripts John Galsworthy's short story "The First and the Last" for Korda; coeditor of short-lived *Night and Day*; writes article on Shirley Temple; withdraws *Journey Without Maps*.

1938 *Brighton Rock*; travels to Mexico; libel case by Twentieth-Century-Fox.

1939 *The Lawless Roads* and *The Confidential Agent*; outbreak of World War II.

1940 *The Power and the Glory*; literary editor, the *Spectator*.

1941 Hawthornden Prize; joins Ministry of Information; leaves for West Africa.

1942 *British Dramatists*.

1943 *The Ministry of Fear*; Charles Henry Greene dies; returns to England.

1944 Director, Eyre and Spottiswoode (until 1948).

1945 Visits U.S.A.

1946 *The Little Train.*

1947 *Nineteen Stories.*

1948 *The Heart of the Matter*; speaks at Catholic conference in Brussels with François Mauriac; travels to Vienna for the writing of *The Third Man*; visits Prague after Communist take over; buys house in Anacapri.

1949 *The Third Man* (film); James Tait Memorial Prize for *The Heart of the Matter.*

1950 *The Third Man and The Fallen Idol*; *The Little Fire Engine.*

1951 *The Lost Childhood and Other Essays* and *The End of the Affair*; travels to Malaya as correspondent for *Life* magazine and to Indochina for the *Sunday Times* and *Figaro.*

1952 *The Little Horse Bus*; Swedish translation of *The Living Room*; travels to Indochina for *Paris-Match.*

1953 *The Living Room* opens at Wyndham's; *Essais Catholiques* and *The Little Steamroller*; travels to Kenya to report on the Mau Mau outbreaks for the *Sunday Times*; establishes with John Sutro "The Anglo-Texan Society."

1954 Visits Vietnam, Cuba , Haiti, and U.S.A.; deported from Puerto Rico; goes to Sweden where he most probably met actress Anita Bjork.

1955 *Loser Takes All* and *The Quiet American*; visits Canada, Monte Carlo, Stalinist Poland, and Hanoi where he interviews Ho Chi Minh. This is his fourth and last visit to Vietnam.

1956 Visits Haiti.

1957 *The Spy's Bedside Book* (with Hugh Greene); travels
to U.S.A. for *The Potting Shed* production and to
Cuba, China, and Russia.

1958 Production of *The Potting Shed* in London; *Our Man
in Havana*; director, Bodley Head (until 1968).

1959 *The Complaisant Lover*; visits Cuba, the Congo,
including a leper colony, and the French
Cameroons where he befriends the Cloetta family;
Marion Greene (his mother) dies.

1960 Travels to Moscow (severe pneumonia), Tahiti,
Canada, and Brazil for P.E.N.; Sir Hugh Greene
becomes director general of the BBC.

1961 *A Burnt-Out Case* and *In Search of a Character*; honorary associate, American Institute of Arts and
Letters; leaves Heinemann for the Bodley Head;
visits Tunis.

1962 Visits Rumania; D. Litt. (Cambridge).

1963 *A Sense of Reality*; visits Berlin and East Germany;
travels to Cuba and Haiti for the *Sunday Telegraph*
and to Goa for the *Sunday Times*; honorary fellow,
Balliol College, Oxford.

1964 *Carving a Statue.*

1965 Visits Santo Domingo.

1966 *The Comedians*; travels to Cuba for the *Sunday
Telegraph*; meets Cuban leader Fidel Castro; made
Companion of Honour; leaves England to settle in
Antibes and Paris.

1967 *May We Borrow Your Husband?*; visits Sierra Leone
and Dahomey; D. Litt. (Edinburgh); Chevalier,
Legion of Honor (France).

1968 Visits Israel.

1969 *Collected Essays* and *Travels With My Aunt*;
Shakespeare Prize (University of Hamburg); visits
Prague for the first time since 1948—travels to
Paraguay and Argentina for the *Sunday Telegraph*.

1970 Resigns as honorary associate, American Institute of
Arts and Letters, in protest over the Vietnam War.

1971 *A Sort of Life*; travels to Chile for the *Observer* and
to Argentina.

1972 *Collected Stories* and *The Pleasure Dome*.

1973 *The Honorary Consul*; Thomas More Medal
(Chicago); visits South Africa.

1974 *Lord Rochester's Monkey*; visits Panama at the invitation of General Torrijos.

1975 *The Return of A. J. Raffles*; visits Panama.

1977 Visits Northern Ireland and Dublin; accompanies
the Panamanian delegation to Washington, D.C.,
for the signing of the canal treaty.

1978 *The Human Factor*; visits Panama.

1979 D. Litt. (Oxford); travels to Panama, Belize, and
Nicaragua; suspected cancer.

1980 *For Whom the Bell Chimes* receives its first perfor-
mance; *Doctor Fischer of Geneva or The Bomb Party*;
Ways of Escape; Dos Passos Prize and City of
Madrid Medal.

1981 Visits Jerusalem to receive the Jerusalem Prize.

1982 *J'Accuse* and *Monsignor Quixote*.

1983 Visits Nicaragua; Grand Cross, Order of Balboa
(Panama).

1984 *Getting to Know the General*; Companion of
Literature, RSL (Royal Society of Literature);
Commandant, Order of Arts and Letters (France).

1985 *The Tenth Man*; visits Nicaragua.

1986 Order of Merit; visits Moscow for the Union of Writers.

1988 *The Captain and the Enemy.*

1989 Travels to Dublin for the GPA book award, his last public appearance.

1990 *The Last Word and Other Stories.*

1991 Graham Greene dies 3 April in Vevey, Switzerland, at the age of eighty-six.

1992 *A World of My Own: A Dream Diary*, edited by Yvonne Cloetta.

The Greenes of Berkhamsted

Barbara Greene

. . . Graham and I hardly knew one another, even though we had grown up in the same town. Graham's father, Charles, was the headmaster of Berkhamsted School. He had a brilliant intellect and had originally intended to become a barrister, but he had taken on a temporary job at Berkhamsted while waiting to "eat his dinners," found that he had a talent and a liking for teaching, and simply stayed on. His brother, my father, was very different. He had been removed from school at a rather early age as he was considered to be not at all clever. The eldest brother, Graham, was almost as brilliant as Charles but in a different, hard-working and conscientious style, and he ended his career as Permanent Secretary at the Admiralty.[1] But my poor father, instead of going to a university, was put on a farm by his despairing parents in the hope that he would somehow be able there to make up his mind as to what he intended to do with his life. During his year on the farm he developed an intense love of country life and an inferiority complex, and he suddenly decided that somehow he simply must go off, far far away. By chance

1

he came across an article in some newspaper describing Brazil as the country of the future, and on the spot he decided to go there. He was right to do so. He very soon discovered that he had a genius for business and a true pioneer spirit, and for the rest of his life he loved Brazil. He was successful and became very prosperous and at the age of thirty-four he married my mother, who had just turned seventeen.

My mother's parents, who were German, had emigrated to Brazil . . . .

My father brought my mother to England after their marriage and this shy young bride, so used to a very different kind of life in Brazil, was suddenly surrounded by swarms, literally swarms, of Greenes, all of them full of energy and artistic literary interests, and all of them perfectly convinced that the British way of life was the only true and right one, and firmly determined to teach her this lesson. It could not have been easy for her but she was young and adaptable and too busy with other things to be unhappy. By the time she was twenty-one she had had three children and, after a few years, she had three more. I was the eldest of the second batch.

My father then bought The Hall at Berkhamsted because by this time he had become great friends with his brother Charles, who had married a beautiful cousin and was producing the same number of children, corresponding in age more or less to our family. My cousin Graham belonged to the older group while I was in the lower category, and somehow there was always something of an invisible dividing line between the two groups, though of course we were constantly meeting at family parties, surrounded by endless relatives, and the nurses and governesses one had in those days. I remember my mother saying at the end of one summer that we had never been less than sixteen at table. That, of course, applied to lunch; we children were nearly grown up before we were allowed to come down to dining room dinner.

The nursery regime, both in my family and Graham's, was a strict one and we had hardly any pocket money. Punctuality, bed-times, prayers, and church on Sundays were immovable milestones, but on the other hand we — especially at The Hall — had huge gardens . . . . There was always something going on; the gardens were thrown open at times for fêtes and garden parties in aid of charity, and our maiden aunts were constantly writing plays and pageants for us to act in. We all learnt a musical instrument and got up our own band, singing songs round the piano. Graham kept rather away from these activities at The Hall. His family were not musical, laying more emphasis on books, and reading became an important part of their lives. They were known as the intellectual Greenes and were always far better at school than any of us.[2]

Extracted from the foreword to *Too Late to Turn Back*, intro. Paul Theroux (London: Settle Press, 1981), *vii–x*. Originally published as *Land Benighted* (London: Geoffrey Bles, 1938). *Editor's title.*

Notes
1. Also a Knight of the Bath. Graham Greene gives impressions of his Uncle Graham in *A Sort of Life*, 20–21.
2. Graham Greene's version of the "Greene cousins" can be found in *A Sort of Life*, 18–19.

Charles Henry Greene, Headmaster

Claud Cockburn

Charles Henry Greene, this headmaster, gave the impression of conducting the affairs of the school and viewing life in general with the same smouldering, sometimes explosive intensity which he brought to the chessboard. He was a man of powerful and vivid reactions. Certain events, sometimes major, sometimes quite trivial, seemed to strike his mind with the heat and the force of a branding-iron, and for a long time would remain in the forefront of his consciousness, to be referred to, commented, brooded upon aloud in a singularly sonorous voice, and with occasionally florid eloquence.

His history lessons to the Sixth Form[1] were not so much history lessons as comments on a state of affairs in which history had taken a distinct turn for the worse. For the most part he treated history simply as a series of signposts to the probabilities and possibilities of the present. Most of them pointed to ruin. For Charles Greene was, in the widest as well as the party-political sense of the word, a Liberal, and in the crack-up of Liberalism he saw the mark of doom.[2]

When he looked at the Treaty of Versailles, his slightly bulbous grey eyes rolled, shone and started from his head, and his yellow moustache bristled. It reminded him of every disaster in the history of treaty-making since the errors committed by Pericles. As he spoke of it he sank back in his chair, pulling the mortar-board farther and farther down on his forehead as though to shield his eyes from the sight of so much folly and horror. "When I gaze," he said, "upon the activities of Mr. Lloyd George, when I consider the political consequence of Mr. Clemenceau,[3] my mind, abdicating its intellectual function, shrinks, half-paralysed, from the very attempt to contemplate the abyss which opens, inevitable but unregarded, before us."

Reading the news from Moscow and from the various fronts of the war of intervention, he would sink into an almost luxurious awareness of impending doom. The spirit of Bolshevism, he said, was permeating everywhere, ·and the most ordinary events and contretemps of everyday life confirmed his view.

Bored at the fact that they were mobilized months after the ending of the war, the soldiers camped outside the town became drunker and drunker, and once rioted, breaking into the school itself and threatening to throw the headmaster into the canal. It was Bolshevism.

Prefects neglected their duties; a French master turned pacifist and started teaching his pupils that the whole war had been a monstrous mixture of crime and blunder in which people had been slaughtered for nothing; and a conspiracy was uncovered among the older boys to wear dark-blue serge suits to chapel on Sundays instead of the short black coats which were required by regulation.

All these were manifest indications of the bolshevistic way things were tending.

And then death-watch beetles were found at work in the timbers of the high roof of the Elizabethan Hall. It was horrifying, but in its awful way satisfactory—a climactic symbol of decay and violent collapse. "Once again I have reports of slackness and indiscipline, everywhere I detect a falling off in keenness. The pernicious and destructive doctrines of Marx and Lenin are tapping away at the foundations and at the roof beams of civilization like the death-watch beetle which even as I speak is carrying out up there, invisible to us but none the less menacing for that, its work of voracious disintegration." Since he said all these things with a vivid sincerity, and these extravagances were the product of genuine and agonized beliefs, the effect was not at all grotesque, but as vividly impressive as a revivalist meeting.

He worried sometimes about my political future. He wanted me to have a political career so that I could take a hand at halting the general decline, and possibly reversing the trend. I held strong Conservative views, and he, though a Liberal, thought that on the whole that was probably a good thing—I should enter the Conservative Party and so stimulate its moral sense and moderate crassness. At lunch in the schoolhouse, when no one could leave the table until the headmaster had stood up and said the Latin grace, our arguments on the origins of the Boer War, or the policy of Palmerston, used sometimes to be prolonged for as much as a quarter of an hour after the last crumbs of the suet and treacle pudding had been eaten. The discussion was conducted amid a rising shuffle of impatient feet and the rebellious tinkling of spoons on empty plates. Sometimes he would use his initiative of Grace to cut short an argument which displeased him or to which perhaps he did not see an immediate rebuttal.

"Well, well, Cockburn," he would say, getting slowly to his feet, "I don't see how civilization's going to be saved Benedictus Benedicat."[4]

Extracted from *I, Claud . . . : An Autobiography* (Harmondsworth, England: Penguin Books, 1967), 35–37. *Editor's title.*

Notes

1. Sixth Form is the equivalent of grade 12 in senior high. Most students in Sixth Form are headed for university.

2. Graham Greene describes his father as "unflinchingly liberal in politics and gently conservative in morals." *A Sort of Life,* 24. Greene's consciousness of himself as a "Quisling's son" seems to have affected his relationship with his father. Ronald de Couves Matthews describes both his and Greene's father/son relationship as "disappointing" (see Ronald de Couves Matthews, *Mon Ami Graham Greene* [Bruges: Desclée de Brouwer, 1957], 11). Guy Martin notes that "there seems to have been a wall of misunderstanding between him [Greene] and his father, but he refers to this today only in veiled phrases: 'One cannot understand one's father as long as one is not a father' is typical." ("The Heart of the Graham Greene Matter," *Realities,* December 1962, 60–63). When, in 1968, Christopher Burstall asked him if he got on well with his father, Greene replied: "I loved him most when I was an adult, and when I had children of my own and realised the problems he had." ("Graham Greene Takes the Orient Express," *Listener,* 21 November 1968, 672–74, 676–77). See also Daphna Erdinast-Vulcan's account of fatherhood in *Graham Greene's Childless Fathers* (London: Macmillan; New York: St. Martin's Press, 1988).

3. David Lloyd George (1863–1945), radical Welsh Liberal statesman, was Chancellor of the Exchequer from 1908 to 1915 and coalition Prime Minister from 1916 to 1922. He was largely responsible for the Old Age Pensions Act of 1908, but he could never heal the split in the Liberal Party. His concession of the Irish Free State led to the defeat of the Liberals in 1922.

    Georges Clemenceau (1841–1929), French statesman and leader of the extreme left and twice premier (1906–09 and 1917–20), was intransigent in his opposition to Germany as he presided at the press conference of 1919.

4. "May the Blessed One bless us."

"Sceptical and Blithely Pessimistic"

Peter Quennell

If I had not encountered him as soon as I reached Berkhamsted, it may have been because he was a little older; and in 1920, his autobiography explains,[1] he had been temporarily released from school-work after suffering a nervous breakdown. On his return, however, we became friends, and he used to accompany me on my rides across the Common, where (he writes) "Quennell always rode a far more spirited horse than mine, galloped faster, jumped higher."[2] This is a tribute I was flattered to read; but Graham's memory has played him false. The hack I rode was by no means spirited; and I have seldom taken a jump if it could possibly be ridden round. Far less vaguely I remember our conversations and the books we exchanged — for instance, *Madame Bovary*, not the kind of novel that either his father or mine would have encouraged us to open. His talk had an exuberantly sceptical and blithely pessimistic turn; and his contemplation of the horrors of human life appeared to cause him unaffected pleasure. His pessimism did nothing to sour his temperament; while Evelyn Waugh would change beyond all knowledge, the young and the old Greene have remained relatively consubstantial. At each fresh insight he obtained into human absurdity or wickedness, his pallid, faintly woebegone face would assume an air of solemn glee.

～～～

. . . I went up to Balliol, this time unescorted, on October 10th 1923, was ceremoniously received at the porter's lodge and taken off to my allotted rooms, painted a dark depressing brown, in the oldest quarter of the college. They occupied half a top floor. My sitting-room commanded St. Giles's; my bedroom overlooked the Broad. Though meagrely furnished, they gave me a sense of space and, what was more, a glorious sense of privacy. I had a college servant to attend to my well-being, make my bed, and, if the weather demanded it, build me a huge coal-fire in my Victorian black-leaded grate. But I still needed friends, and therefore sought out the staircase on which my school friend Graham Greene lived.[3] Our reunion, however, was disappointing. Having taken up residence a year earlier, he had already formed his own circle, which, rightly or wrongly, I considered rather tedious; and, after a week or two of sharing their honest fun, I wandered off into a different milieu. Why Graham at Oxford should have so carefully avoided notice is a question that I cannot answer. But perhaps he did well to avoid the showy, expensive world that I myself was soon frequenting.[4]

Extracted from *The Marble Foot: An Autobiography 1905–1938* (London: Collins, 1976), 97–98, 112–13.

Notes

1. *A Sort of Life*, 1971. *Author's note* [pp. 96–103].
2. Ibid., 106.
3. Graham Greene had gone to Balliol for the autumn term of 1922.
4. Graham Greene gives a sketchy account of his life at Oxford in *A Sort of Life*, 134–36.

The School at Berkhamsted: Two Views at Variance

Peter Quennell

. . . Four of my Oxford contemporaries were hard at work becoming successful novelists. Evelyn Waugh, Anthony Powell and the writer who prefers to be called Henry Green[1] I knew best during their undergraduate period; but Graham Greene I had also known at school, the red-brick school where his father was headmaster, of which he has supplied so dramatic a description in a travel-book entitled *The Lawless Roads.*[2] To see a place that one remembers vividly reflected on the screen of another writer's mind is an odd and disconcerting experience. I remember the school as dull, and the town as drab; but the undertones of evil that Graham Greene detected made no impression on my more unreceptive spirit, which often revolted against my humdrum surroundings but never associated my revolt with a sense of sin. After all, the town had a broad and pleasant High Street, which included some dignified ancient houses, though its late-Victorian periphery was certainly rather grim and squalid. Encompassed by the hideous school-buildings was a venerable Tudor hall; and most of the masters attached to the school struck me as respectable, if somewhat uninteresting, men. But beyond the town, above the ruins of its castle, stretched an enormous tract of open common, where larks spun dizzily up from the turf and dark pine clumps stood islanded in acres of bracken and yellow-flowering gorse bushes. It was bordered by the palings of a park that extended for many miles along a ridge of the Chilterns, as far as a bold eminence named Ivinghoe Beacon, crowned with a small prehistoric barrow, which surveyed the placid Vale of Aylesbury. Through the park itself, around Wyatt's battlemented mansion, mysterious deserted rides ran between colonnades of massive beech trees; the gardens of the house, after its owner's death, had lapsed into a romantic jungle, a wilderness of tall grass, unclipped hedges and tumbled statues.

These same prospects I find strangely transmogrified in my distinguished contemporary's recollections. The school that we both attended proves to have been a place of almost unfathomable iniquity, haunted by adults and adolescents "who bore about them the genuine quality of evil. There was Callifax who practised torments with dividers, Mr. Cranden with pale bleached hair,[3] a dusty gown, a kind of demoniac sensuality"; and from such heights "evil declined towards Parlow whose desk was filled with minute photographs—advertisements of art photos. Hell lay about them in their infancy." But I was conscious neither of the hellish atmosphere of the pedestrian life I lived at school, nor of the signs of spiritual degeneracy that I might have run to earth among the adjacent streets. I never glanced into the windows of the "shabby little shop" that sold second-hand copies of a fetishistic weekly paper;[4] and I remained unaware of

"Irish servant girls" (twice referred to by my friend the novelist) creeping from back doors in the early dark to make "their assignations for a ditch." Perhaps I was unduly simple-minded, perhaps unusually self-centered; but the intimations of Evil that seemed to have coloured Graham Greene's youth, and that since then have had so profound an effect on the shaping of his creative talents, failed somehow to enrich mine; with the result that my memories of the school and the town are much less valuable as a source of literary legend. It may be that they are slightly more accurate. But here we come face to face with the unending problem of how an imaginative artist should employ his material.

For the moment I must put aside that problem and return to the author of *The Lawless Roads*. Graham Greene was not, in those days, the careworn and hag-ridden personage whom one might possibly conjure up from a study of his recollections. Tall, lank and limp, with an extremely pallid skin but sharp, cheerfully observant eyes, he would have made an admirable Pierrot[5] in the eighteenth-century Commedia dell'Arte, concealing under his rather woebegone mask a great capacity for cynical humour. He was often exuberant: he could be positively blithe. Nor have the exuberance and the blitheness vanished. And even at the present period, when I re-read his books — those sombre chronicles of sin and suffering, where every form of pleasure is naturally suspect, every love-affair inescapably doomed, and a breath of Evil mixes with the fog that swirls around the lonely street-lamps — I sometimes feel that I am confronting the spirited schoolboy in a more accomplished and more portentous guise. I cannot resist the suspicion that he gets a good deal of fun — lighthearted schoolboyish fun — from causing his own and his reader's flesh to creep, and that he half enjoys the sensations of disgust and horror that he arouses with such unusual artistry. But is his use of these sensations, regarded as the constituents of a work of art, always perfectly legitimate? Are not the scales weighted against his characters a little too heavily and too deliberately? His men and women drag a burden of guilt like prisoners dragging a ball-and-chain; and it is a foregone conclusion that their experiences of physical love will turn out to be squalid and ignominious. No device is ever neglected that might help rub the squalor in. Thus, when the hero and heroine of *The End of the Affair* wish to invent a private code-name for the act of love-making, one is not particularly surprised to learn that the word they choose is "onions."[6] He has caught us there! One imagines the novelist exclaiming, with a delighted smile and a gleeful rubbing of the hands. No doubt we had had thoughts of Proust, of Swann and Odette in the same circumstances and their feebly romantic *"faire catleya"*?[7] But then, Proust's lovers had a sofa and a bed: Graham Greene's are usually condemned to come to grips with passion upon the naked floor.

I must admit, then, that, much as I appreciate his ingenuity and virtuosity and the remarkable aptitude that he shows for plain straightforward storytelling—what could be more effective, to take a single instance, than the episode of the beleaguered watch-tower in *The Quiet American?*—I am often a little uneasy about the means he has adopted to achieve his ends, and am conscious of a touch of artificiality, even of artistic fraud. Yet, considered from a technical point of view, each of his more recent novels is an amazingly deft performance; and the reader's enjoyment is only spoiled by an occasional journalistic trick, which provokes the suspicion that this extraordinary display of cleverness may conceal, at least in some passages, a certain lack of seriousness . . . .

Extracted from *The Sign of the Fish* (New York: Viking Press, 1960), 60–63. *Editor's title.*

Notes

1. Pseudonym of Henry Vincent Yorke (1905–74).
2. See Section 1, "The Anarchists," of the prologue.
3. *The Lawless Roads* reads: "Mr. Cranden with three grim chins."
4. *A Sort of Life* (9) refers to it as *London Life.*
5. A new and popular type, clever and sentimental, created by an Italian actor for the French stage. Both Pierrot and Harlequin took a commanding position when the comédie-italienne flourished in the second half of the seventeenth century.
6. This is not altogether accurate. See pp. 47–48 of *The End of the Affair* for the significance of the steak and onion dinner Maurice and Sarah have before their first lovemaking.
7. Marcel Proust (1871–1922), French novelist, whose *A la recherche du temps perdu* is a masterpiece of world literature. The love of the unhappy dilettante Swann for the courtesan Odette is described in the first volume of the masterpiece, *Du côté de chez Swann,* translated into English as *Swann's Way* by C. K. Scott Moncrieff.

An Early and Incipient Fascination with Dreams

Claud Cockburn

Disruptive tendencies were at work even in the circle of his own family.[1] As was the custom of many old-fashioned people at the period, the Greenes used at breakfast innocently to describe to one another anything interesting, bizarre or colourful they had had in the way of dreams during the previous night. Mr. and Mrs. Greene were unaware that their third son, Graham, had at about this time discovered Freud. He would leave the bacon cooling on his plate as he listened with the fascination of a secret detective. When necessary he would lure them on to provide more and more details which to them were amusing or meaningless but to him of thrilling and usually scandalous significance.

"It's amazing," he said to me once, "what those dreams disclose. It's startling—simply startling," and at the thought of it gave a low whistle.[2]

Extracted from *I, Claud . . . : An Autobiography* (Harmondsworth, England: Penguin Books, 1967), 35–37. *Editor's title.*

Notes

1. Charles Henry Greene, Graham Greene's father.
2. Graham Greene's fascination with dreams began early and continued to grow. He kept a dream diary under the supervision of his analyst Kenneth Richmond when he was sixteen and later in life to deal with a "writer's block" as he explained to Mirion Grindea (*Adam International Review* 46, nos. 446–48 [1984]: 7), to V. S. Pritchett (*Times*, 18 March 1978, 6–7), and to his niece, Louise Dennys (*Sunday Telegraph*, 12 March 1978, 14) to whom Greene has admitted that he was on "intimate terms" with the world's leaders in his dreams. Louise Dennys also notes that by 1978 Greene had three volumes of his dreams "carefully indexed." Two of his novels, *It's a Battlefield* (1934) and *The Honorary Consul* (1973) and several short stories originate from dreams. He also uses the dream as a literary device to reveal and develop character, to influence the course of the action, and to ensure the reader's acceptance of change in the novels. "Sometimes identification with a character," says Greene, "goes so far that one may dream his dream and not one's own." (*Ways of Escape*, 236). A case in point is Querry's dream in *A Burnt-Out Case*. A selection from the three volumes of dreams, *A World of My Own: A Dream Diary* (Reinhardt, 1992) was edited by his friend and companion, Yvonne Cloetta, and published posthumously.

A Tall and Gangling Youth

Cecil Roberts

. . . My former editorial assistant informed me that they had on the *Journal* staff a youth, a Balliol graduate, who had come as a journalistic pupil. He said the young man would like to call on me. Myself once an unpaid pupil of that paper some ten years earlier, I was naturally interested in this recruit and invited him to call. He proved to be a tall, gangling youth of twenty-one. He had recently published a book of verse, *Babbling April*, which he presented to me.[1] As I thanked him for his first offspring, I said: "I wonder if this is a presage. Young poets out of the cocoon often turn novelists—I have!" He shook his head, diffidently. He was shy at first. After all I was an ex-editor, the author of three published novels, and fairly well established. I suppose that in his eyes I represented success. I got him to talk, most intelligently, and after a pleasant hour he left. I expressed a hope that we should meet again. We did not and I have it on my conscience that I was not more hospitable. He must have been lonely, coming recently from the vivid life of a university and now living in grim lodgings in a provincial city. Happily I had just recovered but my mother was now seriously ill. Years later I wondered whether I might have changed his reaction to Nottingham.[2] When I got round to doing something about it, he had left and joined the staff of the *Times.*

Later my visitor's name came up again. I had called on Charles Evans at Heinemann's. A man of impetuous enthusiasm, he gave me a proof copy of a novel. "I believe we've got a winner! I want you to read it and tell me what you think." Evans was right. The book was *The Man Within,* Graham Greene's first novel.[3] I wrote and endorsed his opinion. I added "He came to see me after I was on the *Journal,* three years ago. Do you think one Heinemann author led to another? After all, the old paper has started off Barrie,[4] myself, and now young Greene."

The predictions were fulfilled, Greene's novel won immediate acclaim. It was felt a star was born. Like Barrie, Greene wrote an account of his descent on Nottingham in his story of an African tour.

I had known that same loneliness in a strange lodging in a bleak city when I had gone to my first journalistic post in Liverpool. In his loneliness Greene fell into the hands of a "fat actor-priest."[5] Possibly he was then a "mixed-up kid," fresh from a university where adolescents battle with life's problems, including spiritual ones. If I had been more hospitable to this lonely youth, would his personal history have been different and the tram-line catechism less influential? Perhaps it is a vain speculation and the mind was already set in the mould. I never saw Graham Greene again and retain a feeling that I failed in timely hospitality.

Greene's picture of Nottingham, derived from a mood, is rather a travesty. By general testimony it is one of the pleasantest, cleanest, well-situated cities in the kingdom and famous for its pretty girls whose standard of virtue is no lower than elsewhere.[6] If the future novelist cultivated there, as well as his faith, a taste for fish and chips, he was in good company . . . .

Extracted from Cecil Roberts, *The Bright Twenties: Being the Third Book of an Autobiography, 1920–1929* (London: Hodder and Stoughton, 1970), 257–59. *Editor's title.*

Notes

1. *Babbling April* was published in 1925.
2. Graham Greene's impressions of the *Journal* and of Cecil Roberts are given in *A Sort of Life*, 158–59. Though "not unhappy"—Greene was then very much in love with Vivien Dayrell-Browning, his future wife—his Nottingham days (November 1925–February 1926) must have been very stressful in view of his financial insecurity, uncertain career and his "hopeless" novel. Greene's recollections of Nottingham are to be found in *Journey Without Maps*, 115–16.
3. *The Man Within* was his first published novel. Greene had written two others, both unpublished.
4. J. M. Barrie (1860–1937), Scottish-born novelist and writer, joined the staff of the *Nottingham Journal* in 1883 as editorial writer and reviewer.
5. Father Trollope was the priest who instructed Greene for his conversion, which was completed before he left Nottingham. See Greene's account of his conversion in *A Sort of Life*, 61–67.
6. In his review of *A Sort of Life* (*Books and Bookmen*, 17 October 1971, 28–31), Cecil Roberts takes Greene to task for his remarks on the *Nottingham Journal* and accuses him of being a "careless and inaccurate writer" who might have been an "acute observer of prostitutes" but is inaccurate in his observations on Nottingham.

The Dangerous Worlds of Graham Greene

Nigel Dennis

Half a century or so ago, when I was about 19, I met Graham Greene, whose 75th anniversary we greet this week. He was standing with his wife Vivien in their cottage garden at Chipping Campden,[1] slim figures among summer flowers and fruit trees — or so my memory has painted it. Behind me, up the garden walk, came a telegraph boy. The message he brought, in lettering that is still in my mind's eye, was from the *Spectator:* Mr. Greene was told that six books were being held for him to review. They would be sent immediately, if he had no objection.[2]

I have no idea what happened next. I was dumb-founded; which is why the memory has persisted. First, there was the astonishing discovery that a publication should want a book reviewer (begging letters to literary editors were all I knew about). Second, there was a request for agreement by the reviewer — surely, an astonishing courtesy? Third, and most astonishing of all, there was the promise of six books. I could hardly credit such an immense number: though I had read two of Mr. Greene's early novels, I now recognised his stature for the first time.

Now that I have reviewed more than six books myself (including some by Graham Greene),[3] I have got over my astonishment. I realise too that Mr. Greene was not a king but a drudge, engaged in a struggle that lasted 10 years to support himself as a novelist. But I still regret that he didn't review a good deal more, because only V. S. Pritchett, the man without whom the old *New Statesman* would have been an interminable misfortune, could write so well about the books of others . . . .

Extracted from "The Dangerous Worlds of Graham Greene," *Sunday Telegraph*, 30 September 1979, 16.

Notes

1. Graham and Vivien Greene lived in London after their marriage in October 1927 but moved to Chipping Camden, eighty-five miles northwest of London, in March 1931 where they resided until they settled in Oxford in June 1933.

2. Graham Greene was an occasional reviewer of works of fiction for the *Spectator* during 1932 and the early part of 1933. As of 7 April 1933 and until the end of 1934, he contributed regularly for the "Fiction" columns of the *Spectator*.

3. Nigel Dennis had reviewed, by then, three of Greene's works for the *Sunday Telegraph: Collected Essays* (9 March 1969, 13); *Travels with My Aunt* (16 November 1969, 10), and *A Sort of Life* (19 September 1971, 18).

The Appeal of Unmapped Territories

Barbara Greene

Almost fifty years have now passed since my cousin
Graham and I set off so confidently and so ignorantly to
walk through the jungles of a country that we knew
almost nothing about. Liberia was indeed unexplored territory. Neither Graham nor I had been to Africa before,
nor had we ever attempted a similar expedition. We were
two innocents, our ignorance was abysmal, and we had no
maps — because there were none. I was then twenty-three
and Graham about five years older.

Graham's and my adventure together began when we met
at the wedding reception of his brother Hugh, where we
were all merrily drinking champagne — I think that was in
1935.[1] Graham had already made his plans for going to
Liberia. Travel books to out-of-the-way places were popular at that time, Graham had a family to provide for, and
his publisher had advanced him the money for a new
book. From childhood on he had enjoyed adventure stories and unknown Liberia sounded hopeful, but he did not
like the idea of going alone. He was trying to persuade

someone, anyone, to go with him, and only after everyone else had refused did he ask me and I promptly agreed to accompany him, though I had no clear idea of exactly where he was going to.

Next morning we both rather regretted this champagne decision, I because I was enjoying myself very much in London just then, and Graham because his heart sank at the thought of having to be responsible for a young girl he hardly knew. I told him on the telephone not to worry, my father would certainly forbid it. But now came what was perhaps the most unexpected part of the whole enterprise. "Papa," I said timidly, "I've done a very silly thing. I've told Graham I'd go to Liberia with him." My father, after only a moment's pause, answered quietly but firmly: "At *last* one of my daughters is showing a little initiative." There was never any arguing with my father and Graham was quite in despair. He sent me endless hair-raising reports of conditions in the interior, lists of unchecked diseases, accounts of savage campaigns by local tribes and anything else he could lay his hands on. But he, as well as I, knew that there was really nothing we could do but accept the verdict, and in a fortnight we were going on our way.

Whatever qualms Graham may have suffered, I think that my own reaction was chiefly one of excitement. Everything sailed along so quickly and perhaps I was also a little flattered by the attentions I was receiving. It was unusual then for young girls to adventure off into the wilds—but my father was in many ways an unusual man. Apart from getting my visa and some injections, I really had nothing else to do. I am ashamed now to admit that I had no idea how much work was needed when preparing for such an expedition, how the question of medical supplies (among a hundred other things) had to be gone into with great care, though that proved later to have been rather wasted work as nearly all our medical supplies were left behind in Freetown in the final rush. Graham saw to everything and I felt sure that he knew what he was doing, though I now wonder whether I really thought about it at all. Even my father, after giving Graham a cheque, seems to me now to have taken everything most casually. . . .

Graham and I were both rather shy people; as I have already said, we were really only acquaintances when we set out together and — strange though this may seem — we were still not more than friendly acquaintances when the long journey came to an end after three months. Even under the worst conditions we were invariably polite and courteous to one another; we never argued. If we disagreed on any subject we dropped it immediately, partly because the heat and sheer exhaustion drained all surplus energy. That was probably a good thing, for although it led to long silences the silences never became bitter or resentful. Graham took all decisions and made all the plans. I merely followed. Looking back now I realise also that I was never, at any time, in the least bit helpful, but on the other hand I never, never complained. We got on well, respecting and liking one another, but when at the end we parted to go our separate ways, we said our friendly good-byes with none of those hugs and kisses so common now, and we did not meet again for months — or was it even for years? — though we were always delighted to see each other when it happened.

What, I sometimes wonder, did that journey bring me? Did it enlarge my horizons, change my ideas or character? Unconsciously I suppose it must have done, as till then I had floated lightly on the surface of what I now realise

was a very privileged existence, and I remember clearly
how Graham's wider experience of life and his independent views often amazed and astonished me; but how far
they changed me, or how much the journey itself changed
me, is now hard to judge for I was at the age when every
day opens new windows to wider views. That I was forced
to stick through all difficulties to the end showed no particular merit on my part, for we soon reached the point of
no return. The journey brought to Graham an intense love
of Africa that has never left him and he returned there
whenever an opportunity offered itself . . . .[2]

We got to Freetown at last.

Graham had never done anything like this before either.
It was, in fact, not at all in his line. Although cousins, we
had never had a great deal to do with one another before
Fate and champagne decided to link up our lives in this
way for three months. I got out my diary and wrote down
what I thought of him. His brain frightened me. It was
sharp and clear and cruel. I admired him for being unsen-
timental, but "always remember to rely on yourself," I
noted. "If you are in a sticky place he will be so interested
in noting your reactions that he will probably forget to
rescue you." For some reason he had a permanently shaky
hand, so I hoped that we would not meet any wild beasts
on the trip. I had never shot anything in my life, and my
cousin would undoubtedly miss anything he aimed at.
Physically he did not look strong. He seemed somewhat
vague and unpractical, and later I was continually astonished at his efficiency and the care he devoted to every little detail. Apart from three or four people he was really
fond of, I felt that the rest of humanity was to him like a
heap of insects that he liked to examine, as a scientist

might examine his specimens, coldly and clearly. He was always polite. He had a remarkable sense of humour and held few things too sacred to be laughed at. I suppose at that time I had a very conventional little mind, for I remember he was continually tearing down ideas I had always believed in, and I was left to build them up anew. It was stimulating and exciting, and I wrote down that he was the best kind of companion one could have for a trip of this kind. I was learning far more than he realised.

Graham walked on in front at a most tremendous speed, and I followed at my own pace. It was a habit we started that day and carried on till much later when my cousin fell ill. Then I walked ahead. But in all those weeks we never once walked together. For one thing we would have always wondered if one was keeping the other back, or walking too fast. Also it was too hot. Walking together means talking, or feeling one should talk occasionally. In the heat one needed all one's energy for the sheer physical effort of placing one foot in front of the other for hours on end.

Graham and I had our supper.[3] It was one of our happiest evenings together—one of the last times when we could talk completely naturally to one another, without wondering whether anything we said could possibly hurt the other in any way. So soon after that we had to give up discussing subjects on which we held different points of view. It sounds unbelievably childish now, but in our weariness we got easily impatient with arguments. My tiredness made my brain work even more slowly that it usually does, and I would grope unsuccessfully for the words I needed. Sometimes as I was in the very middle of saying something my strength would give out and I would murmur weakly,

"I expect you're right, really," which must have irritated my cousin profoundly. Graham, on the other hand, would sometimes become rather obstinate, hanging on to some small, unimportant point like a dog to a bone. But we never quarrelled, not once. We knew so well that it was the ghastly damp heat that was lowering our vitality, and we would smile at one another and think, "We won't talk about that again." Politics was the first thing to go. I sometimes heard myself expressing the most extraordinary ideas, professing the strangest beliefs. Words would come out of my mouth which had nothing to do with my own thoughts. I would listen to the tired voice, and think, "What an odd thing to say." Sometimes what I was saying would sound so dull that I could hardly bear to hear it myself, and I would lose interest in the middle of a sentence. So many unfinished sentences; so many words; sounds trailing away into nothingness and floating off into the hot, moist air. One subject after another would be put away, left to one side, marked carefully, "Not wanted during voyage," till gradually practically nothing remained on the last day or two of our trip except the enthralling subject of food. By that time, of course, it was the one thing above all others that really interested us, and we found that we did not irritate each other by longing for different kinds of food. But those days were still to come. In Nicoboozu we did not even guess that they would ever come. We were feeling so well, and not yet tired, and our minds were fresh. Both of us were enchanted with the village, happy and completely under the spell of the African night.

⁓

. . . Graham had a little twitching nerve over his right eye. When he felt particularly unwell it would twitch incessantly, and I watched it with horror. It fascinated me, and

I would find my eyes fixed upon it till I was almost unable to look anywhere else. I did not tell him about it, for I got to know it so well that I was able to gauge how he was feeling without having to ask him. Soon we would have to press on. We would, of course, go straight on to Monrovia from Ganta, but that would be too ignominious. It was the usual route and was taken by all travellers or missionaries to Ganta. It would be humiliating to descend to that. We had come to Liberia to keep off the beaten track and to walk through the unknown parts. But to trek to Sinoe was out of the question so far as we could see at the moment, and so it was better to try for Grand Bassa. We could start that way, and then if Graham got better, we could still branch off. The way to Grand Bassa would be primitive and interesting, but it would be shorter.

I was definitely frightened. In a day or two, I thought, we shall be away from Dr. Harley; and I shall be alone with the twitching nerve, and I understood absolutely nothing about nursing. Graham too felt uncomfortable. Illness in the bush too often means death. And Graham, to his own surprise, found that he did not want to die.[4] He discovered in himself an intense love of life. I watched him put spoonfuls of Epsom salts in his tea. His face was grey, and it was only his tremendous will-power that was giving him his burning vitality.

As we collected our things together in the early morning ready to trek down to Zigi's Town, I wished suddenly that we could stay on in Tappee Ta. Graham looked ghastly, and was shivering. He had a strange, stupid expression on his face, and sometimes he stumbled slightly as though he could not see very well. I was frightened, for I realised that he was seriously ill. It was no good asking him to stay in Tappee Ta till he was better. He had made up his mind that he must get to the coast as quickly as possible. Although he knew that Grand Bassa was a small town and possessed only one white inhabitant, he talked incessantly about it, as if it was going to turn out to be a heaven on earth. I did not argue with him, for I could see that he was determined to press on. He was as obstinate as only a sick man can be. He wanted to get the coast, and he wanted to get there quickly.

To be alone with one companion for several weeks on end in uncomfortable and strange circumstances means that one either becomes very fond of him or grows to dislike him intensely. There is no half-way house. Mere indifference is impossible. Luckily during these last few weeks I had discovered that I liked Graham, and I had learnt to look up to him and respect him.

As I saw him in the early morning light, his face grey and drawn, his hand shaking even more than it usually did as he poured the Epsom salts into his tea, I became scared. I could not bear to see him so ill, and to be altogether unable to help.[5] I felt stupid and useless.

Extracted from *Too Late to Turn Back*, intro. Paul Theroux (London: Settle Press, 1981), *xii–xv*, 6–7, 16, 60–62, 67–68, 118–19, 170–71. Originally published as *Land Benighted* (London: Geoffrey Bles, 1938). *Editor's title.*

Notes

1. This should have been 1934 since their journey for West Africa began on 4 January 1935.
2. The preceding paragraphs are taken from the foreword written some forty-five years or so after the trip. The recollections and impressions that follow have been recorded during the trip or in the days immediately following it.

3. The setting is the village of Nicoboozu, on the first leg of the trip. Nicoboozu was a "wonderful contrast" to Duogobmai, which they had just left.

4. Her "discovery" is quite significant and is further corroborated by Graham Greene's unequivocal confession: "I had discovered in myself a passionate interest in living. I had always assumed before, as a matter of course, that death was desirable." *Journey Without Maps*, 263.

5. Graham Greene notes that he remembers "nothing of the trek to Zigi's Town and very little of the succeeding days." *Journey Without Maps*, 262.

Excursions in Greene Land

J. Maclaren-Ross

It was noon and summer when I arrived at that house eighteen years before, aged twenty-six and carrying a copy of *Brighton Rock* wrapped in a *Daily Express* containing James Agate's review of the novel which had appeared that morning . . . [1]

I glanced round and as I did so Graham Greene himself appeared quite silently in the open doorway. I was startled because not even a creak on the stairs had announced his approach. Seeing me there gave him also a start, and he took a step back. He was wearing a brown suit and large horn-rimmed spectacles, which he at once snatched off as if they had been his hat. He was not wearing a hat and this was the only time I saw him wearing spectacles. I had not expected him to be so tall.

"I hope you haven't been waiting long," he said. He had a spontaneous pleasant smile. "Nobody told me you were here. Would you like a cigarette? Something to drink?"

"Something cold if possible," I said accepting the cigarette avidly.

Greene said: "We could go over to the local, if you won't find that a bore. They'll have ice there, and anyway I've forgotten to get the beer."

Each carrying a large jug, we set off for the pub which was on the other side of the Common[2] and may have been the one afterwards featured in *The End of the Affair*. Greene took long lounging strides and his shoulders were well above mine as we walked across the grass. Though very lean he had high broad straight shoulders from which his jacket was loosely draped as if still on its hanger.

He said: "I've just been asked to do a radio-play myself, so I'm relying on you to show me how to write them."

"I fear I'll not be much use. I've only written one so far and they wouldn't have that." Then fearing that sounded too much like total obscurity and failure, in fact the truth, I added: "They did offer me a job on the strength of it though."

"At the BBC?"

"Training to be a writer-producer, eventually."

"Then obviously your play impressed them. Why wouldn't they take it?"

"Too sordid, was the general opinion."

"Bloody fools. Well they can't say that about mine. It's to be about Benjamin Jowett, the Master of Balliol, you know."[3]

"Never explain, never apologize?" I said, hoping I'd got it the right way round.

"That among other things," Greene said. "Are you going to take the BBC job?"

"When there's a vacancy. But I was warned I might have to wait a year."

"What d'you do meantime? Besides writing radio-plays I mean."

"I sell vacuum cleaners," I said.

He said: "Well it doesn't matter now. Because you'll be writing your own book I expect . . . "

So I said: "I expect I will. Sooner or later," getting out my Brazilian cigarettes, and nine years in fact went by before I did publish a book on the subject.

Greene said: "Oh, splendid," fumbling in the yellow pack with MENZALA on the green band around it. "I'm off to Mexico shortly, so I must get used to smoking this type of tobacco."[4]

"They're rolled in real rice-paper," I told him, but I noticed that he soon let his burn out tactfully in an ash-tray on the bar.

"Mexico sounds exciting," I said. "To get copy for your work?" I was learning the language fast.

"A kind of travel-book," he said, the ice slid down the empty glasses and we were given the beer-jugs, containing some sort of strong pale ale, to carry back across the Common. . . .

"You are yourself a Catholic?" I asked: it must be remembered that much less was known about the author personally in those days, and I'd been unable to obtain so far the semi-autobiographical *Journey Without Maps*, which would have answered my question.

Greene said: "Yes, I was converted in 1926."

I said: "I was baptized one in 1912," which disconcerted him more than the vacuum-cleaners. I suppose a salesman with literary ambitions was strange enough, but a cradle-Catholic literary salesman bordered on the extravagant.

About the meal itself I remember nothing, except that the dining-room was rather dark; the blinds may have been drawn against the sun and it's possible that we had lemon-pudding as a sweet. The housekeeper did not appear in person: heralded by shouts of a shaft, the dishes were borne from below by a dumb-waiter and Greene himself went round pouring out the beer. Mrs. Greene, handsome with black hair, was placid and sedate like a young Spanish matron, and even the repeated crash of the dumb-waiter arriving at its destination in the serving-hatch failed to shake her poise.

From time to time she left the table for brief periods, when she returned from each sortie her husband raised inquiring eyebrows and she nodded reassurance, but the last time she murmured something that I didn't catch; and when she rose from the table Greene said to me apologetically: "It's an awful nuisance, but They are asking to see you I'm afraid. I wonder if you'd mind."

"Why of course not," I said mystified. "I'd like to see Them very much."

"I'm sorry but we'll get no peace otherwise," he said, leading the way up another, darker flight of stairs; I could hear a strange twittering sound coming from behind the door in front of which he halted.

"By the way," I asked slightly nervous, "What are They?" imagining giant parrots or pet vultures brought from Africa, or even elderly female relatives, not quite certifiable but confined nevertheless to their rooms.

"They are in here," Greene said, opening the door for me to precede him, and I found myself facing a large railed cot raised off the floor to about the level of my chest. From behind the bars of this cage two small, extremely pretty blonde girls peered out at me unblinking. They were perhaps aged four and five respectively, and it's a sobering thought that they must be over thirty now.[5]

"Well, come on," Greene said from behind me, "Say hullo politely."

I now had an opportunity to observe him more closely without staring, which I'd been brought up to believe was rude. He must have been thirty-four at the time, his lean face was unlined then, but the skin was rough and a little worn: though his cheeks were carefully shaven there was still a suggestion of stubble. He smiled a lot and the set of his mouth was amiable rather than severe as in the photographs. His lightish brown hair was parted at the side and brushed in a slight curl over a broad bumpy forehead. He sat forward in the low armchair with broad shoulders hunched up high and large knuckly hands hanging down with a cigarette fuming between the long fingers. I had offered him another Brazilian which, saying he'd been smoking far too much, he swiftly refused, then had stealthily taken one of his own. I don't know how he did manage out in Mexico.

We had passed on now to ruthlessness in films, how Hitchcock got away with it often despite the censorship and how Greene himself had tried and failed to slip a ruthless scene past British Lion while scripting for Korda in 1936.[6] From there we arrived at Paramount's prospective film-version of *A Gun for Sale* and who was to play the part of Raven: if made with an American star, then Bogart, Alan Baxter, or Greene's own personal choice Eduardo Ciannelli, the Trock Estrella in *Winterset*, about which we were both enthusiastic.[7]

"Ciannelli lends distinction to any film," I said.

"He does indeed."

"No, no. I was quoting your own words. From a film-article in *Night and Day*."

"Oh, so you've read *Night and Day*."

"Every issue."

Night and Day[8] had been an excellent sophisticated weekly magazine on *New Yorker* lines, edited by Greene

and John Marks the translator of Céline, and Greene had
done the cinema criticism, which led to the magazine fold-
ing because some fool said that he'd libelled the child star
Shirley Temple and there had been a case in court.

He said: "I remember the article now. Wasn't it a review
of *Marked Woman*, with Bogart and Bette Davis?"[9] adding
with relish: "That was a pretty ruthless picture, where the
henchman cuts the double-cross on Bette Davis's cheek."

Now he began to tell me about the Shirley Temple libel
case, which he evidently found less hilarious than his
error about the feudal system, but accepted all the same
with ironical detachment. Apparently he'd been abroad
and incommunicado at the time, and returned to find the
proceedings all wrapped up and judgement given against
him, together with the censure of the judge.

"Two libel suits one after the other," he said. "There was
a case about my Liberian book *Journey Without Maps* too
and Heinemann's had to withdraw the whole edition, so
that seems to have been my unlucky year."[10]

"D'you think you'll write any more Entertainments?" was
my next question; for *Brighton Rock* was first published as
one, as such despite the Catholic angle I considered it, and
only much later did it become a Novel and later still a
Modern Classic.

"I might," Greene answered. "Just one more. Based on
an original idea I started to work on for Korda, only his
outfit thought it would be too dangerous to film. About a
Spanish Government agent who comes to London on a
mission during the Civil War and finds that the war has
followed him here.[11] I try to restrict myself to home
ground if I can, English backgrounds, London whenever
possible: I've always made that a rule."

South America, Istanbul, Stockholm, the Gold Coast, and now Mexico went rapidly through my mind,[12] I could hardly let this pass, but before I could speak Greene said: "Oh I know, I've broken the rule several times. But all the same I think an English novelist should write about England, don't you?"

Presumably They had settled down at last upstairs, for Mrs. Greene came in to join us, though not in the conversation. She sat in the armchair facing her husband, but turned sideways to him, with her legs tucked under her. She busied herself with head bent over some piece of needlework: embroidery, brocade, it may have been but not, I think, knitting.

I remember her speaking twice only: once was when we were talking about American short-story writers and Greene said: "You liked Saroyan, didn't you darling?"

She looked puzzled and said: "Saroyan?"

"You know, the Armenian."

"Oh yes," she said. "The one who isn't Michael Arlen."

The second time she spoke was to remind her husband that the time was half-past four. Greene glanced at his watch and sprang up with an exclamation. I rose also, saying: "James Agate's brother?"

"Yes. I'll walk you to your bus."

On the way up the High Street, past twopenny libraries and plate-glass shops, he told me several anecdotes about the brother, but I remember none of them. The brandy, the beer and the heat had hit me as we left the house and I was struggling with a question in my muddled head. Would it be an imposition if I asked Greene to look at the short stories which I'd written?

A reply came very quickly, as indeed he'd promised. With eagerness I tore open the small grey distinctive envelope, but realised from the first line and a glance at the signature that the letter was not from Greene at all, but from his wife. An extraordinary similarity in the handwriting, due perhaps to the fact that they were cousins, had misled me.[13]

Her husband had returned the night before, Mrs. Greene wrote, extremely over-tired by his trip, and she felt it her duty to prevent him from becoming completely exhausted by taking on more than was necessary. She was sure that he would have liked to read my stories but she was also sure that I would understand why this would not be possible. She was therefore returning the MSS under separate cover and signed herself Sincerely Vivien Greene.

I still have the letter somewhere.

Extracted from J. Maclaren-Ross, "Excursions in Greene Land," *London Magazine*, December 1964, 56–65.

Notes

1. *Daily Express*, 14 July 1938, 12.
2. Graham Greene had moved from his Oxford residence to 14 North Side, Clapham Common, S.W. 4, in June 1935.
3. *The Great Jowett* was broadcast on 6 May 1939 and published by the Bodley Head in 1981; also in his *Collected Plays* (Harmondsworth, England: Penguin Books, 1985).
4. If Maclaren-Ross had visited Greene on 18 July 1938—the date of James Agate's review of *Brighton Rock*—then the statement about going to Mexico attributed to Greene is erroneous. Both Mr. and Mrs. Greene had sailed for America in January 1938, and Graham Greene returned to England from Mexico at the end of May.
5. Greene has two children, a girl and a boy: Lucy Caroline born 28 December 1933 and Francis 13 September 1936.
6. Greene had met Alexander Korda, the Hungarian producer, in the fall of 1936 and began scripting for him a "film story" he had in mind—*The Green Cockatoo*—and then, in collaboration with Basil Dean, adapted John Galsworthy's story "The First and the Last" that Korda released only in 1939 under the title *Twenty-One Days*.

7. In May 1936, *A Gun for Sale* was sold to Paramount for $12,000.

8. With John Marks, Graham Greene coedited the short-lived, weekly literary magazine. Modeled partly on the *New Yorker*, it ran from 1 July 1937 to 23 December 1937. Graham Greene's film review of *Wee Willie Winkie*, deemed libelous by King's Bench in March of the following year, may have precipitated the demise of the magazine which seemed inevitable because of its financial problems. (See *Night and Day*, ed. and intro. Christopher Hawtree [London: Chatto and Windus, 1985]). Its list of contributors included Anthony Powell, V. S. Pritchett, Evelyn Waugh, William Empson, Cyril Connolly, Herbert Read, Malcolm Muggeridge, and Elizabeth Bowen, among others.

9. Warner Bros., 1937. The review in question appeared in *Night and Day* on 9 September 1937. It is now included in *The Pleasure Dome*, 166.

10. *Journey Without Maps* was withdrawn from circulation some eighteen months after its initial publication (London: Heinemann, 1936). It became available from Pan Books in 1946.

11. Later published as *The Confidential Agent*. *Author's note*.

12. I find no evidence of a visit to South America at the time of the interview. Both Mr. and Mrs. Greene made a quick trip to Istanbul when they went on a Hellenic cruise in 1929; Graham and Hugh Greene visited Sweden in 1933; Graham and Barbara Greene traveled to Liberia in 1935; and Graham Greene traveled alone in Mexico in 1938 after leaving his wife in the U. S.

13. An erroneous impression. Greene met Vivien Dayrell-Browning for the first time during his last term at Balliol in 1925. They were married two-and-one-half years later. Graham Greene's father and mother, Charles Greene and Marion Greene, were cousins.

Graham Greene: Perverse Genius

A. L. Rowse

I find this extremely distasteful—this ingratitude for the marvellous gift of life—and incomprehensible after my happy schooldays, deplorable compared with the struggle I had to get to a university at all. I can suggest only that with his fortunate middle-class upbringing—with those clever brothers, Raymond and Hugh Greene, his mother a first cousin of Robert Louis Stevenson—he must have been spoiled. In my working-class background he would have been disciplined, given a regular hiding—instead of that he was psycho-analysed. Really, at sixteen! He admits that the excuse for being away from school, reading on his own in Kensington Gardens, probably did more good.

Then came Oxford.[1] He failed twice to win a scholarship, but his "overburdened father" gave him an allowance of £250 a year, and got him into Balliol. (The three scholarships I had such a struggle to collect made £200 a year in all.) I didn't see much of my contemporary, though we contributed to the same literary papers and went in for the Newdigate[2]—neither Graham nor Evelyn Waugh getting a mention. . . .

Meanwhile Graham was writing novels, with no money and no success—except for the adventitious luck with *Stamboul Train*. He had married Vivien and started a family: when one thinks of the hardihood, the hardships they endured, the perseverance, one can only say how much he deserved his eventual triumph. It does not seem to have made him any happier. All through his work there is this expression of a perverse preference for death. . . .

Vivien was a Catholic, so he became a Catholic. He claims, as did Evelyn Waugh, that this was a matter of intellectual argument, not of emotional leanings. . . .

Father Gervase Mathew, of Blackfriars at Oxford, to whom *The Power and the Glory* is dedicated,[3] was a close friend of both of us. He used to tell me a good deal about Graham; that he would forget the intellectual arguments that had persuaded him, and Gervase would have to remind him what they were. Simply mumbling the "Rock of Peter," as in that book, is mere mumbo-jumbo.

Graham is self-conscious, and on the defensive, about Greene Land, but he derives inspiration from seediness and squalor. About the time of *Brighton Rock*, I commented to Vivien about his remarkable eyes—opened wide and magnetically as if he saw the world with horror, as I suppose he does. I cannot approve: I immeasurably prefer Acton's vision, seeking for beauty wherever and in whatever it may be found.[4] Why? One must always give a reason: the one is an enhancement of life, the other is a degradation.

About this time too I recall a meal in Oxford at Graham's. There was always a strain in his marriage, which I will not get into, though I know the other side. I remember the furniture, the elegant, uncomfortable Regency window-seat Vivien had picked up, but little of the dinner-party. Martin D'Arcy, the Jesuit,[5] another friend (within limits) was there. Conversation did not flow; Graham was silent, I felt like a fish out of water and had nothing to contribute. Martin was reduced to filling in with snobbish talk about his old Irish family. There was a sense of desolation. Not long after, Graham left Vivien.

Extracted from A. L. Rowse, "Graham Greene: Perverse Genius," *Friends and Contemporaries* (London: Methuen, 1989), 241, 243–44, 247.

Notes

1. As an undergraduate, A. L. Rowse remembers Graham Greene's "marvellous china-blue eyes" as well as Greene's "extraordinarily youthful appearance with the curly flax-gold hair and the odd strangulated voice speaking from his Adam's apple as if he had difficulty in producing his voice." *A Cornishman at Oxford* (London: Jonathan Cape, 1965), 206–7.

2. The Newdigate is an annual prize for an original poem on a set subject awarded to an Oxford undergraduate. It was founded in 1805 by Sir Roger Newdigate (1719–1806), M.P. for Oxford.

3. Though both the British and American editions of *The Power and the Glory* were published in March 1940, only the British edition carries the dedication "For Gervase." The American edition carries the dedication: "To Vivien with dearest love." This is perhaps the last time Greene dedicated a work to his wife. *The Heart of the Matter* carries the dedication: "To V.G., L.C.G. and F.C.G."

4. Harold Acton (1904–94), Greene's contemporary at Oxford, belonged to a group of undergraduate reformers known as the "aesthetes" who attempted in late 1922 to revive the ideals of Walter Pater. Acton, "poet, raconteur and man of taste," was the aesthete par excellence. Apart from eccentricities of dress and behavior, Acton's imposing personality and seriousness of purpose had a lasting influence on the Oxford undergraduates, especially with his founding of a new undergraduate magazine, *The Broom*.

5. Martin [Cyril] D'Arcy, S.J., RSL (1888–1976), lectured in philosophy at Oxford and was Master of Campion Hall from 1932 until he became the English provincial for the Jesuits in 1945. Father D'Arcy has written extensively — no fewer than twenty books — on philosophical and religious topics, especially on the nature of belief, humanism and Christianity, and faith and morals.

Melancholy Marked Him for Her Own

Ronald de Couves Matthews

I remember very little of my first encounter with Graham Greene but of one thing I am certain: Graham had to be wearing a brown suit, not well pressed, for that is what he always wears. What was unmistakable was the bulge of the left pocket of his coat—not due to a hidden revolver but to an atomizer for nasal spray. Though his brother is a Harley Street physician, each year Graham continues to carry everywhere his hay fever which is triggered with clockwork precision at the beginning of the season when the breeze carries into the air the pollen of flowers.

. . . Graham and I never lost sight of each other. We undertook a series of excursions which we pursued regularly until the war separated us but we resumed them when it was over.

The pattern of our outings rarely changed except when we went to the countryside for a weekend because both of us were instinctively conservative in our habits. For the most part, we met on Saturday evenings, that time when the London pubs opened their doors. Whenever possible, we chose an interesting district which was unfamiliar to us. After the deafening din of a trip by underground—we both preferred the underground to the bus—we began our round of the small pubs of the district. After several hours of random sampling of beer in different pubs, of listening no less aimlessly to the conversation of the drinkers, we set out once more to the West End to dine in one of its better restaurants—I say better, not elegant or fashionable. By the time we downed our after dinner drinks, it was time to return home by our separate ways.

. . . As far back as I can remember, Graham never visited my digs in Holborn which I kept until the war. As for me, I can safely say that I never visited his house at Clapham Common where he and his family resided until it was destroyed in an air raid. I met his wife; she was very friendly to me, but I can never say where I first met her. The only social occasion at which I recall meeting her was at the party for the launching of *Night and Day*, the swanky London magazine which took the *New Yorker* as its model. Graham was its co-editor and wrote the film reviews. . . .

A friendship for which reasons can be easily given stands a good chance of being no more than a banal acquaintance. It was only little by little over the years that I began to learn a number of things which Graham and I had had in common in our past. We had both had disappointing relationships with our fathers.[1] We had both known at school moments of painful unhappiness. Neither one of us showed the least talent for sports and, on coming of age, we were sorely tempted to scorn such physical prowess but were too English to believe in the sincerity of our contempt. We were both overwhelmed by the appeal of misfortune, of failure, of sad or trivial commonplace events which Gide once loved to note and which I have labelled "fascinating smuttiness." But we shared the same puerile taste in adventure stories and practical jokes. Finally, like Graham, I had embraced Catholicism for the same kind of reasons also unrelated to faith.

Britain was governed by a conservative cabinet[2] which did not even claim that its indifference to the livelihood of people was redeemed by its solicitude for the national honour. An impotent labour party in opposition was too afraid to raise its voice for fear of being caught singing the same tune of earlier communists. Graham and I were of the left in that we were for the hungry against the well fed, for equality versus privilege and preferred the vulgar violence of the poor to the vulgar self-complacency of upstarts who had taken for themselves the best seats at the banquet table. "How can we make our indignation effective on the social level?" Such was the great question which English intellectuals asked themselves in that period.

. . . Graham has said and written that the causes of his pessimism went back to his childhood.[3] He and I talked a great deal naturally about our childhood.

"They call you an unhappy writer," I said to Graham. "But I wonder whether a totally happy person can ever become an artist or writer."

"Are you not getting things confused?" he asked. "I do not think I'm accused of being an unhappy individual who happens to write but a writer who deliberately chooses painful topics."

"In the final analysis," I said, "does it not all come to the same thing? In so far as a writer has any worth or value, is it not true to say that the subjects choose the writer and not he the subjects? The obsession that makes a writer choose painful subjects of any kind does not settle normally on a perfectly happy person."

"Can you, in some Orwellian future, imagine a potential author invited to undergo an 'examination of his state of happiness or contentment' before being granted a membership card to the syndicate of writers?"

"Of course. But I wonder whether sufficient interest in literature will survive in such a future to make the creation of unauthorized bookstalls profitable."

"Not more than I can envision public libraries filling their shelves exclusively with books by contributors to youth weeklies. Name me several sound authors. I mean, real authors not candidates for a membership card in some future syndicate of writers."

"Dickens is generally considered a sound author. I seem to remember receiving several of his books as prizes when I was at school."

"Dickens a sound author? Does it not strike you right-away that the evil characters in Dickens have the reality of a nightmare and the good ones the emptiness of a summer memory? One can almost touch Fagin but one's hand passes through the body of Mr. Brownlow."[4]

"The controllers of thought would not have had much difficulty in eliminating Dickens if they had wanted to. His unhappy childhood was common knowledge: the whole world knew the story of the blacking factory. One knows that though one may survive an unhappy childhood in the same way that one survives the small pox, one carries the scars for life. In this regard, you might pass the test. On the whole, can you say, in fact, that your childhood was unhappy?"

Extracted from *Mon Ami Graham Greene*, trans. (from English) Maurice Beerblock (Bruges: Desclée de Brouwer, 1957), 8–11, 15, 30–31. Retranslated into English by A. F. Cassis. *Editor's title.* The English text was never published and is not available; the only available text is the French translation by Maurice Beerblock.

Notes

1. In "The Heart of the Graham Greene Matter," Guy Martin records his impression that there seems to have been a "wall of misunderstanding between [Greene] and his father." *Realities,* December 1962, 60–63.
2. Stanley Baldwin took over the "national government" from Ramsay MacDonald in June 1935 and was replaced by Neville Chamberlain in May 1937.
3. See "The Lost Childhood" and "The Burden of Childhood" in *Collected Essays* and his prologue to *The Lawless Roads.*
4. "In the Fagin darkness Dickens's hand seldom falters," says Greene and questions whether the "inadequate ghosts of goodness"—that is, Mr. Brownlow or Rose—"can triumph over Fagin, Monks, and Sikes." See "The Young Dickens," *Collected Essays,* 107–8.

One-and-Ninepenny Lunches

~~~~~

H. E. Bates

By this time Madge and I were expecting a third baby[1]
and it will give some idea of the high state of my finances
if I say that one day I accepted with alacrity an invitation
from Graham Greene to lunch with him at a restaurant he
had just discovered: "You can eat for one-and-ninepence."
The place was in fact that splendidly Edwardian pub in
the heart of London's theatre-land, all brass and red plush
and mirrors and beer-engines and snug corners, The
Salisbury in St. Martin's Lane. Graham, as impecunious
as I was, had discovered with delight that for one-and-
ninepence you could get soup, a large plate of boiled or
roast beef, roast lamb or pork, some sort of pudding or
cheese with magnificent celery. It was all excellent.

Neither of us had enjoyed, up to that time, anything
more than a *succès d'estime,* to which on my behalf
Graham had contributed a generous appraisal of *Cut and
Come Again,*[2] the volume of stories containing *The Mill.* In it
he had compared me fairly and squarely with Tchechov,
saying that he didn't think me the lesser artist. In consequence my literary stock now stood pretty high and I

therefore felt that the time had come when I should attempt to build something of ambition and solid worth on these foundations.

～

. . . One day at lunch with Graham Greene I had mentioned to him my arid literary predicament (I hardly think his own was all that much better) and he had suggested that my talents surely had their correct place in the Ministry of Information, for which he himself was doing certain work.[5] Very kindly he promised to put in a word for me in the right place, which he duly did, and in due course I went along to the headquarters of the Ministry, then housed at London University.

I was there ushered into the presence of a gentleman who informed me that he had been a school inspector: a tribe of whom, I understand, the teaching profession is not particularly enamoured; and after my experience with one I cannot say that I wonder why. We had scarcely begun to talk when he was called away to another room for a telephone call, leaving the interview to be carried on by an office boy. The following illuminating conversation then took place.

"What kind of work do you do?"

"I am a writer."

"Do you mean you actually write?"

"I actually write."

"Oh! really? What have you written?"

"Books."

"Oh? You mean you have actually written books?"

"Yes."

"You mean the sort of books that are published?"

"The sort of books that are published."

"Oh! Good heavens. And have they actually been published?"

I rose and walked out, not waiting for the return of His Majesty the school inspector.

Graham Greene's fury at this nonsense, when I told him of it, was so great that he may well have communicated it to Cecil Day-Lewis.[4] He certainly communicated it to someone at the MOI and as Graham Greene isn't noted for using stale suet for words I do not doubt that the echoes of protest reverberated acidly.

Extracted from H. E. Bates, *The Blossoming World: An Autobiography.* Volume 2 (London: Michael Joseph, 1971), 123, 176–77. *Editor's title.*

Notes

1. Bates's third child, Richard Lucas, was born in July 1937.
2. Graham Greene's review appeared in the *Spectator*, 22 November 1935, 36, 38.
3. Graham Greene worked at the Ministry of Information before he was posted to West Africa in December 1941.
4. Cecil Day-Lewis (1904–72), Irish-born poet and prose writer, became poet laureate in 1968.

Chivalrous and Courteous

Kathleen Raine

I met there Antonia White;[1] far more experienced in the ways of such non-places than I was, and incomparably more skilled at impersonating the person she was expected to be. She was, I am bound to say, very kind to me; and certainly she, and Graham Greene, who presently appeared in the Department[2] (for this kind of thing was, as he himself admitted, "copy" for the books he wrote or might write) influenced the course of my life at the time. . . .

Graham Greene too was a Catholic. I had reviewed books for him at the time he was editor of the *Spectator*;[3] and now in the Department it was a pleasure to see him tilting against bureaucracy, a game of skill which he played as others play chess, or poker, perhaps. Graham was, towards both Antonia and myself, invariably chivalrous; like a knight who does battle with every champion, but shows courtesy towards women. I cannot say that I at all understood Graham either; he was not of my own imaginative kindred, but the association was, at the time, a very pleasant one.

⌐⌐⌐

. . . Of Catholicism as a culture I may have had some conception; but of Christianity as a way of life, something simple not to be found in books at all—that secret I had not discovered.

Graham Greene too was tormented by "doubts," though less subtle than Antonia's, for he was a convert, and his mind had been formed, as had mine, on simpler lines than those fine Jesuitical intricacies which James Joyce so nostalgically depicts. I remember his saying to me once (we were walking together through some woods and fields near Berkhamsted and I can remember his voice and his look as he quoted the words, one of my few flashes of imaginative insight into Graham Greene) "Unless I shall see in His hands the print of the nails, and put my finger into the print of the nails, and thrust my hand into His side, I will not believe." It was from Graham also that I first heard of Padre Pio,[4] who bore the stigmata. It is obvious that for one of the types of mankind, this proof by physical evidence is crucial; to me, I must confess, it really had no importance whether the Incarnation had, as historical fact, taken place or not.

Graham insisted that Catholicism is essentially a "magical" religion.[5] I did not quite see what he meant, but had nothing against magic, as such. Transubstantiation, however, did not strike me as a magical, but as a metaphysical doctrine . . . .

Extracted from Kathleen Raine, *The Land Unknown* (London: Hamish Hamilton, 1975), 178, 180–81, 184. *Editor's title.*

Notes

1. Antonia White (née Botting, 1889–1980), journalist, novelist, short story writer, and translator of many works from French,

was a friend of Greene whom she seems to have first met in 1935. She was also one-time fashion editor of the *Daily Mirror* and drama critic of *Time and Tide*.

2. Ministry of Information.

3. Greene had become literary editor of the *Spectator* in 1940 but his editorship was interrupted by his wartime service.

4. Greene had seen the stigmata "from a few feet away as he [Padre Pio] said Mass one early morning in his monastery in South Italy." (*Ways of Escape*, 116). He had also spoken about it to Malcolm Muggeridge. See *Like It Was: The Diaries of Malcolm Muggeridge*, sel. and ed. John Bright-Holmes (London: Collins, 1981), 374. For a more detailed account of Greene's experience, see the John Heilpern excerpt "On the Dangerous Edge" on p. 253 and his statements to John Cornwell in the "Why I Am Still a Catholic" excerpt on pp. 463–65.

5. See also his comments on this topic to Marie-Françoise Allain, *The Other Man: Conversations with Graham Greene*, trans. Guido Waldman (London: Bodley Head, 1983), 156–57.

Nature's Displaced Person

Malcolm Muggeridge

Graham Greene, who had also joined the Ministry of Information wartime staff, as characteristically took a highly professional view of what was expected of us, coolly exploring the possibility of throwing stigmata and other miraculous occurrences into the battle for the mind in Latin America to sway it in our favour. In the way of duty, he also had access to a file of letters from successful writers like Hugh Walpole, Michael Arlen and Godfrey Winn offering their pens for King and Country. Dipping into this gave us much pleasure. He was staying near the Ministry in a little mews flat where I spent an occasional evening with him, the invariable supper dish being sausages, then still available. Whatever his circumstances, he has this facility for seeming always to be in lodgings, and living from hand to mouth. Spiritually, and even physically, he is one of nature's displaced persons. Soon after his house on Clapham Common had been totally demolished in the Blitz, I happened to run into him. There was no one in the house at the time, his family having moved into the country, and he gave an impression of being well content with its disappearance. Now, at least, he seemed to be saying, he was homeless, *de facto* as well as *de jure.*[1]

~~~

The Blitz was a kind of protracted debauch, with the shape of orderly living shattered, all restraints removed, barriers non-existent. It gave one the same feeling a debauch did, of, as it were, floating loose; of having slipped one's moorings. Once, in an access of folly, I drove round and round Piccadilly Circus the wrong way to celebrate the absence of all traffic. Restaurants were often almost empty; it was possible, for instance, to dine at the Cafe Royal—still with marble-topped tables and red-plush seats—when there were no more than a dozen or so other patrons present, the five or six waiters on duty scurrying to and fro as though engaged in a game of musical chairs, and the music about to stop at any moment. From time to time, some shattering explosion nearby made the walls shake and the tables rattle and the windows crumble. Even at the much-boosted Windmill Theatre there would be just a handful of dedicated addicts in the auditorium, gazing balefully at the nudes;[2] rather pinched and ravaged in the footlights' glare, yet still bound by law to keep absolutely still. Almost the only stillness to be found in all London those nights.

I went once with Graham Greene. The spectacle appealed to him for its tattiness and seediness; the guise in which he most likes the Devil's offerings to be presented. He explained how the cognoscenti knew just where to sit to get the best view, and how, as the front rows cleared, spectators at the back pressed forward to take their places; wave upon wave, like an attacking army. For expeditions in the Blitz, he made a special act of penitence and other appropriate liturgical preparations in case death came upon him unawares. It made me feel uneasy, and even envious; like travelling in a first-class railway carriage with a first-class ticket-holder when one has a third-class ticket oneself. I imagined Graham being carried away to paradise, and I left behind in purgatory, or worse. Ever since I have known him, he has seemed to me to possess some special quality of aloofness and detachment from the passions he so concerns himself about in his novels, and, for that matter, in his life. If you come upon him unawares — as I sometimes have, catching a glimpse of him from the top of a bus, or walking in or out of Albany, where we both for a time resided — an expression in his face of isolation from everything and everyone around him, makes it seem almost as though he were blind. One almost expects him to have a white stick, and to need a friendly guiding hand to see him across the road. I once without thinking said of him that he was a saint trying unsuccessfully to be a sinner, and I a sinner trying equally unsuccessfully to be a saint. The remark, which was widely quoted, annoyed him, not so much because it credited him with being a saint (a role for which he has no taste), as because of my pretensions to be a sinner. What sort of sinner are you? he asked scornfully, as though I had claimed some quite undeserved achievement or beatitude.

By this time Graham Greene had left MI6 and joined the publishing firm of Eyre and Spottiswoode, calculating — as it turned out incorrectly, as far as he personally was concerned — that the aftermath of the war would be a time of great difficulty for writers, in which it would be well to have some secure economic base. The precise occasion of his leaving MI6 was very characteristic; as part of his machinations inside Section Five, Kim Philby[3] wanted to

promote him — something that Greene considered an outrage, and indignantly refused to countenance, to the point
of resigning. At the Eyre and Spottiswoode office in
Bedford Street, he sat in a room with Douglas Jerrold,
where I several times visited them. It would be difficult to
imagine two more strangely assorted human beings; both
Catholic converts, certainly, but Jerrold induced thereby
to move to the extreme Right, as a supporter of General
Franco, and Greene to move ever further Leftwards as a
fervent advocate of Catholic-Marxist dialogue. If I had
occasion to talk with one of them, I was keenly aware of
the other's presence; a telephone call by either produced a
sort of anguished silence in which a third person found
himself listening intently to every word spoken into the
receiver, however softly. Even their appearance made a
striking contrast. Jerrold gave an impression of being
enormous. He dressed in an old-fashioned conventional
way — black coat, striped trousers, stiff collar, foot-wear
noticeably hand-made for him by Lobb. His head was
tiny, thinly covered with sparse hair, and altogether he
looked, as Kingsmill[4] used to say, like an inflated hors
d'oeuvre. Greene, on the other hand, was tall and slight,
with the look of a perennial undergraduate engaged in
working out some ingenious joke or impersonation. It is a
tribute to both their characters that they managed to survive this strange proximity without a serious quarrel.

   Knowing that I was going to Paris, Greene asked me to
seek out François Mauriac[5] and get him to agree to
English translations of his books, to be brought out in a
uniform edition by Eyre and Spottiswoode. This I gladly
agreed to do, and in the very early days of the Liberation
made a special point of calling at the office of Mauriac's
publisher, Grasset . . .

Extracted from *Chronicles of Wasted Time. Chronicle 2: The Infernal Grove* (New York: William Morrow and Company, 1974), 78–79, 104–5, 236–37. *Editor's title.*

Notes

1. Malcolm Muggeridge's diary entry for 13 January 1949 (see *Like It Was: The Diaries of Malcolm Muggeridge*, sel. and ed. John Bright-Holmes [London: Collins, 1981], 316–17) suggests another reason why Graham Greene was "well content" with the disappearance of the house on Clapham Common.

2. The Windmill Theatre, near Piccadilly Circus, remained open throughout the war and, before its conversion into a theater restaurant, it was customary in the thirties and forties for the Windmill Girls to appear in nude tableaux.

3. Harold Adrian Russell "Kim" Philby (1912–88), British intelligence officer and a successful Russian spy, defected to the Soviet Union in 1963. Philby details his exploits in *My Silent War* (London: McGibbon and Kee, 1968). After his return from West Africa, Greene, then responsible for "counter-espionage in Portugal," worked under Philby. He seems to have remained in contact with Philby after his defection for he sent a copy of *The Human Factor* to his "friend Philby, and his reply interested" Greene. *Ways of Escape*, 257–58.

4. Hugh Kingsmill (1889–1949) English novelist, biographer, and literary editor, deserves wider recognition for his criticism.

5. For François Mauriac (1885–1970), French novelist, see note 4 on p. 81 of the Jean Duché excerpt, "A 'Jansenist' Writer of Thrillers" and Greene's comments to Bernard Violet in the excerpts from "A Rare Occasion: Graham Greene on TV" on pp. 351–52. Greene never made a secret his interest in, and admiration of, Mauriac but he tended to deny his "influence" on him.

Graham Greene in Paris

Jeanine Delpech

Graham Greene could play the role of one of his characters whom he brings forth from the thick fog or the darkness of night as bearers of a mysterious message or an
explosive piece of news. He has a tall lean body, a supple
movement and a voice that one attributes to ghosts. One
imagines him fitting easily in a gambling den as in the
most exclusive London club. Yes, the look of a sleep-
walker perched on the edge of a roof, eyes accustomed to
darkness, and the timid politeness are indeed those of a
man who, in books unforgettable like certain dreams,
brings us face to face with the gentle assassin, or with children playing hide-and-seek with death disguised in a
policeman's trenchcoat, or with courteous dynamiters
exchanging passwords against a background of gipsy
music. If I had met him on an international train, I would
have guessed that he held in his slender hand the threads
of an amazing conspiracy.

It is ten in the morning: in the lobby, I am not standing
beside an anxious traveller but beside the greatest novelist from England, a writer who is not yet well known in

France but whose three novels *Brighton Rock, A Gun for Sale* and *England Made Me* will be soon available.[1]

"As far back as I can remember, I've always been writing. But since all around me expected that I would make a profession of my hobby, I decided to become a business man. I resisted my calling for fifteen days."

"Your first book, *The Man Within*, was an immediate success."

"It would be well to forget the two or three that followed.[2] In them, I was carried away by my romanticism. . ."

"The sin of youth."

". . . which I tried to correct with *A Gun for Sale* and *England Made Me* in 1937."[3]

"Of all your books, it [*England Made Me*] is the only one where a woman figures as prominently as the hero."

"I tried to make tangible the force and the subtlety of the relationship that unite brother and sister. But I do not know how to 'do' women. It is so difficult. Victorian writers had good reason to present them as disembodied creatures, angels or demons, without physical bodies. And then D. H. Lawrence came along and revolutionized English literature with disastrous consequences. He has shown us women who heed the body and are absorbed by its desires, pleasures and demands. Do you not then expect a writer to shake with fear when he introduces in his works creatures as terrifying? I was quite happy to be able to write a book like *The Power and the Glory* without women."

"Your first book, a wonderful example of the psychological novel, left little doubt that you would be tempted by the 'thriller.' "

"I like the detective novel because I see in it something like the creation of a legend: it entails making people believe a story where the truth and the psychological intensity of the characters give credibility to situations and incidents without much verisimilitude."

"It is because you have succeeded so well that films are now being made of several novels: *Stamboul Train, A Gun for Sale* and *The Confidential Agent* with Charles Boyer. . ."

"Fritz Lang has adapted *The Ministry of Fear.* Until now, all these adaptations were made in Hollywood, but Sidney Box in England will shoot *The Man Within* in technicolor and Alexander Korda *The Power and the Glory.* I am a little curious about what they'll do. Curious and a little worried, too."[4]

"How do you explain that Hollywood has succeeded so badly with English writers?"

"I think they are victims of a paradoxical situation in America. With large sums of money at their disposal, writers are frightened by their responsibilities, that is, if they still retain any scruples. On the other hand, they are constantly aware that their work, their performance, is watched with eagle eyes. This feeling of being a Napoleon spied upon by bookkeepers must put them in an unpleasant state of nerves."

"Does that mean that you will not go to Hollywood like Huxley and others?"[5]

"Not for all the money! I am trying out an experiment at the moment with the Boulting Brothers. We are shooting a film of *Brighton Rock.*[6] It's a cooperative venture where each does his work and we share the profits."

"That seems fair."

"And a little frightening, too. To be able to say that one is betrayed by one's director is always convenient!"

"You have not written many short stories which is rather unusual for an English author."

"I've written less than twenty in twenty years. I do not find the genre attractive: one is forced to know beforehand what will happen. What's exciting about the novel is that after the preliminary concept of plot and the principal characters, one is almost always surprised by the emergence of unforeseen characters. I love to see my characters escape me; one cannot allow that in a short story."

"Is it true, as some would have it, that you have been strongly influenced by Kafka?"[7]

"I've read several of his books and I admire him. But our critics like to find him everywhere. They have found my designation of the hero by a single initial in *The Confidential Agent* 'Kafkaesque.' The truth is that I did not wish to specify, by the use of a Spanish or German surname, the imaginary country in which the action unfolds in that novel which was written in1939 in an atmosphere of war."

"To me, your work has more in common with Bernanos[8] than Kafka, perhaps because you are both Catholics."

"I admire very much *Sous le soleil de Satan* and *Le Journal d'un curé de campagne.*[9] I did not quite understand *Monsieur Ouine.* Perhaps it was difficult to write such a book in Brazil because the place in which one writes has an influence on the novel. I began *The Ministry of Fear* in 1943 on my voyage in a convoy on its way to South Africa.[10] I meant to write a cheerful novel. And then, in spite of me, the fantastic action got hold of me and as I continued writing, alone with the mosquitoes and black servants in a house surrounded by marshes, the novel turned out far from cheerful . . ."

"But quite haunting! One gets the impression from your novels that you read much poetry. Am I wrong?"

"No. But it seems to me that as one grows older, one can only read living poets who are older than one or not more than five years younger. I am unable to appreciate our poets who are now twenty-five. I'd like to believe it is my fault not theirs."

"Are American writers as successful in England as they are in France?"

"No. Intellectually, the gap between the United States and England is increasing. I do not want to dwell on the political reasons behind this gap but as a publisher, I find fewer talents in this generation than the previous one. American publishing is moving, more and more, towards the creation of successful serials, of which *Amber*[11] remains the most deplorable example. I hope the French who always have fine taste will not like that book. But I am told it is widely read here."

"Yes. Like England, I think."

"Alas! In the meantime, the public is recovering the taste for good authors: Dickens and above all, Trollope, have come back now that we have begun to move away from D. H. Lawrence . . ."

It is neither to facilitate the task of his director nor to pander to the taste of the public for secret agents, luxury trains and dead bodies that Graham Greene borrows the techniques of the so-called "sensational" literature. But his modesty makes the best of this modern disguise which he imposes on his romanticism. To him, as to Bernanos, there is no fervour without violence; mystical flights are not exclusive of humour as they were for Chesterton whom Greene frequently recalls but whom he surpasses by his psychological acuity and richness of invention . . .

But the man who creates *A Gun for Sale* and *The Confidential Agent* also knows how to give life to the allegories of *The Power and the Glory*. He does not seek, like Huxley today, a many armed god in Indian philosophy;

Greene discovers the hand of God wherever believers like himself find that the blasphemies, the fear and the indifference to death never fully succeed in hiding it altogether in the heart and the flesh of man. And this is why he leaves, on the screen as on the pages of his novels, that enormous desire to recover the grace which continues to exist even in the suspect regulars of smoke-filled London pubs and the frequenters of sleeping cars on the Orient Express.

Extracted from Jeanine Delpech, "Graham Greene à Paris," *Nouvelles Littéraires,* 19 December 1946, 1–2. Trans. A. F. Cassis.

Notes

1. French translations of the three novels appeared in 1947. *Le Rocher de Brighton,* trans. Marcelle Sibon (Laffont), *Tueur à gages,* trans. René Masson (Laffont), and *Mère Angleterre,* trans. G. de Tonnac-Villeneuve (Laffont).

2. Greene's first published novel, *The Man Within,* appeared in 1929. Later, he withdrew from circulation the two that followed, *Rumour at Nightfall* (1931) and *The Name of Action* (1930).

3. *England Made Me* was published in June 1935 and *A Gun for Sale* in July 1936.

4. *Stamboul Train* retitled *Orient Express* (Twentieth-Century-Fox, 1934). Produced and directed by Paul Martin. Starring Heather Angel, Norman Foster, Ralph Morgan, Una O'Connor, and Herbert Mundin.

   A Gun for Sale retitled *This Gun for Hire* (Paramount, 1942). Produced by Richard Blumenthal. Starring Alan Ladd, Veronica Lake, and Laird Cregar. James Cagney directed a remake in 1957 entitled *Short Cut to Hell.*

   The Confidential Agent (Warner Bros., 1945). Produced by Robert Buckner. Starring Charles Boyer, Lauren Bacall, Peter Lorre, Katina Paxinou, and Wanda Hendrix.

   The Ministry of Fear (Paramount, 1943). Directed by Fritz Lang. Produced by Seton I. Miller. Starring Ray Milland, Marjorie Reynolds, and Alan Duryca.

The Man Within (Rank Productions, 1947). Retitled *The Smugglers* in U.S. Directed by Bernard Knowles. Produced by Muriel and Sidney Box. Starring Richard Attenborough, Michael Redgrave, Joan Greenwood, and Jean Kent.

There may have been talk with Alexander Korda about *The Power and the Glory* but the only production of the novel in the forties is *The Fugitive* (R. K. O., 1947). Directed and produced by John Ford. Greene was not involved in the scripting of any of these films. He came across *Orient Express* in Teneriffe when he was on his way to Liberia, and he describes his reaction in *Journey Without Maps*, 19–20.

5. Aldous Huxley (1894–1963), English novelist and essayist, settled in America in 1938. Worth noting is his assessment of Greene's first published novel as "most remarkable . . . Much better (between ourselves, for it's a heresy!) than Virginia's *To the Lighthouse*. It's the difference between something full and something empty; between a writer who has a close physical contact with reality and one who is a thousand miles away and only has a telescope to look, remotely, at the world." *Letters of Aldous Huxley*, ed. Grover Smith (London: Chatto and Windus; New York: Harper and Row, 1969), 330.

6. *Brighton Rock* (Associated British Picture Corporation, 1947). Directed and produced by John Boulting. Screenplay by Graham Greene. Starring Richard Attenborough, Hermione Baddeley, and William Hartnell.

7. Franz Kafka (1883–1924), Austrian novelist born of Jewish parents in Prague whose works and views on society, published posthumously, seemed to have exerted great influence on Albert Camus and Samuel Beckett, among others. "Kafka makes me feel bad," said Graham Greene. "I appreciate his way of writing, but I feel when I read him, a pain between the eyes . . . just like what one feels when one chews on a piece of ice." Ronald de Couves Matthews, *Mon Ami Graham Greene* (Bruges: Desclée de Brouwer, 1957), 125.

8. George Bernanos (1888–1948), French novelist with strong Catholic sympathies, lived in Brazil from the late thirties until 1945 when he returned to France.

9. Translated into English and published as *The Star of Satan* (Pamela Harris, trans. [London: John Lane, 1940]) and *Diary of a Country Priest* (Pamela Harris, trans. [London: Borriswood, 1937]).
10. Greene left for West Africa in December 1941. The novel was published in May 1943.
11. Kathleen Winsor's novel *Forever Amber* (New York: Macmillan, 1944), an inversion of the romantic book, was such a commercial success that it was printed eleven times in one year and its film rights purchased by Twentieth-Century-Fox. The French translation by Edith Vincent was titled *Ambre* (Paris: Editions du Pavois, 1946).

A "Jansenist" Writer of Thrillers

Jean Duché

"What would you like to drink?"

His lanky body bent forward without apparent effort. Here we are sitting at the end of the Pont-Royal bar with Greene's knees sticking up above the stool.

"A dry martini."

"How do you find Paris after the strike?"

"Oh! the same as always. I noticed many dustbins in the streets but one does not want to use dustbins to judge a political situation. Isn't that so?"

We talk in English. Graham Greene assures me, like any self-respecting Brit that he does not speak another language. I was surprised he was a member of the panel awarding the Denyse-Clairouin prize for the best translation.[1]

"One must consider the original text," he said, "so that one does not end up with an excellent translation of an author who is not worth a nickel at home. A case in point is the 'great' English novelist Charles Morgan in France.[2] The English cannot understand how many wonderful people admire him here!"

He laughs and the sparks of malice twinkle in his grey eyes.

"Please don't let me say nasty things about my colleagues."

"In that case, let's have another dry martini and talk seriously."

"A writer can then afford to live by his pen in England."

"We also have the reading public of the Empire and the United States. An author should easily clear fifteen thousand copies. At nine shillings a copy, the twenty per cent royalties adds up to a sizeable amount of money."

I was fascinated by the twenty per cent.

"But before the war an author made twenty-five per cent."

. . . I congratulated Greene for his success as a novelist and also as a publisher for the last three years. He had introduced Julien Green, Louise de Vilmorin, Daniel Rops[3] and Mauriac to the English.

"The great majority are Catholic. One can see that you are one."

"*Thérèse Desqueyroux* will appear in one volume with *La Fin de la nuit* and should sell thirty thousand copies."[4]

"How do you know?"

"The volume has been chosen already by a Book Society."

"Ah. So you too have this American system."

"Fortunately not to the same degree. Otherwise, a publisher would have to take his cue from readers' clubs."

"Why do you not publish your own novels?"

"It is not bad for a writer to submit his work to the critical judgment of an editor and publisher."

"Do you seriously believe that a publisher would refuse a work you have submitted? Or ask you to rewrite it?"

My Jansenist friend laughed. I had never seen a Jansenist laugh as much. Can one imagine Pascal writing thrillers at Port-Royal-des-Champs? . . . [5]

"When I reached the end of *Brighton Rock*," he said, "I perceived that the book was divided in half by the assassination of Hale. I couldn't bring myself to rewrite the first part."

These are things a writer says himself but which he does not like being told. I made the unusual remark that the reader could see that clearly.

"I begin my books without knowing where I am going."

"Do you believe in Fatalism to such an extent?"

I observed his profile: his snub nose and thin but sensuous lips. He looked like a big kid who loves the most harmless of barley sugar sticks, not the barley sugar sticks which, when broken, show Brighton written on them—or your fate. He said with the same detached voice and veiled humour:

"I did not invent Fatalism. I found it in me."

"If the Boy wanted to escape his pursuers," I continued, "he could easily have taken the train. It is only stubbornness that kept him there."

"He is afraid of losing his identity by abandoning the territory."

"Gide,[6] if one can imagine him in such company, would never have hesitated to take the train. He would never have lost his identity."

"Yes, a gratuitous act . . ."

"No, not a gratuitous act but the act of an intelligent man who weighs the consequences and knows that he is strong enough to be himself. The courage of the Boy is nothing but presumption."

"It is true, he is weak."

"Rimbaud, Gauguin[7] know better and would have taken the train."

"I, too, took the train," said Greene softly. "I took the train as far as Sierra Leone. I was impatient with myself. I don't think one escapes one's destiny. Some may perhaps. I do not speak for all the human race."

"This is something I would like to say to you: You are a Jansenist writing detective stories."

He sat back and held one of his knees in his long hands. His eyes were bloodshot.

"Besides, I shall never write more detective novels. I would be repeating myself. There, I can change colour at least. You were saying . . . Jansenist?"

"You know, these austere men who think that they can only be saved by Grace and that God gives that Grace only to the elect."[8]

"I think," said Graham Greene, "that man cannot be saved without a miracle."

He said that in the offhand manner of one asking for a light. . . .

"By the way," I said, (one can see that the transition was rather subtle), "C. E. Magny maintains in her Introduction[9] that the function of fatalism—a useful function—is 'to prevent the novel from breaking up, from reducing itself to a tale told by an idiot, full of sound and fury signifying nothing.' I know, so does she, that you are deeply attached to this fatalism. Predestined as you are, you are now locked into the 'situation' of Sartre and grappling with a world that is as absurd as it is to Camus."

"Absurd?" repeated Greene, surprised. "What does that mean?"

"Roughly speaking, it means that we do not know who we are, where we come from, or where we're going."

"Oh!" said Greene—and here the Jansenist facing his destiny never lost his sense of humour—"I know only too well where I am going."

Thereupon, he left me for his next meeting, more positive and surely less tragic I hope, for it was time to dine with an English painter, a friend of his, living on President Wilson Avenue . . .

Extracted from Jean Duché, "'Je n'écrirai plus de romans policiers,' nous dit Graham Greene," *Figaro Littéraire*, 20 December 1947, 6. *Editor's title.* Trans. A. F. Cassis.

Notes

1. Award for the best French translation of an English-language work.
2. Charles Langbridge Morgan (1894–1958), English novelist, playwright, and essayist whose popularity and fame on the Continent seemed excessive to English critics. He is the author of *The Fountain* (1932), which won the Hawthornden prize and *The Voyage* (1940), which won the James Tait Black Memorial prize.
3. Julien Green (1900–), novelist, born of American parents in Paris and writing in French.

    Louise de Vilmorin (1912–69), French novelist and poet.

    Daniel Rops [Henri Jules Charles Petiot] (1901–65), French educator, editor, and fiction writer, noted for his support of the Catholic faith. Among his popular works is *Jesus in His Time*, trans., R. W. Millar (London: Eyre and Spottiswoode, 1955).
4. Two novels by French novelist François Mauriac (1885–1970) whose fiction is dominated by problems of religion. Mauriac's warm appreciation of *The Power and the Glory* and his tribute to Greene appeared in *Figaro Littéraire* (30 October 1948): 1, 3. It was influential in establishing Greene's reputation with the French public.
5. Blaise Pascal (1632–62), French mathematician and moralist, fell under the influence of Jansenism.
6. André Gide (1869–1951), outspoken French novelist and critic, and recipient of the Nobel Prize in 1947.
7. Arthur Rimbaud (1854–91), French poet noted for his contribution to the Symbolist movement.

    Paul Gauguin (1848–1903), French post-Impressionist painter who moved in the Symbolists' circle in Paris.

8. Jansenism was a movement within the Church founded by the Bishop of Ypres, Cornelius Jansen (1585–1638). It rejected the Catholic notion of freedom; that is, the power to choose at any time between good or evil and asserted merely the existence of freedom from external constraints. Denial of the freedom of the will also entailed the notion that interior grace is irresistible— there is no possibility of resisting Divine Grace. This theological system, condemned by the Church in 1653, contended that even the just cannot always keep some of the commandments. Further it maintained that Christ did not die for all people, but only for a chosen few. The heresy acquired a strong foothold at Port Royal near Paris where Blaise Pascal was among its more brilliant apologists. See note 5 on p. 356–57 of the Bernard Violet excerpt, "A Rare Occasion: Graham Greene on TV," and note 20 on p. 428 of the Maria Couto excerpt, "The Solitude of the Writer and Political Involvement."

The Manichean tradition rejects the notion of a moral fall and a personal conviction of sin; the soul suffers from contact with matter, and the evil it allows itself to commit are regarded as physical not moral, miseries not sins. The tradition upholds the "doctrine of the two principles" eternally opposed: God and light versus Satan and darkness. Because free will and sin are denied, the Incarnation is rejected even though the Divinity of Christ is recognized. The young Augustine (A.D. 354–430) was one of the many intellectuals attracted by it.

9. "Graham Greene," *Poésie* 32 (May 1946): 32–37, in which she posits that Greene has substituted an inexorable fatality by "traditional psychological motivation" and associates him with Sartre and Camus.

Graham Greene: Saint or Cynic?

Richard McLaughlin

A tall, slightly stooped, loose-limbed Englishman, looking as though he had just stepped out of a Beerbohm drawing, rushed into the lobby of the Algonquin about a month ago. He was traveling incognito and was apparently doing such a successful job of it that none of the guests milling about in the hotel lounge suspected that a distinguished English novelist was in their midst. Wearing a mackintosh (it was raining outside), hatless, his face flushed, his eyes feverishly bright, Graham Greene stalked through the crowded lobby.

This forty-four-year-old Oxonian, novelist, editor and publisher . . . appeared at once so shy and tense and remote against a modern New York hotel setting. But when he spoke, apologizing for being delayed at a cocktail party, all my impressions of his being youthful evaporated. Behind that soft, cultured speech one caught the faint Oxonian drawl; it was a voice which could have belonged to an ingratiating worldly host or a diffident scholarly don, or perhaps to both at the same time. Certainly nobody could say of Graham Greene what is said of one of the characters[1] in his novel, *The Heart of the Matter*, that "the lines that make a human being" had yet to be drawn on his face. Close up, the burning eyes, the long, ascetic face, read like a battleground, where the conflict between the flesh and the spirit, reason and faith, had left their ineradicable marks.

After chatting in a gay, almost bantering manner over bourbon and soda, we made our way to the dining room. Greene said he was enjoying the current trip, despite the fact that it was only to be four days this time. He was particularly pleased that he had succeeded in shunning publicity on this visit, and boasted like an errant school-boy about the way he had eluded certain luncheon engagements.

One knew instantly that his desire for privacy was not a pose. Notoriety, rewards and the patronizing by book clubs might be regarded by him as dubious prizes for his artistic efforts but, so long as his privacy was not too often encroached upon, Greene could adapt himself to the ways of a practical man of affairs. A wife and two children to support, a house in Oxford and a flat in London, and the special enjoyment he derives from being able to hop into a plane and go to Paris and New York for brief jaunts, make it somewhat easier for Greene to accept all that adaptations of his nine novels for the movies, for example, entail.[2]

At different times a journalist, staff member on the *Times*, film critic for the *Spectator*, literary critic for Lord Beaverbrook's *Evening Standard*, and now editor and director of Eyre and Spottiswoode, British publishers, Graham Greene's progress in professional circles would appear to belie the modest, retiring, sensitive man that he really is. However, after talking with him over dinner, and continuing our talk after the theatre until nearly dawn at the apartment of a friend who was curious to discuss with

Greene some of the theological points behind his novels, *The Power and the Glory* and his latest work, *The Heart of the Matter*, I am firmly convinced that Graham Greene is no ordinary novelist. Not only is he one of our finest craftsmen writing today, but he is so preoccupied with man's inner struggle to save his soul that he is comparable only to our greatest literary masters. His moral fervor, his peculiar concern with man as beset by evil and yearning to reach God through a maze of despair and anguish pervades his writing; but what is even more awesome is to find it so evident in the man's mien and conversation. All my earlier suspicions that Greene perhaps fancies himself as a zealot, even a martyr in the style of Savonarola or Jeanne D'Arc,[3] came hurtling back as I listened to him talk that night.

Mr. Greene sat back in a big, comfortable armchair and stretched out his long legs. My friend and I were pleased to find that neither our questions nor our sometimes dogmatic statements ruffled our distinguished guest. The common fallacy that all Britishers traveling abroad carry their arrogance like a shield or banner was proving itself as fatuous as ever. Greene did not bridle when my friend asked for an unofficial explanation of Britain's official attitude and behavior toward the Palestine situation. Instead, he answered inquiries and veiled accusations alike with admirable calm and forbearance. His remarks were always intelligent and often authoritative, since Greene had conducted highly confidential missions for the British Government in West Africa during the war, and later in London with the Ministry of Information.[4]

When we veered to the topic of Greene's pet likes and dislikes, both literary and sundry, another facet of his personality, however, came sharply into focus. Book clubs,

Shirley Temple,[5] publicity of any sort, American publishers' habits of changing British titles,[6] might all fit into the category of his pet hates at one time or another. There are no halfway measures with such a man. Life and literature and morals are black or white; there are no neutral or mauve tints in the fabric of his existence.

Mr. Greene proved that he could be quite caustic in his comments on Aldous Huxley, Maugham, Bromfield[7]—not that they do not deserve sharp re-evaluation now—and conversely almost zealous in his defense of Henry James, Evelyn Waugh and Ivy Compton-Burnett. Of Henry James, Greene says he has read everything the master has ever written, and *The Turn of the Screw* is a great favorite with him. Speaking of Waugh and Ivy Compton-Burnett, he reveals his own satirical weapons: Miss Compton-Burnett is "one of our English ladies," complete with Kensington drawing-room, tea-caddy and late Victorian cake-rack, a gifted English novelist who "writes historical novels from the modern viewpoint." Greene suggests that her remarkable dialog is rather Restoration, out of Congreve, if anything. When asked what he thought of the much discussed *The Loved One*, a mischievous gleam came into his eyes. "It's a nice little book," he replied, and then proceeded to explain that its niceness mainly lies in the writing rather than in the subject material—with which we are all inclined to agree.

It did not take very long to find out, however, that Graham Greene is not completely devoid of English traits. Insularity might be considered one of them, were it not for the fact that he is a moralist. Writing modern-day parables, though the urge may be a very personal one, he necessarily encompasses the universal scene in his probings into the depths of man's conflict with himself and the problems of good and evil.

The insularity I speak of comes closer to the surface in Greene's religious beliefs. His attitude toward Roman Catholicism has something of a sectarian ring to it. I suppose this is often the case with converts, particularly intellectuals like Greene and Evelyn Waugh.[8] They have a zeal which is likely to be looked upon—by folk who do not have to choose Catholicism but are born to it—as unnecessarily feverish, even fanatical. How else can one explain a statement Greene made while two men sat speechless, pondering over the devious path of thought their eminent visitor must have had to travel to arrive at such startling, not to mention frightening, conclusions on his religion and the future of the Catholic Church?

It seems that every age produces men who think that, through persecution and travail, man is purified—regenerated. It is the old test-by-fire formula, the stony path, etc. Mr. Greene solemnly holds this belief concerning the future of the Church. He had seen priests celebrating Masses underground in Mexico,[9] and was inspired to write *The Power and the Glory.* It is a romantic but dangerous idea that he harbors when he expresses hope that all good English Roman Catholics, if they have to choose between the United States and Russia, will choose Russia so that the Catholic Church will be driven underground and there survive as a fighting spiritual force.

Greene raises a question here to which few of us have heretofore given much thought. Are there really distinguishable contrasts between the Catholic Church in England, the United States, France, Belgium, Italy, et al? That he has detected them in his travels and his theological pursuits does not alter the fact that these differences, if they exist, may rest mainly with certain ecclesiastical disputes or canonical departures which do not directly affect the average Catholic worshipper. One would not ordinarily bring up such a topic; it arises here because Greene's *The Heart of the Matter* is so intrinsically a Catholic novel, dealing so specifically with a Catholic's dilemma, with his faith and the passions that drive a man to deception, evil and, finally, self-destruction.

Looking back on that evening spent with Graham Greene, I can only feel a sense of gratitude that circumstances permitted it to happen. In addition to showing forth that steady flame of faith which one beholds so rarely (which may account for the shock we experienced on seeing it burning so clearly in a lower Manhattan drawing-room at two o'clock in the morning), Graham Greene could not help but awe us as we listened. Perhaps it is the stuff of which genius is made—this driving conviction Greene undoubtedly has that runs roughshod over our weak-kneed answers, our smug compromises, no matter what religious sect we belong to.

When Graham Greene very quietly said, "I would like to be a good Catholic some day," he was voicing a modest enough resolution at the time; but now, on re-reading his magnificent *The Heart of the Matter*, one is able to sense the pain and the debate between the intellect and the heart that lurked behind these words. Saint or cynic, poet or psychologist, Graham Greene seems to have all those contradictory traits which make up the whole of the thinking man. Showing as painstaking a devotion to his theological concerns as to his writing craft, it is no wonder that Greene should produce at once a masterful piece of writing and at the same time be able to lift such a bright torch in the abyss which separates thinking man and God today.

Extracted from Richard McLaughlin, "Graham Greene: Saint or Cynic?" *America*, 24 July 1948, 370–71.

Notes

1. Reith, the chief assistant colonial secretary. "Nobody had yet drawn on his face the lines that make a human being." (*The Heart of the Matter*, 24).

2. By 1948, seven of Greene's novels and two of his short stories, "The Basement Room" and "Went the Day Well," had been adapted to the cinema.

3. Girolamo Savonarola (1452–98), Italian Dominican priest and political and religious reformer whose rigorism and claims to prophecy led to excommunication, charges of heresy, trial, and hanging.

   Joan of Arc (1412–31), French patriot and martyr, rallied her countrymen to raise the seige of Orleans but was captured and later sold to the English who burnt her for heresy and sorcery. She was canonized in 1920.

4. Greene had worked for the British SIS and was stationed in Freetown in West Africa during the war.

5. On 28 October 1937, Graham Greene reviewed *Wee Willie Winkie* in *Night and Day*. Twentieth-Century-Fox deemed the review libelous. The case appeared before King's Bench on 22 March 1938, with Greene in absentia and the judge ruled the libel as a "gross outrage" and approved the terms of the settlement. See *Ways of Escape*, 45–49.

6. By 1948, the titles of four of Greene's books had been changed by Viking Press, his American publisher: *Stamboul Train* became *Orient Express*, *A Gun for Sale/This Gun for Hire*, *The Lawless Roads/Another Mexico*, and *The Power and the Glory/The Labyrinthine Ways*. In 1953, *England Made Me* was reissued as *The Shipwrecked* and in 1972 *The Pleasure Dome* as *Graham Greene on Film*. When in 1969–1970 Viking requested that he change the title of *Travels with My Aunt*, Greene refused and switched over to Simon and Schuster.

7. Louis Bromfield (1896–1956), American novelist and journalist, lived in France after World War I but returned to Ohio in 1939.

8. Both Graham Greene and Evelyn Waugh were converted to Catholicism in 1926 and 1930, respectively.

9. See chaps. 6 and 7 of *The Lawless Roads*.

A Jekyll and Hyde Character

Malcolm Muggeridge

February 24, 1948

Usual visit to Heinemann. Discussed Graham Greene's new novel, *The Heart of the Matter*, about which Bruce Marshall has written an amazingly adulatory letter. Felt slight pang of envy, which soon passed. Greene's previous novel, *The Power and the Glory* I consider to be one of the best contemporary novels, and this is in the same genre. I dislike the gangster books, like *Brighton Rock*, despite their remarkable competence. Greene, we agreed, is a Jekyll and Hyde character, who has not succeeded in fusing the two sides of himself into any kind of harmony. There is a conflict within him, and therefore he is liable to pursue conflict without. I remember him saying to me once that he had to have a row with someone or other because rows were almost a physical necessity to him. This pursuit of disharmony is wrong, just as the pursuit of harmony or love is the source of all the finest achievements of human beings, whether in perfecting their own characters or in expressing the idea of perfection beyond the world. All the same, Greene is a very loveable character, and a very remarkable writer, who entirely deserves the success this new book will bring him.[1]

Our lives have always run in a curiously parallel way. He succeeded me at the Ministry of Information; when he was in West Africa in SIS, I was in East Africa, and we used to communicate with each other in cipher. Then he went to Eyre and Spottiswoode[2] and became my publisher, and I went to Heinemann's and became his. I always say to him that the greatest quest of his life has not been virtue but sin, and that this quest has been completely fruitless. He is a sinner manqué. In the blitz we used to spend a good many evenings together, and I remember the longing he had for a bomb to fall on him, but of course it didn't, and I told him it wouldn't. . . .

April 30, 1948

. . . Read Graham Greene's *The Heart of the Matter* about which Tony has to write a "middle" in the *Times Literary Supplement.*[3] Novel, like all his work, is excitingly written, but in many respects absurd. It is about the period during the war when he was in Freetown on the west coast of Africa and I was in Lourenço Marques on the east coast, doing the same job. We used to communicate with each other in cipher. Thus I was able quite easily to pick holes in the narrative. I said to Tony that reading the novel was like going into a Roman Catholic church in some out of the way place in France or Italy. The immediate impression is distasteful—the half-light, the stale smell of incense, the garish figures of the Calvary. But after one becomes acclimatized to the atmosphere, it becomes interesting and even moving. All the same, when one comes out again into the light of the sun, it is a great relief.

Tony and I were able to identify most of the characters. There is every reason for the book to have the enormous success it is set for.

~~~

September 13, 1948

I ran into Graham Greene, whom I hadn't seen for a long time. We were affectionate with an undercurrent of hostility. Greene described having a hemorrhage in New York. He seemed to me in poorish shape on the whole, talked a lot about how Russian domination would be less terrible than American, etc. I mentioned the Church and he said Russians only destroy its body, whereas the Americans destroy its soul. Altogether, he's as difficult as anyone I know, but I still like him. . . .

~~~

January 13, 1949

. . . Then went on to dine with Graham Greene and his brother Raymond, who is a doctor, rather like him in appearance. Graham looks more melancholic than ever. He told me that he had now definitely separated from Vivian [sic], which I thought was rather a pity. He spoke about *The Heart of the Matter* in a surprisingly objective manner. I said that, in my view, it certainly wasn't his best book, but that one had to consider a writer's work as a whole, and that if one part of it received a reward it mightn't deserve, other parts received less than they deserved, so that over all it was just.

Another thing Graham said was that when he heard that his house at Clapham Common had been destroyed in the blitz he experienced a sense of relief because there was a mortgage on it and it had represented a heavy financial liability. He described arriving there, and finding the part where the house had been roped off. When he told Vivian, he said, she rebuked him for mentioning what had happened in front of the children, which seemed to him unreasonable. I said I didn't think it was unreasonable, because, obviously, Vivian felt that the destruction of their house was an outward and visible manifestation of the destruction of their marriage, and that Graham's satisfaction at the destruction of the house was not really because it released him from a financial burden, but because he saw in it the promise of being relieved of a moral one. I said that everything that happened had to correspond with what was, and that's why life is at once so fascinating and so terrible.

January 19, 1950

. . . Dined with Graham Greene. Graham talked about a certain Father Pio in Italy whom he'd seen, and who, according to Graham, has stigmata. Graham described these in his usual lurid way. Said miracles were done constantly by him, and that, in his view, the heavenly and devilish forces in creation were now exceptionally active in preparation for busting up the universe by means of the hydrogen bomb. Told him that, to my Protestant sceptical mind, no catastrophic solution or ending to human affairs seemed to me likely.

Typical of Graham that he has made a collection of small whisky bottles which are now prominently displayed in his flat.

Said that he was bored by all the réclame over *The Heart of the Matter*, especially the manner in which it had been taken up by the Catholics, a long article appearing about "La damnation de Scobie."[4] Graham said that Evelyn Waugh is now writing a book about some female saint, which is very good. Really prefer his conversation when he discusses means of evading stigmata. . . .

Extracted from *Like It Was: The Diaries of Malcolm Muggeridge*, sel. and ed. John Bright-Holmes (London: Collins, 1981), 248–49, 270–71, 297, 316–17, 374. *Editor's title.*

Notes

1. Muggeridge is referring to *The Heart of the Matter.*
2. Greene became a director of Eyre and Spottiswoode in 1944.
3. [Anthony Powell], "West African Rock," *Times Literary Supplement*, 29 May 1948, 302.
4. Raymond Jouve, "La Damnation de Scobie," *Études*, no. 263 (1949): 164–77.

Interview with Graham Greene

Robert Ostermann

Graham Greene and I spoke together for some four hours one evening in an England advancing into a troubled Autumn. This little paper is simply my impression of him as he revealed himself during a casual and unplanned conversation; it is not critical, nor have I tried to relate the man in any way to contemporary events. We spoke as persons; and this ought to have an interest for other persons. Since he has written so frequently of London, it seems appropriate to present them together; because the impact on me of both of them was new, it may perhaps be instructive to associate them.

If all this appears unfactual, or over-imaginative, it will be precisely because my visit was not a professional one; thus whatever I have written will suffer those disadvantages of incompleteness, obscurity and diffusion which are the particular conditions accompanying any human contact.

At half-past eight in the evening I finally got through to him at his flat. London was hot, the phone box steamed, a few yards down the road a palace guard went sweating on his rounds; and then dimly down the line came the voice one had waited so long to hear, saying, "Hello there, how are you? I've been wondering when you'd call."

We had exchanged several letters and the final weeks in September had been tentatively selected for a meeting. He hadn't forgotten, he remembered instantly the arrangement; but still one was astonished at the ease with which everything was progressing.

It wasn't to be all as simple as one thought. "You've come at a bad time," he said. "How long will you be in town?"

I said I had three days before returning to Sussex and he said, "I'm working on a play with Basil Dean and we're facing a deadline.[1] We're at it night and day." A woman rapped urgently at the side of the box; I waved at her and smiled reassuringly and Greene said: "I'm terribly sorry. Basil has to get the play to New York next week. Will you be coming through again?"

It so happened that I would next Monday, but I musn't have sounded very hopeful, because the voice floated back, trying to be helpful, "Call Monday before you come up from the country. We'll try to arrange something."

We said good-by and I broke the connection. Something certainly would have to be arranged, since I was leaving for Ireland in a week and had no idea when I'd be back again . . . .

～

Sometimes it takes no more than a moment to establish the particular character of hours. This is the way it was when I rang the bell and Graham Greene came thumping down the stairs to open the door. We shook hands and he said, abruptly, "Excuse me, the phone's ringing," and disappeared up ahead of me into a first floor flat. He told me a few moments after that someone had called earlier and asked for me; he had thought this call might also be mine.

But he was too late; there was no one on the line; and he became apologetic, was troubled, he hoped it wasn't anything important. During the next four hours he would express again and again concern for this friend who had never succeeded in making contact.

A thin man with graying hair and a worn, strained serious face that didn't resemble anyone else's, this was his way. And I would remember this night in terms of gentleness and courtesy and a spontaneous Christian regard. Even in those centuries which we like to call the ages of faith, it must have been like a miracle to find Christianity at work in even one human soul.

We sat in a large room full of books and light and we talked, trying to locate each other. It was a human maneuver at which I had every advantage: I knew his work and he knew nothing of me. He asked several questions, politely; I tried to decide, as the conversation proceeded, exactly what was being added by personal communication to the impression I already had from a close study of the books.

Greene hooked a leg up comfortably onto his chair (one was instantly at home) and began to speak of those things which authors might be supposed to have interest in: Jack Yeats, one of whose canvasses—very dark with burning patches of fierce and somber colors—was the only painting on the walls; modern literature; Kafka. Greene said that Prague was as full of tortured turnings and unexpected disclosures as Kafka's own tormented mind and stories.[2] He mentioned with interest and sympathy and a sense of debt Ernest Hemingway; he thought him more important in American literature than Faulkner.

He had been to Sweden in the middle thirties[3] and he spoke with a kind of horror of its tidy sick suicidal civilization, apartments like glittering hives, the absence of heart, a social order so perfect that they'd had to exclude a part of man.

He joked of his latest film, *The Third Man*[4] ("an interesting thriller"), but I disagreed, because I had seen it a few days before and I thought it a profound expression of the truth of the Mystical Body.[5] (There is a third man involved in every sin, every act, and that man is each one of us.) But as this exchange continued, one noticed that what had been in the beginning a kind of diffidence was now marked uneasiness. It wasn't obtrusive, it was simply quite obvious that only forbearance and convention carried us forward.

Then abruptly—I wasn't able to specify the transition—we were moving in a new world of broader loyalties and more profound problems; that region—this life—where man is restless and unhappy for heaven, where the greatest reality he knows is the hell he makes for himself, the hell he anticipates. These, one knew instantly, were the important things; the casual, the superficial, the conversational, all had been left behind and one was at home in a Catholic world.

⁓

. . . I was going to have trouble getting back to my hotel. But just the same I delayed: one really couldn't leave without saying something about the last Greene novel, *The Heart of the Matter*. Not that there was very much that could be said; but I did admire it and I wanted at least to say so. There certainly wasn't sufficient time to discuss it in any adequate manner.

"Oh, yes," he said, and smiled. I had repeated the accusation familiar in some circles that he was only *using* the faith for the purpose of his work. He went on with mild cynicism: "I was a Catholic before I began to write novels, but no one seemed to care particularly. The critics, especially the Catholic ones, are a little confused."

"What do you mean?" I said, and he told a story about the *Tablet*, a British weekly Catholic review which had commissioned a moral theologian to criticize the novel. It was a hard review, but what is most interesting was the response it evoked from clergy and laymen in its defense and the attempts made to enunciate what the novelist's position might be.[6]

"It's quite possible," Greene suggested, "that a novelist ought to be acquainted with moral theology; I'll concede that he ought to know a decent amount of general theology. But he isn't writing a moral treatise, that isn't his purpose. If it were, he wouldn't write a novel and he wouldn't be a novelist. But he is a novelist. That's what most of the critics forget. They're enthusiastic about the faith but they mix jobs too easily.

"Ethics, and other subjects like it, are concerned with what ought to be, and the only material the novelist has is what is, human material. What he sees in it, how deeply he sees, are something else again; you can't prescribe for them without imitating Moscow. Do you know what happens," he said pointedly, "when you wish the world to be neat and orderly and precise, a closed, untroubled place? You try to make it that way. And when people don't respond (and they don't), you end up with Belsen."[7]

Extracted from Robert Ostermann, "Interview with Graham Greene," *Catholic World*, February 1950, 356–61.

Notes

1. Basil Dean (1889–1978), English actor, producing manager, and director, collaborated with Graham Greene in adapting John Galsworthy's story "The First and the Last" for the screen. It was

released as *Twenty-One Days* in 1939. The play referred to is the dramatization of *The Heart of the Matter* for Rodgers and Hammerstein that opened in Boston. It was such a flop that the New York opening was cancelled. See Basil Dean, *Mind's Eye: An Autobiography 1927–1972* (London: Hutchinson, 1973), 305–7.

2. Greene visited Prague in 1948 for one week during the Communist takeover.

3. Greene visited Sweden in 1933 with his brother Hugh.

4. *The Third Man* (London Film Productions, 1949). Produced and directed by Carol Reed. Screenplay by Graham Greene. Starring Orson Welles, Joseph Cotten, Trevor Howard, Alida Valli, and Wilfred Hyde-White.

5. This is a rather far-fetched interpretation that probably made Graham Greene uneasy.

6. It all began when Evelyn Waugh ("Felix Culpa?" *Tablet*, 5 June 1948, 352–54) reviewed the novel and maintained that to will one's own damnation for the love of God is either "a very loose poetical expression or a mad blasphemy." He was followed, in the same issue, by the comments of Canon Joseph Cartmell on Scobie's sin. This prompted a flurry of letters to the editor: Philip Hughes's (19 June 1948) deploring Greene's "Shelleyism," Father B. C. Butler's disagreement with Waugh and rejection of Hughes's charge, and C. C. Martindale's defense of Greene and acknowledgment of his "insight and pity for human nature" (26 June 1948). They were followed by Ronald Brownrigg's letter arguing humorously, I think, against the publication of the novel (10 July 1948), W. J. Igoe's support for the novel (17 July 1948), and, finally, Evelyn Waugh's letter admitting the error in his review (17 July 1948, 41). For a searching commentary of the novel from a Catholic viewpoint, see Illtud Evan's review in *Blackfriars* 29 (July 1948): 344–45.

7. Nazi concentration camp in World War II.

Hypnotized by the Church

Rose Macaulay

I am interested in the novels you are reading.[1] I don't much care for Hugh Walpole really, tho' he wrote a capable story. I think *The Cathedral* is a better novel than *The Prelude to Adventure*; more mature.[2] I wonder if you have read it, and what you thought of it as a picture of Life in a Cathedral Close. His father became a Bishop, of course. But I feel the picture is exaggerated. Graham Greene is somewhat different! I was dining with him last Friday. An amusing little company . . . It was in a restaurant, and . . . I was upholding the Anglican point of view against Graham's assertions that only R.C.s were capable of real sin because the rest of us were invincibly ignorant . . . . I never quite know what is his view of sin; I sometimes get the feeling that with him it is largely a matter of absolution or the reverse, and that he doesn't really think so much about the actual sin. But I may wrong him. So many questions that one would like to ask one's not-very-intimate friends, and of course can't. I told him what I felt about his position in my review in the *Times Literary Supplement* (unsigned) of his last book.[3] Someone had told him it was by me, and we discussed it.

⟞⟋⟍

Yes, Graham Greene is not New Testament but R.C. The
N.T. hasn't got those *magic* solutions—being saved (or
damned) at the last simply by whether you repent at the
moment of death, etc., etc., and everything depending on
joining the right Church.[4] G.G. wouldn't understand or
approve of "not everyone that saith 'Lord, Lord,' shall be
saved, but he that doeth the will. . ." Doing the will means
less than nothing to him, compared with saying Lord,
Lord, before the right altars. That gets you to heaven,
doing the will doesn't. No, St. John VIII (I have just been
reading it) wouldn't mean a lot to him. It is all about *our
Lord* being all that matters, the light, the truth, the giver of
freedom—personal commitment to Him, not to the for-
mularies of any Church. The Church (one section of it) is
all to G.G., one feels. He has been hypnotized by it.
Indeed, where should we be without it, but it's not the
infallible dispenser of salvation that he thinks (or writes).
It's the essential channel that God uses—but the Church
is a much larger sense than G.G. knows. I find it (the
Church) enlarges one's comprehension of God all the
time—comprehension, apprehension, in both their senses.

⟞⟋⟍

Do you ever come across or read any of those huge
American novels—*The Sheltering Sky* and others, which
are full of horrors and obscenities and the nasty talk of the
Common Man (usually a soldier). You wouldn't like
them—but their popularity is a portent. Actually, I don't
read them myself, but I am told they are very "powerful"
and impressive. So is G. Greene. I half forget *The Ministry
of Fear.* But how completely those war years were his
milieu. He loved walking the bombed streets, wrapped in
a shabby mackintosh, admiring the craters, the fires, and

the tumbled buildings. It is his setting. But to him the world was always horrific, squalid, sordid. No, he would have no affection for the C. of E. [Church of England] of his childhood; it was much too temperate and mild and benign for him. The R.C. church broke in his ears with a darker, more catastrophic thunder, and caught him up in it. Had he lived in *l'an mil*,[5] he would have lived daily in expectation of the End of the World. . . .

Extracted from Rose Macaulay, *Letters to a Friend, 1950–1952*, ed. Constance Babington Smith (London: Collins, 1961), 124, 218–19, 338–39. *Editor's title.*

Notes

1. Rose Macaulay (1889–1958), English novelist, essayist, and poet, is here in a letter dated 8 May 1951 addressing the Reverend John Hamilton Cowper Johnson, of the Cowley Fathers' Community in Boston, Massachusetts. She had known him for several years in London before they lost touch with each other in 1916. They renewed their acquaintance by mail in 1950.

2. Sir Hugh (Seymour) Walpole (1884–1941), English novelist and critic, is the son of an Anglican canon who became Bishop of Edinburgh in 1910. *The Prelude to Adventure* (1912) is one of his early novels and *The Cathedral* (1922) owes much to Trollope.

3. This is Macaulay's review of *The Lost Childhood and Other Essays* ("Dark Lantern," *Times Literary Supplement*, 6 April 1951, 208).

4. In view of the date of her letter, 13 November 1951, one may assume that at the back of Rose Macaulay's mind is Greene's *The End of the Affair*, which makes use of the miraculous.

5. *L'an mil* literally means the year 1,000. In the Middle Ages, there seemed to be a widely held belief or superstition that the world would come to an end by the year 1,000.

An Inner View of Graham Greene

Kenneth Tynan

Some people are able, over the years, to build up a fairly
secure resistance to alcohol. Graham Greene has never
been able to build up a resistance to sin: no sooner has a
nip of it reached his stomach than the hangover begins.
This prompt and unfailing reaction has moved him to
undertake, over the last two decades, an exhaustive examination of sin in all its forms; but especially sin the plea-
sure-giver, sin the pain-inflictor and sin the unholy
paradox. Like several other modern Catholics who have
been articulate on the subject, Greene believes that sin
holds within it the seeds of virtue, and the paradox of evil
breeding sanctity, of dunghills sprouting daisies, has
become one of the trademarks of his work. William Blake
found eternity in a grain of sand; a Graham Greene character is more likely to find it in ten grains of cocaine.
Greene finds it easier to share his sympathies with sinners
than with the moderate, diurnally good people, who, with
their self-confidence and blunt certainties, manage to
repel him, making him glad to return to the shy, guilt-
riven souls whose reticence and loneliness he shares.

He was converted to Catholicism in 1926, when he was twenty-two. His subsequent explorations into the problems of the soul-racked have rewarded him in no beggarly fashion: his business sense, as everyone concedes, is as highly organized as his sense of sin. Although he is rich, he remains lonely, a sequestered, roaming man who can afford to travel where he likes and avoid whom he wishes. At present he writes for only ten weeks in each year, and his purposes are nearly always strictly didactic. As he admits, his aim is the single and unmistakable one of demonstrating, as graphically as he can, the truths of his religion; but, unlike most didactic writers, he could never be called a demagogue. Greene is the most notable case in recent literary history of the unhealed physician. Self-accusation, amounting almost to self-flagellation, is second nature to him, a trait in which many of his detractors have smelled morbidity . . . .

Your interpretation of Greene's life depends simply upon your allegiances. It is either a Catholic pilgrim's progress, or it is the tale of a man diseased, who has come to define his sickness as health. There is no third conclusion, nor would Greene wish there to be: he wants to challenge our powers of choice, to remind us that all decisions are decisions between absolute good and absolute evil, to point out that there is a theological element even in ordering lunch. For every minute of our lives we are, to his mind, oscillating between salvation and damnation, and not, as most of us would say, between ease and unease, satisfaction and discontent. The object of psychiatry being to remove the unease and the discontent, Greene regards it cooly, wondering whether it may not be designed to pour the baby of creativeness away with the bath of neurosis.

He was born forty-eight years ago, one of four brothers, all of whom have since telescoped up to heights of
more than six feet. At six-feet-three, he comes a poor second to brother Hugh, who is six-foot-seven and the head
of the BBC Eastern European Service. His father was the
headmaster of Berkhamsted School, near London, where
all the boys were educated, and it is no coincidence that
Greene's loathing of authority extends with particular
venom to the public school system. He hated most of his
youth; and when, on an early journey to Africa, he saw his
first masked Devil-Man, his instinctive response was to
liken him to Dr. Arnold of Rugby.[1] It was at this period
that Greene took up Russian roulette, the sport in which
you load one bullet into a revolver, spin the chamber, put
the barrel in your mouth and press the trigger, giving
yourself what he has since described (a little carelessly) as
a six-to-one chance. By the time he left school he had
become a connoisseur of oppression. Or so he felt; the
sense of victimization is not uncommon. Greene's
uncanny distinction is that he can express it with no con-
cessions to self-pity.

He won an Exhibition—a sort of junior Scholarship—to
Balliol College, Oxford, where he took a second-class hon-
ors in history and edited a mushroom magazine called
Oxford Outlook.[2] In his first year he became a probationary
member of the Communist Party, into whose funds he paid
two shillings, and under whose wing he remained for
exactly four weeks. This first, brief loyalty to anything outside himself recoiled on him when, twenty-nine years later,
he was classed as undesirable on the strength of it and
refused admission to the United States.[3] Greene, who was
left kicking his heels at Saigon, was irritated, but not

wholly dismayed at a chance to pour scorn on what he now
calls the U. S.'s "cellophane curtain." He reminded the
press of the fact that most of his books had been banned in
Russia, and added tartly that the atmosphere of panic he
found in New York on his last visit recalled to him nothing
so strongly as that of England in the late seventeenth century, when the persecution of Catholics was at its height.
Greene is still perfectly willing to "rob the robber barons,"
as he puts it, by writing for the richer American magazines;
his two consciences, the craftsman's and the moralist's,
function with a quite magnificent independence.

His search for external loyalties came to a second and
final halt in 1926, when he was admitted to the Catholic
Church. In the next year he married Vivien Dayrell-
Browning at St. Mary's in Hampstead,[4] and left Oxford a
settled dogmatist on most of the larger questions of human
existence . . . .[5]

Greene's Oxford years had proved to him that the best
of English literature, from Shakespeare to James Joyce,
had always been produced from a Christian standpoint. It
infuriated him to hear men like Stephen Spender deploring
the dearth of politically conscious novelists in England.[6]
Political novels, said Greene in the course of a public
wrangle with Spender, were aimed at an attainable objective, and once that objective had been gained, all passion
died. Look, he exhorted his audience, at the later Russian
cinema. Religious novelists, on the other hand, could never
gain their objective, and accordingly their care and passion
never diminished. Greene had always preferred a sense of
passionate inadequacy to a sense of fulfillment, and this
debate with Spender (which ended in the latter's rout)
helped to explain why. It also explained the basis of his

bitter contempt for the gentler, unaspiring, job-trot English novels of the thirties; he is still fond of quoting one contemporary critic, who spoke approvingly of them as "good, wholesome books that leave no taste in the mouth."

Greene's story sounds like one of success, but to meet him you would think it represented failure. He looks retiringly pedantic, and sits hunched, with hands and knees crossed, peering out at the gray flux of circumstance with bright, moist, hopeless eyes. His face is pouchy and veined pink, and he will rouse himself from time to time to venture some little riposte in a petulant, time-stained voice which still has trouble with its r's. A man, you might suppose, who feels he has disappointed life as much as life has disappointed him: the impression he leaves, as he wanders rangily off along a crowded street, is one of acute solitariness. His talk is not so much kindly as commiserating, and his demeanor is that of a scholar at a jam session, rather than a saint in the market place.

His only hobby is a sad one, a cheerless atonement for his existence; in it there can be no fulfillment, and only the least, most momentary shreds of triumph. It takes a compulsive form: like Bendrix in *The End of the Affair*, Greene collects car numbers.[7] You must spot first the figure 1 by itself, and then numerically upward: the first hundred are the hardest. It demands the utmost honesty, this treadmill pastime, since it leads nowhere save toward an ever stronger temptation to cheat. After a few hours in his flat, Greene goes out to stare intently past car headlights. God knows what, if anything, he is expiating; some day, perhaps, we all will; meanwhile the speed and zest of his storytelling will continue to bustle us past the question . . . .

Extracted from Kenneth Tynan, "An Inner View of Graham Greene,"
Harper's Bazaar, February 1953, 128–29, 209–10, 214–15.

Notes

1. Graham Greene describes the "masked devil" at Kolahun as "a
   headmaster with rather more supernatural authority than Arnold
   of Rugby ever claimed." *Journey Without Maps*, 99.

2. *The Oxford Outlook* was first established in 1919. Graham
   Greene was acting editor in 1923 and editor in 1924. Among the
   contributors when he was editor were Edmund Blunden, Louis
   Golding, Louis MacNiece, W. H. Auden, Cecil Day-Lewis, and
   Rex Warner.

3. Early in 1952, Graham Greene, named winner of the 1952
   Catholic Literary Award, decided to visit Hollywood to check on
   the filming of *The End of the Affair* and to consult with the editors
   of *Life* for whom he acted as correspondent. His application for a
   visa in Saigon was turned down under the McCarran Internal
   Security Act until the State Department intervened and "cleared"
   him to visit the U. S. "If I wished to visit the United States,"
   writes Greene in *Ways of Escape*, "I had to get special permission
   from the Attorney General in Washington—this took as a rule
   about three weeks and my stay was limited to four. I had to
   inform the authorities on which planes I would arrive and leave,
   and mysterious letters and numbers were inscribed on my temporary visa which always ensured a long delay at immigration."
   Ways of Escape, 180–81. This situation continued until John F.
   Kennedy was president.

4. 15 October 1927.

5. Graham Greene left Oxford in June 1925 before his views on
   Catholicism had taken firm hold.

6. Stephen Spender (1909–), English poet, editor, professor and
   critic. In *The Destructive Element* (London: Cape, 1935;
   Philadelphia: Saifer, 1953) Stephen Spender maintains that writers like Henry James, T. S. Eliot, W. B. Yeats, and D. H.
   Lawrence hovered on the verge of the destructive element or
   political chaos fostered by capitalism and conventional liberalism
   but sought refuge by withdrawing into their personal worlds; he
   therefore advocates the search for a system of values that are

the same way as Nature is real." Such dedication to an outside order does not sit well with Graham Greene's belief in the "virtue" of disloyalty. Greene does not seem to have been an admirer of Stephen Spender.

7. "I've been so bored," says Bendrix to Henry Miles at the end of the novel, "I've even collected car numbers." *The End of the Affair*, 231. Ronald de Couves Matthews also describes Greene's preoccupation with car numbers and his great delight in discovering no. 276 which he was missing! See *Mon ami Graham Greene* (Bruges: Desclée de Brouwer, 1957), 90–91.

A Lapsed Catholic?

Evelyn Waugh

Graham came June 12th [1953]. He is full of theatrical projects but, it seemed, in an unhappy state. He told the Italian ambassador, as excuse for not visiting conference at Florence, that he was "no longer a practising Catholic." He asked for a biscuit before Mass as though to provide (like his hero in *The Heart of the Matter*) a reason for not taking communion, but went off to early train fasting on Monday. He told me the plot of his new play is a priest who "sacrifices" his faith in order to restore a boy to life.[1] But very sweet and modest. Always judging people by kindness.

London, Thursday 21 July 1955

I went to London by the breakfast train from Kemble and drove straight from Paddington to Garrard's carrying the Vuillaume movement for regulation. Walking back along Vigo Street I turned into Albany on impulse and called on Graham Greene. I found him alone and *désoeuvré* having completed a novel and a play,[2] now waiting to take his daughter to Canada[3] in search of cattle and a husband. He told me he has the beginning of cirrhosis of the liver and is on a strict regime. Also that he has broken with Korda who guillotined the Monte Carlo film[4] just as it was ready for shooting.[5]

Thursday 28 July 1955

To Bath to meet James and Graham Greene. We reached Stinchcombe to find the Jesuit who is taking duty during Father Collins's holiday, waiting for luncheon. He seemed disposed to spend the afternoon with us and addressed Laura twice as "mummy." On the first occasion I thought my hearing was playing a trick on me. The second was unmistakable. Graham was genial and full of repose, deep in a condemned book by an Italian theologian who holds that mankind was created to redeem the Devil.

Extracted from *The Diaries of Evelyn Waugh*, ed. Michael Davie (Boston: Little, Brown, and Company, 1976), 721, 731, 733. *Editor's title.*

Notes

1. *The Potting Shed* was first performed at the Bijou Theater, New York, on 29 January 1957 and opened at the Globe Theatre in London on 5 February 1958.
2. The two works in question are *The Quiet American*, published December 1955, and *The Potting Shed*.
3. Interesting to note that though Greene had traveled to Canada, he makes no reference to the journey in any one of the interviews he has given or in his two volumes of autobiography.
4. *Loser Takes All* (Rank Productions, 1956). Directed by Ken Annakin. Produced by John Stafford. Screenplay by Graham Greene. Starring Rossano Brazzi, Robert Morley, and Glynis Johns.
5. "I suppose I was having a bit of liver trouble and dramatized it to Evelyn. Just as he dramatized my visit to Canada which was in search of a small ranch and not of a husband. I had a temporary

quarrel with Korda, who refused to allow Alec Guinness to play a part in a film *Loser Takes All*—part based on himself." Graham Greene in a letter to the editor of the *Diaries*, [Michael Davie], November 1975.

Sex on His Mind!

Otto Preminger

Am I sorry I made the film?[1] No. For I loved working on it. I met another delightful man through the picture: Graham Greene, who did the screenplay. He is a great writer and a delightful companion. Though he gives the impression of being controlled, correct, and British he is actually mad about women. Sex is on his mind all the time.

When Graham Green read this, he wrote me an amusing note protesting: "This sentence doesn't seem quite fair to me. If it were true, I would not have written so many books."

We had an interesting time together in London but he kept telling me, "Wait until we get to Paris. I know a stupendous place there. You have never seen anything like it in your life."

On our first evening in Paris, Greene hurried me into a taxi. "The lady who runs this establishment has amazing resources," he explained to me. "You can go to any show in Paris and if there is a girl you fancy you have only to make a note of her. For instance, you tell the madame that you want the fourth dancer from the left and she will be delivered to you right after the show."

I made no comment when he gave the taxi driver the address of the extraordinary establishment. We arrived and were admitted to a lavishly furnished anteroom. Graham Greene prepared to introduce me to the madame as she entered but before he could do so she rushed past him and embraced me. "Monsieur Preminger!" she cried. "How wonderful to see you again!"

Extracted from *Preminger: An Autobiography* (New York: Doubleday and Company, 1977), 153–54. *Editor's title.*

Notes

1. *St. Joan* (Wheel Productions, 1957). Produced and directed by Otto Preminger. Screenplay by Graham Greene from the play by George Bernard Shaw. Starring Jean Seberg, Richard Widmark, Anton Waldbrook, and John Gielgud. The film was a failure. The tendency was to blame Jean Seberg for her inexperience and the script for showing Joan as a crude miracle worker, but Otto Preminger maintains in his autobiography that he misunderstood "something fundamental" about Shaw's play, that it was not a dramatization of the well-known legend but a "deep [and] cool intellectual examination of the role religion plays in the history of man." In a letter dated 14 September 1957, Greene responded to the "rather offensive suggestion" of the *New Statesman*'s film critic that he had been brought in to "de-Protestantize" Shaw's *St. Joan.*

Graham Greene on
"The Job of the Writer"

Philip Toynbee

It was a sunny, rather quiet London day of early September, but the sudden cool and hush of the Albany arcade was an astonishing change from Piccadilly. Graham Greene received us in his bright, tidily-untidy upstair room with every sign of extreme nervousness. He looked with dismay at the camera and the shorthand pad which my colleagues were carrying, gulped once or twice and made hastily for the fine array of bottles on top of a bookshelf.

Drinks put us both at ease, and after a few preliminary courtesies Mr. Greene began to answer my questions with readiness and eloquence.

PHILIP TOYNBEE: *Shall we begin by taking the most appalling and least escapable event of our times namely the extermination of the Jews? Do you think that this frightful crime and tragedy has had any direct effect on novels and poetry in England?*

GRAHAM GREENE: Not direct, I should say, but certainly an indirect one. I rather think we were already living, before that, in a climate which made that kind of thing not only possible, but probable. After all, the thirties was the great period of engaged literature in this country.

I must admit that I was sitting next to an American woman in a plane the other day who said to me, speaking of Auschwitz,[1] "Don't you think that all that was just propaganda?"

PT: *Yes, that's rather terrifying. I'm inclined to think, though, that there's a considerable difference between the climate of the thirties and the one we've been living in ever since the war. Twenty years ago writers like Auden and Spender[2] deliberately set out to involve themselves in the public issues of the times. Nowadays, many young writers seem to be involved almost against their will—certainly not by any deliberate choice.*

GG: That may be so. But the effect of this climate is very obscure. I don't see how the novelist can write about anything of which he hasn't had direct personal experience.

PT: *Well let's take your own case. I suppose it would be possible to describe nearly all your novels as "engaged." But I very much doubt whether you ever set out deliberately to write a novel in defence of any particular political attitude.*

GG: The nearest I came to it was in *The Quiet American.* But that was really only because I had seen so much of the country and got to know the issues over a period of years.[3]

PT: *So you really feel that any deliberate decision by a writer to engage himself is rather nonsensical?*

GG: It is to me personally. On the other hand, if anybody can write a good book by doing so, then I think he is thoroughly justified.

PT: *Well, can you envisage a young man nowadays writing like Firbank[4]—who is, I suppose, about the most disengaged novelist one can think of?*

GG: No, I can't. But I should be very glad if it happened.

PT: *Shall we take another example of your work? It would be possible, though rather crude, to describe* The Power and the Glory *as a study of the conflict between Church and State in Mexico.*

GG: Yes, but I see that only as the background of the book. It is really an attempt to understand a permanent religious situation. The function of the priesthood. I was much more interested in the theological point of view than in the political one.

PT: *I suppose one might say that your religious convictions are themselves a form of involvement.*

GG: I wonder. It wasn't until ten years after my conversion in 1926 that anyone noticed any trace of it in my novels. The reason for this is quite a simple one. I simply hadn't had sufficient experience of how Catholics think or behave, and therefore I couldn't write about them.

PT: *Of course, any book can be described in so many different terms.* Brighton Rock *was the first of your novels which specifically dealt with a Roman Catholic theme. Yet it could also be described as a study of juvenile delinquency.*

GG: Yes, and the Catholic element in that book was really an afterthought. It grew up after I had begun the novel.

PT: *Let's get back to Firbank. You say that you wouldn't feel any offence if a writer of today wrote a good book in that sort of manner?*

GG: No; I'd be delighted. I hate the idea that any sort of duty is imposed on the writer from outside. It savours of Communism. I see in to-day's paper that Mr. Khrushchev has just fulminated against Russian writers for not paying enough attention to collective farming and engineering projects.

PT: *Yet one might say that simply as a human being the man of to-day who was totally unconcerned about public tragedies would have something wrong with him. He would not be fully human, and I suppose one can say that good writers must be full human beings.*

GG: A modern Firbank would certainly be a rather different Firbank. There would inevitably be a difference of tone in his books.

PT: *Perhaps a note of defiance?*

GG: Or of despair. Or even of optimism.

PT: *Let's take a very extreme example. A Hungarian writer who had lived through the revolution of last October[5] would really have to be a freak if that experience had had no effect upon him.*

GG: I think the most likely effect of the Hungarian Revolution would be to drive writers to silence. After all, how much effect did the French Revolution have on French writers?

PT: *Very little effect I suppose. Yet the Russian Revolution has proved a lasting inspiration to Russian writers and film directors. Of course, this was partly due to direction from above.*

GG: I think it was. After all, you do get your disengaged writers in the Russia of the early 1920s. Books like *The Little Gold Calf* and *The 12 Chairs*.

PT: *That was one of the natural reactions. Some writers wanted to forget the whole bloody business.*

GG: Or was it an attempt to be anarchical in an over-organised society?

PT: *Very likely. And I think this raises an interesting new point. If you belong to a society—belong to it organically I mean—you cannot rebel against it when the society is really threatened. For example, a great many naturally anarchical writers became ardent French patriots during the Occupation.[6] On the other hand, when your society is really strong and healthy, it's a natural tendency to rebel against it.*

GG: Which is what seems to be happening in Russia now. One example might be Dudentsev's novel *Not By Bread Alone.*[7]

But I suppose we must also remember that there is such a thing as the good conformist writer. Someone like Trollope, or possibly Kipling. For all I know, there may be such writers in Russia to-day who genuinely thrive on following the Party directives.

PT: *What it perhaps boils down to is that unless the writer has a strong sense of pity he is bound to be in some sense a maimed writer.*

GG: I prefer the word charity. Pity always sounds rather superior.

PT: *Well, then, would you agree that lack of charity in a writer would be destructive?*

GG: There are times when one would welcome a bit of destruction. Especially in a Welfare State.

PT: *I mean destructive of literature. The lady in the plane who said wasn't it all propaganda about Auschwitz would probably have been a pretty bad novelist.*

GG: Yes, I agree. And we were all guilty of the same thing after the First World War. We didn't want to think about all the horrors any more.

PT: *Exactly. It wasn't until about ten years after the war that the public was willing to read about it.* Journey's End[8] *was the first popular war play, and it was produced, I think, in about 1929. But wouldn't you say that it is one of the writer's jobs not to forget?*

GG: Yes, it is. It's also the writer's job to try to engage people's sympathy for characters who are outside the official range of sympathy. For the traitor for example.

PT: *And you have certainly succeeded in doing this in many of your novels.*

GG: But not as a duty; simply from interest. To do this sets one a slightly more difficult task. It also makes people see something which they have failed to see. That the apparent villain is in fact human, and deserves more compassion than the apparent hero.

PT: *It is certainly a major function of the writer to make people experience emotions which they haven't experienced before.*

GG: I rather feel that if one has anything direct to say about politics or society one should channel it into journalism. When I wrote about the Mau Mau in the *Sunday Times*[9] it was quite obvious that my sympathies were engaged by the Africans and not by the White Settlers.

PT: *And it didn't occur to you to write a novel about that issue?*

GG: No, I had no wish to at all.

PT: *Yet* The Quiet American *was stimulated, surely, by an equivalent journey?*

GG: I knew the scene far better. I must have spent four winters there.

I should like very much to go to South Africa as a reporter. But the hero and villain of such non-fictional writing might well turn out to have their roles reversed in a novel.

PT: *You mean that, although you wrote with great sympathy for the African cause in Kenya in your capacity as a journalist, a novel on the same subject might well have had a British settler or official for its hero?*

GG: Yes, exactly. It's in this way that one's function as a novelist seems to differ so much from one's function as a reporter of events.

PT: *Do you think this special sympathy you have always shown for the sinner, for the apparently unsympathetic character, is due to your religious beliefs?*

GG: I don't know. To tell the truth I find it very difficult to believe in sin. Reviewers always talk about my sense of sin or evil, but doesn't that belong to some of my *characters?* Personally I find I have very little sense of it. What it really adds up to is that I write novels about what interests me and I can't write about anything else. And one of the things which interest me most is discovering the humanity in the apparently inhuman character.

Extracted from Philip Toynbee, "Literature and Life — 2. Graham Greene on 'The Job of the Writer,' " *Observer*, 15 September 1957, 3.

Notes

1. Polish site of notorious Nazi concentration camp.
2. W[ystan]. H[ugh]. Auden (1907–73), English-born poet, settled in America in 1939. He was regarded as a leading radical and antifascist in the thirties before his poetry became overtly Christian in the late forties and fifties. He was the major figure of a group in the thirties comprised of Stephen Spender (1909–), Christopher Isherwood (1904–86), Louis MacNeice (1907–63), and Cecil Day-Lewis (1904–72), with whom he shared opinions and collaborated. Chap. 3 of Bernard Bergonzi's *Reading the Thirties: Text and Context* (London: Macmillan, 1978) stresses the "affinity" between Greene and Auden and the latter's influence on Greene's prewar fictional prose.
3. Graham Greene had visited Vietnam four consecutive winters beginning in 1951 as a reporter for the *Sunday Times* and *Figaro.* His visits culminated in an interview with Ho Chi Minh.
4. [Arthur Henry] Ronald Firbank (1886–1926), English novelist. His "disengaged" approach to novel writing stems from his *fin de siècle* aestheticism.
5. On 23 October 1956, Budapest students demanding economic and social reform were joined by the people and the army. They forced Soviet troops outside the capital and called upon Imre Nagy to form a coalition government. When early in November

Nagy denounced the Warsaw Pact, Soviet tanks rolled into
Budapest and, after savage fighting, quelled the revolution.

6. Jean-Paul Sartre and Albert Camus, for example, were active
members of the French Resistance against the German occupation of France in World War II.

7. Vladimir [Dimitrievitch] Dudentsev (1918–), Russian novelist.
This 1956 novel, translated by Edith Bone, was a literary sensa-
tion because of its indictment of Soviet bureaucrats—only possible under the relative tolerance of the post-Stalin era.

8. A very successful war play by R. C. Sherriff produced at the
Savoy Theatre and published in 1929.

9. "Kenya as I See It," *Sunday Times*, 27 September 1953 and 4
October 1953.

Self-pity at Success

Evelyn Waugh

31 December 1960 – 1 January 1961

The *Daily Mail* sent me an advance copy of Graham Greene's *A Burnt-Out Case* asking for a review for which, I suppose, they would have paid £100. I have had to refuse. There is nothing I could write about it without shame one way or the other. Coming so soon after his Christmas story[1] it emphasizes a theme which it would be affected not to regard as personal—the vexation of a Catholic artist exposed against his wishes to acclamations as a "Catholic" artist who at the same time cuts himself off from divine grace by sexual sin. The hero of *A Burnt-Out Case* is a bored, loveless voluptuary who hides his despair in the most remote place he can find—a leper settlement in the Congo—recovers a spark of humanity but not his "faith" and dies in an absurdly melodramatic way. The efficient doctor is an atheist. The faithful missionaries have given up all attempt to impose the moral law and are interested only in building and finance. A grotesque Catholic layman seeks to impose mystical ideas on his adolescent wife. There is an excellent sermon by the Father Superior and a splendid creation of the heat and remoteness of the leproserie. The journalist intruder is a sham — "Quote — Wordsworth." It is the first time Graham has come out as specifically faithless — pray God it is a mood, but it strikes deeper and colder. What is more — no, less — Graham's skill is fading. He describes the hero's predicament three times, once, painfully, in a "fairy story" which is supposed to take up a whole night but is in fact told in ten minutes. The incident of Deo Gratia's attempted escape and rescue is poorly handled. Graham can't carry corn [?]. His early books are full of self pity at poverty and obscurity; now self pity at his success. I am not guiltless as one of those who put him in the odious position of "Catholic artist." He complained of the heat of his sexual passions, now at their coldness. A book I can't review.

4 January 1961

I wrote to Graham saying that taken in conjunction with his Christmas story, his new novel makes it plain that he is exasperated by his reputation as a "Catholic" writer. I told him in all sincerity how deeply sorry I am for my share in his annoyance. Twelve years ago a lot of Catholics were suspicious of his good faith and I officiously went round England and America reassuring them.[2] I pray that the desperate conclusions of "Morin" and "Querry" are purely fictitious. It has been a bad year for the old steeplechasers — Elizabeth Bowen, John Betjeman, Lesley Hartley down and out of the race; Nancy Mitford and Tony Powell just clinging to the saddle. *A Burnt-Out Case* will be a heavy fall.

21 June 1961

. . . I was the guest in London of the BBC, Christopher Sykes acting as host.[3] Unlike other great businesses they

have no motor cars available. Christopher had to stand at
street corners waving at taxis. They were unable to obtain
theatre tickets for me. The Director-General, Graham's
brother, had me to dinner at Shepherd's Bush in a new
"Television Centre." This was well-found. Graham in a
state of euphoria such as I have never seen him in. He
spends Christmas in Addis Ababa. We may expect a
Communist rising there before Easter.[4]

I am reminded of the time Graham and I went to
Rheims with a mixed party of celebrities to visit the champagne houses. At the air office we were given a list of fel-
low-guests. Alan Pryce-Jones among them.[5] Graham said:
"I am not coming. I won't go with that man Jones."

"What do you mind about him?"

"I absolutely detest him."

"Well he isn't here. He always accepts all invitations
and decides on the most attractive at the last moment.
He's obviously chucked."

So Graham got into the bus. But Alan was at the aero-
drome, having motored there. It was then too late for
Graham to escape. He had a bottle of whisky with him
and swigged for comfort. He swigged throughout the *vin
d'honneur* and the banquet. At 11 o'clock the dinner party
broke up. Graham wanted to find a brothel and would not
believe they had all been closed. I went to bed early. We
had an early start for Epernay in the morning. Alan
Pryce-Jones was in the hall, fresh and elegant, looking
eighteen years old. Graham lurched out of the lift with
bloodshot eyes and pallid face and trembling hands.

"I sat up till 4 drinking whisky," he said.

"Who with?"

"Alan Pryce-Jones."

Extracted from *The Diaries of Evelyn Waugh*, ed. Michael Davie (Boston: Little, Brown, and Company, 1976), 774–75, 778. *Editor's title.*

Notes

1. "A Visit to Morin." After its appearance in *London Magazine*, this short story was published by Heinemann and distributed as gifts, Christmas 1960. See R. A. Wobbe, *Graham Greene: A Bibliography and Guide to Research* (New York: Garland, 1979), 120.

2. In his 1948–49 U.S. lecture tour, Evelyn Waugh used Greene as one of his lecture subjects. In autumn 1953, Greene, indignant at the McCarthy measures that restricted his freedom of travel in the U.S., mentioned that it would be "fun to write about politics for a change and not always about God." Waugh retorted: "I wouldn't give up writing about God at this stage if I was you. It would be like P. G. Wodehouse dropping Jeeves half-way through the Wooster series." Christopher Sykes, *Evelyn Waugh: A Biography* (Boston: Little, Brown, and Company, 1975), 357.

3. Christopher Sykes was later designated as the "official" biographer of Evelyn Waugh by the Waugh family. His biography of Waugh gives interesting insights into the relationship of these two very different temperaments and characters.

4. Perhaps an uncanny premonition of the military coup d'état of 1974! Waugh was familiar with Ethiopia; he was special correspondent for the *Daily Mail* in 1935 and wrote about his adventures there in *Waugh in Abyssinia* (London: Longmans, 1936). I am, however, unable to corroborate that Greene spent Christmas 1961 in Addis Ababa.

5. Alan Pryce-Jones (1908–), English writer and editor, was editor of the *Times Literary Supplement* (1948–59) before settling in the United States. and becoming book critic for the *New York Herald Tribune.* I am unable to determine the reasons for Greene's rather uncharitable attitude; it may be that Evelyn Waugh is dramatizing the situation.

A Pantheon of Contemporary Writers

George Adam

It was the first time in my life that I heard a celebrated novelist speak to me with such unconstraint about his last book.

"It's a joke!" declared Graham Greene referring to *Our Man in Havana*. The novel, translated like all the others by Marcelle Sibon, is a new addition to at least fifteen others in France, several of which have been admired world wide by very demanding critics.

In a short prefatory note, Greene presents the book as a "fairy story." Such confidence! One can only interpret "it's a joke" to mean "a tall story," "an entertainment."

The setting was most appropriate for this widely travelled man whose Albany apartment in London or house in Capri rarely sees him: a small red sitting room adjoining the room he occupies for 48 hours in an hotel on the Champs-Elysées, within a few steps of our Rond-Points.[1] He was snugly ensconced at the end of the couch, bending forward, with his knees crossed under him. It is not much to say that he is tall! He is very tall and, when standing, is almost obliged to bend forward out of concern for his interlocutor. He inclines his well-groomed head with its thin pale red hair turning silver at the edges, always with a gentle and assured glance from his sunken faded grey eyes. He takes a sip of strong black coffee—he had asked for strong coffee. And a glass of cognac.

"I got up this morning with . . . a hangover. Some friends gave me a huge breakfast and I'm quite sure I'll be having a big dinner. One must make room."

I couldn't ask about his collection of miniature whisky bottles—over a hundred of them from all parts of the world—or whether he used it to play checkers, a trait he had given one of his characters in the novel to which I have referred.[2]

"It's a joke!" he repeated. *"It was the same story with* The Third Man."*

He was then making a film in postwar Austria where the producer had frozen assets.[3] While Carol Reed, the future producer, was trying to familiarize himself with the setting of the new film, Graham Greene created the story in which Orson Welles starred.

Some fifteen years later, the same combination of author and producer was reconstituted, this time in Havana where Greene set afoot his amazing spy story in those turbulent days when Fidel Castro and his partisans were preparing to launch their final assault. Had he not, in collaboration with his brother Hugh Greene, written *The Spy's Bedside Book?* He has just spent six weeks there with Carol Reed adapting, on location, the script, scenario and dialogue.[4]

"Oh, I don't like this kind of work! You know what it is like!" and then confidingly adds: *"One talks, one drinks: one drinks and one talks even while adjusting details continually. It's very tiring."*

Nevertheless, he echoes my laughter at this perspective. Alec Guinness in the role of Wormold. The small English salesman of vacuum cleaners turning spy in spite of himself. Agent "5,2000 stroke 4"[5] who perceives that his expense account will make affordable a suitable education for Milly, his daughter. Sends to London reports of unexistent installations with plans that are really sketches of vacuum cleaner parts. The reports are accepted, money is forwarded and Wormold is launched for good into the obscure but well-paid spy trade.

I told him that the convent-reared Milly who plays the part of a pure angel and aggravates her father deeply belongs to the fictional world of his best characters. Even in this sketch of a film, the novelist of *Brighton Rock* and *The Power and the Glory* points discreetly to his inner preoccupations.

"Oh, no! She is just a mischievous young lady, and her mischief is characteristic of her age!"

As I had just mentioned Scobie, I thought that *The Heart of the Matter* occupied an important place in the writer's secret preferences but Greene quickly corrected me. No, he no longer likes that book. In a word, he finds it too "protestant." Scobie has escaped him somehow; the novelist believes he has erred in focussing attention on Scobie's case, his self-importance and his inner woes.

Exeunt "our man in Havana" and poor Scobie, too! Graham Greene is gracious enough to sympathize with his visitor. He was described to me as a person difficult to approach; but there he sits at his end of the couch, relaxed, even laughing, warming his glass of cognac in his hands. And yet, there is that subtle reserve . . .

He remembers, with joy, his first stay in Paris around 1923. The high light at the time? He was able to purchase a copy of James Joyce's *Ulysses*—then banned in England—and just published by Sylvia Beach. The wonder of it! He recalls, by a gesture, the form and size of the book: "Like the Bible and just as rich!"[6]

The name of Ford Madox Ford crops up in the course of our conversation. We regard him, I said, as the occasional collaborator with Joseph Conrad on *Romance,* a novel translated by Marc Chadourne but which found, I am afraid, few readers.

"Come on! It's a wonderful book," says Greene, warming up. (We exchange views with equal enthusiasm on this masterpiece which promises to live up to its French title *L'Aventure.*) *"Ford's part is much larger than people think. It is quite conceivable that Conrad owes him his particular understanding of time in that narrative. Ford is also the author of* The Good Soldier *which isn't at all about war but is one of the first novels in England that touches upon the problems of sex."*

I make my way slowly to certain questions I had in mind since the beginning of our meeting. I ask Greene his opinion on Virginia Woolf, D.H. Lawrence and Aldous Huxley, those inter-war English novelists to whom, at some time in our youth, we were attached. (Greene is only 54.)

He pursed his lips. He does not go so far as to tell me that they have lost their importance to him, but close enough. *"Is it now possible to believe"* he asked, *"in the grand designs of Lawrence and the myth of his plumed serpent?"* I suggested that the author of *Sons and Lovers* will survive thanks to Huxley's fascinating portrait of him in *Counterpoint.*[7] But with one gesture, he indicated that the book had no merit for him.

I asked him which English writers he would include in a small, personal and contemporary Pantheon.

He joined willingly in this little game. Let's see. An old friend first, one whom he meets at most, twice a year:

Evelyn Waugh. Then Ivy Compton-Burnett. And, above all, his namesake, Henry Green.

"He's the best stylist in England to-day. He always chooses one word titles for his works: Loving, Back, Doting, Nothing *... Waugh is more in line with the traditional novel than Green who, under cover of action-packed narratives, reveals himself as a metaphysical writer. A fully humorous book like* Back *uses words like musical themes: note, for example, 'Rose.' "*. . .

Perhaps to a few attentive readers, these names may not be significant discoveries. Three novels by Evelyn Waugh, among them the charming *The Loved One,* have appeared in the "Pavillons" collections of Armand Pierhal. Ivy Compton-Burnett's *Men and Wives* has recently aroused more interest than the preceding ones (in "Le monde entier" collection of Gallimard). And Henry Green was honoured with a translation of *Love* (1934) and *Nothing* (1956).

Graham Greene sees Muriel Spark at the gate of his Pantheon. *"A good candidate with her novel* Memento Mori" and, bursting out laughing, adds: *"All the characters are over seventy."* And finally Greene opens wide the doors for certain poets: D.[W.] H. Auden, Ezra Pound, T. S. Eliot—but only for his early poems up to *The Waste Land*—and Robert Graves whom he rates higher than Eliot.

Many other names come up but Greene dismisses them with a smile after weighing them. We're not citing any other names so as not to offend or to make a choice following other criteria. The Pantheon is closed.

It seems to us in Paris that among the rising generation there is a group that is making quite a splash. One of them, John Osborne, has had his play *La Paix du Dimanche*[8] performed at the "Mathurins." That group has just published a collection of statements which has the tone of a manifesto: *"The angry young men are talking to you."* Are we here speaking of a new school? Ten years down the road, will their revolt against world weariness be regarded as the English equivalent of the anxieties, let's say, existential, of our Saint-Germain-des-Prés?[9]

"A literary school? Come on! The label 'Angry Young Men' was given them by newswriters of the day casting about for copy. I see nothing profound in their alleged rebellion. This group comprises two good authors: Osborne, justly so, and Kingsley Amis. The others, for the time being, are sowing their wild oats. They belong to the times . . ."

They are, all the same, I ventured to say, full of sound and fury.

"You mean the one thing they have in common? They have accepted the age and have yielded to it!" he concluded with a note of disapproval. But to attenuate a little the harshness of his judgment, he continued: *"Literary groups have much less importance in England than in France. Writers live in isolation and often avoid the company of their confrères and literary circles, except for playwrights who find contact with directors, actors and the public essential."*

It is precisely for this kind of activity that Graham Greene returns to London tomorrow. He is, first and foremost, a novelist. Why then does he turn to the theatre? *"Well, to try something else."* It is enough to think of *The Living Room* which the Jean Mercure company had put on lately in Paris and which had met with great success. His second play, *The Potting Shed*, has not been translated yet. But his third, *The Complaisant Lover*[10]—in rehearsal this week in London—is currently being adapted into French by Jean Anouilh. This is a judicious choice because, according to the author, it is *"a comedy . . . a little black!"*

The mention of Jean Anouilh's name in conversation helped us slide from English literature to French. After

being a powerful force in the publishing house of Eyre
and Spottiswoode until 1949, Greene joined the Bodley
Head as literary consultant. At his request, the Bodley
Head will publish a translation of Leautaud's *Petit Ami*.[11]
He is quite proud of his choice just as he was when earlier
he set up an English edition of the complete works of
François Mauriac.[12]

One can justly apply to him his very words on Mauriac:
"He is a writer for whom the living world around him has
not ceased to exist, whose characters have the solidity and
importance of men with souls to save or lose. He is a
writer who claims the traditional and essential right of a
novelist, to comment, to express his views . . ."

I said to him that for the present French generation in
their forties and fifties, the disappearance of Mauriac's
great contemporaries, André Gide, Claudel, Valéry, and
Roger Martin du Gard, had left a void which does not
seem to have been filled.

"And George Bernanos," he added.

I conceded to Bernanos without reservations and asked
whether the French knew their real merit and credited
them with their real worth.

"I just can't follow you!" he said. *"How come? You have
Camus, Malraux, Sartre and Montherlant! What else do you
need? I'd give all Gide for* La Chute *and* Les Noyers de
l'Altenburgh.[13] *I won't say anything about the generation
that's coming. You see, I can only read your authors in translation and one must take into account that they take at least
five years, often more, to reach one. Roger Vailland? I hardly
ever think of the Italy of his last novel . . . Ah! I found great
pleasure in Peyrefitte's* Clés de Saint Pierre;[14] *but mind you,
only as a popular writer!"*

He returns to Sartre from whose works he values *Huit
Clos* most highly.[15]

*"The first time I saw that play, I had to leave the theatre dur-
ing the performance and go and sit on a bench, my head
between my hands. I was choking with emotion! "*

Coming from a Catholic like you, I said to him, there
could be no better tribute! To think that the unbelieving
Sartre has succeeded in giving you a frightening picture of
hell . . .

He acquiesces. He also recognizes that for materialists
like the author of *La Chute,* the spiritual life can only be
founded on the notion of justice. As he gets ready to rise
from the couch—his glass of cognac now empty—he
seeks a way to help me share his beliefs. His delicate hand
traces an invisible but impeccably straight line from the
back of his seat to the table.

*"God has a scientific and total knowledge of us. He is a
mathematician, not a judge. Having said that, I've more confidence in the charity of a mathematician than a judge!"*

George Adam, "Graham Greene établit son pantheon des littératures
anglaise et française . . ." *Figaro Littéraire,* 2 May 1959, 4. Trans.
A. F. Cassis. *Editor's title.*

Notes
1. The offices of *Figaro Littéraire* were then located at 14 Rond-
Point des Champs-Elysées.
2 In *Our Man in Havana,* Wormwold and Captain Segura play
checkers with miniature bottles: twelve bourbon confronting
twelve scotch.
3. Hungarian-born Sir Alexander Korda (1893–1956) was then
production chief of London Films, and he had asked Greene to
write a film "about the Four-Power occupation of Vienna" for
Carol Reed, director and producer of *The Third Man.* (*Ways of
Escape,* 103).
4. *Our Man in Havana* (Columbia Pictures, 1959). Produced and
directed by Carol Reed. Screenplay by Graham Greene. Starring
Alec Guinness, Noël Coward, Burl Ives, Maureen O'Hara, and
Ernie Kovacs.

5. It is "Agent 59,2000 stroke 5."
6. ". . .the size of a telephone directory" is how he describes it in *A Sort of Life.*
7. D. H. Lawrence is favorably portrayed as Mark Rampion in Huxley's *Point Counter Point* (London: Chatto and Windus, 1928).
8. This is the French title for *Look Back in Anger.*
9. This old abbey on the left bank of the Seine and the adjacent coffeehouses have been associated with existentialist thought in French literary circles.
10. *The Complaisant Lover* was first performed at the Globe Theatre on 17 June 1959. Sir John Gielgud directed the play with a cast that included Paul Scofield, Phyllis Calvert, and Ralph Richardson. It premiered at the Ethel Barrymore Theater, New York, on 1 November 1959. The play was also translated into French by Jean Anouilh and his wife Nicole as *L'amant complaisant* (Paris: Laffont, 1962).
11. Three of Paul Leautaud's works—*Le Petit ami, In Memoriam,* and *Amours*—were translated into English by Humphrey Hare and published by the Bodley Head in 1959 under the title *The Child of Montmartre.*
12. *The Collected Edition of the Novels of François Mauriac,* trans. Gerard Hopkins (London: Eyre and Spottiswoode, 1946–58).
13. Albert Camus's *La Chute* (1956) and André Malraux's *Les Noyers de l'Altenburg* (1943) were translated as *The Fall* (1957) and *The Walnut Trees of Altenburg* (1952). In an open letter to Malraux in *Le Monde* (23 June 1960) protesting against torture in Algeria, Greene, after quoting a passage from *Les Noyers de l'Altenburg,* asked how Malraux could still belong to a government that was responsible for such torture. See Marie-Françoise Allain, *The Other Man,* 84.
14. Pierre Roger Peyrefitte, *The Keys of the Kingdom,* trans. Edward Hyams (London: Secker and Warburg, 1961).
15. Sartre's play *Huit Clos* (1943) was translated by Stuart Gilbert as *In Camera* (U.S. title *No Exit*) and published, with three other plays, by Hamish Hamilton in 1946. Jean-Paul Sartre (1905–80) was a French postwar novelist-dramatist-philosopher and an exponent of existentialism.

The Business of the Writer

Madeleine Chapsal

MADELEINE CHAPSAL: *What do you think of your last novel?*

GRAHAM GREENE: *Our Man in Havana?* Of course, I consider it an entertainment.

MC: *It is excellent.*

GG: I only hope it made you smile!

MC: *When did you write it?*

GG: Last year. I began it in November 1957 when I was in Havana.

MC: *Do you write quickly?*

GG: No, very slowly. When I'm working on a book, I aim at 500 words a day but I am often held up.

MC: *Where do you work? In London?*

GG: No, not in London. Too many telephone calls, too many people! . . . Generally speaking, I write in the country. Or else I go to Brighton, by the sea, and work in my hotel room where no one can join me and if I get too bored, well London is not too far. . .

MC: *I am sure this question has been put to you often. Why do you give your books, even the most serious, the pattern of a "thriller"? Of a detective novel?*

GG: I like detective novels and take great pleasure reading them. John Buchan was one of my first favorites when I went to school.[1] And from then until today, life looks a little like a detective novel. Do you not find it so? Especially since the war?

MC: *Do you have the whole plot in mind when you start writing a book?*

GG: I see the beginning and the end but there is much that is obscure in between. And fortunately, too, or the book would be already written. This is why I do not write short stories because one must know in advance what one will say and there are no discoveries to work out. I like a book to grow.

MC: *Will you be writing books that are not just "thrillers" like* The Heart of the Matter *and* The Power and the Glory?

GG: I am tired of being considered a Catholic novelist and persecuted for that very reason . . . This is why there is no Catholicism at all in my last two novels. I also have a play currently running in London which is nothing but a comedy. This is just to throw people off. It is difficult to do so because once they've decided that you're a Catholic novelist, a whole group of well meaning people is around, to put pressure . . .

MC: *What is the theme of your play?*

GG: It is called *The Complaisant Lover* and that says it all.

MC: *Do you think so?*

GG: It is impossible to explain the plot . . . All plots have a sterile air about them. But I found it very amusing to write that play. I have written three plays until now and I think this is the best. M. Anouilh is presently translating it into French.

MC: *What do you think of the films made from your books?*

GG: I detest them all, except the ones whose scripts I have written, *The Third Man* and *The Fallen Idol*. Did you see *The Quiet American*?[2] It is awful. The American is wholly right and the Englishman wholly wrong. The American is the embodiment of wisdom and heroism. It's terrible! I've just finished writing the script of *Our Man in Havana*. They are currently shooting the film there with Alec Guinness. I have just returned from Havana.

MC: *For whom do you write?*

GG: For myself, I think.

MC: *Do your readers not interest you more than that?*

GG: No. I believe that in writing, each writer has in mind an imaginary reader who is the ideal reader.

MC: *What is yours? Man or woman?*

GG: A hermaphrodite, probably! In reality, when one writes a play or a film script, one must think of one's audience because one is dealing with a public art form. But writing a novel is a private act and it is not necessary to think of one's readers.

MC: *Has the great success of your books not had any influence on you?*

GG: I would hope not, especially for one's self-preservation. One must work hard, do all that one can, struggle with one's self. That's all. Besides, I was always interested in storytelling, in technique. Perhaps too interested.

MC: *Did you study the technique of other writers?*

GG: Yes, when I was young.

MC: *Whom do you admire most as storytellers?*

GG: Henry James, Joseph Conrad and a writer who is not well known, Ford Madox Ford. There was a time when he was more famous in France than in England because he lived in France. He's a good writer. He died around 1940. His best book is *The Good Soldier*. I do not know whether it has been translated.[3]

MC: *Whom do you like among the contemporary French writers?*

GG: I regret to say that I do not read them in French. I very much like Malraux, especially *Les Noyers de l'Altenburg* and *La Chute* by Camus. They remind me of Rilke a little.

MC: *And Sartre?*

GG: I like certain plays of his. *Huit Clos* is a wonderful play. I find his novels to be very much influenced by John Dos Passos.

MC: *John Dos Passos was, in effect, one of our post-war discoveries.*

GG: To me, he is a little dated; he belongs to the twenties—newspaper clippings, large headlines and all that— he is tedious, very tedious.[4]

MC: *Do you follow contemporary English literature?*

GG: A little. There are one or two young authors whom I admire but, on the whole, I do not read many novels. Above all, I must admit that the only two contemporary authors whose last novels I can open, absolutely certain that I shall find them pleasurable, belong to an earlier generation like myself: Evelyn Waugh and Henry Green. I am always certain that I will spend an agreeable time in their company.

MC: *Don't the young authors ever give you a picture of the modern world, their world, that is meaningful to you?*

GG: I don't feel that at all. Perhaps a woman, Muriel Spark. But when all's said and done, I do not read very much.

MC: *You say very little of yourself in your books. Is that intentional?*

GG: But yes, I do speak of myself! In my travel books. It is true though, I neither like confessions nor confession boxes.

MC: *You give the impression that you do not like the modern period very much. You seem to think that its mores, customs and machines endanger the inner life.*

GG: I do not think this is altogether true. Certainly, if one were to write on something . . . let's say something ugly, one can describe it affectionately and meanwhile the reader may perhaps see only the ugliness . . .

MC: *What is it that you dislike in today's civilization?*

GG: America. And by America I mean many things that have nothing to do with America itself: television, gadgets, cellophane wrapped vegetables, frozen foods, all sorts of things . . . It's not just America; I use the term to identify and point out these things.

MC: *Why do you not like television?*

GG: One is conscious of what it has done to one's friends. Once people appear on television, they become "stars."

MC: *And you?*

GG: I have never accepted the idea of seeing myself on it. I don't want to. The business of the writer is not just to be recognized. All those people you see on television will be recognized on the street . . . A writer should have a sort of protective cover that prevents people from recognizing him, that's for sure.

MC: *You have travelled much. Why?*

GG: It's neurotic. I say this because last year I found out that I travelled 44,000 kms by plane.[5] This is too much. It's a form of neurosis . . .

MC: *You do not like refrigerators but you like aeroplanes?*

GG: I like long-distance flights. I like to hear a voice on the loud speaker announcing Damascus, Khartoum, Hong-Kong . . . But I do not like small planes; I prefer the train.

MC: *You often choose in your novels the same kind of hero: social failures and outcasts. Are these what you also prefer in life?*

GG: I cannot say yes because all my friends will feel insulted! It is rather as acquaintances that one values these questionable individuals, like those one encounters in a bar or on a train and to whom one speaks for half an hour. There are so many people who love to tell their life history. It's extraordinary the number of stories one hears from fellow travellers on a plane.

MC: *Have any of these encounters ever served you as starting points?*

GG: No, the starting point always comes from oneself. For example, for *The End of the Affair* I saw a man sitting on a balcony in a particular spot in Freetown.[6] There were two ways to get him to leave that balcony and I had to choose between them because each could have been the starting point of a wholly different story resulting from the image of that same man on the balcony. It was necessary to kill one of the stories to allow the other to take off. I did not know which to sacrifice. One was a detective story and the other is the story I have written.

Sometimes I see the first scene and the last scene but do not know how to fill in the rest. Likewise, for this story which I hope will get moving, the first scene is situated in the Belgian Congo: I see a man walking towards the camera; he is a doctor. I've already written the last lines he must speak in the novel. But the middle is still missing. It's difficult and I'm not sure it will ever get done. One must wait. This idea struck me before I even saw a leper colony and I felt it incumbent upon me to go and see one in the Belgian Congo. I did and stayed there several weeks. I stayed six weeks in that leper colony so that my character would have a proper setting. It was he I was thinking about first.

MC: *What is it that attracted you to lepers?*

GG: There exists in leprosy what is called the "burnt-out case": when a person has lost his fingers perhaps, or his nose, or his ears; he is finished but so is the disease also. It is burnt out. I was interested in making the analogy to a man who is psychologically burnt out, who finds himself on the edge of his profession, for example, or his faith, and though one is cured, one is also finished . . . I just don't want to think about it. At the moment, I'm busy with the play and have put away the novel in a drawer; I might take it out this summer. I don't know.

MC: *Have you written the books you always wanted to write?*

GG: Certainly not. When I was young, I wanted to write historical novels in the manner of an English novelist, Marjorie Bowen whom I liked very much.[7] I certainly did not want to write the books I've written. I wouldn't like to read them either if I were a reader. I find them a bit too gloomy.

MC: *Do you not think the public likes gloomy stories?*

GG: I don't know . . . I don't.

MC: *You said that you did not like to be classified as a Catholic novelist. Do you think that Catholics are a special lot?*

GG: Only insofar as they are believers. The effect of an act that is contrary to their beliefs often engenders a conflict, or the seeds of one, and that is of interest to the novelist. But things happen in the same way with all kinds of people who believe in something: like the communist, for example. There are communists in my novels.

MC: *It has often been said that your books deal with the conflict between good and evil, that your novels are an illustration of the power of evil.*

GG: I don't understand what that means! Someone coined that phrase in connection with evil and it has been reiterated ever since. When one has a label tied round one's neck, one finds it extremely difficult to get rid of it ... This was an additional reason for writing a comedy, an attempt to get rid of the label.

MC: *Do you think you will succeed?*

GG: It may take long ... I became aware of it at the first performances of my plays. People who come to see a specific show refrain from laughter; they think it improper. They believe a play must be solemn and they have decided not to be amused. One must struggle, struggle with the public to make it laugh despite itself. All this because one has had the label "serious writer" hung round one's neck. But perhaps now that I've called my last play a "comedy," I may still have an opportunity to see the public more disposed to be merry.

Extracted from Madeleine Chapsal, *Les Ecrivains en personne* (Paris: René Julliard, 1960), 109–17. Trans. A. F. Cassis. *Editor's title.*

Notes

1. John Buchan (1875–1940), Scottish novelist and one-time Governor General of Canada, is best remembered for *The Thirty-Nine Steps*. Greene reviewed his last work, *Sick Heart River*, in 1941. See *Collected Essays*, 223–25.

2. *The Quiet American* (United Artists, 1957). Directed and produced by Joseph L. Mankiewicz. Screenplay by Joseph L. Mankiewicz. Starring Audie Murphy, Michael Redgrave, Claude Dauphin, and Georgia Moll. Greene condemned the film adaptation as a "complete travesty" and as a "real piece of political dishonesty." " ... One could almost believe," writes Greene "that the film was made deliberately to attack the book and the author." See "The Novelist and the Cinema—A Personal Experience," *International Film Annual*, No. 2, ed. William Whitebait (New York: Doubleday, 1958), 55.

3. *Author's note.* Translated by Jacques Papy and titled *Quelque chose au cœur* for the French Book Club.

4. John [Roderigo] Dos Passos (1896–1970), American novelist, playwright, and journalist whose monumental trilogy *42nd Parallel* (1930), *1919* (1932), and *The Big Money* (1936), often regarded as the great American novel, presents a view of contemporary United States in a kind of prose montage derived from newsreels, posters, and songs.

5. Greene notes in his "Congo Journal": "In 1957 I travelled more than 44,000 miles." See *In Search of a Character*, 33.

6. The novel in question is *The Heart of the Matter* not *The End of the Affair*. See the introduction to the collected edition of the novel or *Ways of Escape*, 100–101. Eight years later, in an interview he granted V. S. Naipaul, Greene explains the same situation in very much the same words. See "Graham Greene," *Daily Telegraph Magazine*, 8 March 1968, 28–32.

7. "Marjorie Bowen" [Gabrielle Margaret Vere Campbell: Mrs. Arthur Long] (1886–1952), American-born novelist and author of some 150 works. *The Viper of Milan* (1906) is her first novel.

Graham Greene:
The Man and the Message

Charles Rolo

As a novelist and as a man, Graham Greene is a figure surrounded by paradox, ambiguity, and surprise. To begin with, he has a dual literary personality: for twenty-nine years, he has been a writer both of serious novels and thrillers, which he labels "entertainments." Although he is widely regarded in Catholic circles as a leading Catholic novelist, Greene's theology has been the subject of endless controversy. His admirers include atheists, who maintain that his books unintentionally show up religion as a blight; existentialists, who claim that he is one of them; the Moscow journal *Soviet Literature*, which sees Greene as a social critic boldly exposing the corruption of capitalist society; and tens of thousands of book buyers who find his storytelling irresistibly readable.

In his autobiographical writings, Greene has frequently expressed a profound attachment to failure—"seedy" has always been his favorite adjective. Yet his own career presents a picture of phenomenal industry and unflagging purpose. From the outset, he made it a rule to write five hundred words a day ("stepped up to seven-fifty as the book gets on"), and today his output totals eleven novels, seven "entertainments," three plays, two travelogs, two collections of short stories and one of essays, and a volume of verse—twenty-seven works all told, plus children's books, film scripts, and a good deal of journalism.

Personal impressions of Greene vary considerably. Physically, he is a tall lanky man, with arresting blue eyes, who likes to appear slightly seedy; he looks weather-beaten—as though he had spent a long time in the rain. Some interviewers have seen the novelist faithfully reflected in the man; they have spoken of his "tormented smile" and "neuralgic agony" of spirit. Others, perhaps too literal-minded, have found Greene's social manner and his way of life more worldly than his works had led them to imagine. Two young magazine editors who visited Greene in London were disconcerted to discover that his so-called "hole in the ground" was an extremely snug, well-appointed flat in the aristocratic heartland of Mayfair. "What worries us," one of them blurted out, "is that you yourself seem so much happier than we expected."[1] Those who know Greene well do not doubt that the inner man is a battleground on which punishing campaigns are constantly being fought. They emphasize his exceptional kindness, but they also see in him a streak of the schoolboy who delights in mystification and play-acting—Greene is an inveterate and elaborate prankster. But for all his contradictions, one thing is certain about Greene: at the basis of his work there is a deeply passionate and searching concern about the human situation. He is unmistakably, a man and a writer who puts the Four Last Things first: death, judgment, hell, and heaven.

Extracted from Charles Rolo, "Graham Greene: The Man and the Message," *Atlantic*, May 1961, 60–65.

Notes

1. Martin Shuttleworth and Simon Raven, "The Art of Fiction," *Paris Review* 1 (autumn 1953): 25–41.

The House of Fiction

Frank Kermode

Miss Murdoch,[1] then, finds it clear that the trouble nowadays lies in an over-willingness to depend upon "myth," and that this premature dependence is falsely consoling; that it takes the bitter flavor out of reality, reduces the identity of characters, and, morally speaking, is a self-indulgence on the part of the writer. Mr. Greene uses the term "myth" differently, and accordingly sees the whole problem in another light. In fact he almost echoes Turgeniev [sic], who said, "I would, I think, rather have too little architecture than too much—when there's a danger of its interfering with my measure of the truth."

FRANK KERMODE: *Mr. Greene, in the book in which you describe the genesis of your last novel,* The [sic] Burnt Out Case, *you make this remark: "Am I beginning to plot, to succumb to that abiding temptation to tell a good story?"*[2] *I'd like to ask you, if I may, in what sense the abiding temptation to tell a good story is to be regarded as inimical, as it presumably is, to the production of a good novel?*

GRAHAM GREENE: I'm not sure that one can generalize on that; I feel it's inimical to my producing a good novel.

My own wish always is to produce a central figure who represents some idea of reasonable simplicity—a mythical figure if you like. And the simplicity often gets damaged by plot making. For instance, if I can just illustrate a point from a book I don't like much called *The Heart of the Matter*, where one wanted to draw a fairly simple portrait of a man who was corrupted by his sense of pity. But in the course of that book, perhaps because one was rusty, not having written for some years during the war, one began to over-load the plot, and I felt the effect of the character was whittled away.

FK: *This is a curious comment on the terms plot and myth, because we have had Iris Murdoch telling us that she regarded myth as the great temptation to self-indulgence, when what one ought to be concerned with was the texture of reality. And you are really saying something which is not quite the opposite, but quite close to the opposite, aren't you?*

GG: Yes, very nearly the opposite.

FK: *And it's interesting in that connection that Miss Murdoch's stories do, as she would put it herself, descend into myth-making from time to time, whereas you are a plot-builder, are you not?*

GG: And I would like to ascend into myth, but find my boots so often muddy with plot. My own feeling is that the nearest I came to hitting the mythical element was in *The Power and the Glory*, where I feel the plot was sufficiently simple for the main purpose of this story to remain clear throughout.

FK: *May I mention a novel of yours, which I especially admire, and which I dare say would incur your own criticism that it's too heavily plotted in a slightly different way? That's* The End of the Affair. *What do you feel about that?*

GG: I like a lot of the book, but I made an appalling mistake, I think, in the last third of the book, which has always spoilt—though I don't read my books—any retrospective enjoyment I might have.

FK: *It would be very interesting to know what you thought that mistake was.*

GG: The introduction of something which had not got a natural explanation. I had intended a much longer last part of the book after the women had died, where there was to be a succession of coincidences, until the lover became maddened by the coincidences which would not cease. I found it very difficult to continue the book with the loss of the principal figure, and I foreshortened badly by introducing something which was not easily accountable for in natural terms.

FK: *This encourages me to believe that I am right in my own view of the book, which is that it is in a way a novel about plot making, isn't it—not only about a novelist making a plot, but about God making a plot?*

GG: Yes.

FK: *And if you had put in these additional coincidences, you would have strengthened that element?*

GG: Yes.

FK: *Of course I think in* The End of the Affair *God the novelist is quite a strong figure in the myth, as it were.*

GG: Yes.

FK: *In* A Burnt-Out Case, *for example, you didn't feel that your plot had that kind of function as a kind of mirror image of providence?*

GG: No.

FK: *So this is a different case, in that the element of plot in it tends to be destructive rather than to augment the myth?*

GG: Yes, in a curious way it was more simple plotting, wasn't it, than, say, *The Heart of the Matter*—less details, less events, less action. And yet what little action there was seemed to take too strong a part. Perhaps it would have seemed less plotted if there had been more plot.

FK: *I had intended to ask you whether you feel that there is a point beyond which you can't dispense with plot. I mean there obviously is such a point, but where does this point lie? On what you said at the beginning of our conversation, it would seem that the less plot a novel had, the better it was likely to be, broadly speaking.*

GG: Yes, in a way I agree—but that's my feeling often when I'm trying to write a novel which conflicts with passionate liking for melodrama. And a reaction, when I was a young man, I suppose a reaction from the books of Virginia Woolf, where the narrative was very subordinated to mood. And I still have a liking for action in the novel.

FK: *But on the whole you think that the representation of reality, of the real truth about the world, in a novel is primarily the burden of what we have agreed to call myth?*

GG: Yes.

FK: *And that plot on the whole is in opposition, at any rate, has to be controlled.*

GG: Yes, it must be controlled. Because after all in *Tom Jones* there is a tremendous amount of plot, but it's subordinated the whole time to the main character, isn't it?

FK: *I suppose it's a good case of a novel in which you have a strong myth of a rather ethical cast, and also an extremely complex plot, well timed, and thoroughly worked out and so on.*

GG: Yes.

FK: *Without any sense that the things collide; in fact when they do seem to collide, as in the case of Sophia's muff on the bed,[3] for example, they have a very strong ethical flavor.*

GG: Yes.

FK: *And this is the direction in which you would like to . . .*

GG: I would like to be able to write.

FK: *So in fact there is no real argument against having very complex plots?*

GG: No, as long as it does not damage the mythical center.

Extracted from "The House of Fiction," *Partisan Review* 30 (spring 1963): 65–68.

Notes

1. This excerpt is part of a series of conversations with seven contemporary British novelists: Iris Murdoch, Graham Greene, Angus Wilson, Ivy Compton-Burnett, C. P. Snow, John Wain, and Muriel Spark. The conversations generally revolve around the relation between fiction and reality in terms of the novelists' struggle to be faithful to themselves as perceivers and as seekers of the truth.
2. *In Search of a Character*, 57.
3. In Fielding's classic novel *Tom Jones*, Bk. 10., chap. 6, Sophia asks the maid to leave the muff so that Tom would know that she had been there.

The Real Africa

~~~~~

Martin Tucker

I asked Graham Greene in his flat in London whether he
thought the kind of book he wrote about Africa could continue to have an audience.[1] Since he is a modest man, he
only folded his hands and smiled, but he did say he was
hoping to write still another novel set in Africa, and it
would NOT be a political, "New Africa" book.

"I have no interest in the political novel as such. My
interest is in my characters."

Did Greene have any idea where he would place the
novel, in what area or milieu?

"I'm still fascinated by what is called black Africa. All I
know is that it won't be set in North Africa, which I detest,
and I'm not really interested in South Africa. I know West
Africa well, having lived and worked there, and I've visited
East Africa as a correspondent for a newspaper."[2]

Could Greene explain why West Africa has produced
such a relatively vast native literature, especially in
French, while British East Africa has produced practically nothing of consequence by a native-born African.

"I think the reason is that the British came to stay in
West Africa. They came only to exploit the land in East

Africa. The African influenced by French civilization in the Western part has an advantage over the British-educated African of the East. The French brought a solid block of culture united by their Catholicism, while the British brought polo, Sunday school teachers and ministers. I don't mean this as a religious comment, but as a cultural observation. The Catholic attitude gave a unity and a purpose, and thus a permanence to the French African teachings."

In his first book on Africa, *Journey Without Maps*, published in 1936, Greene said "everything ugly" in Africa "was European." The Coca-Cola signs, the wooden houses, the fences, the depressing neon lights. Would he still give the same criticism?

"No, I think there are some pretty cottages in Africa, just as there are in America. Things have changed for the better."

What English writer has written the best modern book on the old Africa, within the colonial framework?

"I'm not sure. But I have always liked Joyce Cary.[3] I think he understood Africa and the Africans. I liked *Mister Johnson* very much."

What African writer did he admire?

"I haven't read too many of the West Africans, you'll have to excuse me. But I enjoyed Amos Tutuola, although he relies more on dreams than people. As far as South Africa goes, I admire Laurens van der Post's first novel, *In a Province.*"[4]

What did he think of *The Story of an African Farm*, by Olive Schreiner, universally acknowledged as the classic novel of South Africa?

"I haven't read it."

Did he think the great African novel, the one which would really capture the spirit of the turbulent conflicts, could be written by an Englishman, or must it be written by a Negro? Could only a Negro illuminate the dark areas of the African soul?

"I don't see why a visitor couldn't, if he was a true observer, write a perceptive novel about Africa. I think a black African will write one kind of novel, and an Englishman another. They'll be two sides of the same story, but each will reveal the true Africa. A writer should know something about his locale, but a recent prize-winning story was written by a man who had never come near the continent. And as far as the great African novel is concerned, I object to the concept. What is a *great* novel? I think Americans looking for the great African novel are like Jews, they're all waiting for the Messiah."

The final question I put to him was in the nature of a speculation. The rich turmoil of Africa has pervaded all its affairs, and even independence has not vitiated the color question. Independence has often merely turned color prejudice around: instead of barriers against blacks, there are now barriers against white. Did Greene believe, as some other novelists have said, that miscegenation was the solution? That the racial question in Africa would only be solved when whites and blacks intermarried?

"Miscegenation may be the answer. I've no personal objection, but it must be fifty-fifty. It must not only be the white man marrying a black woman, but the black man marrying the white woman. But the question is too big for me to solve. The first novel I wrote, which never got published and never will—it's a very bad book—is about a black boy born to white parents in England.[5] It's based on the Mendelian principle that a characteristic will come out sooner or later. The principle is out of date nowadays; you hear mainly that children in a black-white marriage get whiter and whiter."

What happened to the child?

"I've forgotten. Besides, it wasn't a very good novel."

Extracted from Martin Tucker, "The Real Africa: Heart Before Politics," *New York Herald Tribune*, 23 September 1962, 11.

Notes

1. By 1962, Greene had published four works about Africa: a travelogue, *Journey Without Maps* (1936), two novels, *The Heart of the Matter* (1948) and *A Burnt-Out Case* (1961), and his "Journals," *In Search of a Character* (1961).
2. Greene's first visit to West Africa was in January 1935. Later, as an agent of MI5 during World War II, he spent two years in Freetown, Sierra Leone. Greene visited Kenya in 1953 to report on the Mau Mau rebellion for the *Sunday Times*.
3. Joyce Cary (1888–1957), English novelist. *Mister Johnson* (1939) is the last of his three novels dealing with Africans.
4. Amos Tuotola (1920–), Nigerian novelist and short story writer.
   Laurens Van der Post (1906–), South African novelist and traveler. *In a Province* (1934) is his first novel and deals with the theme of racial discrimination.
5. The novel in question is *Anthony Sant* that Greene wrote during his student days at Oxford but it "never found a publisher." See *A Sort of Life*, 146.

Interlude in Bombay

S. V. V.

One cannot escape the confusion a schoolboy feels in the immediate presence of his favourite movie actor, when one greets Graham Greene. The "entertainments" one has read in the last three decades, the films one has seen based on his stories and scripts, the novels and plays that have presented the "pathetic martyrs" of our time and gathered in bouquets all the fragile fragrance of the *fleurs du mal*, make Greene as much a perplexing personality as an absorbing author.

Lanky, loose-limbed, sprightly even at sixty, Greene puts out his hand in easy friendship, with no trace of formality in his stance or speech and, soon, one is unmindful of the numerous characters he has created, but acutely aware of being in the presence of one of the most gifted novelists of England today.

Once inside the hotel room, Greene quickly removed his coat, with an "excuse me," which also made it clear that he was in need of some rest, having had but just a few hours to meet all the demands for appointments and calls in Bombay.

It was indeed a pity that he was not free to discuss all the questions noted down.

"Are you chiefly concerned with the presence of evil?"

"I don't consider myself a Catholic writer. Of course I am a Catholic. But, in so far as my works are concerned, perhaps, only 4 or 5 out of 30 books have anything to do with religion. Such attitudes as the sense of guilt are not, in my opinion, specifically Christian. They are common to all humanity."

It is, in a way, surprising that so many critics have evaluated the contribution of Greene solely from the viewpoint of Catholic criteria of sin and salvation. This has resulted in the lopsided argument that Greene's vision is sustained largely by Christian theology. But one must remember that Greene's concern, as a writer, is more with humanity than with God or religion. Long ago he had made it clear when he observed: "If my conscience were as active as M. Mauriac's showed itself to be in his essay 'God and Mammon,' I could not write a line."[1] Again he is on record as having remarked that his being in the Catholic Church "would present me with grave problems as a writer if I were not saved by my disloyalty."[2]

Talking to Greene one realises that he is far from François Mauriac, who can certainly be categorized as a Catholic writer, and even from other minds such as Aldous Huxley to whom the thought of a godhead became a reality involving him in a passionate pursuit of the perennial philosophy.

Properly viewed, Graham Greene, as a writer, is only interested in sin and evil because they exist in all lives and even the most sinful sinner is aware of the spiritual self.

"I suppose you are not against a certain amount of experimentation with the mind and use of drugs to unravel new visions?"

Greene has written so freely and frankly about his experiments with opium that one need not feel any moral compunction in discussing the subject.

"I am all for opium. I like alcohol, too. But, any day, I prefer opium to alcohol. I have nothing against anyone taking any drugs as long as a person is not responsible for others."

"Have you tried hashish?" I asked him, since I had an occasion to study the limits of the mind under the influence of this alkaloid.

"I did, some time ago in the Near East, but without any effect. I took it in the form of pills."

Greene appeared to be interested in my tip to grind the stuff into a paste and mix it with milk. There is a certain childish curiosity that he maintains, apparently, in such "disloyalty" to self and one can readily sense it as his clear blue eyes sparkle as he talks of opium — "no exciting drugs for me."

"Have you any views on Indo-Anglian writing? And do you think that the question of a foreign language presents any insurmountable problem to the Indian writer, or is it only the lack of imaginative vision that makes several works in this field remain mediocre?"

"I am not very conversant with Indo-Anglian literature. I can only recall reading Rabindranath Tagore long ago. I suppose he is now being rediscovered. But, for some reason, I don't very much care for Tagore. The only author in this group I can talk about is R. K. Narayan. To me he appears the best among those from India writing in English. I have referred to him as the Indian Chekhov. The strange setting of his stories — just as in Russian literature — and Narayan's sense of humour, as also the underlying sadness in his works, make me think of Chekhov.[3] There are certain points that appeal to me while reading him — for instance the way certain friends do not see each other for years and are then brought together.

"Regarding the difficulties presented by a foreign language, I suppose each has his own problem. Narayan told me about the trouble he has with the use of articles. But eventually a good writer evolves his own individual style, and Narayan does have an idiom of his own. Personally I will not think of writing in any language except English, for I am bad at languages. Of course in literature one can talk of Conrad and Nabakov — to cite instances of those who have overcome the tremendous difficulty of handling alien languages."

"Have you read Raja Rao, especially *The Serpent and the Rope?* There is a lot more of the Indian mind and philosophy in it than any other Indo-Anglian work."

"I am not particularly interested in philosophy. Anyhow I haven't read Raja Rao."

"Who among contemporary authors appeal to you most?"

"If I may pick from the immediate dead I would say William Faulkner. Among the living I find Evelyn Waugh very interesting."

"What about Durrell?"[4]

"Oh, he is the Charles Morgan of the present day. I thought it was a little presumptuous that one of the novels in the *Alexandria Quartet* used the title of Marquis de Sade's classic *Justine.*"

It appeared to me that Graham Greene is not a very reliable critic. Moreover I do not think he makes any claims to be recognised as one.

There would be many readers, I thought, who will not agree with Greene's estimate of Durrell, though everyone will be ready to use the phrase "Charles Morgan of the present day" to deride a novelist with whom they differ.

"Have you any acquaintance with Hindu philosophy or Buddhist thought?"

"Hindu philosophy? No. But I have some contact with Buddhist thought, since I have stayed in Viet Nam."

Every passing minute made me feel guilty, for I was holding Greene from his siesta, which he appeared to need badly after having motored down to Bombay from Goa and with a night in the plane now facing him. It made me feel disappointed also, for nothing would have been more rewarding than a long talk with Greene on his idea of religion—which must certainly have had a meaning for all, for he can combine the opposites and make a sinner a saint, and a saint a lover.

It is easy to put these lines from *The Power and the Glory*, for instance, in a novel by D. H. Lawrence—only, one has to appreciate that both the lover and the priest seek in the main a sense of spiritual fulfilment in the course of their search:

> What a fool he had been to think that he was strong enough to stay when others fled. What an impossible fellow I am, he thought, and how useless. I have done nothing for anybody. I might just have never lived. . . Tears poured down his face: he was not at the moment afraid of damnation—even the fear of pain was in the background. He felt only an immense disappointment because he had to go to God empty-handed, with nothing done at all. It seemed to him, at the moment, that it would have been quite easy to have been a saint. It would only have needed a little self-restraint and a little courage. He felt like someone who has missed happiness by seconds at an appointed

place. He knew now that at the end there was only one thing that counted—to be a saint.[5]

But a saint could be found anywhere—one does not have to go to the mountain caves to look for him in penance—for one can come to sainthood at any place. And that is why among the earliest declarations of Graham Greene—to be exact in 1930—he announced that he hoped to have time in future "to become thoroughly acquainted with such strange and slightly sinister suburbs as Brixton and Streatham Hill."[6] And it must be stressed again, that in Greene's vision, just as Remy de Gourmont also visualised in a story, the "whisky" priest can be a saint. It may sound strange, but Greene, perhaps, would say that it does not matter whether God reprimands or rewards one.

What would be Greene's future literary projects? He himself cannot be certain, for he has the talent of picking his characters from any crowd, the tact to make any headline yield a story, and the imagination to turn any setting into a locale for a dramatic situation.

Presently he appears to be a little involved with the theatre, and a play entitled *Carving a Statue* is due for publication. But I am almost certain that some day he will produce a novel on his namesake who has led him to strange encounters.

This other Graham Greene, an adventurous type according to reports, has often crossed the novelist's path, but the two have never met.

Graham Greene has maintained a dossier of the interesting incidents that the elusive character has staged. And not for nothing would Greene have decided to explore accidental contacts with the acquaintances of the other, once even studying "a horse-faced woman" from one end of the bar after having invited her to a drink in this mix-up of names and requesting an intermediary to impersonate him.

Extracted from S. V. V., "Graham Greene," *Illustrated Weekly of India*, 19 January 1964, 22–23. *Editor's title.*

Notes

1. "If my conscience were as *acute*. . ." Graham Greene's letter to Elizabeth Bowen, *Partisan Review* 15 (November 1948): 1189. Also in *Why Do I Write?*
2. Ibid.
3. In his review of Narayan's *The Financial Expert*, Greene describes Margayya as one who has "the hidden poetry and unrecognized pathos we so often find in Chekhov's characters who on the last page vanish into life." See "The Town of Malgudi," *Collected Essays*, 207.
4. Lawrence [George] Durrell (1912–90), Indian-born English novelist and poet. See also note 4 of Shenker excerpt on p. 219.
5. *The Power and the Glory*, 253.
6. "Save Me Only from Dullness," *Evening News*, 23 January 1930, 6.

Graham Greene: The Next Move

J. W. Lambert

"Yes," he said. "It's true. I'm packing up. Leaving England, going to live abroad. In France.[1] What do you feel like eating? Most things are pretty good, but of course it's a fish restaurant really."

Fish? A memory stirred—the young policeman in *A Gun for Sale:*

> A man at the next table had been eating fried plaice and now, he didn't know why, he associated a certain kind of pain with the smell of fish.[2]

Raindrops shivered on the window.

"Good evening, Mr. Greene." The waiter hung about. "I come here a lot, use it as a club, almost. But I can't bear real clubs. Well, that's not true, really. I like going to them as a guest, but as soon as I get elected to one I can't bring myself to go in. You know how it is, one has a good meal, an amusing time, a bit too much to drink. 'You ought to join us here, you know.' And there one is, paying the subscription. I've resigned from five London clubs. Shall we have a glass of sherry?"

The very thought of having resigned from five London
clubs inspired an understandable mood of genial triumph.
The face that sometimes shows its sixty-two years suddenly whipped off forty-five of them. Mischief darted
from blazing blue eyes.

"I don't feel at all apologetic about going to live abroad.
There are plenty of reasons why a man in my position might
want to live somewhere else. Remember I'm going to
France, not Switzerland. There's something not quite . . .
well, not Switzerland.

"For years now, anyway, I've only spent four months of
the year in England. And after I went to Moscow in 1960 I
had a very severe pneumonia. Since then every winter I've
suffered from bronchial and chest troubles—so my doctor
not surprisingly says I should avoid the London smog.

"I shall live partly in Paris and partly in Antibes. I've
written several short stories about Antibes,[3] and I've been
attached to Paris for a long time. I don't know particularly
why—well, when I was young I suppose I was attracted
by the brothel life and that sort of aspect . . . ."

Another echo: in the first novel, The Man Within, this
attraction was put to work. "I would," thought young
Andrews—

be creeping out of the house on the sly to visit prostitutes. The cool air of early morning touched him in
vain. He was hot with shame and self-loathing.[4]

The blue eyes were now clouded and a little rueful. "In
those days, in the late Twenties, I went naturally for all
that Left Bank life; but nowadays, somehow, I seem to
spend most of my time in Paris on the Right Bank.

"What shall we drink with the sole? The Sancerre's
rather good."

A finger bristled over the wine list:

35: Sancerre *(Mont Damné)*

Wine from the Damned Mountain . . . h'm. Sure enough, mischief was back in a glint of self-parody. This was the boy that his school-fellow Peter Quennell described:

> . . . he would have made an admirable Pierrot in the eighteenth-century Commedia dell'Arte, concealing under his rather woebegone mask a great capacity for cynical humour. He was often exuberant: he could be positively blithe.[5]

He could be so still, was being so at the moment. But this was also the boy who ran away from that school of which his father was headmaster, who dreamed of suicide; and who also

> became aware of God with intensity . . . anything might happen before it became necessary to join the crowd across the border . . . And so faith came to one — shapelessly, without dogma, a presence above a croquet lawn, something associated with violence, cruelty, evil across the way. One began to believe in heaven because one believed in hell . . . the pitchpine partitions of dormitories where everybody was never quiet at the same time; lavatories without locks . . .[6]

The mischief-lightened boy's face grinned challengingly now over the wine-glass. Was it even at this moment peering out of Hell? This was the boy who mopped up every adventure story in sight, in whose mind, as he read Rider Haggard, Africa flowered, a vast, blank enticing space the shape of a human heart, so that at nineteen he was studying the appointments list of the Colonial Office and very nearly joined the Nigerian Navy, who at thirty-one set off on a near-fatal journey to Liberia, in the war found himself working in Sierra Leone and seven years ago was back in the Belgian Congo.

This was the boy who at fourteen read Marjorie Bowen's historical novel *The Viper of Milan* and recognised that "human nature is not black and white but black and grey."

And then again

I was not on the classical side or I would have discovered, I suppose, in Greek literature instead of in Miss Bowen's novel the sense of doom that lies over success—the feeling that the pendulum is about to swing.[7]

Or, as one of his characters put it more than forty years later

You can't cure success. Success is a mutilation of the natural man.[8]

Or again, as he put it over the sole and Sancerre. "One has had a certain measure of success and it separates one from one's material. I mean, wherever I go—if I turn up in Rio there's the British Council at the door or some kind host on the telephone.

"Anyway, it was Marjorie Bowen who really set me off writing. A play, yes—well, the beginning of a play. Poems. And at Oxford I wrote a novel on what turned out to be a quite fallacious subject—a black child born to white parents, a throwback: it isn't possible, of course. Still it was a projection, an attempt not to write autobiography, or at least to express one's sense of isolation and loneliness through consciousness quite different from one's own. But of course one can't escape.

"Next I tried a historical novel under the influence of Conrad's *Arrow of Gold*, about Spanish exiles — Carlists — conspiring in Leicester Square. And then a detective story about a murder committed by a child. The idea was that a child would leave very few clues, or at least clues hardly recognisable as such to an adult mind. But they were to have been recognised by a priest.

"Nothing much came of all this. In fact one way or another — and I got married quite young — I was steadily in debt for years. But when I was twenty-five and working as a journalist Alexander Frere of Heinemann, the publishers, accepted *The Man Within*, my first novel to be published."

"Shall we have a glass of port? *The Man Within* went quite well, in fact it was reprinted almost immediately — though in those days you could and did print very small editions, and I don't suppose it sold more than eight hundred copies all told.

"But on the strength of it Frere offered me, so that I could give all my time to writing, £600 a year for three years — a very respectable sum in those days. Needless to say my next two books did progressively worse. I had to do something to save the situation. I determined to write a book that would sell: and I did."

Conrad did it with *Romance*. Faulkner with *Sanctuary*. Priestley did it with *The Good Companions*. Greene did it with *Stamboul Train*, chuntering across a wintry Europe with its cargo of crook and chorus-girl, currant-merchant and crazy idealist, running into snowdrifts, death and degradation.

"Even if it hadn't sold, I believe Frere would still have supported me—and I wasn't the only one by any means that he was helping in this way. It has been marvellous to have this kind of support, much more than merely financial. One may have outgrown one's own father, but one still likes to feel that there's somebody there.

"Well, now I'm not with Heinemann any more.[9] Control of the business changed hands; and not being under contract I left.

"I was a publisher, with another firm, for four years myself, and I never tried to keep an author who wanted to leave—even when he most unjustly wanted to go. But if one does want to go, one should be allowed to go completely. As it is Heinemann still have the handling of almost all my books, and I feel as though I'd left a limb behind. I'm still struggling to buy them back.

"It isn't, of course, that I'm losing financially. Funny how one goes through a sort of financial sound-barrier. *Brighton Rock*, I remember, published in 1938 and really rather a success for a writer like me, sold 8,000 copies at 8s. 6d. each. Well . . . and now all sorts of other things crop up, apart from film rights and paperbacks and so on, which hardly amounted to much then. I know some people were rather surprised when I sold the manuscript of my last play, *Carving a Statue*, even before it was produced.[10] Well, why not? They were having a sale of manuscripts and it seemed the right moment. Just as well, perhaps, as things turned out.

"Shall we have another glass of port?" Greene's career in the theatre has suffered something of a setback. . . .

Once again the years dropped away. A vast grin spread from ear to ear. The thought of the failure of *Carving a*

Statue seemed to produce intense gratification — no danger of mutilating the natural man there.

"But of course I was sorry, for everybody's sake. It was altogether" — the light strong voice seemed to purr a little despite itself — "a painful business. But I *should* like to see it produced as a farce — I think that's what I meant it to be."

Failure, seduction, indecent assault, a fatal car accident?

"Well, but a farce about human inadequacy, not what it seemed to turn out to be, a small big play about a man seeking God. I mean, the character Ralph Richardson played was supposed to be a really bad sculptor, something like the painter Benjamin Robert Haydon, only without even his capacity to make a tragic end — a man absurdly driven on by his daemon to practise his art, but with practically no talent at all.

"Still, I've enjoyed working in the theatre. I wrote my first play, or started writing it, when I was sixteen, but I didn't try again until I wrote *The Living Room*. Of course I was a theatre critic for a while in the 1930s. But I didn't enjoy that much. I suppose it's good to see a play with one's critical faculties alert, but — knowing one has to write about it, thinking of phrases all the time . . . .

"Really I suppose I came back to the theatre via the movies. Good money, of course, and at first I found it rather fun, playing about with the dialogue — but it soon came to seem the most awful drudgery. So the theatre turned out to be a real refreshment, when I was beginning to feel I was written out.

"But it's true I don't actually go to the theatre very much. Not for the usual intellectual's reasons, the shame at so to speak having to join in as a member of the audience — certainly I love sharing a belly-laugh. No, it's more

. . . well, deciding when to go, finding somebody to go with, getting the seats booked, and all that. And then, I hate intervals—talk, talk, and the play has to warm up all over again.

"Besides—" again the grin, again the gleam, "I like the secrecy of the cinema. You can go when you feel like it, sneak in in the dark, take a girl friend and nobody need know.

"As for the other things—I've talked on the radio,[11] but it's true I've kept clear off television. I still think the writer should be as unrecognisable as possible. And the horrible danger of TV is that one might be a success."

Out went the spark, the blue eyes widened in puckered dismay, like the sea shrinking from a squall.

"Wasn't it Osbert Lancaster who said 'Radio tends to corrupt, television corrupts absolutely'? It might—'a kind of speculative hope dawned behind the dismay, a momentary glimpse of an untried possibility'—it might be a salutary experience to go on television and be a hopeless failure. But . . . no, whatever happens there you are, in the position of an actor, aware of being looked at, of being the toy of technicians, of applause and criticism. Even in a good cause, to advance something one really believes in . . . no, no, I can at any rate make a stand about television. Writing articles and letters to the papers is one thing, putting one's face in a million homes is quite another."

A shudder.

"Let's go back and have some brandy."

A fat man scowled at a fat woman. Otherwise the restaurant had emptied. Down in the wet street a tramp nuzzled a dustbin. Piccadilly shimmered, the Albany courtyard waited, withdrawn, patrician . . . the high room hung shadowed above the dim lamp. Over the mantelpiece, commanding the room, a painting by Jack Yeats, also shadowed, but glowing. A man on horseback, roughly wrapped, moved away towards a village huddle.

"It's an Irish scene, of course. But to me it brings back a moment in Mexico when I rode in on a mule one evening, utterly exhausted, to a village pretty much like that."

He gazed into the picture, down the lawless road, on the heels of the whisky-priest, the outlawed wreck who like several of Greene's characters turned back to death in *The Power and the Glory* in a Mexico where priests were persecuted and all but he had fled.

"I seem—" he gazed speculatively into the brandy glass—"to have swung about a bit in politics. Certainly in the middle 1930s although I'd been a Catholic for quite a long time I was politically well to the Left of centre."

"The Spanish War was a bit of a problem, yes. As a Catholic I simply could not do what so many other people were doing—rush off and join the Anarchists or the International Brigade or whatnot. But then I personally didn't feel I could go and join Franco either. In fact there was only one place in Spain where I could go—Bilbao, the only area that was both Republican and Catholic. I set off—but of course I never got there. I did get as far as Toulouse, and I was going to fly on; but the pilot—a tiny little pilot—lost his nerve or something; anyhow he wouldn't go on. Tiny little man."

At this distance of time the man's size seemed to amuse and console him still. Over his shoulder, dimly looming in a painting by Henry Moore, flowing figures in a landscape mysteriously sighed . . . .

"Now that the Stalinist period is over I've swung back to the way I used to feel when I was young. I can't imagine, for instance, how the East can realise itself except through Communism. Or better, in some kind of accord between Communism and Christianity.

"I've spent four or five winters out there, and I've come to feel that in their apparently different ways it's only the priest and the commissar who treat these people properly. In the churches, at the services, even at fearfully dull lectures arranged by the Communists, one could see that they were realising themselves as human beings. The Church and Communism, quite apart from their faiths, have techniques which are going to bring those people more satisfaction."

West Africa (*The Heart of the Matter*), Cuba (*Our Man in Havana*), Haiti (*The Comedians*), the Belgian Congo (*A Burnt-Out Case*), South-East Asia (*The Quiet American*).

Here . . . you could love human beings as God loved them, knowing the worst. . . .

Only when you get back to zero, to the real ugly base of things, there's a chance to start again, free and independent.[12]

"But I don't think I've suffered from disillusion. One's always coming across people in dreadful situations who inspire respect. Surely my books are full of them?

"I remember George Orwell attacking *The Heart of the Matter*[13] because, for one reason, he claimed that no Commissioner of Police would be so humane as to object to hanging. But I knew one in Freetown who after an execution couldn't eat meat for a fortnight.

"Not that I want to defend *The Heart of the Matter*. I don't like it, though I like some parts of it. It was written at the end of the war, too soon. I wasn't up to it. I know it's been very successful, and I know writers often come to dislike their most successful work—partly out of a sense of fair play for the rest, partly because they simply get tired of hearing about it. It's certainly true that I got very tired of hearing about *The Heart of the Matter*—and people kept missing the point, which must be my fault.

"All these discussions about whether Scobie stood a chance of salvation after his suicide—not what I meant at all. I meant Scobie as an object lesson, if I 'meant' him to be anything at all, showing how awful pity is—I mean pity as opposed to compassion—and how it is really the expression of a kind of pride. But everybody seemed to take the book as the story of a good man driven to self-destruction by his dreadful wife. Well, as I say, it must be my fault.

"The balance was wrong somehow. I know I left out one scene for Scobie's wife, after I'd written it, which might have helped in this way. But I couldn't see how to get it in without holding up the flow of the story. . . . [14]

"I think I was aware of a great liking for melodrama, and I wanted to canalise it out, which is one reason for the 'entertainments'—not but what on the whole they sell rather less than any other books. On the other hand I think I consciously reacted against the Virginia Woolf style—well, I quite liked *To the Lighthouse* but I couldn't bear *The Waves*.

"I don't think any of my books have been explorations of purely personal affairs, they've all had some connection with the world in which its characters live. Naturally I've felt like rebelling a bit against this conception of Greene Land. Still I can't deny what I have written. Don't want to. This isn't a world I've dreamed up. It does exist, in fact it's the world of a large part of the earth's inhabitants.

"I've explored it, depicted it, with a sort of love . . . well, I've been doing a series of introductions for French and German editions of my books—I did some for Sweden too, a couple of years ago—and I realise that these too add up to a kind of autobiography."[15]

A rueful grin.

"A sort of life, I suppose. And one has sought the life one has lived. What one does for fun one does for work. Remember that line of Masefield's—'The long defeat of doing nothing well'? I know I said in the front of *A Burnt-Out Case* that I thought another full-length novel might be beyond my powers. But still, up came this new one, *The Comedians.* If it were nothing more, and of course it is, writing has been a way out of accidie; one had to try something, one needed to prove that one could. . . ."

The clock stuck one.

In the hall, the first signs of departure and disorder, piles of discarded books . . .

"I shall be sorry to leave here. But then I'm looking forward to France . . . the fear is, you know, that one will make another home there—and have to run away from that."

Extracted from J. W. Lambert, "Graham Greene: The Next Move," *Sunday Times,* 16 January 1966, 41–42.

Notes

1. In 1966, Graham Greene left England to live in Paris and Antibes after being appointed Companion of Honour.
2. *A Gun for Sale,* chap. 3, *iv,* 103.
3. "May We Borrow Your Husband?," "Beauty," "Chagrin in Three Parts," and "Two Gentle People" in the volume *May We Borrow*

Your Husband? and Other Comedies of the Sexual Life (London: Bodley Head, 1967).

4. *The Man Within*, 184.

5. *The Sign of the Fish* (New York: Viking Press, 1960), 61–62.

6. *The Lawless Roads*, 4–5.

7. "The Lost Childhood," *Collected Essays*, 18.

8. Dr. Colin, *A Burnt-Out Case*, 253.

9. *A Burnt-Out Case* (January 1961) is the last of Greene's novels to be published by Heinemann. Greene moved to the Bodley Head with his next work *In Search of a Character* (October 1961).

10. *Carving a Statue* was first performed at the Haymarket, 17 September 1964 and, in spite of the pulling power of Graham Greene and Sir Ralph Richardson, it was greeted with a chorus of criticism. It also opened at the Gramercy Arts Theatre, New York, on 30 April 1968.

11. For a list of Greene's radio broadcasts, see R. A. Wobbe's *Graham Greene: A Bibliography and Guide to Research* (New York: Garland, 1979), 407–11.

12. *The Heart of the Matter*, 31.

13. George Orwell, "The Sanctified Sinner," *New Yorker*, 17 July 1948, 66, 69–71.

14. The scene Greene refers to was reintroduced as Part 2, chap. 2, *i*, in the Collected Edition of the novel. See Greene's remarks in the introduction, *xiv*.

15. In a review article on the first four novels in the Collected Edition, Philip French described these "beautifully wrought, sly, ironic, simultaneously guarded and revealing" introductions as "piecemeal autobiography from the twenties." (*New Statesman*, 10 April 1970, 516). They make up, in Greene's words, "rather less than half" of *Ways of Escape*.

Friendship, Sex, . . . and a Sense of Doom

David Lewin

Graham Greene was talking. "I want to see—and I need to see—the body," he said. "This world which people say I have created . . . this Greene Land . . . doesn't exist. I do not deal in fantasy or imagination. I deal in fact. The body is fact.

"The mother and child dead in a ditch between the lines in Vietnam in *The Quiet American*—I saw them. I was alone beyond the front line and for the moment I was lost and I was very afraid."

It is hard to believe that Graham Greene, a muscular, well-built man, can be afraid, although he does deal in fear in his books.

We were arguing one night in the South of France— Peter Glenville, who is to direct and produce the film version of Greene's latest best-selling novel,[1] *The Comedians*, Graham Greene and I—about this Greene Land.[2]

It is, Glenville believes, a special, uncomfortable territory, carefully selected by Greene himself. "You have a perfect example in *The Comedians*," Glenville, a boyish-looking, extremely intelligent man, was saying.

"A bogus major, a lapsed Catholic sitting in a Haitian cemetery at night and sharing a sandwich almost as a sacrament and watched by a starving cat.[3]

"No one but you, Graham, could find a scene like that."

Greene had argued against us. Then the next morning, sitting on the terrace looking out across the calm sunlit water, a young American on his first trip to the Côte d'Azur joined us and said: "Isn't it beautiful. So very beautiful."

At that very moment a glint of sun reflected itself from a car windscreen on a viaduct. Greene looking at it said bleakly: "I remember—it must have been four years ago—on New Year's morning, a car was taking a party of young people across that viaduct.

"The car crashed over the edge and smashed into the rocks beneath. Their bodies had to be picked up in sacks."

We were silent for a moment. Then: "And you say there isn't a Greene Land?" said Glenville.

Greene is a man who does not like to discuss himself, but Glenville and he had invited me down to talk and watch them work.

It is not always easy to find Graham Greene: the finest English writer living, he approaches work like a foreign correspondent, researching his books in the places where they are set.

For his 26th novel *The Comedians*, a striking plea for commitment in the struggle against a vicious dictatorship in Haiti, he went there to see that wretched country for himself with its ruler "Papa Doc" Duvalier and his sinister "Ton Ton Macoute" henchmen.

For *Our Man in Havana* he was in Cuba before Castro; he spent months in Mexico for *The Power and the Glory* and he was in a leper colony for *A Burnt-Out Case*.

He is now 61, a tall man with eyebrows which curl up and exceptional eyes that are large and wary—and then can crease in fun. On his 60th birthday he started to keep a diary of what he considered would be his last decade on earth.

"I felt the wall was nearer," he said, and he meant the wall of death. I had not heard it used in that way before.

"I thought that as I was nearer to death I would jot down what I felt. I completed nearly two pages and gave it up.

"The sense of death is not with me any more. If anything, as I grow older I become less manic and less depressive than in my 50s.

"Death has always interested me. As a student I played Russian Roulette with my elder brother's revolver. You had one chance in six that the bullet would fire and kill."

With me in the relaxed air of the South of France he said: "Before and during the war one had dreams about death. They gradually became worse with the H-Bomb.

"I remember the dreams vividly. Then, when Krushchev came to power in Russia, the fear lifted, and I have no dreams of that sort any more.

"Mr. K. was a good, cheerful sort of man. I miss him."[4]

I asked him then: "What are the dominant forces in your life?"

He answered immediately: "Friendship and sex. Oh, and politics. I have seven or eight really close friends and many acquaintances. I even find that in my 60s I can still make friends which I never expected.

"Sex—well, that is always there, although it does create problems. One's recollection of visiting Paris for the first time at 16 was the brothels.[5] They are not there any more and it is duller.

"And politics. As I grow older instead of becoming more Conservative, I find myself getting more to the Left where I started as an undergraduate in Oxford.

"I don't really plan ahead, I say I can't or won't write another book—but then I do. Writing takes a lot out of me. *The Comedians* took me two years with a break in the middle to do my play *Carving a Statue* which wasn't a success. You can't keep it up all the time."

~~~

Greene will spend two months on the script of *The Comedians* — his first film since *Our Man in Havana* seven years ago.

"I don't mind cutting or rearranging. I would have preferred to wait another year because after I finish a book I've had it.

"In a year I'd be fresher. The dangerous period for me is when I say, 'Keep the money — I don't need it. Why should I do it?' I never write consciously to amass money. I wrote only two novels, *Stamboul Train* and *Confidential Agent*, because I needed money at the time.

"With *Stamboul Train* I was down to my last £20 in the bank and living with my wife in Chipping Campden. When a cheque from America came for $1,500 we just went for a walk in the country to celebrate. And we said nothing."

The hero in any Greene novel appears to be on the run — physically and spiritually. There is frequently a sense of sin in his characters. Now Greene adds a deep sense of commitment to a political cause — *The Comedians* are the flotsam in the world without any commitment at all.

He said: "The sense of sin may be in my characters — but not in me. I may feel guilty, but I have no sense of sin.

"What I want to do in books is to evoke sympathy for people outside the borders of public sympathy — the Communist in America; the capitalist in Russia."

He may not like my use of the adjective, but Graham Greene is a GOOD man in a world where that rarely happens.

Excerpted from David Lewin, "Friendship, Sex, . . . and a Sense of Doom," *Daily Mail*, 22 March 1966, 8.

Notes

1. *The Comedians* (Metro-Goldwyn-Mayer, 1967). Produced and directed by Peter Glenville. Screenplay by Graham Greene. Starring Richard Burton, Elizabeth Taylor, Alec Guinness, Lillian Gish, and Peter Ustinov.

2. Arthur Calder-Marshall seems to have been the first critic to introduce that now familiar term that Greene disliked. See his discussion of "Greene Land" and its "seedy ingloriously vicious" inhabitants in "The Works of Graham Greene," *Horizon* 1, no. 5 (May 1940): 367–75.

3. *The Comedians*, Part 3, chap. 3, *iii*.

4. Nikita Khrushchev (1894–1971), responsible for the de-Stalinization campaign begun in 1956, became first secretary of the Communist Party in 1955 and premier in 1956 of the Soviet Union. He was removed from leadership positions in 1964.

5. Greene was *not* sixteen but nineteen and three months when he left for Paris with Claud Cockburn after Christmas 1923. See *A Sort of Life*, 132–34.

A Brief Encounter

Roy Perrot

"Monsieur Grin?" said the concierge, peering out into the courtyard. She indicated the tenebrous stairway opposite, winding upwards, its carpet patterned in old-fashioned black and red. "Second floor, on the left."

Mounting the stairs, I rather wished I had read more than a few lines of Henry James, could grasp Conrad better, two of his major influences. A shade too late now, foot on the top stair. I pondered the fact that Graham Greene was supposed to guard his privacy like gold-dust. I rang the bell, several weeks before I was quite ready.

He opened the door with a welcoming swing, weight on the back foot, as though he had just used it to play an enjoyable cricket stroke. A tall, lithe figure in grey, chalk-striped suit, with shrewd and somewhat anxious eyes.

I said I had come over on the boat-train because I was tired of the anonymity of airports. But there was still all that clanking at Dunkirk to endure in the middle of the night. "Hm," he said, holding up a glass to the glinting light coming in from the boulevard, to get the measure right. "I quite like vodka, don't you?"

Yes, he said, he was fond of trains too. Also those cargo ships carrying about a dozen passengers, which went plodding over the ocean, where you could read the books you had been meaning to, and ruminate a little.

Now in his flat in the north of Paris—a rather modest place, considering his success—Greene said he had moved into one of his more ruminant phases, his new novel out tomorrow,[1] and the autobiography of his early years, *A Sort of Life*, now in the final polishing stage.

I studied the bright Cuban paintings on the walls, the row of his favourite Victorian poets in the bookshelf. He looks like a man who has been a long, long way down in his time, I thought. But he still manages to get across, personally, as in his writing, an inner buoyancy, some ultimate optimism, or belief, that has fortunately—or unluckily, as some Greene characters might mordantly say—kept pushing the coward he has often told us about back into the front-line trenches.

It must have needed endurance. But even a casual visitor can sense that he has that. Now 65, the craftsman inside him remains a most exacting taskmaster. All the time you are with him, whether he is fumbling in the fridge, being the attentive host, or showing you his books, he is always, all the time, thinking with part of his mind about his craft, and where is the right place to put a comma.

"You know," he said coming back, "boredom has always been my problem. That's probably what has made me travel so much. My roots are in rootlessness. Living out of a suitcase has never bothered me. In a way, my suitcases are my flat here and my place in Antibes. When I get on the move I can write in hotel rooms and feel quite at home with it.

"Yes, ennui is the thing. Writing's certainly hard work but it occupies only a couple of hours a day. I used to try for 500 words in a morning. Now I aim at about 200. It's tiring on the inner eye trying to follow the movements of your characters. Even if they're not on stage you feel you must know what they might be doing. Don't you think?"

I wondered what he did most evenings. He gave a short rueful laugh. "Well, when I can face it after a drink I polish the 200, of course." He writes in minute handwriting, almost illegible to anyone else. Then a final version goes into the dictating machine for the typist.

~~

There is a big change between his early and later work. The river is no longer boiling so intensely through the rapids; it has broadened out and moves with understanding. "What was the turning point?" I asked. "When did you start feeling like the writer you wanted to be?"

"Well, there was a review of my ghastly second novel by Frank Swinnerton.[2] A bit savage, I thought at the time. But you know how people sometimes alert you to flaws in yourself? Before that I was on the way to becoming another Charles Morgan, all terribly soft and easy. I began to shake myself out of that dreadful romantic dream world, a sort of disease I'd got by absorbing all the worst influences of Conrad. So I wrote *Stamboul Train*. Not great, but not bad. It meant I was getting in touch with life."

"But in the late thirties your work becomes almost different in kind. The cleverness goes and something stronger comes in . . . ?"

"Yes, there was a big change. In 1938 I went to Mexico and saw the Catholic priesthood under persecution. My religion had been purely intellectual till then. But I became emotionally involved and, of course, that changes one's writing, one's whole life."

"Did a writer's apartness sometimes feel like common or garden loneliness?"

"Oh, I've plenty of good friends. Well, yes, of course it does. Isn't it part of the job? But let's go and have some lunch. I usually eat at a little place round the corner. Since you're paying we'll go somewhere nice."

We walked down the boulevard to the cab-rank, people taking their aperitifs at the corner café, warm sunshine sprinkling down through the trees. I made some banal remark about the fine weather. "Mm, a bit ominous wouldn't you say?" with a wary glance at me. "Trouble, trouble. Think of that long, hot summer of '39, eh?" The interviewer felt he was being gently ribbed: that Greene was lobbing up a too-easy cliché about himself, just for net practice. It would glide straight off the bat into the note-book: "Author remarks on implications of doom in rising barometer."

I recalled that he had once entered a *New Statesman* competition, under a pseudonym, with a brilliant parody of his "seedy" style. But no. I am sure his reaction was sincere. Surprising, really. I had hardly expected Greene to be Greene.

In the cab I said I'd been reading Hemingway's book on Paris, *A Moveable Feast*, and wasn't it fine how his prose slowed the pace down?

"Mm, yes, and how enchanting *Farewell to Arms* was. I hardly dare read it again in case I find all sorts of faults in it. I went to his place in Cuba once. Taxidermy everywhere, buffalo heads, antlers . . . such carnage."

He gazed reflectively out of the window for a moment. "And look how that hairy-chest romanticism could betray him. *For Whom the Bell Tolls*, for instance, one of those things that gets famous and is rather bad. So the guerrilla-band has to have a pretty girl in it; and she has to fall for the handsome American instead of some swarthy Spaniard; and she conveniently has to have that sleeping-bag . . . . It is so self-indulgent isn't it?"

Easiness in anything, whether in living or in writing, is obviously a most unpleasant taste on the palate for Greene. The only bad people in his books—not so much villains as recipients of his scorn—are the neutral and the bland, the ones who are aloof from struggle. "I find myself always torn between two beliefs," he once wrote, "that life should be better than it is, and the belief that when it appears better it is really worse."

We saw a couple of hippies standing on a corner, just past the Madeleine. "Remarkable," he said, "they all look like that distant relative of mine, Robert Louis Stevenson. Same hair and everything."[3]

He chortled loudly at an image of so many young and hopeful Hemingways toting around sleeping-bags, with space to let. The driver hesitated for a moment, thinking the laugh a command to halt. "They've rejected the technological dream society. Quite right, too. A sense of values does keep bubbling up from somewhere in England, though the politics has become so weary and meaningless there now, wouldn't you think?"

Then, from something I said, he detected in me a half-suspicion that he might move much in literary circles, attend salons, hold occasional court at the Lapin Agile.[4] The idea amused him. "After all, what have writers got in common: what could we possibly talk about? Evelyn Waugh was my great friend but we never discussed writing."

The restaurant was not as smart as all that. He chose a corner table, out of the way. After a few moments a tall, pin-striped diplomatic figure came over and, with a slight stoop from the hips, presented his card and his compliments, as though it might be an invitation to a duel. But it was only to ask Greene to look in for a drink at some embassy or other. The card remained sticking half out of his top pocket, a pale pennant signaling reluctant membership of the social whirl.

I asked Greene about his new novel, *Travels with my Aunt*. He searched his mind but could not remember how it had germinated. "It puts a few characters together to see what happens, the first free-wheeling book I've done. The theme? I don't think it's got one."

I said I had found it very subtle and funny. "Mm, but it caused me more hell to write than any other. I had to scrap whole sections and start again. I had the same problem with *Our Man in Havana*. And just before I started it I'd chucked away 20,000 words of another novel. About the Secret Service. Completely gave it up. I'd read Eleanor Philby's book about Moscow and the description was so good I felt I couldn't better it."[5]

I asked whether he laughed out loud when he wrote a funny line. "Goodness, no! Same old neurotic groans coming up from the table, trying to get it right. Comic writing is so demanding, the timing's so hard to measure properly . . . ."

In his comedies, as in his other books, Greene's purpose has been all of a piece. Always living on the dark frontier, he has spent his time bringing unlikely people in from the cold just as once, long ago, that empty and indifferent nihilist had to be found a place nearer the fire. He is fond of cowards, partial to the desperate, loves the uncertain Hamlet in forceful men. "A writer's job," he once wrote, "is to engage sympathy for people outside the official range of it"; and "The apparent villain deserves more compassion than the apparent hero."[6]

There is a minor war criminal in the new novel, to whom Greene extends the charity of making him comic. I wondered how far a writer could go in redemptive sympathy, whether he would not need to be really saintly to feel for, say, the bigger crooks of Nuremberg. "That would be rather factitious, synthetic. On our level there are limitations. We just do what we can."

"Then again," I said, "isn't it impossibly hard to make up one's mind about such figures as Ho Chi Minh or Fidel Castro? You describe Uncle Ho as a charmer[7] and I know you're a friend of Fidel. But Ho must have knocked off a few thousand opponents on his way to the top, and one can't forget Castro's political prisoners . . . . "

"No, it's never easy. I think one has to depend on human instinct about it. Ho was a human being, not a bureaucrat, though he may have done great crimes against humanity. Morality has to take account of intentions," Greene said with great firmness, "and the aim of the bureaucrat to make a neat solution is not at all the same as someone fighting for an ideal."

I asked how his views generally had changed. "Well, I'd still fight for Cuba. Though I think one becomes steadily more neutralised. Catholicism becomes rather less interesting the more permissive it gets. You know, I went to Paraguay to get material for the new novel. I wanted a place that was both Victorian and violent, somewhere that seemed stuck in time. The authorities gave me a warm welcome until I started addressing students in favour of Fidel, the pill, and so on. Ha!

"I want to go to Samoa next. There's a quaint restaurant there called Aggie Grey's where they serve the wine in bottles labelled Armagnac for some reason. Tastes like syrup of figs." Something in Greene obviously prefers that vintage, in a way, to the best chateau-bottled. He is always noticing small incongruities and ironies around him; on the boulevard, in the restaurant, everywhere; and, when he does, he lights up a little. They seem to reassure him that life does have a rough edge that can be gripped; that it does not slide smoothly by, as it did for Querry [in *A Burnt-Out Case*], leaving him unaffected.

We take a cab back to his flat. He waves from the stairs. The door quietly closes. The craftsman resumes his task.

Extracted from Roy Perrot, "Graham Greene: A Brief Encounter," *Observer*, 18 November 1969, 25.

Notes

1. *Travels with My Aunt.*
2. Frank Swinnerton reviewed Greene's third novel, *Rumour at Nightfall.* See "People We All Know," *Evening News*, 20 November 1931, 10.
3. Graham Greene's mother, Marion Greene, was a first cousin of Robert Louis Stevenson.
4. Lapin Agile, a famous cafe in the Montmartre section of Paris, was a favorite haunt of writers and artists, especially from 1900 to 1914.
5. *Kim Philby, The Spy I Loved* (London: Hamish Hamilton, 1968).
6. See the Philip Toynbee excerpt, "Graham Greene on 'The Job of the Writer,' " on pp. 121–28.
7. In "The Man Pure as Lucifer," Greene describes Ho Chi Minh as one who gave "an impression of simplicity and candour, but overwhelmingly of leadership. There was nothing evasive about him: this was a man who gave orders and expected obedience and also love. The kind remorseless face had no fanaticism about it." *Collected Essays*, 402–4.

Graham Greene: On
the Screen—An Interview

Gene D. Phillips

Graham Greene is one of the first major literary talents of our time to have shown serious interest in the motion picture medium. Consequently, it was about his interest in the screen as well as in writing fiction that I questioned him when we met in his home in France.

GENE D. PHILLIPS: *When did you become interested in the cinema?*

GRAHAM GREENE: At Oxford, in the days of silent films. There was a review, long since defunct, called *Close-Up* which dealt with all the major directors of the time.[1] [He showed me a bound volume.] Besides writing film criticism in the 1930's, I did two film scripts around 1937. One of them, *The Green Cockatoo*, was terrible.[2]

GDP: *In 1938 you contributed an article to a collection of essays called* Footnotes to the Film, *in which you said: "The cinema has got to appeal to millions; we have got to accept its popularity as a virtue, not turn away from it as a vice. The novelist may write for a few thousand readers, but the film artist must work for millions."[3] You added in 1939 in your* column in the Spectator: *"A film with a severely limited appeal must be—to that extent—a bad film."*[4]

GG: I think I should stand by that. By limited appeal, I mean a flop. A good film is seldom a complete flop. Whereas a book can be very good and still be a flop.

GDP: *Do you agree with those of your critics who feel that your narrative style has been affected by your script writing for the screen?*

GG: I don't think that my style as a writer has been influenced by my work for the cinema. My style has been influenced by my going to the cinema. *It's a Battlefield* was intentionally based on film technique, and it was written before I did any film scripts. It is my only deliberate attempt to tell a story in cinematic terms, and it is one of the few novels which I have written that has never been filmed.

GDP: *What is your favourite among the scripts which you have done?*

GG: *The Fallen Idol* is my favourite screen work because it is more a writer's film than a director's. *The Third Man,* though it was more popular because of the song, "The Third Man Theme," is mostly action with only sketched characters. It was fun doing, but there is more of the writer in *The Fallen Idol.*

GDP: *Do you retain much of your original dialogue when you adapt your own fiction to the screen?*

GG: I use actual dialogue from the novel when it seems to fit. Often in the first version of the script a great deal of the original dialogue is kept. But it is slowly whittled away, in order to reduce the dialogue as much as possible. What has the right rhythm in the book because of the surrounding paragraphs may seem unreal on the screen and must be modified. Dialogue in fiction must have the appearance of reality, without having to be real, while on the screen the camera emphasizes the reality of the situation: you have to be closer in a film to real-life conversation in order that the dialogue will match the realistic settings.

GDP: *The critic Jack Gould wrote of the 1967 Laurence Olivier version of* The Power and the Glory *(which was released in Europe as a commercial film)[5] that the "omission of the climax of Mr. Greene's novel—the arrival of the new priest to replace the cleric who had just perished before the firing squad—was especially unfortunate." Although John Ford's 1947 film of the same novel, called* The Fugitive *departed greatly from the book, that film did at least have the shadow of the new priest falling across the doorway.*

GG: More than the shadow of the priest should be there. It is important to have the dialogue of the new priest with the child to show the change of mind in the child toward the dead priest, whom he did not respect until his death, and also to indicate that the Church goes on.

GDP: *Father John Burke, the technical adviser for the film of* The Heart of the Matter *(1953) has told me that against his advice the suicide of the policeman Major Scobie was greatly obscured in the film's ending because the film makers thought Catholics would object to a Catholic taking his own life. Instead Scobie is killed trying to break up a street brawl.*

GG: I tried to persuade the company to leave it in. Trevor Howard, who played Scobie, and who is an intelligent actor, said he would do a re-take of the ending without charge. I even figured out a way of doing it without Trevor Howard: I wanted to show Scobie writing a suicide note with the gun at hand, thus making it clear that he intended to take his own life. At that moment he would be called away to the police action and be killed, apparently with the intention of suicide in his mind. I disclaim the ending of the film as it is. At any rate, I do not like the novel, and have never re-read it.[6]

GDP: *I have often wondered why films like* The Heart of the Matter *which include peculiarly Catholic concepts like the sacrilegious reception of Holy Communion, appeal to the large non-Catholic audience.*

GG: For the same reason that they seem to buy my books on which the films are based. Any author writing for a Catholic audience would not reach a large public. It goes back to what I said in the *Footnotes to the Film* essay which you mentioned earlier: if you excite your audience first, you can put over what you will of horror, suffering, truth. This is still true and applies to the novel as well as to the film. By exciting the audience I mean getting them involved in the story. Once they are involved they will accept the thing as you present it.

GDP: *You once were quoted as saying, with reference to the controversy over the meaning of* The Heart of the Matter: *"I wrote a book about a man who goes to hell* — Brighton Rock — *another about a man who goes to heaven* — The Power and the Glory. *Now I have simply written one about a man who goes to purgatory. I don't know what all the fuss is about."*[7]

GG: What I really meant was that, for example, *Brighton Rock* is written in such a way that people could plausibly imagine that Pinky went to hell, and then I cast doubt upon it in the ending. The real theme of the three novels is embodied in the priest's phrase at the end of *Brighton Rock:* "You can't conceive, my child, nor can anyone, the . . . appalling strangeness of the mercy of God."

GDP: *Would you say that the period of your Catholic novels is over?*

GG: For one period I did write on Catholic subjects: from *Brighton Rock* to *The* [sic] *Burnt-Out Case*. But the majority of my novels do not deal with Catholic themes. One only began with a Catholic subject because one found it a great interest of the moment. *The Comedians*, for example, is not a Catholic novel. Brown happens to be a Catholic; it was this formation that made him the type of person he was. But Brown, as I said in the preface, is not Greene. *The Comedians* is essentially a political novel. My period of Catholic novels was preceded and followed by political novels. *It's a Battlefield* and *England Made Me* were political novels. I was finding my way. Even the early thrillers were political: *The Confidential Agent* deals with the Spanish Civil War. *The Quiet American* and *The Comedians* are political novels. One has come full circle in a way. I am not taking anything back from my Catholic novels. The fact that Brown seems to continue in disbelief at the end of *The Comedians* should not be thought to mean that.

GDP: *Didn't* The Burnt-out Case *explore both belief and unbelief? Incidentally, that is one of the few novels which you have written that was never filmed.*

GG: Plans to film that novel were abandoned when we could not get the director and the cast that we wanted. In *The Burnt-Out Case* I wanted to show various grades of belief and disbelief. The hero's faith was lost temporarily and came back. There was a fanatical believer in the novel; a good believer, the superior of the mission, who was too busy to concern himself with doubt; and the doctor, who had a real belief in his atheism.

GDP: *To get back to* The Comedians, *how did you conceive that the screenplay should be written?*

GG: For purposes of the screen I had to leave out Brown's whole past. Beginning with the present, without the past, he would not have any character. But slowly, bit by bit, I brought out different sides of his character and developed them in dialogue. My big problem when adapting one of my novels for the screen is that the kind of book I write, from the single point of view of one character, cannot be done the same way on the screen. You cannot look through the eyes of one character in a film. The novel was told from Brown's point of view. Brown remains the character who is on the screen more than any of the others. His comments on others are often there. But we still do not see others completely from his point of view as we do in the novel. For example, Martha's husband is despised by Brown in the book, but on the screen he is seen by others as a noble character.

GDP: *Since the title story of your most recent volume of short stories,* May We Borrow Your Husband?, *is being filmed, I am reminded of a review of the book in which a British critic raised once again the old charge of Jansenism in your work, referring to what he called your habit of damning or exulting characters "in either case for capricious, Jansenist reasons."*

GG: People who think they are getting at Jansenism in my novels usually do not know what Jansenism really means. They probably mean Manichaeism. This is because in the Catholic novels I seem to believe in a supernatural evil. One gets so tired of people saying that my novels are about the opposition of Good and Evil. They are not about Good and Evil, but about human beings. After Hitler and Vietnam, one would have thought good and evil in people was more understandable. Still, I do not wish to judge any of my characters. I would hope it was common to most of us to have sympathy for the unfortunate part of the ordinary human character. As I once told another interviewer, I'm not a religious man, though it interests me. Religion is important, as atomic science is.

GDP: *Even though your fiction has turned more toward politics than religion, will religion continue to be an important element in your work?*

GG: Space hasn't influenced my views of religion. I don't look for God up there, do you? He's not up there. He's down around here.

Extracted from Gene D. Phillips, "Graham Greene: On the Screen — An Interview," *Catholic World*, August 1969, 218–21.

Notes

1. *Close-Up* was a film magazine of the late twenties and early thirties, edited by Kenneth Macpherson and Winifred Bryher to which filmmakers such as Marc Allegret, Vsevold Pudovkin, and Sergey Eisenstein contributed.

2. See note 6 on p. 42 of the Maclaren-Ross excerpt, "Excursions in Greene Land."

3. Graham Greene, "Subjects and Stories," *Footnotes to the Film*, ed. Charles Davey (London: Lovat Dickson, 1938), 64.

4. Graham Greene, review of *Goodbye Mr. Chips*, *Spectator*, 16 January 1939, 1036. Also included in *The Pleasure Dome*, 228.

5. The "Laurence Olivier version" of *The Power and the Glory* was a television adaptation for CBS in 1961, not 1967. According to the author, it was aired on 29 October 1961. See Gene D. Phillips, *Graham Greene: The Films of His Fiction* (New York: Teachers College Press, 1974), 112.

6. Also quoted in *Graham Greene: The Films of His Fiction*, 123.

7. "Shocker," *Time*, 29 October 1951, 66. (Canadian edition).

Graham Greene at Sixty-six

Israel Shenker

Driving along the Riviera coast from Nice, caught in the slow crawl that passes for traffic each summer, I had lots of time to think about the man I was going to see. I recalled that Graham Greene had not been in America for years, and vaguely I remembered a fitful sniping back and forth—Mr. Greene squeezing off bursts of disenchantment with America's imperial role, and an occasional defender of the trans-Atlantic faith returning fire.

But we had hardly said hello before he told me that he was planning a visit to America this month—after an absence of eight years. It was a long time, considerably longer than the period he spent in the Communist party, which is what bothered American officials during the seizures of the cold war.

"Four weeks at the age of 13,"[1] said the 66-year old Mr. Greene, laughing. He had just fixed a drink for himself. Setting it down on the coffee table, he fitted his long frame into an easy chair. His large comfortable apartment takes up one floor of a modern white building which overlooks the old port here.

"I used to go to New York because I had plays coming on," he said. "But one had to plan quite a bit in advance. I had to get permission from the Attorney General in Washington, and one had to say which plane one was arriving on and which plane one was leaving with, and I would have a three-weeks visa. During the Kennedy period it was altered—I got a permanent visa."

Now he expected to find himself rather at home in an America where so many oppose the Vietnam war. "One can really say that one is pro-American now," Mr. Greene acknowledged. "One is pro—at any rate—half America. In the days of *The Quiet American* I was accused of being very anti-American, but now one finds one is on the side of so many Americans."[2]

His visit this time is not for a play by Graham Greene, but to visit his new American publisher; after years with Viking, the author has moved to Simon & Schuster. "I switched after the last book," he said. "What irritated me was a telegram saying that the travellers [salesmen] didn't like the title of my book [*Travels with My Aunt*] and would I change it to something else, and I came back saying it was easier to change the publisher than the title."

The current Greene book, *A Sort of Life*—which comes out this week—is his autobiography up to age 27. "There was a certain amount of material in manuscript," said the autobiographer, "because about 20 years ago during a period of nervous depression I went to a psychiatrist, and he told me to start writing out my memories of childhood. I had 20 or 30 pages before I stopped—well, not cured, but I stopped bothering.

"When my mother died I got a whole box of letters that I had written to her—which was quite useful for checking up things and also for remembering. Like all old men I have a better memory of the far past than the recent past. I sent the manuscript to my elder brother[3] and he said his memory coincided completely with it.

"One is afraid, one wants to be as accurate and as close as possible—that's the fun of it in a way. I wasn't censoring the thoughts, I was letting them flow. I cut out quite a bit partly because the patches didn't fit into the frame. They were just there because they'd happened, and they interrupted the general flow. One is writing a book. One isn't just spilling out everything one can remember."

Since World War II Mr. Greene has found it harder and harder to spill or to write. It all takes longer and longer. "Age," he said, as though it were as painfully simple as that, and then he added: "Also one's afraid that one's said it oneself before. I find I forget a book very quickly after I've finished it, and then people write some critical work or other and point out the similarity between this situation in Book 3 and the situation in Book 2. It's boring. One wishes that one had remembered.

"My chief sickness is getting easily bored—a symptom of manic depression. What I cherish most is probably escape from boredom, especially from oneself. That can come from loving somebody, or from a good wine, or from travel. Or from getting involved in something which isn't one's own problem—the days when I used to go to Vietnam in the French war. Something that will make the adrenalin work, too."

It does not seem to him to work very well as he writes. Before he attacks the difficulties of a new book, he moves restlessly about his apartment, constructing in his mind the story's essentials. "I hate sitting down to work. I'm plugging at a novel now which is not going easily. I've done about 65,000 words—there's another 20,000 to go. I don't work for a very long time—about an hour and a half. That's all I can manage. One may come back in the evening after a good dinner, one's had a good drink, one may add a few little bits and pieces. It gives one a sense of achievement. One's done more than one's thought.

"There are certain writers who seem to write like one has diarrhea—men like Durrell for instance.[4] Perhaps their bowels get looser and looser with age. I'm astonished at someone like Conrad who was able to write 12 hours on end—it's superhuman, almost.

"It's like a strain on the eyesight. I find that I have to know—even if I'm not writing it—where my character's sitting, what his movements are. It's this focusing, even though it's not focusing on the page, that strains my eyes, as though I were watching something too close.

"I found it difficult to adjust to the passage of 60, as I dare say I felt at 50, too. Nothing good occurs to me about growing old. All I can see are the handicaps. One can't walk as far, one gets tired more easily, one gets more irritable. I write less and it's more difficult to have the energy.

"In the old days, at the beginning of a book, I'd set myself 500 words a day, but now I'd put the mark to about 300 words." Did he mean that literally—a mark after every 300 words? Precisely. With an x he marks the first 300 words, 600x comes next, 900x after 900 words.

"I generally have the beginning, the middle and the end in my head, and hope that there are some surprises in between to amuse myself. The end sometimes alters. One's got to leave enough liberty to one's characters. One can't be absolutely sure what point they'll have reached at the end of the book.

"At the opening of a book one is thinking of the mood in which the whole book will move—the signature tune.

In something written as an entertainment, one wants a quick mood, to excite the reader, keep him on the edge of his chair. For a book that is going to be slightly brooding I think one wants to prepare by a slow movement at the beginning. For depressed moods it becomes very unpleasant writing."

In Mr. Greene's novels, good and evil appear to be strong motive forces; he has been accused of obsession with evil at the expense of concern with good. But he demurred. "I'm interested in human beings," he said. "They aren't saints and they aren't evil men as a rule. I should have thought that only in one book had I tried to write about a wholly unpleasant character, and then at the end one put in a doubt whether even he was as theologically damned as he seemed.[5]

"Some people would say that there was a sense of morality inculcated into man at the beginning, that conscience is inherited in most people. I don't think I've ever met anybody who was without a conscience. Environment would have an effect, a religious belief would have an effect. Happiness and misery have their effect, too. Unhappiness isn't always purgative; it can destroy a man. And happiness isn't always selfish; it can make a man less selfish."

For the work now in progress,[6] Mr. Greene has been devising, for the character presented as an ex-priest, a theology which accommodates evil. "God in this theology is evil as well as good," explained the author. "So there's a night side and a day side, and we contribute to both. We are part of the evolution of God—and Hitler obviously aids the dark side of God, while Gandhi, John XXIII and Chavez aid the day side.

"Talking as a Catholic, I would argue that Christ was a kind of overpowering expression of the day side—which was a guarantee that the day side could never be swamped. If God is torn as we are between the dark and the bright — and therefore suffers a certain division and anguish as we do — it makes Him a more sympathetic figure."

"This is just playing with words, you know, just an amusing speculation," Mr. Greene added, as though he wanted to retreat, revise, or at least hand the ancient problem of evil to the ex-priest and let him puzzle and try for surprises.

Can one be sure that Mr. Greene is not speaking with tongue in cheek? He has shown delight in hoaxes — as when, for example, he entered a contest which called on participants to write a parody of Graham Greene. But he said that he has pulled his final hoax.

"The last one was too successful, you see," he explained. "I was in Edinburgh with a friend of mine and we met two nice Texan girls, whom we took to the theater. The next day, in the train coming back, we drank a little bit too much with our lunch, and I said, 'Why don't we have an Anglo-Texan Society?'

"I wrote a letter to the *Times* saying that we were proposing to found the Anglo-Texan Society in view of the special cultural and historical links between England and Texas.[7] Then I went off to East Africa, and when I got to Nairobi I had a telegram from my companion saying that the letter had appeared in the *Times*, and that there had been 60 applicants to join on the first day, including the Attorney-General, Sir Hartley Shawcross.

"I found an excuse over Suez to resign. I wrote a letter saying that owing to the appalling conduct of America over Suez[8] I was resigning from the Anglo-Texan Society. But it still goes on, for the worst thing that could happen did — the hoax became so deadly serious that they now have dinners at the House of Lords, and the Duke of Edinburgh attends. Nobody has ever asked what were the special cultural links between England and Texas."

I asked Mr. Greene if he could summarize what he had done with his life. "I think I've accomplished a little bit and I've failed a good deal," he replied. "I've written about two or three good books. *The Power and the Glory, Travels with My Aunt*, I think I'd put amongst them, and after that I'm not sure. I think *The Quiet American* is not a bad book.

"One fails in all sorts of ways in life, doesn't one, which are much more important than writing books. In human relations and that sort of thing." There are many things that bother Mr. Greene about the character he takes to be his own: "I'm not nice to live with. One is impatient, one is irritable, one is unjust, one is probably intolerant."

"What bothers you about the world?" I asked him, as I got up to leave.

"That's a terrible question," he said. Mr. Greene has extraordinarily pale eyes, and the thought went through my mind that if eyes are mirror to the soul, anyone who intended to plumb the depths of this man's soul had his work cut out.

"There are so many things that bother one about the world," he said. "Injustice, intolerance. And that it all comes to an end."

"Graham Greene at Sixty-six," *New York Times Book Review*, 12 September 1971, 2, 26.

Notes
1. At the age of nineteen, not thirteen.
2. Graham Greene has often been accused of harboring a strong antipathy toward America. When in 1958 Madeleine Chapsal asked Greene what he disliked in today's civilization, he replied:

"America. And by America I mean many things that have nothing to do with America itself: television, gadgets, cellophane wrapped vegetables, frozen foods, all sorts of things . . . It's not just America; I use the term to identify and point out these things." (See excerpt from Chapsal on p. 147.) This sentiment has not been alleviated by the glitter and glamour of Hollywood and its treatment of literary classics nor was it dispelled by the insensitive and heavy-handed application of the McCarran-Walter Act of 1952 to Greene who, on one occasion, was actually deported from Puerto Rico. (See Greene's humorous account of the episode in *Ways of Escape*, 180–85). *The Quiet American* aroused great indignation in the United States and was always denounced as an "angry," anti-American, "crude and trite," "pettish and fretful" attack on America (the perception was limited to the immediate political situation.) A few, however, like Ralph Freedman in the *Western Review* (21, no. 1 [1956], 76–81) and Neil Brennan in *Accent* (16 [spring 1956], 140–42) rose above the chorus of disapprobation and regarded the subject matter of the novel and its implications as extending to "wider moral and religious issues affecting the basic problems of awareness, action and existence." Now that the Vietnam experience is over, one tends to regard *The Quiet American* not only as prophetic but also as one of the best novels, if not the best, on Vietnam. Greene's much maligned and rather provocative statement in his letter to the *Times* (4 September 1967) indicating his preference for life in the Soviet Union over the United States of America has often been quoted out of context. In his conversation with John Vinocur, Greene stated (*New York Times Magazine*, 3 March 1985, 36–39) that the remark was meant to be "ironic":

> I would end my days much quicker in Russia than in California, because the Russians take writing seriously, so I would soon find myself in a gulag, which is in a way a compliment to a writer. Whereas one might drag out one's years in a California in some backwater.

For Greene's conception of America as it appears in his writing, see James Hazen's "The Greeneing of America," *Essays in*

Graham Greene: An Annual Review, vol. 1, edited by Peter Wolfe (Greenwood, Fla.: Penkeville Publishing Co., 1987), 1–24.

3. Dr. Raymond Greene.

4. It is not altogether unusual for a writer to speak so unflatteringly, occasionally, about a confrère. But Greene seems to be disturbingly candid about his dislike for Durrell's works. Cf. his earlier derisory reference to Durrell as "the Charles Morgan of the present day" (see p. 170 of the S. V. V. excerpt, "Interlude in Bombay"), and his unflattering remarks to Marie-Françoise Allain that "Lawrence Durrell and his cloying prose is the Charles Morgan of his generation." *The Other Man*, 171.

5. Pinkie in *Brighton Rock*.

6. *The Honorary Consul*.

7. Letter to the editor, *Times*, 22 August 1953, 7. In a subsequent letter dated 23 December 1953, after his return from Kenya, Greene not only announced the inauguration of the Society but also the "strong response" received and the enrollment of members such as "Mr. Samuel Guinness and Sir Alfred Bossom, M.P." Greene resigned his presidency of the Society on 1 April 1955 and describes later in "A Thorn in the Yellow Rose" (*Daily Telegraph*, 22 November 1974), the circumstances surrounding the formation of the Society and his resignation.

8. One wonders whether Greene's statement about the "appalling conduct of America over Suez" refers to the denial of American funds to Egypt to build the High Dam at Aswan that led to the nationalization of the Suez Canal or to the pressure of the United States on Britain to end quickly the brief Suez War. The latter seems more likely. That would put his resignation as "president" of the Society in 1956.

"Le Bon Dieu Made Me a Writer"

Alex Hamilton

They were sleeping six in a bed in Antibes when I met Graham Greene on his home patch. The sweated outline of bodies were imprinted on unrucked sheets as clear as factory cut-outs. But that first hint of it as a seedy milieu was straightaway discounted by the town, and by Greene himself, who should know.

I came round the old seawall one evening, where the restaurants spreading along narrow fissures of rock look in their variegated intensity of umbrella and tablecloth as if they had themselves burst the stone open, and half the world was facing in from the ramparts to watch the other half playing boule in the grit. All but a dog, who had no choice but face the sea, since his head and neck were encased in plaster. Antibes is the innocent one of the Riviera, said Greene, his theory being that it's the HQ of the Mafia, and they don't want their own nest fouled.

He emerged suddenly and unexpectedly into my line of vision, as if from a fog, in canvas parka and soft shoes, a tall figure slowly leaning his way up the slope, Isaac Deutscher on Trotsky under his arm.[1] We wouldn't drink where I'd been drinking, he said, a terrace from which I'd been reflecting on the absence of tarts on the waterfront, Vauban's fort like a worn molar across the water, and the mass of white yachts from Panama and Liberia. He had a feud there, he said, we'd go round the corner where the Mafia drink. He poured just enough water on his whisky to varnish it and looked round hopefully. But the Mafia were playing boule.

My own book was *The Lawless Roads.* Yes, he said, it was one of two watersheds in one's writing, the other being *Journey Without Maps.* They both gave one a kind of switch, and rivers ran a different way afterwards. He talks in the unhurried manner of his generation and class, pulling out the diphthongs, and his sentences bending to an expiring cadence, while the frequent Yesses which patrol your own comments are largely noncommittal. Only some of the harsher consonants, gritted out, give a spikiness to a voice like a sharpening steel.

He had just flown in from his house in Capri, where he'd been labouring on a new novel,[2] and spoke of the biographies which seem to sell so much better than novels. He spoke too of biographers and his dislike of the amateur historian, and of publishers and how one noted Catholic publisher would be so much better as the central character of the comic novel than of any other medium.

He said he was glad of the chance encounter, it had taken the chill off. We'd go on next day, at his home, only give him time to write his few words of fiction after breakfast, and without prepared questions, one so much preferred just to talk. He'd had an interview with the Pope himself,[3] and it had been very dull. Well, he was a dull man, who'd been given a copy of *The End of the Affair* and the only comment reported back from His Holiness had been "this man has problems." Perhaps the whole Church was getting duller. He commended Lulu's to me as a place to dine. One ought to have a companion there, but the coastguards used it.

We talked the next day of chance encounters, and the luck that follows a writer. "An unexpected encounter," he said. "You think nothing is going right. I've got nothing to write about. Then out of the blue somebody comes across and the whole thing starts." Like who came across?

"Like in Liberia. I arrived with my carriers in a small town called Tapis and one found there the commander of the frontier force, the villain of the League of Nations, a man called Colonel Benes, who'd committed many atrocities. One was invited to dinner with them, he drank my whisky, and one had met the villain of the piece without going out of one's way to do so."[4] Had he the capacity for going out of his way, for getting to grips with a complete stranger? "No, I wait for him to come to me."

It's a long while since the rivers changed courses in Liberia, Mexico, Malaya, Vietnam, the Congo, Cuba, Haiti. The shyness persists, he's never found a formula for breaking out? "I find things happen somehow, now as then. Recently I was in a town in North Argentina where I didn't know a soul. I came down from my hotel room for a quiet dinner by myself and a mysterious figure came and said he had an invitation for me to a camp outside the city. I asked how he knew I was there, and he said he lived in the hotel I originally booked into, before the Governor decided I'd be more comfortable in the one I was in. From there I found myself sitting down to a dinner at a table loaded with seven people. I hadn't had to approach anybody."

That city, let's call it Aguadiente, is the setting for the novel he is writing, *The Honorary Consul.* The foolscap sheets rest on a table by the balcony of his fourth-floor flat looking over the port. Foolscap because he wants it tightly written, as contrasted with the loose quality of *Travels with My Aunt* which allowed him to break with precedent, and use ordinary plain paper. He writes very, very slowly, and the callous on his forefinger is a tiny hemisphere.

Of course Aguadiente is a frontier town, bordering Paraguay. The frontier has been a symbol of excitement for him since childhood, when as the son of the headmaster of Berkhamsted he ventured as a Quisling across the border from private side to school side. He'd not actually run his nail down frontiers in search of a site, but he'd been attracted to Aguadiente passing through at night on a boat up the Paraná. He'd returned without a story, but he did have a dream to work within. As with so many of his stories, it was the dream that began it.[5]

And somehow things happened. The Paraguayan consul of the province was kidnapped in Buenos Aires, a priest was excommunicated, there was the house arrest of the Archbishop, a bomb in the cathedral, a car overshot the ferry, a suicide in the river. And lastly a dead man in a field, though that could have happened anywhere. The dream had ceased to be necessary.

No more about this novel, said Greene. The saving grace in the hell of writing was the surprise: "Characters hide points." Sometimes they hide themselves altogether, erupting to alter the whole structure, like Minty in *England Made Me.* Erupted to the good, he thought. Also he liked to forget. "I always say I'd be a good priest because stories come in one ear and go out the other. The power to forget is part of the created thing too. It comes back from the unconscious in another form. It's the difference in a way between the job of a reporter, and that of a novelist. It's yours to remember, mine to forget. In a way what one

forgets becomes the unrecognised memory of the future."
Afterwards I remembered who said "Literature is a contrived process of forgetting": Conrad.

So anecdotal people would be of little use to him? "I like overhearing more than being told. I love eavesdropping. That was the penalty in South America, that my Spanish is too bad for good eavesdropping." The peculiar value being that getting it out of context gave it a curious dramatic interest? "Exactly. Also it eases one's conscience. One gets a story which is completely untrue and therefore can't be identified."

Twilight piled upon isolation. With his predisposition to boredom, did he not suffer a certain angst, arbitrarily lodged on some alien sandbank? A certain timidity, he acknowledged. When he knew where he was going, he took his books. As in the Congo *leproserie*. The first day was rather grim. He had a hut, with table, mosquito net, and bed. He could not speak the African language of the leper who looked after him, though he alternated lunch with the Belgian father and doctor. But when he spread out his books he thought, "This is my study, this is my home."

The experience inspired *A Burnt-Out Case*, the novel about a refugee from his own creative talent for architecture once he has lost his faith. For a time after that book Greene seemed written out. Should one make a parallel? "No, one had a mental block, caused by fatigue and perhaps living with a downbeat character like Querry for two years. Relieved by writing out one's dreams . . . When I was 60 I had a strong sense of my age. I started a nonfiction book called 'The Last Decade' and after I'd written four pages I forgot about my age. One is aware though, you know, at 66, that the wall is there, that if one wants to finish this novel, one mustn't start playing around."

Had he ever felt, playing around in wars, that he might not get out for external physical reasons? "Only once, two years ago in Israel. I spent two nights in an Israeli mess at El Kantara,[6] borrowed a jeep to look at positions all down the Canal, and everything was peaceful as you could wish until our return. Then everything broke loose from the Egyptian side. What worried me after we ran to the dunes was when the Israelis eventually replied, because I thought the Egyptians will now learn they've been over-shooting. The mortars didn't come in, but there I thought, 'This is a bit silly to be mixed up in somebody else's war at my age, and be lying three hours on a dune on a hot afternoon, without a hat.'"

He'd wanted to survive then. Different story in our own war with the Axis. He reckoned then there was a very strong sporting chance of not surviving: the blitz, toing and froing to Africa, submarine warfare, the diseases of Africa, all stacked up to a promising prognosis of death. But because it was a wish fulfilment, one had miscounted the chances, the casualties weren't that heavy. In those years (which immediately follow the close of his autobiography *A Sort of Life*), his writing became rusty with misuse and disuse.

I said diffidently that I supposed accidie to be a form of sin. It might be, he agreed, but he had never been against sin. Anyway his wish not to survive had been less accidie than the apathy of a personal situation. (I remembered the preface to *The Confidential Agent*—1939—written in six weeks while slowly moving *The Power and the Glory*—1940—forward, where he attributes the break-up of his marriage to the spleen resulting from that "Benzedrine" effort.) But he'd not say the same today. On the whole he'd fight to survive now. The Suez adrenalin had been a notable gush compared with the blitz trickle.

"I have a certain pleasure in being frightened," he said. "It makes one rather cheerful afterwards." But each variety of Russian roulette can be played only so often, before the adrenalin peters out? "Yes," he said, with that quiet thoracic chuckle that accompanies particularly his more baleful remarks, "and one is merely afraid of being sick on the back of the pilot."

We talked of areas of the world where his re-entry would promote too much adrenalin. He'd been banned in South Vietnam for *The Quiet American*. He wouldn't risk his life in Haiti. He didn't think General Stroessner would welcome him back in Paraguay. He wasn't sure they'd let him back in Czechoslovakia,[7] after his recent airing of his views in Prague, but they might, since they're still publishing him. In Russia he'd bitten off his nose to spite his face, by putting an interdict on publication of his work, over Daniel and Sinyavsky. People had criticized that as an empty gesture, but they were misled, the Russians had been very scrupulous over royalties. Yes, he concurred with Pyle's view in *The Quiet American* that an opinion is an action, especially if the Russian tanks are about. An individual could do more than a committee, or a writer's union, because there need be no compromise.

He could go back all right, to Freetown, setting of *The Heart of the Matter* (very popular book, except with its author) but the trouble there was . . . the chance encounter. He'd in fact gone back and, coming out in the dark from his hotel, had his arm viciously gripped. A high hearty voice said "Helloooo, Greene! I'm Scobie!"

I mentioned the old story of his being banned from Butlin's for peeping through a knothole and he professed never to have heard it. "I did fall down on the dance floor," he conceded. "That was the depth of my disgrace. I went with Edward Ardizzone[8] and arriving at Clacton we were encouraged when the taxi-driver said 'That brothel,' but it was sadly not a bit like that. It was very much like the place that I'd anticipated years earlier in *The Confidential Agent*.[9] The effect of charm wore off by breakfast on the second morning."

People who wondered at him as a writer alienated from England should remember, he said, that half his work was laid there. In his earlier years a book would take nine months and the idea for the next reared up when he was two thirds through. Now it takes two years or more, and nothing splits off but a few ideas for short stories, in which however he takes more pleasure than he used to, expanding them to give room for a surprise. He once could walk up a character, but now travel, the anodyne to boredom, is the necessary locomotor urge to his imagination. He never read theses on his work, because that only had the effect of making him self-conscious. He reads the reviews of a new book until sickened by rereading his own plot adumbrated. The one stimulus that comes from criticism is a perceptive essay on another writer, like Erich Heller's book *The Artist's Journey into the Interior*,[10] which reawakened the excitement of writing.

There'll be no more plays after the debacle of *Carving a Statue*.[11] Previously he'd been rather spoilt in the theatre, but there he had a horrible difference of opinion with the players. He thought he'd written a black farce, his best play, but the actor was resolute not to be funny, he thought it an Ibsen piece on God the Father. The English sometimes get the mood wrong, as with his novel *Travels with My Aunt*. They reviewed it as merely funny,[12] whereas it was laughter in the shadow of the gallows, as a perceptive Swede had said.

There'll be no more autobiography after *A Sort of Life*, except the prefaces to the Collected Edition.[13] He has little memory of his work, and revisiting them now is almost always a painful business. Does he not fear the inevitable double-decker from somebody else on his life?[14] "I hope that as the Vietnam War may cease, this desire for huge biographical tomes should also . . . . I used to enjoy the old Victorian three-deckers. One felt one was making one's own biography out of that material. Something rather fascinating in a boring book. Every 56 pages something interesting — like looking for precious metal with a Geiger counter."

The problem with *A Sort of Life* had been what to leave out. In the end he had been run by his conscience as a novelist, and dropped a long section on prostitute life in London in the twenties, not to break the story line. We talked about that, the two or three girls he had known personally, how Soho had gone downhill from girl into clip-joint, how Butler had proved himself the worst of Home Secretaries with his so-called Cleaning the Streets Act,[15] how Maupassant had been the only writer to get the whore in fiction, until he said I was providing just the disequilibrium he had avoided. But yes, it might yet make a good monograph.

Any kind of start now is a horror, but not to write is worse horror. "One becomes disagreeable, one fidgets, one can't stay alone, one can't read a book with comfort. One feels a layabout." There remain the attractions of Scylla and Charybdis, communism and the Catholic Church. In either, he said, he would have been a Protestant.

He has never been as far Left again as in his Oxford days. "I've wavered, that's all. In Malay I was anti-Communist. It was a war waged by purely mercenary

Chinese, against the Malayan population. I had great deal of sympathy for the French in Vietnam, but I swung back, and with the American intervention I became even more a Communist sympathizer. On the other hand the combat with Russia, even post-Stalin, has made one dislike that form of communism."

He remains with Freud rather than with Jung, whose kindliness makes him suspect. And just as he long ago did his technical homework on the prefaces of Henry James, Conrad, etc., so he no longer has an interest in theology, having done his homework on Newman, Bonhoeffer, St. John of the Cross, and the only book he liked by Father D'Arcy, *The Nature of Belief.*[16] Trying to talk of the pathology of the urge to martyrdom was something of a cul-de-sac.

"And why not take the symbols from human love, when they're the nearest we've got to equate? Some of Crashaw's poems might be absurd, but not when they're felt." He's suspicious of mysticism and (long pause) doesn't want to believe in revelation. "I've seen somebody who had the miraculous element, Padre Pio in South Italy. He was no mystic, but a solid peasant who happened to have the stigmata. I'm slightly on my guard against mysticism because it approaches fake poetry. Juliana of Norwich I don't appreciate, nor Evelyn Underhill.[17] Eastern mysticism is a closed book to me. I can't appreciate Milton. I mean, there have got to be blind spots in me."

But the usefulness of being a Catholic remains all-embracing. "The Church has the best intelligence service in the world." Wherever he goes he feels he has a visiting card to the best-informed member of the community. The encounters are not chance. "One learns a great deal from priests." And from women? "Not as much as from priests," he replied quickly. I waited. "From women," he said slowly, "one learns about oneself. And that is important for a writer." He had said once that fear and sex interconnect. "I don't think of myself as fearsome. I'm a victim, not a producer of fear."

Could he feel any positive sediment in the whirlpools of human passion? "I shouldn't want to watch my friends in one. One of them being myself—one has experienced the obsession on various occasions, which has gone too far, and now I would like to control the obsession, a lot easier with age . . . .

"I wouldn't be frightened of sadness or grief for a particular thing. The hysterical misery scares me, too many emerge on the far limits of the pool as suicides. This is a self-preservation instinct in me." Shouldn't other people be allowed to make up their own minds? "Oh yes, it was Scobie's fault that he didn't."

And can a writer plead privilege? The chuckle this time came from a lot farther down. "I always say before Le Bon Dieu: 'Well, you made me a writer, and if I got into more scrapes than others, it is because You did.'"

I thanked him for a sort of interview, and sort of began to go. We chatted about gambling, and he said he had won £250 at the tables at Nice and been tempted to put it all then on red or black, but had been dissuaded. Because he had a girl as a mascot? "Yes, actually. I also won £190 at Beaulieu though, with my publisher Max Reinhardt for companion. The only superstition I have is to play 19 and wait around on it until I focus lines and squares." He made that sound like the Clapham omnibus.

The afternoon sun pressed. I was sorry to leave his spare quarters with the table, sofa, two chairs, bookcase, and three paintings. There was a deck of cards on the table. Patience? I asked. "Gin rummy," he replied. He smiled. "A game for two."

Alex Hamilton, "Graham Greene," *Guardian*, 11 September 1971, 8.
Editor's title.

Notes

1. Isaac Deutscher wrote a sympathetic three-volume biography of
   the Russian leader, Leon Trotsky, from a neo-Marxist perspective. The reference here most likely is to the third volume, *The
   Prophet Outcast: Trotsky 1929–1940* (Oxford: Oxford University
   Press, 1963).
2. *The Honorary Consul.*
3. Pope Paul VI.
4. This is presumably "Colonel Davis" whom Greene describes in
   Journey Without Maps, 243–55.
5. See note 2 on p. 18 of the Claud Cockburn excerpt, "An Early
   and Incipient Fascination with Dreams."
6. A small town on the East Bank of the Suez Canal.
7. In a letter to the editor of the London *Times* dated 5 July 1969,
   Greene writes: "The day of ideals — and ideologies which are their
   expression — are certainly over. The invasion of Czechoslovakia
   by the Soviet Union and her allies was an echo of the invasion of
   the Dominican Republic by the United States and her allies . . . .
   The convenience of the major powers now is all and morality
   counts for nothing in international politics."
8. Edward Ardizonne (1900–79), painter and illustrator and the
   author of numerous children's books.
9. In his introduction to *The Collected Edition* of the novel, Greene
   recalls how he and Ardizonne went to Clacton and "spent two
   extraordinary days before we packed secretly and fled from the
   red blazers of the prefects of the dining halls, . . . and the grey sea
   which no one visited." Greene anticipated the Butlin-type
   resort — the family-oriented Butlin holiday camps were scattered
   throughout Britain — in *The Confidential Agent* when he described
   the Lido which seemed to D. "more like a village than a hotel . . .
   circle after circle of chromium bungalows round a central illumi-
   nated tower — fields and more bungalows . . ." (233).
10. Erich Heller, *The Artist's Journey into the Interior* (New York:
    Random House, 1965; London: Secker and Warburg, 1966).

11. In spite of the assertion that there would be no more plays, Greene came up with *The Return of A. J. Raffles* in 1975, the curtain-raiser *Yes and No* and *For Whom the Bell Chimes* in 1980 (although they were both published in 1983), and *The Great Jowett*, published in 1981, which was first written as a radio play for the BBC in 1939.

12. Greene's characterization of the reaction of the English is generally true; but it is also true that several reviews noted the combination of irony, compassion, and wit with "the hint of tears" (*Illustrated London News*), the "sad humour" of the novel (*Irish Times*), the "chill" that its "pure and infectious" humor brought in its wake (*Punch*), and even regarded the novel as Greene's *"De Senectute* turned upon age and death" (*New York Review of Books*).

13. In spite of this assertion, Greene published his second volume of autobiography, *Ways of Escape*, in October 1980. It incorporates the prefaces to the Collected Edition.

14. The first volume of the "inevitable double-decker" appeared in 1989. This is Norman Sherry's 783-page *The Life of Graham Greene Volume I: 1904–1939* (London: Jonathan Cape; Toronto: Lester and Orpen; New York: Viking Press).

15. Baron Richard Austen Butler (1902–82) served as Home Secretary from 1957 to 1962. The Street Offences Act of 1959 prohibited street solicitation and loitering by prostitutes. Greene ridicules Mr. Butler's "new look" of London in a letter to the editor of the *Daily Telegraph* dated 2 September 1959.

16. Martin Cyril D'Arcy, *The Nature of Belief* (Dublin: Clonmore and Reynolds, 1958).

17. Juliana Norwich (1342–1416) was an anchorite and celebrated English mystic who had written about the revelations of Divine Love; Evelyn Underhill (1875–1941) was an English mystical poet and author whose works have helped establish the respectability of mystical theology among intellectuals.

The Pain of Writing

Elizabeth Easton

As I sat in the subdued grandeur of the lobby of London's
Ritz Hotel, a variation of an old nursery rhyme kept running through my head:

Pussy cat, pussy cat, where have you been?
I've been to London to visit Graham Greene.

About to meet Mr. Greene, I was apprehensive. He had
the reputation of being austere, shy, remote. Would he
answer questions? My frame of mind wasn't helped by the
problems I had encountered in trying to arrange an interview. Before leaving New York, I learned from Michael
Korda, Greene's New York editor, that an interview date
might be difficult to fix. "Greene may be in Antibes, or
Paris, when you're in London," Mr. Korda said gloomily.
But he agreed to inquire.

The day of my departure approached without word
from Mr. Greene. I called Mr. Korda. "I absolutely can't
telephone him," he said. "Is he so difficult to deal with?" I
asked. "No," said Mr. Korda, "he's not difficult at all, but

he's a very private person." Finally, a cable came. Yes, Mr. Greene would be glad to see me in London on a given day.

I put the nursery rhyme out of my mind when he came up to me in the Ritz lobby, a tall man with blue eyes and a gray suit that matched his gray hair. We sat in his second-floor quarters, the sun streaming in the windows and Sunday crowds strolling along the edge of Green Park outside. We began to talk about *The Honorary Consul.*

ELIZABETH EASTON: *Do you have trouble beginning a book?*

GRAHAM GREENE: I can't begin a book until my characters have names. The moment when I was able to begin this book was when I'd got the name of Fortnum, who is the honorary consul, and of Plarr, the doctor. They came in the space of a day, suddenly, like that—when I was doing something else. Then one could begin the book. Names, as you know, have a curious value. In Africa, a boy from a tribe has three names. He has a name if he comes to be a "boy" working for a European—he has a name which the European calls him by. Second, he's got his tribal name. And he's got a name which only his parents have known, which he doesn't tell anybody. And there is a curious, I think mystic, thing about names. If you call your character by the wrong name, he doesn't come alive. You can't get on with it.

EE: *Do any of your characters in* The Honorary Consul *represent you yourself?*

GG: Probably bits of one's self are distributed all the way through.

EE: *Do you see people who sometimes give you ideas?*

GG: Yes, and dreams also give me ideas. Dreams are perhaps too important to me, because sometimes a whole story is based on a dream.

EE: *Was that true of* The Honorary Consul?

GG: *The Honorary Consul* began with a dream. It began with a dream about an American ambassador, in fact. What I dreamed was completely different from what I've written in the story, though.

EE: *Do you have a sense of playing God with your characters?*

GG: No. I have much more of a sense of their playing God with me.

EE: *How's that?*

GG: Because sometimes the story suddenly alters in a way which one had not intended at all. The characters are controlling me rather than I'm controlling the characters. I've had a character run away from me.

EE: *Which one?*

GG: That was Minty, in a book called *England Made Me,* which is now in America called *The Shipwrecked.*

EE: *That was one of your earlier books.*

GG: Yes, and the character called Minty was a minor character and became much too important.

EE: *What did you do about it?*

GG: Nothing. I just let him have his way.

EE: *How does your writing go?*

GG: I used to be able to write 500 words a day, whilst I was working, with intervals of holiday in between. Now I set myself about 300 or 400 words a day. But one rewrites that and rewrites that. When I say rewrite, I mean with corrections so extensive that the page becomes unintelligible. I write longhand, and the longhand becomes unreadable even to my secretary. So I have to dictate it.

EE: *Do you find writing fun or is it agony?*

GG: There are moments of pleasure when one feels that something has worked—but mostly it's a pain in the neck.

EE: *What do you do when you finish a book? Take a vacation? Or do you yearn to start another book?*

GG: I don't yearn to start the next one. You know, at my age, which is 69, the thought of beginning a book which may take three years is daunting, and one prefers to try and do little things.

EE: *Where was* The Honorary Consul *written?*

GG: Mainly in Antibes, but I write wherever I am.

EE: *What makes a place a good place for you to write in?*

GG: That's a mystery. There are places which I've never succeeded in writing in. London I always found difficult. I could much easier write in a hotel than in the flat I used to have in London. I can write in Antibes; I wrote most of *The Honorary Consul* there. But I haven't yet been able to write continuously, except just for revisions — small things — in Paris, where I've got a flat. It's a mystery, I don't know. . .

EE: *Do you go off alone or is your family with you when you write?*

GG: Well, I'm separated from my wife. But no, in any case I'm alone. When one writes, one's alone.

EE: *In the Introduction to that collection called* The Portable Graham Greene[1] *the editor discusses the importance of political frontiers in a number of your novels, and frontiers play a part in* The Honorary Consul, *too. Do you use this symbolism deliberately?*

GG: I think I'm conscious of it, probably because of my critics.

EE: *What's your favourite European city?*

GG: I think Bath. And Edinburgh, perhaps.

EE: *Why Bath?*

GG: I think it's one of the most beautiful cities in Europe.

EE: *Shades of Jane Austen.*

GG: Curiously enough, I do not like Jane Austen. I've never been able to read her. The humor of Jane Austen has always struck me as being so overplayed and so obvious. I suppose it's one of my blind spots. We all have blind spots—like I can't read Milton. Jane Austen is my blind spot in the novel. I read certain novelists whom I admire and like.

EE: *Who are they?*

GG: Well, one recently died—Evelyn Waugh, whom I liked very much and was very fond of. It's very difficult—whenever one is asked for names, you know, they all disappear out of one's head. But one has one's admirations, and one's admirations in the past—Henry James, Conrad, Ford Madox Ford—sort of, as it were, images in a side chapel.

EE: *I read somewhere that you admire François Mauriac.*

GG: Yes, up to a point. His views of Catholicism and mine differ enormously, like my views of Catholicism and Evelyn Waugh's differed enormously. But one or two of his books I liked enormously.

EE: *I believe Mauriac once said, "Every novelist should invent a style for himself." How would you describe your own?*

GG: I'd say one doesn't consciously invent a style, but one tries to say something as plainly and clearly and in a few words as possible, and out of that perhaps a style becomes detectable. I don't know.

EE: *You have a reputation for being a very private person, and yet you've been a newspaper correspondent. How do you explain that?*

GG: I've only been a newspaper correspondent for a few months at a time, in the space of a few years. I was a newspaper correspondent in Vietnam during the winters for four years. I was a correspondent for *Life* in Malaya, but that was only a question of three months. I've done special newspaper assignments, but they wouldn't amount, in effect, to more than at most two years of my life, if one put them end to end.[2]

EE: *Do you think that* The Honorary Consul *departs from the mainstream of your other novels?*

GG: No, I would have thought that it was very much in the mainstream; I would have thought it was in the mainstream of *The Power and the Glory* and *The Comedians*.

EE: *Which of your books means the most to you?*

GG: I think probably *The Power and the Glory*. I think *The Honorary Consul* is good, but I'm very fond of *Travels with My Aunt*.

EE: *Why did you put* The Power and the Glory *first?*

GG: Because I think . . . technically perhaps, I think it's my best book.

EE: *A lot of people would agree, but they haven't read* The Honorary Consul *yet. Would you care to say anything about your future plans?*

GG: No. I have no future plans.

EE: *What more would you like to accomplish as a writer?*

GG: I don't know. Just write a good book.

Elizabeth Easton, "A Conversation with Graham Greene," *Book-of-the-Month Club News*, fall 1973, 4–5. *Editor's title.*

Notes

1. Philip Stratford states that Greene is "irresistibly drawn to frontiers" and draws attention to the "physical frontier" in his novels and, more important, the "sense of conflicting allegiances that it breeds." Introduction, *The Portable Graham Greene*, ed. Philip Stratford (New York: Viking Press, 1973).
2. Graham Greene's activities as a newspaper correspondent are, in the main, confined with one exception to the first part of the fifties when he was correspondent for *Life* in Malaya, of the *Sunday Times* and *Le Figaro* for several winters in Vietnam, and

of the *Sunday Times* in Kenya in 1953. See also *Ways of Escape*,
119. Other "special newspaper assignments" were in the mid- and
late sixties when he went to Cuba on two occasions (1963 and
1966) and to Paraguay (1969) for the *Sunday Telegraph,* to Goa
for the *Sunday Times,* and to Sierra Leone in 1967 and Chile in
1971 for the *Observer.*

On the Dangerous Edge

John Heilpern

"What was he like?" asked the actress about Graham Greene.

And I talked a little about the man she had known, with his gallows humour and haunted eyes. And the actress laughed, laughter of recognition. "That's him!" she remembered fondly. "That's him, all right." Yet she had not met him for 20 years.

Perhaps people never change, not even in a lifetime. They become more themselves. But with Graham Greene, whatever the circumstances of his life, young or old, successful or not, you sense that he would always remain the same. It's bound to be so with people who live out their lives in near-despair.

He's 71 now. "Getting on a bit," he said when we met. "Last decade. One doesn't know but one hopes."

Last decade?

"We're a very long-lived family, unfortunately. My mother died in her mid-eighties. I had an uncle who fell out of a tree at the age of 90. It fills me with horror to think I might have to go on much longer."

What age did his father die?

"Oh, he died the normal age. About 75."[1] He began to laugh. "It's a biblical age, isn't it? Three score years and ten . . ."

He looked fit, a man of 60 perhaps. How old did he feel?

"More than a hundred. Life does seem to have been inordinately long. Perhaps it comes from travelling about so much. Would you like a drink?"

What he calls the curious individual Berkhamsted face looked at me hopefully — "pointed faces like the knaves on playing cards, with a slyness about the eyes, an unsuccessful cunning." It's also the face of a watchful man: vulnerable and sympathetic. He's inquisitive, giving the impression of a good listener. It's why he says he would have made a good priest: in one ear, out the other.

"Help yourself," he said, pouring gin into a tumbler. "I think I've got everything." I felt relieved. I hadn't expected him to be quite so welcoming. He's notoriously private and shy, rarely giving interviews to much length. With Samuel Beckett he shares a unique distinction among famous men. He's never appeared on television.

I met him in his flat in Paris near the Champs Elysées, though he lives most of the year in Antibes since he left England over a decade ago. Both homes are surprisingly modest for a wealthy man: reminder of his rootlessness perhaps. The Paris flat could have been almost anywhere in the world. Functional furniture in the sitting room, a simple oak table, a television set tucked into a corner, scarcely used, and many books in neat shelves — Conrad and James, Victorian poets, row upon row of thrillers. One eccentric object: a table croquet set, a present from his son (who's a publisher). Only the art in the room was remarkable: a tiny Graham Sutherland, two pictures back from Haiti, a Sidney Nolan, a bleak Lowry seascape, a bronze maquette bought years ago from his friend Henry Moore for £150. It must be worth about £10,000 now.

On the oak table a copy of *The Return of A. J. Raffles*, his new play for the Royal Shakespeare Company. By its side, the unfinished manuscript of a novel to be called *The Cold Fault*.[2] It was handwritten in a minute, practically illegible scrawl. He counts the words meticulously as he writes. In mid-sentence over the word "said" was written the number 40,000. It takes him two to three years to write a book.

"Perhaps it is only desperation which keeps me writing," he wrote in *A Sort of Life*, "like someone who clings to an unhappy marriage for fear of solitude."[3]

Surprisingly, he never wanted to be a writer. He told me that contrary to popular belief his strongest instincts were against the whole idea. He wanted to be a businessman and joined the British-American Company, destined for China. He lasted two weeks. But he still might be a contented sub-editor on the *Times* if his first novel hadn't been accepted. He doesn't understand what finally produced the compulsion. He knows his compulsion to write reveals itself in the misery of not being able to.

He has blocks? "Yes, and they're very painful. I have periods of complete sterility. They're not happy times either for oneself or one's friends or the people one lives with. The other day I was in Budapest and met a Hungarian friend, over 80, a writer. We were talking about blockages. He told me that a recent block of 10 days was for him a period of horror. But my goodness! I sometimes go for six months or a year—nothing, unable to do it."

When he left his friend he said to him: "Please pray for me that I can write. That I only have a block of 10 days like you."

"But it's simple!" came the reply. "All you have to do is drink three whiskies and sit down in front of a piece of paper and write."

"Write about *what?*" asked Greene.

"About life," replied his friend. "But take your three whiskies first."

Throughout his life he has written for just two hours a day. Two hours of work! But the work is so highly concentrated he finds that he's practically spent. Always he's limited himself to only 500 words a day, though is content now with 300. At night, he revises the manuscript for an hour or so. It seems a lonely ritual of constant re-writes, chipping and hacking at a stone until a shape slowly begins to emerge.

"It's like having your face covered with boils," he said unexpectedly. "One doesn't exactly yearn for them. Yet one gets uncomfortable without them. In the writing game."

Where's the fulfilment? "Release of pressure."

Had he ever totally captured in words the thoughts he struggled to express? "Nearly, sometimes, just occasionally. What's that line from Shelley? 'To hope, till hope creates from its wreck, the thing it contemplates.'"

He writes just before sleep and as soon as he wakes. He lets his subconscious work for him. Dreams have always been a vivid element in Graham Greene's life and sometimes they help. Two short stories came from dreams. So did the seeds of *The Honorary Consul.* He used to keep dream-diaries, though no outsider has been allowed to see them . . . .

⁓

"When was the last time you leapt in the air and shouted,'It's good to be alive,'" I asked.

"When was there ever a time?" he replied, and laughed again.

Why is life so depressing for him? True, his childhood had been unhappy. And writing can sometimes be agony for him, as if he'd become the victim of his own inventions. Still one couldn't help feeling his life ought to have its compensations. Two or three hours of work a day, time, freedom, travel, friends, success, a flat in Paris, another in the South of France: it could be worse. And yet throughout his life he's been suffocated by boredom, what he calls "the boredom-sickness." It envelops him like a shroud.

"Boredom is another word for depression," he explained. "I think my temperament is manic-depressive. And it happens without reason. The real melancholic invents reasons for his despair. He might put it down to jealousy in a love affair. But one knows one's inventing an excuse and it's what makes it worse. My moods are more even nowadays. I'm not so manic, not so depressive. I've reached the plateau of old age."

A few years ago he was in a state of such hopeless depression that he visited a psychiatrist for the first time since his childhood. He asked to be given electric shock treatment. The psychiatrist advised him to delve into his upbringing instead. He went away and wrote *A Sort of Life*. And the bleakness passed.

Just after the war, he went to stay with his friend Evelyn Waugh. But he was manic then and spent his visit collecting car numbers to which he formed emotional attachments. "Evelyn was rather worried," he said.

His father's father was a manic depressive. His mother's father was an Anglican clergyman who suffered from an exaggerated sense of guilt and unfrocked himself in a field. It so happens.

It is the "boredom-sickness" that has been the curse and most powerful motive of Graham Greene's life. Apart from his work, the two major escape routes from his own temperament have always been books and travel. With his conversion to Catholicism, they shaped his life.

He reads 15 books a month on average. But it was his childhood reading that foretold his future. "In childhood," he wrote in an essay, "all books are books of divination."[4] Wasn't it the fascination of the ancient African witch in *King Solomon's Mines*, he asked himself, which led to Sierra Leone where he conceived *The Heart of the Matter?* Had he not encountered at 14 Marjorie Bowen's *Viper of Milan*[5] would he have followed the revolutionary roads of Mexico and written *The Power and the Glory?* Even *The Return of A. J. Raffles*, his new play based on the Edwardian crime stories of E. W. Hornung, has its unlikely antecedent there in the twilight. The first book Greene ever read was called, *Dixon Brett, Detective.*

And travel: more desperate form of flight. When he was at Oxford he played that dice with death invented by bored Russian officers at the turn of the century: Russian roulette. He found a gun belonging to his brother, spun the chambers, pointed the loaded gun to his head and squeezed the trigger. It helped pass the time. The first attempt was out by one. The bullet was next in line. Miraculously, every successive gamble with his life cheated death too. And his initial jubilation turned into boredom. Travel replaced Russian roulette. Countries in chaos and revolution became the new prescription—danger, corruption, evil, betrayal, the whisky priest, the sympathetic coward, smell of fear, thrust of the knife. *Our Man in Havana, The Comedians, The Quiet American* are some of the results.

"A kind of Russian roulette remained too a factor in my later life, so that without previous experience of Africa I went on an absurd and reckless trek through Liberia; it was the fear of boredom which took me to Tabasco during the religious persecution, to a *léproserie* in the Congo, to the Kikuyu reserve during the Mau-Mau insurrection, to the emergency in Malaya and to the French war in Vietnam. There, in those last three regions of clandestine war, the fear of ambush served me just as effectively as the revolver from the corner-cupboard in the life-long war against boredom. . ."

He's been sniffing round Portugal of late.

"Is the *Observer* paying for lunch?" he asked suddenly. "Oh, good. We'll go somewhere nice."

People imagine that Graham Greene has a taste only for the "seedy," but it can't be so. The restaurant he chose, Le Voltaire, is a favourite with antique dealers.

The taxi dropped us on the other side of the road to the restaurant. Just as we were about to cross over, the lights changed and the traffic came revving down the road. I stopped automatically but to my astonishment he started to dash across. It was as if he'd been attracted towards the traffic like a moth to a flame. I yelled, "NO!" but he didn't seem to hear. I watched him pirouetting round the Renaults until he was somehow safely across the road. Russian roulette again. He looked cheerful.

He ordered *sole meunière* for us both and a bottle of Sancerre, speaking almost fluent French in his correct English accent. "Merci, Monsieur Grin," said the patron.

By chance I remarked on the gold ring he wore on his left hand and it led to an unexpected story. The ring has a heraldic design on its surface: a gryphon. His father gave it to him for his 21st birthday. But when he worked for the Secret Service in Sierra Leone during the war, the ring took on a special significance. It became his secret seal. He used to dip it in wax, sealing all correspondence with the secret seal of the gryphon.

"Silly business," he said, beginning to giggle at the memory.

He took a bit of a risk with the secret combination to his secret safe. The combination was 0499, the only sequence he was certain he could remember. 04 was the year of his birth. 99 was 99 Gower Street: then the address of the *Spectator*. He used to be its literary editor.

His boss in MI6 was Kim Philby and they were friends. Recently, he read an interview in which Philby was asked what he would wish for if he had a magic wand. "Graham Greene on the other side of the table," he replied. "And a bottle of wine between us."

When Greene was in Budapest earlier this year, he tele-grammed Philby inviting him over for the bottle of wine. He didn't make it.

. . . Over the years he's been involved with political causes, admiring Castro, Ho Chi Minh, Allende—men he's met and liked. But for Greene the writer's instinct is essen-tially heartless, what he calls "the splinter of ice." When I asked him if he could remember what he did when he learnt that war had been declared, he answered: "Write." He heard the sirens and assumed that it would be the fin-ish of London. He went to look out of the window of his Hampstead flat and could see over the city. Immediately, he began to take notes. There was a woman walking her dog in the road outside. He noted down: "Sirens gone for air raid. War declared. Woman walking dog. Pauses by tree." He laughed as he told the story.

It's almost as if he has a distaste for what he does or has been singled out to be. Once, he was in hospital with appendicitis and a child died in his ward. When the parents came to the child's bedside everyone else in the ward put on their ear-phones to avoid hearing the terrible distress. To his own wonder, he was the only one who didn't. He lay in bed, listening.[6]

Nothing, one knows it, could have been easy in this writer's life. And perhaps least of all that struggle for ultimate meaning in a life of bewilderment and pain: his search for God. "I couldn't have undertaken it," he said casually, "if it hadn't been for my disloyalty."

He converted to Catholicism when he was 22, though more to share his future wife's beliefs rather than from deep personal conviction. (He was separated from his wife some 20 years ago.) The turning point came in the 1930s when he witnessed the religious persecution of Catholics in Mexico. As a result he wrote *The Lawless Roads* and *The Power and the Glory*. Since then, perhaps no Greene novel would have seemed complete without God as a leading character. It's something Greene was aware of himself and it led to a famous story. In 1953 he was eating in White's with Evelyn Waugh and mentioned it might be fun to write about politics in future. "Oh, I wouldn't give up writing about God at this stage if I were you," said Waugh. "It would be like P. G. Wodehouse dropping Jeeves half way through the Wooster series."[7]

Greene laughed as he recalled the story and when we returned to his flat he made an interesting observation of Waugh. "What I liked about him was that he insulted you to your face. The good things he said behind your back."

Does Greene believe any more? The depressive has a strange battle with God. If he discovers a reason to believe, he might feel cheated of his own condition. If he cannot believe, he feels worse. I sensed there was something of that in Graham Greene, though the battle has subsided for him now. Although he still attends Mass regularly, he no longer follows the strict practices of his faith. He no longer believes in mortal sin, damnation, or the value of confession. When I said to him that he seemed a curious kind of Catholic, he replied: "Evelyn Waugh would rebuke me for not being a Catholic at all. But then," he added with a smile, "The Pope doesn't."

It was a nice point, for approval doesn't come much higher. Eight years ago, Pope Paul asked to meet him and the two men talked informally in the Vatican. The Pope told him that he'd read *Stamboul Train* and *The Power and the Glory.* "But Your Holiness," said Greene, "*The Power and the Glory* has been condemned by the Holy Office." "Mr. Greene," the Pope replied, "You will find that parts of any book you write will offend some Catholics. And you shouldn't bother about it."

So he doesn't.

"I have very few beliefs now. But I continue to have a certain faith. I have the faith that I am wrong. And that my lack of belief is my fault. And that I shall be proved wrong one day."

Does he believe in salvation?

"One thing I feel sure, if there is such a thing as life after death it won't be a static state. I think it will be a state of movement and activity. I can't believe in an ultimate happiness which doesn't include a form of development."

What kind of development? "A kind of evolution. Evolution of the spirit. And an eternity of evolution."

"But do you believe in God?"

"I believe sometimes. I know that I'm wrong in not believing. Over and over again I find at times when my belief is practically extinct inexplicable things which I can't dismiss. Most of the time now I don't think about my belief, or lack of it. One will know soon enough. Except sometimes in extreme disbelief I remember wonderful incidents and I think, 'My God! Perhaps I'm *wrong.*' "

A few years ago, he heard of a Franciscan priest who awoke one day with the stigmata in his hands, his feet and his side. The priest was called Padre Pio and lived in a poor village in Southern Italy. Three doctors studied his case, a Catholic, Protestant and Jewish doctor. None could give any explanation even after the most exhaustive study. Nor was the stigmata of Padre Pio judged hysterical or self-inflicted. A suspicious Vatican refused permission for him to say Mass except at a side altar at 5 a.m. each morning. It was an attempt to reduce the pilgrims. But thousands flocked to see him anyway, and to pray with him. Greene was one of the pilgrims. He watched Padre Pio enter the church, a short, stocky man, a peasant figure, bearded. And the Mass began. He expected it would take the customary forty minutes or so and believed when the Mass ended that it had. To his amazement, he found it had taken two and half hours. He looked at Padre Pio and saw that he tried to keep his robes over his hands. But the robes slipped and he saw the wounds of Christ on his hands.[8]

Since then, Graham Greene has prayed to Padre Pio. And his prayers have been answered. As he approaches the end of his life, belief is less important to him. But at such times he believes that life has meaning, and hope.

Extracted from John Heilpern, "On the Dangerous Edge," *Observer*, 7 December 1975, 17–8, 21, 23, 25.

Notes
1. Charles Greene, Graham Greene's father, died in 1943; Marion Greene, his mother, in September 1959.
2. No novel, with this title, exists. One wonders whether this is a tentative title to what turned out to be *The Human Factor*.
3. *A Sort of Life*, 63.
4. "The Lost Childhood," *Collected Essays*, 13.

5. For "Marjorie Bowen" see note 7 on p. 151 of the Madeleine Chapsal excerpt, "The Business of the Writer."
6. Graham Greene describes this incident in more detail in *A Sort of Life*, 184–85.
7. Christopher Sykes, *Evelyn Waugh: A Biography* (Boston: Little, Brown, and Co., 1975), 357–58.
8. Norman Sherry, Greene's biographer, also records Greene's rather vivid account of this visit in *The Life of Graham Greene*, vol. 1, *xix–xx*.

Graham Greene in Antibes

Michael Mewshaw

Graham Greene is well over six feet, and if he does stoop slightly at the shoulders, it is not as if bowed by years—he is seventy-two—but as though to incline his ear and listen closer. Only his eyes betray his age. Moist, large, and often fixed on something in the distance, they also seem sad. But then they have seen an awful lot.

I apologized for being late, and blamed the traffic I had run into returning from an exhibition of Nicholas de Staël's[1] painting in St. Paul de Vence.

"There's where he killed himself, you know." Greene waved through his livingroom to a narrow balcony. But he was gesturing toward the squat fortress at the mouth of the harbour. "He jumped off the wall. It doesn't look high enough, but it worked."

He led me onto the terrace to have a look. Though we stood four or five floors above the street, the noise was nearly deafening, and we had to raise our voices.

What time did he start working? How long did he stay at it? I asked, sounding like the rawest amateur hoping to discover some secret in the details of his schedule.

"I'm usually awake by six and keep going until I have a hundred words. That means about five hours. I have to be strict with myself or I'd never get anything done. I used to write five hundred words a day, but as I get older, I found that was too much. So I cut down to three hundred, then to a hundred, just to keep my hand in." When he smiled, his eyelids creased and the moistness of his pupils seemed about to spill out. "I never lose track of where I am. Sometimes I stop smack in the middle of a paragraph."

Difficult as this was to believe, Greene swore it was true. "Of course I used to work much faster. When I was young I liked to bring out a new book every year. It was a conscious reaction against the Bloomsbury people,[2] most of whom seemed content to do a few things, build a huge reputation, and rest on it. But even then I always had to revise my novels again and again to get them right. Now it takes me years to finish a book and sometimes it still isn't right."

I remarked how strange it was that practice and experience didn't make life much easier for a novelist. "You'd think once a writer had been through it a few times and developed confidence in his talent . . . "

"One has no talent," Greene interrupted. "I have no talent. It's just a question of working, of being willing to put in the time."

Greene has long had this sense of timeliness, an instinct for stories which afterward seem prophetic, and a tropism for troubled corners of the world. In Africa, in Saigon and Hanoi, in Malaysia, in Haiti, in Central and South America, he had produced not only dozens of novels, short stories, and travel books, but controversial articles on the Mau-Mau uprising in Kenya, influential reviews of hundreds of movies and books, and interviews with Ho Chi Minh, Diem, and Castro.[3]

It would be difficult to think of any author who has written more often and more effectively about the bankruptcy of colonial and post-colonial regimes, the abuses of political power, the threat of unrestrained intelligence agencies, and the repression of personal and religious beliefs, whether by the Left or the Right. In a world which likes to pay lip service to writers who are fiercely independent, politically engagé, and who risk great danger to do their jobs, no one except Solzhenitsyn—certainly not Hemingway, Camus, Malraux or Sartre—can make the kind of claims which, interestingly enough, Graham Greene declines to make for himself.

As the lights in Antibes began to blink on, we went inside. The livingroom walls were lined with books, but there was very little to suggest who lived there. Perhaps the personal memorabilia is in Greene's apartment in Paris or his house on Capri. Or then again, maybe he prefers to keep his personal life tucked away, his day to day existence unencumbered by the past.

While Greene mixed us each a Scotch and Perrier ("you Americans like ice, don't you?") I told him I always enjoyed his books, but admired even more his energy, courage and commitment.

He dismissed the compliment, saying straight out that he was a coward. He was frequently afraid and suffered from a long list of phobias. "I'm terrified of water, for example. Always have been. It's all I can do to splash my face in the morning and rinse away the shaving cream."

As he proceeded to tell of spending months in Tahiti scuba diving every day in a vain attempt to conquer his fear,[4] I pointed out what appeared obvious. It was a triumph of bravery to spend hours in the ocean if you were pathologically afraid of water.

Greene shook his head. He was still a coward, he said, even though he'd forced himself to go diving. In a way it was a replay of his attitude toward his talent. Inverting the Biblical homily, Greene in effect claimed you couldn't judge him by his works, but only by the weaknesses he felt within. Perhaps this paradigm of his reasoning explained the paradoxical nature of his fictional characters who have to be strong because they know they are weak, who are good because they are sinners.

After the discussion of cowardice, there came an uncomfortable moment and we quietly sipped our drinks. Greene has a reputation of resisting interviews, being unco-operative in conversation and chary of personal disclosures. It may simply be that people hold unrealistic expectations of writers and assume that anyone whose medium is language must be perfectly at ease in conversation. But the connection between the spoken and written word is tenuous at best, and many novelists, loquacious though they may be by nature, have learned the hard way to avoid idle conversation with journalists.

"It's got so I hate to say who I am or what I believe," Greene admitted. "A few years ago I told an interviewer I'm a gnostic. The next day's newspapers announced that I had become an agnostic."

For Greene, the anecdote appears to provide a more comfortable vehicle for exploring past experience and a most effective means of communicating with strangers. Certainly he is seldom as animated or interesting as when he is telling a story. When, to break the silence, I said I liked the painting on the wall behind his couch, he explained it had been a gift from Fidel Castro and suddenly we were launched for several hours.

Greene had visited Cuba while Castro and his men were fighting in the mountains, and through intermediaries he managed to contact the rebels and arrange a meeting. When the interview went well, he asked if there wasn't some way he could return the favour, and Castro had said yes. Come back often and bring warm clothing. It was cold in the mountains, especially at night, and his men were freezing.

Since Greene suspected he was being watched by Batista's police, he didn't see how he could smuggle supplies over the circuitous route to their rendezvous point. There was also the danger of compromising his journalist's neutrality.

But Castro convinced him he didn't need a truckload of contraband, just sweaters, pairs of socks and trousers. Greene could wear several layers of clothing and take them off after he arrived. Nobody would notice, and even if they did, Greene could claim he was cold. Weren't the English always cold, even in the tropics?

So each time he set out to meet Castro, Greene bundled up like an Eskimo, suffered through the sweltering heat of the lowlands, reached the mountains and molted a few layers of clothing, then returned to Havana pounds lighter.

Years afterward when Castro was in power, Greene came back for yet another interview, presumably more appropriately dressed for the occasion. It was then that Castro presented him with the painting in gratitude for his help during the revolution.

I asked how Cuba had changed, and Greene said, "Oh, for the average Cuban it's a far better place. But . . . well, it's too bad about Havana. It used to be such a lively city. Now it seems rather dreary."

Then abruptly we were discussing Haiti. Perhaps there was a transition. If so, I was unaware of it. Yet I had no sense that Greene was taking tangents. For one thing, as an accomplished raconteur, he had the ability to control a listener just as skilfully as he sets up a reader. His hands in particular he used to good effect, clasping them in his lap, then letting them fly out at dramatic moments. For another thing there was a kind of cartographical logic to his vignettes and he connected distantly spaced dots on the map and circled the globe as unerringly as a latitudinal line.

It was inevitable, I suppose, that I would eventually try to work the conversation around Viet Nam. Greene knew the country and conflict as few people did, having gone there before Dienbienphu and defined the tragedy taking shape for America long before the Marines arrived, before Tet and the truce and last spring's sudden unravelling.[5] But at this subject, his volubility faltered. He could do an imitation of Diem's hysterically high-pitched laugh, and he told a final, self-deprecating tale, this one about his meeting with Ho Chi Minh, which had made him highly nervous beforehand so that he smoked a pipe of opium and went to the rendezvous stoned. Judging by the resulting interview, the opium must have sharpened his perceptions.

But as for the war itself, and America's military policy, he had little to say. What was there to say that he hadn't said before? In the opinion of most experts, *The Quiet American* is still the best novel about the war, and when one considers that it was published over twenty years ago it seems all the more appallingly prophetic. So Greene would only repeat that he loved the Vietnamese and especially the city of Saigon which in those days had a laundered look each morning and smelled flowery and full of life. When asked if he'd like to go back, he said he preferred to remember it as it had been.

The scent of charcoal smoke had insinuated itself into the room. Out on the balconies everybody was barbecuing. It promised to be a long restless night and a difficult morning for Greene. As I got up to leave, I asked what he was working on now. I had waited until the end so he would feel free to duck the question.

But he said he had recently picked up a novel which he had set aside years ago. Although he was making progress, he wasn't sure he would finish it or how it would turn out if he did. "I put the book away when that Kim Philby business blew up. I was well into it by then, but there are certain similarities between my plot and the Philby affair, and I didn't want anyone to think I had drawn on that. There has already been enough nonsense about my friendship with Philby. Perhaps now the novel can be read on its own terms."[6]

As we headed for the door, he added that he was also collecting some of his autobiographical sketches.

A sequel to *A Sort of Life?* I asked. Not exactly. Just isolated pieces and a few articles that still seemed worthwhile to him.[7]

In the hall now, I said if the anecdotes he had told me were in the collection, it was bound to be a fascinating book.

"I don't know. Interesting experiences, fascinating people you meet in extraordinary places — of course that's all very enjoyable. But they don't make one a better writer and they don't always make for good books." As we descended in the elevator, Greene went on, "I sometimes think failure and boredom, the feeling of loneliness, of being flat and empty, have more influence on a novelist."

When we reached the lobby, we shook hands, and then I was out on the street, wondering about the final paradox Greene had presented. In the elevator he seemed to have been suggesting that although he wrote successful and compelling novels, it was out of a sense of failure and boredom, although he had led an exciting life, it was just an effort to overcome a feeling of hollowness and drift.

But it seemed to me Greene had indulged in self-deprecation one time too often. If anything had become clear that evening, it was that Graham Greene is a good man because he has a moral compass, a courageous man because he is willing to go where the compass points, and a gifted writer because he has the ability to make the reader understand and follow the compass too.

The town of Antibes may have changed since Fitzgerald, and all those who came after him, prowled this coast searching for some vision of grace and dignity that would endure after innocence ends. But Graham Greene has lasted and will last.

Extracted from Michael Mewshaw, "Graham Greene in Antibes," *London Magazine*, June–July 1977, 35–45.

Notes

1. Nicholas de Staël (1914–55), Russian-born French abstract painter, who committed suicide.
2. A group of London writers and artists between 1915 and 1935 — including Virginia and Leonard Woolf, Lytton Strachey, and others — with strong communal interests who achieved distinction but incurred contemporary disapproval by their unorthodox principles and assumption of intellectual superiority.
3. See *Sunday Times*, 27 September 1953, 4, and 4 October 1953, 4, and *New Republic*, 16 May 1955, 10–12.
4. Greene went to Tahiti in 1960.

5. The reference is to the rapid collapse of the U.S.-supported regime of President Nguyen Van Thieu in the spring of 1975, which was followed by the reunification of Vietnam under the leadership of the Viet Cong-dominated Provisional Revolutionary Government.

6. The novel in question is *The Human Factor*, published in March 1978.

7. *Ways of Escape*, published in October 1980.

The Private World of Graham Greene

J. W. Lambert

Greene in his 74th year is lithe and limber in baggy trousers, cardigan, open-necked shirt, the eyes in the weathered, sometimes almost chubby, face at once amused and accusing. He is a solitary, but by no means a recluse, this fascinated investigator, in book after book, of the exhausted spirit, the man on the run, the double life— all three of these among the themes of *The Human Factor*.[1]

He himself has put it differently—a compelling desire, he has suggested, drives him "to evoke sympathy for people outside the borders of public sympathy."[2] This desire hardly extended to Papa Doc in Haiti, but a year or two ago, and fulfilling a notion vaguely held for some time, he went to Panama and found himself to be much taken with its current ruler, General Torrijos, grappling with his own fairly disorderly people and with the Americans, who run the canal zone and a questionable network of South American commercial and political manoeuvres.[3]

"He isn't in the least a typical military dictator. He's coping with a pretty impossible situation and maintaining a genuine private life"—again, one of the themes of *The Human Factor*, which Greene was then writing. One day the General said to him, "Like you I am self-destructive"—but, added the beaming Greene, "I'm not sure what he meant."

But though it's a small country, Panama has much more to it than the politics-dominated sheets of Colón and the Canal Zone.[4] "Some of it is very beautiful—Portobello Bay, for instance, which is where some people think Drake lies dreaming all the time of Plymouth Hoe, rather than Nombre Dios. I must say I used to enjoy quoting Newbolt[5] in Panama."

A glance to the bookshelves which fill the far wall. "Somehow, when one's living in two places, the books one wants are always in the wrong one. I've got most of my poetry here. Mostly I read Hardy, Yeats—oh, and Arthur Hugh Clough ("Say not the struggle naught availeth"?).

"Still, at least the books are there. Early in the war we—that's my first wife[6] and I—had a house in Clapham which we'd bought—well, taken out a mortgage on—in the mid-1930s. During the blitz the family was evacuated, but most days I used to go back to Clapham at lunchtime to see if the house was still there. One day it mostly wasn't. The back was almost completely destroyed. And there were all my books, absolutely inaccessible—or so it seemed. But months later a lot of them, mostly with inscriptions from their authors, turned up at Sotheby's. Some adventurous thief had thought them worth getting, and somehow or other got at them."

Time for lunch. "Let's go down to a place I rather like." The rain has stopped. Coatless despite bronchitis, Greene sways into a sharp breeze. At last a taxi, rattling us down to the rue du Faubourg St. Honoré, its smart shops glittering. The restaurant is cosy, quiet, with wooden rustic decor. Cage-birds twitter beside our table. With our sole, a bottle of Montrachet.

"I like food to be all right, but really—well, I don't want to give a false impression, but I suspect I only eat to have something in my stomach to mop up drink. Not, really a vast amount of drink, but I do like it regularly. And when I'm working well, I write in the morning, don't have a drink then; but in the evening a vodka and a half-bottle of wine sharpen my mind up to sit down and correct what I've written.

"I still read a lot—but let's not have a brisk run over present-day writers, shall we?" No indeed. But now that he's dead, what about Nabokov? After all Greene virtually launched Nabokov into fame when he named *Lolita* as his book of the year in the *Sunday Times* back in 1955.[7] But after that? "Well, I liked *Pale Fire* and *Pnin*, but I couldn't get through *Ada*. Perhaps I could have done, once. But now—well, I shall never be able to re-read Lowry's *Under the Volcano*.[8] For that matter I tried to re-read *Ulysses* but I couldn't, I simply couldn't.

"When I read fiction I suppose I have a sort of professional interest, but in the end I think I read fiction for the same reason as everybody else. Well, sometimes a novel will excite me because it seems to have something to say about a state of affairs, or an attitude of mind, that I'm particularly interested in at the moment. But mostly people read novels for—yes, escape, which everybody needs as they need drugs, including alcohol.

"That's why novels should have if not dull then level patches. That's where the excessive use of film technique, cutting sharply from intensity to intensity, is harmful. Not in moderation, it's helpful to keep a sense of movement, and we can't now do with many of those static nineteenth century descriptive passages done like paintings. But the writer does not need level passages for his subconscious to work up to the sharp scenes — and then of course it sometimes works up in a quite different way from what one thought one intended. And the readers need those level passages too, so that they can share in the processes of creation — not by conscious analysis but by absorption.

"Oh yes, I have used a first-person narrator quite often, it's true. I don't know, sometimes one wants to present things through one consciousness, sometimes — especially in short stories — a bit like one's own, sometimes not. No, I haven't used the first person in *The Human Factor*. It's very difficult to bring off. I still get extremely irritated by the way Proust cheats — there are far too many scenes which his narrator couldn't possibly have known anything about. But I do admire the extraordinary variety of tone Dickens managed with it in *Great Expectations*."

The last mouthful of airy apple tartlet disappears with the last mouthful of Montrachet. Outside, it has started to rain again; hunched in an archway we wait for a taxi and watch the scurrying shoppers. Was he ever recognized? "Yes, sometimes. Being occasionally approached by strangers isn't so bad, but I could do without all these other Graham Greenes, who get me a bad name. I don't mean my nephew the publisher,[9] but these other people who keep cropping up — in Jamaica, or at Geneva airport even, all apparently pretending to be me. Then there's this man who calls me Dear Graham and talks about meeting four years ago; rather a menacing letter, that one.

Back in the flat the talk turns to the theatre. "I love working in the theatre — because such absurd things happen there. Well, for example, you remember that in *The Living Room* Eric Portman played a priest confined to a wheelchair. One night it caught on something and he was tipped out of it. I hope it was an accident. Anyhow he took it very well, though he was often terribly peevish, downright angry indeed.

"Actors really are extraordinary. Look at Ralph Richardson. A fine actor, obviously. But in *The Complaisant Lover* he set about completely altering the character of the dentist-husband. Naturally the result wasn't in the least what I meant—but then it was highly praised, so I suppose he thought he knew best.

"But he's an amazing man as well as a great actor. One day, talking about long runs and keeping fresh, he said to me 'Some nights I try to freshen myself up by imagining I'm not in a Graham Greene play at all, but one by, say, Pinter. But don't worry old boy, if I'm ever in a Pinter play, I shall probably try to give it something different by imagining as I speak the lines that it's by Graham Greene.'"

His most recent adventure in the theatre was *The Return of A. J. Raffles*. "That was really splendid. Such fine acting—Denholm Elliott right exactly, though a bit inhibited by the 'leading role' business, and Paul Rogers really uncannily good, absolutely first-class. But I must say I wasn't at all prepared for the sense of shock some people seemed to feel at that momentary nudity. It certainly wasn't meant. Anyway those were some of the nicest weeks of my life.[10]

"In a very different way I enjoyed Malcolm Williamson's operatic version of *Our Man in Havana*—in fact I came to its defence, some people were very unkind to it, quite wrongly I thought.[11] It had some good tunes—must have if I enjoyed it. I don't seem to get much out of music. Even in church services the music's just a vague general enhancement. Well, of course I enjoy jolly musical comedy sort of stuff, but none of it actually means anything to me.

"Fact is, I have no musical memory. I suppose the way one's mind works depends on how one's brain works. Either way it's a mysterious business, what goes on in there. Dreams, for instance. Yes, I'm interested in dreams. There do seem to be pre-cognitive dreams . . . . "

A thoughtful pause, as though he were recalling a moment in *The Third Man*, when the writer Martins "suddenly saw in that corner of the mind that constructs such pictures, instantaneously, irrationally, a desert place, a body on the ground, a group of birds gathered. Perhaps it was a scene from one of his own books, not yet written, forming at the gate of consciousness . . . . "[12]

"Yes; and of course there was that odd business when I was writing *A Burnt-Out Case*, and got stuck. Then I dreamed a dream, not a dream telling me what to write exactly, but a dream my principal character could dream, and that provided the missing link between one part of the story and the next.

"And then again," he added, peering mischievously over his glass, "I'm one of those people given to dreaming about the Queen. She always figures as very—well, attractive. One of my dreams about her actually recurs. We're both in church, and there's a priest giving a ridiculous sermon. I catch the Queen's eye—I'm almost bursting out laughing, she puts her hand to her mouth in a gesture of jokily suppressing a yawn. And in another one, I remember, I was just getting on very well with the Queen when Prince Charles came in dressed in Boy Scout's uniform . . . . "

Time to go. It was still raining a little in the grey boulevard outside. We stared down through the shivering trees at Parisians scuttling along, heads down. Above the sodden windy scene, arching over the street, a perfect rainbow signalled its unlikely promise, a celestial vulgarity right on cue. Hurriedly, before it could fade, I left him.

Extracted from J. W. Lambert, "The Private World of Graham Greene," *Sunday Times*, 5 March 1978, 37.

Notes

1. The interview was occasioned by the publication of *The Human Factor* in March 1978.
2. Graham Greene, *Why Do I Write?*, 47.
3. Graham Greene visited Panama in 1974–75 at the invitation of the Panamanian leader General Omar Torrijos.
4. Colón, situated on the Atlantic coast and outside the Canal Zone, is the most important urban center after Panama City. Its principal paper is *Atlantico*.
5. Sir Henry Newbolt (1862–1938), English barrister and poet, long remembered for "Drake's Drum" (*Admirals All, and Other Verses* [London: Elkin Matthews, 1897]) and "Clifton Chapel" (*Clifton Chapel and Other Poems* [London: John Murray, 1908]).
6. Greene was only married once.
7. Vladimir Nabokov (1899–1977), erudite Russian-born writer and critic, settled in the U. S. in 1940. His best-seller was *Lolita* (1955), which was followed by *Pnin* in 1957. *Pale Fire* (1962) is a novel consisting of a poem and a long commentary on it by a mad critic and *Ada* (1969) is a novel much of whose life depends on interlingual puns.
8. Malcolm Lowry (1909–57), English-born novelist whose most successful work, *Under the Volcano* (1947) at whose center is an alcoholic Englishman, was inspired by Mexico. See Douglas W. Veitch's *Lawrence, Greene and Lowry: The Fictional Landscape of Mexico* (Waterloo, Ont.: Wilfrid Laurier University Press, 1978) and Ronald G. Walker's *Infernal Paradise: Mexico and the*

Modern English Novel (Berkeley, Calif.: University of California Press, 1978).

9. Graham Carlton Greene (1936–), Sir Hugh Greene's son, is the director of Jonathan Cape and a trustee of the British Museum (1978–).

10. *The Return of A. J. Raffles* opened at Aldwych Theatre, London, 4 December 1975. Denholm Elliott played the part of Raffles and Paul Rogers the Prince of Wales.

11. The operatic version of *Our Man in Havana*—libretto by Sidney Gilliat—was first performed on 2 July 1963. Greene's defense of the opera and his disagreement with the *Times'* critic is recorded in his letter to the editor, *Times*, 4 July 1963, 13.

12. *The Third Man*, 47–48.

The Greene Factor*

Louise Dennys

He has always guarded his privacy carefully, but it has not always been easy. After the publication of *The Heart of the Matter* in 1948, he was besieged by "cries for spiritual assistance." "Priests would spend hours in my only armchair while they described their difficulties, their perplexities, their desperation," Greene recalls. "I was like a man without medical knowledge in a village struck with a plague."

He has lived in France since 1966: British taxes don't encourage the successful writer to stay at home. "I speak French very badly," he remarks, "but I feel perfectly at home here. The only things I miss are English sausages and English beer." He is 73 now, but his vitality belies his age. He is a tall, attractive man with that long-legged awkward English elegance. In a sense one knows him from his books. The weariness and melancholy, the glimpses of innocence, the intimacy with the human heart and the shadows of damnation, the irony and the comedy, are all here. With him, one also becomes conscious of his kindness and lack of pretension.

Greene does not enjoy talking about himself and is uneasy being interviewed; he sits in the chair as if driven back into it, tensely restrained. Yet for all his reticence he is immensely sympathetic. "One is inclined to be evasive," he smiles. "It's my natural instinct, I'm afraid."

It's also his natural instinct to avoid any analysis of his own work that might make him conscious of "the pattern of the carpet." "In writing—and I'm talking only as a novelist—one is using the unconscious without being conscious of it, not trying to forget about it but driving blindly, trusting the horse to lead you.[1] There obviously are attitudes to life in every book but I don't want to think about them. I think I've written somewhere that the good writer is always a victim of an obsession, and that gives a family likeness to his work.[2] But I don't want to discover what my obsessions are. Let them be unconscious. One doesn't want to remember one's own books. One wants the last book to be the unique book, the only book one's written.

"Of all the books *The Human Factor* has probably been the most difficult to write—that and *The Honorary Consul*. It's an albatross off my neck. I started it 10 years ago and abandoned it after I'd written 25,000 words.

"I abandoned it because it deals with the subject of a double agent in the secret service and 10 years ago the Kim Philby book came out and I thought everybody would assume, as I knew him and had worked with him, that I was basing my book on him. But there's no connection. The character has absolutely no resemblance to Philby, the situation and the motives are completely different, and there's a strong element of fantasy that is inevitable in writing about a secret service." His eyebrows lift in amusement. "Otherwise one would be breaking all kinds of official secrets, I suppose. Anyway, I wouldn't know them because I've been out of it for so long."

"He betrayed his country—yes, perhaps he did," Greene once wrote, "but who among us has not committed treason to something or someone more important than a country?"[3]

"The subject of divided loyalty is one I've dealt with a lot and which is psychologically important to me," he says of the new book. "The human factor is, in this case, the effect of family life on a man working day by day in the Secret Service, which draws him in a completely different direction from what the authorities would like. I mean love for his wife, love for his adopted child. I mean a greater loyalty than the loyalty of country, as it were."

After dinner, we return to his flat: it feels different at night, the sea and the sky just a dark expanse beyond the large window. Objects within it take on more prominence—the books on simple shelves across two walls, the few small paintings (one a gift from Castro), the lamp on the writing desk. "There are places that have a certain magic power for letting one work," he says. "Here I work steadily. Brighton used to be a great place for writing. But, alas, Brighton is not what it was.

"When I used to be absolutely blocked with writing, because I was stuck hopelessly or hadn't got a book to write, I'd keep diaries of my dreams. I seem to have been on very intimate terms with nearly all the world's leaders in my dreams. I used to dream of atomic warfare about three times a year, but when Khruschev came to power those dreams stopped and I used to dream very friendly dreams about Khruschev.

"And the Queen, I used to have quite a number of fanciful dreams about her. There's one in which I was going to a service in the Guards' chapel with her and the clergyman was making a very long and silly sermon and I found it difficult not to laugh and the Queen, also finding it difficult not to laugh, made motions to me not to. I felt as if I were getting along well with her—there was a communion of spirit. And then, alas, the Duke of Edinburgh arrived and she said you must push up one seat to make room for the Duke. He was dressed as a Boy Scout and I didn't feel at all sympathetic to him."[4]

Dreams and the workings of the unconscious have long interested Greene. When he was 15, after a long period of rebelliousness, loneliness and conflicting loyalties suffered as a boarder at the school where his father was headmaster ("a country in which I was a foreigner, a suspect"), he was sent to a London psycho-analyst—"an astonishing thing in 1920." Intermittently over the years since then he has recorded his dreams. There are three volumes, carefully indexed. He lifts them from the shelf. "There are all kinds of characters in here and I thought at one point of doing a mock book about the people I've met."[5]

On another shelf is a neat row of small hardbound books—the old Nelson Sevenpenny series. He has been collecting them over the years, hunting them out in secondhand bookstores. It's the excitement of the search, the surprise of discovery that he enjoys. "My happiest dreams," he says cheerfully, "are of finding old Nelson Sevenpennies. I think if I hadn't been a writer, I would have liked to have been a secondhand bookseller."

The struggles of his early years as a writer (his publishers dared print only 3,000 copies of The Power and the Glory, his 10th novel) are long over, but for Greene success is an uneasy word. "There's a line from 'Dauber' a poem by John Masefield, that I've often quoted: 'The long despair of doing nothing well.' There's a little bit of that feeling."

"For a writer as much as for a priest," Greene once wrote, "there is no such thing as success."[6] "The priest," he says now, "can never come close enough to his own idea of sanctity, and a writer can't get close enough to writing well in his own eyes. There's always that ambition to do the perfect book. There's always that failure.

"I think I've changed as a writer. I've simplified, simplified, simplified. What I would like is to achieve an unnoticeable style."

Greene has often been called a Catholic writer. The label exasperates him. He converted to Catholicism when he was 22, before any of his novels had been published. It was not until *Brighton Rock* (his sixth book)[7] that anyone took notice of his faith or began to confuse it with the beliefs of the characters. He is not a Catholic writer, he protests, but a writer who happens to be a Catholic.

Greene does however make a claim for the value of a "religious sense" in fiction. It is something he has long admired in the great 19th century novelists, in Henry James, in Evelyn Waugh. "I think the religious sense does emphasise the importance of the human act. It's not Catholicism, it's simply a faith in the possibility that we have eternal importance. A religious sense makes the individual more important and therefore it helps to put the character on the page."[8]

Faith in itself is an intermittent thing for Greene. "It's like Browning's poem 'Bishop Blougram's Apology.' You call the chessboard black and I call it white. You have moments of faith diversified by doubt, or moments of doubt diversified by faith. I think my moments of faith decrease rather than increase. I think that to hope is as far as one can go. Catholicism has given me a standard of failure, not a standard of success. I don't mean in a literary way — I know where I've gone right and wrong in a book. But one thinks of what one could have done and hasn't, of the suffering one has caused, the failure one has had in human relationships. At least that's what I think of at night in bed before sleep."

Extracted from Louise Dennys, "The Greene Factor," *Sunday Telegraph*, 12 March 1978, 14.

Notes

1. Greene believes that the unconscious is that "part of the mind which nourishes creativity." See *The Other Man*, 15.

2. In an essay on Walter de la Mare's short stories, Greene writes: "Every creative writer worth our consideration, every writer who can be called in the wide eighteenth-century use of the term a poet, is a victim: a man given over to an obsession." *Collected Essays*, 141.

3. "Reflections on the Character of Kim Philby," *Esquire*, September 1968, 111.

4. Both J.W. Lambert, "The Private World of Graham Greene," p. 270 and Michael Meyer, "Greene Test," *Listener*, 3 January 1980, p. 10, describe this episode in more detail.

5. "Eight hundred pages, begun in 1965 and ended in 1989," is how Greene describes it in his introduction to *A World of My Own: A Dream Diary*, published posthumously, with a foreword by his friend and companion, Yvonne Cloetta (London: Reinhardt Books; Toronto: Alfred A. Knopf Canada, 1992). For Greene's interest in dreams, see note 2 on p. 18 of the Claud Cockburn excerpt, "An Early and Incipient Fascination with Dreams."

6. "The Soupsweet Land," *Collected Essays*, 463. Greene argues that for a writer "success is always temporary, success is only delayed failure." *A Sort of Life*, 215.

7. *Brighton Rock* (1938) is Greene's sixth published *novel* if one excludes *The Name of Action* and *Rumour at Nightfall* which Greene withdrew from circulation. Two other books, *The*

Basement Room and Other Stories (1935) and *Journey Without Maps* (1936), had also been published by 1938.

8. According to Greene, it is the "religious sense" that saves James's novels from "deepest cynicism" and lends the "importance of the supernatural" to the struggle between the "beautiful and [the] treacherous." *Collected Essays*, 50.

Graham Greene into the Light

V. S. Pritchett

. . . If he does settle for a month or two, he will be either in a flat in Paris or Antibes, and that is where I caught him. On the telephone the flat, conspiratorial, laughing voice which, of itself, makes him the best company I've known in the past 40 years, welcomed me as usual with a quotation. He'd just found the right words in Conrad for his state of mind. He had done no work for weeks — he was waiting for his new novel, *The Human Factor*, to appear — and "felt the leaden weight of an irremediable idleness." Writers love words: the word "irremediable" spoken with his curious near-French "r" and its overtones of glee in being beyond hope, was Greene in vintage condition. He is a quarter Scottish: Robert Louis Stevenson was his mother's cousin and the Balfours were close to his family; he has a D. Litt. from Edinburgh if he has also one from Cambridge and is a Companion of Honour.[1] For a writer, only the Order of Merit could be better.[2]

Still, he is a Londoner through and through. I see him as one of those tall, long-legged Englishmen, wearing the dark grey suits of club members and a look of misleading anonymity common to members of the professional class, coming out of White's, the Reform or the Athenaeum.[3] They are the natives of that state-within-a-state which lies between Pall Mall, St. James's and Albany—where he used to live—and which extends to the rather bohemian neighbourhood of Covent Garden. On the way there, if you dropped into Rule's Restaurant,[4] you might see him lunching with his brother, Sir Hugh Greene.[5]

The only difference between Greene's London appearance and his Antibes look was that he was wearing a discreetly modish casual brown suit, something between a track suit or battle dress, fastening with a drawstring cord at the neck. When we met, we swore we had not changed at all over the years and boasted about our ages and good health, as old codgers in their seventies do. We had reached the decade when every birthday had better strike a note of farce, especially in my case. I am four years older than he.

The flats are spacious and functional, exactly the place for a man living and working a good deal alone. The sitting room where he worked is as simple as an office. Close to the large ceiling-to-floor window was a small table with nothing on it but a toy wooly animal—a squirrel or rabbit, perhaps—two or three folders, a lamp and nothing else. "Doesn't it tire your eyes working straight into the light and the blinding white paint of the yachts?"

"You get used to it," he said. "What tires my eyes is continuously looking at my characters."

On the pale, dun-coloured walls of the room are a few pictures of the bleak and sensitive kind, one abstract exploding with colour and a droll print of Lunardi making his ascent in a balloon in 1789. On the other two walls there are, I would say, 2,000 books on the white shelves, in very orderly regiments, many complete editions. He has several thousand more in his flat in Paris. (He keeps his poetry there: he can quote large chunks of Clough, Browning and Hardy.) Greene is not only a writer and a vast reader, he used to be a director of the Bodley Head,[6] and knows his titles, dates and first editions. He is more interested in the trade of literature than most authors are and is something of a collector of curiosities: he has, for example, "collected" a long line of the famous little red Nelson's Sevenpenny hardbacks we used to buy about 1910 and feels as sentimental about them as I do. He is very proud of a vituperative attack on his Haitian novel and himself, which the Haitian government sent out to all their embassies, in a large splashy volume.[7]

At 73, Graham is lithe and has the shyness of genially subversive men. His grey hair is short and his head bald here and there. If there are deep rings under his eyes, the eyes are blue, red-rimmed, intent and parrying—the eyes of a fencer. The florid patterns on the pale face are now more sculpted, nothing slack there. For the first time I noticed his hands: they are strong and narrow, as capable as a craftsman's, and the fingers are extraordinarily powerful and long. The voice is as it always was: it has grit in it; there is the pleasant sound of a good razor blade on a beard when a barber is at work—a Sweeney Todd, but on holiday. The human nose usually conveys that it is living an independent life of its own: his is neat, pink at the tip and evidently alert for textual error.

He is a man of the fixed habits of one who lives a good deal alone. Breakfast is quickly over, he picks up a pen and starts work soon after 8 a.m., spends the next two or three hours slowly writing his daily 200 words—only 200 now he complains, it used to be 400. "Do you find one gets slower? Two or three years to finish a book?" (I do.) He slips out to a restaurant—his favourite one is closed for January—for the main meal of the day, sometimes with one or two of his French friends. He eats very little. At the other meal probably he will simply eat a little pâté at home. At this cold time of the year, he drinks Kir rather than pastis[8] and, of course, wine. The meat at Antibes is only so-so, but duck, rabbit and fish are good, especially the loup de mer grilled with fennel. He would really prefer a good English chop, and he is rather off garlic nowadays.

In the afternoon there is the siesta. And then he'll spend an evening with a French couple now and then, playing gin rummy with them. Sometimes they drive him out to one of the good Provençal restaurants in the hills behind Nice. But most days he will be revising his 200 words, covering the hand-written manuscript with a Balzacian spider's web of corrections. That is when ideas develop. He is not a torrential writer; every paragraph has to be exact and settled. He then reads his pages into the dicta-phone Alexander Korda[9] gave him and eventually sends a bundle of tapes to England, where they will be typed. He hates the noise of a typewriter. In view of the delays and strikes of the French post office, his method sounds risky.

"You prefer the foreign political crises to the English ones?"

"English parliamentary politics don't interest me, but my new book is set in London. One makes small irritating mistakes. I mentioned buses going down St. James's when now they go up. I had to put that right."

"Why do you travel so much?"

"To kill boredom."

Boredom? the most ingenious, inventive and exciting of our novelists, rich in exactly etched and moving portraits of real human beings and who understands the tragic and comic ironies of love, loyalty and belief—is he really bored? Or is he putting on a defensive mask? I know him as an affectionate and interested man.

I think Greene feels the boredom of all writers who live by their imagination. You finish your story, the people vanish, emptiness flows in. He travels to re-populate himself and he has an appetite for experience and especially for out-of-the-way people. For example, he is an astute collector of picaresque priests. In the last two or three years he has been going to the north of Spain with an eccentric cleric[10] whose chief interest is in discovering peculiar vintages of white wine. They have a rollicking time.

Now, he says, he is probably "a manic depressive." Many writers are: the profession is very hard on the nerves; one catches fire at the beginning of the day and burns out by the end of it. The paradox is that he sprang out of a jolly and very intelligent family, indeed a whole clan of congenial successful Greenes, all very close and proud of one another.

"There is often a child in your novels who finds himself exposed to pain or is the witness of corruption—the private detective's son, for example, in *The End of the Affair* or the boy of *The Basement Room*."

"I made a point of visiting a private detective's office," he told me years ago. To see for himself is necessary to him.

Still, he has written books for children.[11]

And a fine essay of his called *The Lost Childhood* shows childhood was as important to him as it is to most artists. He quotes from a poem of Æ[12] which goes to his own heart:

In ancient shadows and twilights
Where childhood has strayed
The world's great sorrows were born
And its heroes were made.
In the lost boyhood of Judas
Christ was betrayed.

～

But the loner and the writer was too restless for the bonds of family life, and after 20 years the marriage broke up. Precisely why—he thinks rightly—is his private business. One can only guess that the need for what Benjamin Constant[13] called "the wilderness of my liberty" is very strong in him and that his work is his overwhelming passion. Once or twice, he has said, he half-wished he could have had the dedication of a priest or even to have been a sinner-turned-saint.

But, in his honest way, he now says his conversion was really a sort of gamble with God and the Church. His actual induction into the Church depressed him. He found himself making secret reservations as he made his vows. The theology had its fascination, for he hated Calvinism, as his hero Robert Louis Stevenson had done: it was enjoyable for the Protestant to feel now that the English Catholics had been "disloyal" and "traitors" and that, morally, English Protestants put the satisfactions of knowing right from wrong before the Catholic preoccupation with good and evil. Also, one must remember, only 10 per cent of the English population is Catholic—he knows that 10 per cent is a lot—and a large proportion of those are Irish "rebels." Characteristically, Greene had chosen a minority. This cheered him, and in his early years as a Catholic writer, he was very much the fighting convert.

But the lasting result of his conversion can be seen in a letter he wrote to me in 1948—published in a correspondence
between his great friend Elizabeth Bowen and myself.[14]

"You used to strike us as a very Protestant Catholic, a sort
of Jansenist," I said.

"No, I wasn't," he said, and, holding his arms above his
head, added, "In the Jansenist picture of the Crucifixion,
the arms are raised above the head."

I did not know this.

"We thought Mauriac influenced you."

"I didn't read him until long after I had started writing
novels as a Catholic and even then I wasn't thought of as
a 'Catholic novelist' until *Brighton Rock*."

"It was very explicit there. You couldn't stand the
Protestant barmaid who was out for justice."

"Yes, I underlined too much in that book, and I did the
same in *The Heart of the Matter*. It's my most popular book
but I don't like it any longer. I don't like many English
Catholics. I don't like conventional religious piety. I'm
more at ease with the Catholicism of Catholic countries.
I've always found it difficult to believe in God. I suppose
I'd now call myself a Catholic atheist. The English
Catholic I admire is Alexander Pope."

"A rather privileged and discreet Catholic in a rational
age?"

"And Newman of course," he said. "As a writer I have
often been criticized by the pious. Cardinal Newman
answers them."

He put his case more thoughtfully when he wrote of his
conversion: "Later we may become hardened to the formu-
las of confession and sceptical about ourselves: we may only
half-intend to keep the promises we make, until continual

failure or the circumstances of our private life finally make it impossible to make any promises at all, and many of us abandon Confession and Communion to join the Foreign Legion of the Church and fight for a city of which we are no longer full citizens."

"I travel because I have to see the scene," he said. "I can't invent it." (That line of brown fume or cloud which marks the Paraguayan frontier in *The Honorary Consul*[15] had to be seen in order to evoke a country by a sentence.) "Some of my travel has been by invitation or accident. I don't always write about places I go to. I went to Kenya at the time of the Mau Mau but I didn't write a novel about that. I can't go to Chile because I was a friend of Allende. I walked across the Liberia long before the war; it was only when I was stuck in the Secret Service during the war that I started *The Heart of the Matter*. Often an unlikely dream will start me on a book or a story. *It's a Battlefield*, which you praised, was started by a dream."

He went to a Catholic psychiatrist once when he had a writer's block and was told to write down his dreams. That started him off again and he has always written down his dreams since. "I've got a book of them." Querry's dream of a lost priesthood and the search for sacramental wine in *The* [sic] *Burnt-Out Case* was the exact account of a dream he had when writing the book.

Technical questions are what pre-occupy him most now. He doesn't write with a film in view; the novel is a much richer form—but perhaps he has learnt something from cutting and visualizing his story. In his Conradian days his style stultified the characters and narrative. They did not move. He had to cut out this influence before he could master scenes of action. Action has to be clean; no adjectives. If a book is started in the wrong way, it will never be finished. One has to hesitate a long time before plunging in, but by the time you have spent two years living with a book, you come to terms with your unconscious and you know the end.

"You have the art of seeming to be personal in your books. You have even made your narrator a novelist in *The End of the Affair*, particularly; also in *The Comedians*, the opinions of the narrator, like that aphorism about violence and indifference, seem to be your own," I said. "What Turgenev called the novelist's privilege of private self-castigation."

"Well, I am not the son of a bankrupt speculator who has never known his father and whose mother is a tart! A novelist can easily unself himself. He can write as a woman or a child. The opinions in my novels are not mine: they are the opinions of my characters. Readers are very stupid about this. I do not take people straight from real life in my novels. A novel is not a work of travel or auto-biography. (Even these are re-creations.) I shall never write my own reminiscences because I have a poor memory. Real people are crowded out by imaginary ones, that is why I have to stare at them for so long. There has once or twice been a little straight reporting in my novels — there was some in *The Quiet American*, but no real people. Real people would wreck the design. The characters in my novels are an amalgam of bits of real people; one takes isolated traits from many; they are fused by the heat of the unconscious. Real people are too limiting."

"I remember that in *The Quiet American* there was a Buddha in the room. I thought it made the God look rather dubious. Some think *The Quiet American* is your best book."

"The innocence of Pyle gave me an exaggerated dislike of America, that was a fault. I prefer *The Honorary Consul.*"

There was talk of brothels—they crop up a lot in his talk.

"I have been reading *Clarissa.*[16] The brothel scene is wonderful," he said. "People say Lovelace was a devil. He is a magnificent and unique character and such a witty talker."

"Not the devil; but he did want to destroy Clarissa, didn't he?" I said.

"Only," he snapped back, "because she put too high a price on her virtue."

That brought us to love and sex. He said he was not good about "in love"—no D. H. Lawrence in him—but he is far more interested in the habits, circumstances, quarrels and jealousies of ordinary love. Brown's love in Haiti is wrecked by nagging jealousy, touchiness and egoism. The girl prefers the shady and lying con man who has the merit of being easily human; he can make her laugh. He can even make her dull husband and her tiresome child laugh.[17]

The peculiar attraction of husband and lover for each other is a frequent theme. He is alert to the love affair that is also a hate affair. *The End of the Affair* is a hate affair which has its happy sexual scene, but it is conditioned by the fears of the doodlebug[18] period in London and the lover's suspicions and malice. He records the irony by which relationships turn into their opposites. Cynicism turns into compassion or pity becomes cruel. We must not be too sure of our virtue; charity he admires most, and tolerance of the inescapable mingling of good and evil.

We debated the handling of sexual scenes. There is a close relation between a writer's sexual life and the creative imagination, for him as for myself. The danger which the modern novelist runs into in evoking the sexual act is that the act is so strong a subject that it may unbalance a scene or book, if not managed with care. He hates Genet,[19] for instance; but is not against pornography. *Fanny Hill*, for example, is elegant, well-mannered and is about the baroque quality of sexual fantasy. He mentioned a pornographic story he had read to some of us 20 years ago at his house in Anacapri. It was really about secrecy and the hurt of innocence as far as I can remember it.

How shall we sum up Greene as a person? One side of this man with the sad tolerant mind is a joker. In daily life he is a great practical joker who delights in risky pranks with a thrill in them. He once, for a lark, stole some letters sticking out of the letter box of a London sex shop, dashed off to a club to read them hoping to find some sexual revelations, found them dull and then, characteristically, enjoyed the alarm of trying to stuff them back in the letter box unseen.

Tired of fashionable clubs, he joined a moribund one because "it was the only place, in those days, where one could get a bed to sleep in in the afternoon." Also, people had torn pages out of the out-of-date *Who's Who*. He liked that. But he is not a roaring bohemian or an exhibitionist. He likes belonging to the opposition, to be the odd man out, and to make his own flesh creep.

And to laugh. The world is too complacent. Let us catch it out. And don't run away with the idea that he is a cynic or a mocker or a man in a temper: he is a very gentle, serious, self-centered enquiring artist, and a man of great charity.

Extracted from V. S. Pritchett, "Graham Greene into the Light," *Times*, 18 March 1978, 6–7.

Notes

1. Greene was awarded the D. Litt. from Cambridge in 1962 and from Edinburgh in 1967. He was named Companion of Honour in 1966.
2. Greene was awarded the Order of Merit in 1986.
3. Three old and distinguished "gentlemen's" clubs in London: White's, on St. James's Street, was established in 1693; the Athenaum and the Reform are both in Pall Mall and were established in 1834 and 1836, respectively.
4. Rule's, established in 1798, is located at 25 Maiden Lane. Among its distinguished patrons—mostly actors and actresses and writers—were Charles Dickens, H. G. Wells, and Edward VII.
5. Sir Hugh Carlton Greene (1910–87) was Graham Greene's younger brother. Following school at Berkhamsted, he went to Merton College. After coming down from Oxford in 1935, he worked as newspaper correspondent for several London papers. In 1939 he joined the BBC and later served as director general from 1960 to 1969. He was an avid collector of first editions of early detective novels and edited with Graham Greene *The Spy's Bedside Book* (London: Hart-Davis, 1957) and *Victorian Villainies* (London: Viking Press, 1984; New York: Viking Press, 1985). See his "Childhood with Graham," *Adam International Review* 46, nos. 446–48 (1984): 8–14.
6. Greene was one of the directors of the Bodley Head from 1958 to 1968.
7. *Graham Greene demasqué. Bulletin du Departement des Affaires Étrangères* (Port-au-Prince, 1968). The English version is entitled *Graham Greene Finally Exposed.*
8. Kir is a drink made of white wine and a liqueur de cassis; pastis is an aniseed apéritif.
9. The Hungarian born producer whom Greene first met in 1936. See note 6 on p. 42 of the J. Maclaren-Ross excerpt, "Excursions in Greene Land."
10. Presumably, Father Leopoldo Duran, a Spanish Jesuit scholar who accompanied Greene on his journeys through Spain for several years. See *Adam* 46, nos. 446–48 (1984): 7. Father Duran has written extensively on the subject of the priesthood in Greene's works.

11. Greene has published four children's books: *The Little Train* (London: Eyre and Spottiswoode, 1946; New York: Lothrop, Lee, and Shepard, 1958), *The Little Fire Engine* (London: Eyre and Spottiswoode, 1950; New York: Lothrop, Lee, and Shepard, 1953), *The Little Horse Bus* (London: Max Parrish, 1952; New York: Lothrop, Lee, and Shepard, 1954), and *The Little Steamroller* (London: Max Parrish, 1953; New York: Lothrop, Lee, and Shepard, 1955).

12. "Æ" [George William Russell] (1867–1935), Irish poet and writer.

13. Benjamin Constant de Rebecque (1767–1830), French novelist and philosopher, mostly remembered for his intellectual and passionate liaisons, especially with Mme de Staël.

14. Greene, *Why Do I Write?*

15. "The years had changed nothing except by adding the line of smoke which . . . had not yet been hung out along the horizon on the far side of the Paraná." *The Honorary Consul*, 9.

16. This is Samuel Richardson's masterpiece of 1748.

17. In *The Comedians*, Brown's impotence sometimes "lay in his body like a curse which it needed a witch to raise" (154). Later in the novel, Martha somehow fancies Jones.

18. World War II slang for flying bombs, the German "Vergeltungswaffe," the self-propelled projectiles used by the Germans in the latter years of the war to bomb London. The dreaded V1 and V2 rockets feature in *The End of the Affair*.

19. Jean Genet (1910–86), French novelist and black-comedy playwright, wrote about the criminal underworld and expressed a profoundly pessimistic outlook.

Graham Greene: Our Man in Antibes

Gloria Emerson

. . . Mr. Greene is now seventy-three: there is nothing very old or very sad about him. He does not even have a cough or a tremble. I had not known he has such a wonderful smile; perhaps women always try to make him laugh, and are pleased when they do. But it is hard, even for the brashest or the most respectful, to know what to say at first to the Englishman who has written so often, like no one else, of deceit and love, of divided loyalties, of the sick conscience, of honor and of the havoc it can bring, of pity and the admission of failure that changes people as much as a gas that reaches the lungs.

"I used to feel a certain homesickness for Vietnam until the American war," Mr. Greene said. "It would have been too depressing . . . it would have been difficult feeling completely against one side. One wants to have a certain sympathy. I used to feel homesick for Africa but now Africa has gotten into such a mess. How many African countries now are not dictatorships? The African dictator has not been a very pleasant man so far." He gave the names of some unpleasant men for he is well informed. There is a television set in the living room, with its two walls of books, the oil painting that Fidel Castro gave him hanging above a couch clearly past any prime. He likes to see the evening news from Paris at 7:45; he waits for foreign reports and there is never much.

"France is the most insular country in the world," he said. A Haitian painting is in the hall but there is nothing from Asia and his Vietnam library is in his Paris apartment. *The Quiet American,* published in the United States in 1956, was not well received. A. J. Liebling wrote a review for the *New Yorker,*[1] in the voice of an outraged patriot. . . .

~

"Nobody liked it in America at the time. They only began to like it when they became involved. Then I got lots of nice letters from people and correspondents who were there. But before that I don't think I had any good reviews when it came out in America," Mr. Greene said of his novel.[2] "My publisher, Harold Guinzburg, was alive in those days. He wrote me an absurd letter saying, 'On page so-and-so I think you've made a little bit of an error because your character [the English reporter, Fowler] . . . compares colonialism with the colonialism of America. As I understand colonialism I think what you should have said was dollar diplomacy—because, after all, colonialism in my eyes is taking possession of something on which you haven't got a land frontier. . . .' And I wrote back and said, 'But have you got a land frontier with Hawaii? With the Philippines in the old days? With Puerto Rico today? Don't you call what the Russians have done with Estonia and Latvia colonialism?'

"He wrote back and said, 'Oh well, I accept that it's an English character speaking and they don't understand. . . .'"

Boredom—his name for the relentless enemy that has stalked him everywhere—has lessened with age, Mr. Greene said. He has described, in terrible detail, the peculiar torture it once caused him. A young, and more despairing, Graham Greene found his boredom so unbearable that, in 1923, he played Russian roulette, alone, with a loaded revolver "to make the discovery that it was possible to enjoy again the visible world by risking its total loss." It was boredom, too, that made Mr. Greene once insist that a dentist extract a healthy tooth because he so wanted the ether that was used. And it has pushed him to witness and write about foreign wars, to still travel like a man both pursued and in pursuit.

"I get restless if I'm in the same place too long . . . it may be an effect of the war. One was cooped up in England, except for the period in Africa, one couldn't travel to Europe at all," he said.

"My favorite now," I said of *The Honorary Consul*, remembering Father Rivas, the revolutionary priest who leaves the church, ashamed to have to preach the Gospel in the barrio while the diocesan archbishop gorged with the fat army general, and drank French wine. The priest, with other men, plans to kidnap the American ambassador in Buenos Aires and to ask for certain prisoners as ransom. The dilemmas—theological, social, political—that confront Father Rivas confront priests throughout Latin America and political kidnappings now are common. He is eerily ahead of the times.

"So is it mine," he replied, perhaps relieved to be praised for recent work not one of the early novels,[3] although he is hardly displeased that *Brighton Rock* (1938) has sold more than a million copies in paperback. Mr.

Greene said that he had asked a friend, a Spanish priest who teaches English literature,[4] if he had not found the character of Father Rivas "a little bit off the rails."

"But he said, 'Not a bit of it, not a bit of it—perfectly Catholic, perfectly acceptable,'" Mr. Greene said. "You know, Father What's-His-Name in *The Honorary Consul* had the idea of a night side of God and a day side of God, you know—God's evolution and God as evil. God and the Devil are the same person. I invent this for him because he's got to have his theology, as it were, as he had left the church and married. Well, I thought it would probably not be acceptable to the Catholic Church."[5]

What is forgotten about Greene Land—a name he intensely dislikes—is that people in it are often heroic, have humor, make choices even if they are wrong, and are sometimes braver than most. His characters demand our respect and they always have his. It was once said of Mr. Greene that he spent his life looking for hell and always found it again in each new novel. But it is a hell with real prisons, real huts, real diseases and real fear.

He thought the term "Greene Land" had been first used by a man who used to write rather good novels, who was at Oxford the same years he was there.[6]

"It irritates me," he said. "I want to say—BUT THESE THINGS HAPPEN. IT'S NOT RURITANIA."

He did go back to Panama last summer after all and he did come to the United States although no one here knew it. Perhaps it is what he wanted. In September a letter from Antibes explained: "I did enter America as the general [Torrijos] wanted me to go to the signing of the treaty and I went to Washington with a Panamanian passport and

returned by Concorde—a terrible disappointment. The
food was worse than the average tourist class and the only
advantage I could see in it was speed and who wants to be
as speedy as that."

The treaty between Panama and the United States, trans-
ferring the canal to the Panamanians by the year 2000, was
signed with immense fanfare during three days last June of
meetings, parties and grinning. Some 2000 people—including a foreign fascist or two, a group of the most powerful
U. S. senators and the Joint Chiefs of Staff no less—were
unaware that in their midst at the ceremony in Washington
was the celebrated novelist, the radical Catholic, whose
political views remain the same as those he expressed in a
letter to the *Times* of London ten years ago: *If I had to choose
between life in the Soviet Union and life in the United States I
would certainly choose the Soviet Union just as I would choose
life in Cuba to life in those southern American republics, like
Bolivia, dominated by their northern neighbor. . . .*

It probably delighted him to go unnoticed—he prefers
it. That day in Washington, he was not awed by the company he kept. "It was curious seeing the all-star cast at the
signing," he wrote. "The only star who seemed to be missing was Elizabeth Taylor. Two rows in front of me was
Andy Young and five rows in front all in a row were
Kissinger, Nelson Rockfeller, Ladybird, Ford, Mrs.
Carter and Mondale. Somehow these political stars all
seem to be like dwarfs when you see them in the flesh."[7]

The Human Factor is not a novel with his usual fine touches
of wit (even *The Quiet American* had a funny scene, there
was humor in *The Comedians*) but he thinks perhaps the
critics will not grieve. For two earlier books, a collection of
stories called *May We Borrow Your Husband?* (1967) and a

hilarious novel, *Travels with My Aunt* (1969), were comedies that went largely unappreciated. He thinks he knows why.

"The critics—well, they certainly don't like me to be funny," he said. "They want one to stick to Greene Land. And of course they are apt to complain of the Catholic element in my books. Now the Catholic element is very small. It was large in about four books but then it hadn't been large before and it hasn't been large after. But then they rather resent that, I think. I can't help reading the notices [reviews]. Bad ones don't awfully depress me because they're written by people I don't have any opinion of. The good ones sometimes cheer me up."

"There's no such thing as success for a writer and priest," I said, quoting Graham Greene to Mr. Greene.[8]

"There isn't a success that one can settle on."

There was a time when Mr. Greene liked danger, felt cheerful facing it, thrived on the threats of ambushes on the road, and said so. But fear is one thing, he said, it can have sexual overtones, but terror and panic are something else: hateful and sickening. You lose all reason. He still remembers a night on patrol with French paratroopers in the north of Vietnam, in Phat Diem, finding himself separated, lost, uncertain of who was closer, the Viet Minh or the French. But much worse than that, he said, was seeing a bat with a broken wing fluttering on the ground in the passage of a temple in Angkor Wat: there was no exhilaration of danger to that, just terror and sickness. The bat caused him more anxiety than war, as bats did in the Congo, when he was on a small steamer and saw a cloud of them trailing the boat.

"And birds—yes, birds, too. If a bird was in this room I'd freeze. When I was very young and being patronized by a rather bad writer—who invited me down to stay with her in the country—at the first lunch a bird flew in at the window and I got under the table. It didn't do much for my ego.

"But one can deal with fear, can't one? Fear is something that can go on and on several hours—and then one gets bored with it. One gets bored with it and then one loses it. Because it becomes just boring."

He is still pushed to see if danger is different, in the meanest and saddest of places. It was Graham Greene, of course, obsessed with espionage, who first noted that the novelist and the spy have something in common: both are always watching, overhearing, seeking motives, analyzing character. He is, in some ways, the best sort of spy, a man forever investigating the weather of the soul.

"I went to Belfast last year for five days only. But I must say I was more frightened than I've ever been in Indochina or during the blitz or anything. Because I felt in a very ambiguous position, you see. I came purely out of curiosity. The government let me have a car and a driver. All the numbers of government cars are known, of course. And I was a Catholic and therefore a traitor from the IRA point of view. . . . And my past, I felt, was against me, I mean being in MI6. It was terribly depressing. I went on down to Dublin and it was like heaven. I mean, seeing the girls sitting on the grass with their boyfriends. . . ."

The famous anti-Americanism of Graham Greene—which now seems very mild compared to the real thing—has been exaggerated, although he has had good reason, aside from Shirley Temple, to find us a peculiar and menacing people.

⌇

Many of his admirers in this country think Graham Greene remained silent during the American war in Vietnam, sensing there was nothing he could do after having sent out the first great warning in his novel. Not quite: he resigned from the National Institute of Arts and Letters and the American Academy of Arts and Letters—those prestigious institutions in New York—and also tried to persuade other foreign members to join a mass resignation. And some did although a number considered that the war was not an affair with which a cultural body need concern itself. In his own letter of resignation, Mr. Greene wrote ". . . I disagree profoundly with the idea that the Academy is not concerned. I have tried to put myself in the position of a foreign honorary member of a German Academy of Arts and Letters at the time when Hitler was democratically elected chancellor. Could I have continued to consider as an honor a membership conferred in happier days?"

During a visit to Chile, when the late Salvador Allende was president, he received a telephone call on his first night in Santiago. We're waiting for you, said an American voice.

At intervals, when he has not been able to work, Mr. Greene keeps a diary of his dreams, so as "to keep my hand in." He indexes them very carefully.

He thought he had only voted once in his life for a "half-Socialism," which didn't seem to work and now he is not sure he would vote Communist. We were talking about the Stalinist years in the Soviet Union, when he said: "In a curious way, it may be easier for a Catholic to mentally survive that because we went through our Stalinist periods, thousands of them—Torquemada and the Spanish Inquisition. But it didn't alter the fundamental idea, as it were. And so"—he gave his small smile—"one still has the hopeless hope of a human face of Communism."

There is only one of his books, *The Heart of the Matter*, which seems to irritate, and after it came out, he received disturbing mail, some from people inviting him to shed his blood for Christ which he did not feel like doing. The source of irritation is Scobie, a very decent policeman in West Africa, who is unfaithful to his wife with a young girl, a child really, rescued in a shipwreck and, in the end, Scobie betrays them all and God as well by killing himself.

"There's something wrong with it, that's why I don't like it," Mr. Greene said. "It carries a kind of Protestant exaggeration, which makes people say that he's saintly. That was not the intention at all, he's meant to be a man suffering from pride. I'd done another book, *The Ministry of Fear*, which is where one talks about pity—pity bombing cities, pity killing. And Scobie was an extension of that idea. And pity is a sense of superiority, isn't it? Unlike compassion. You have compassion for an equal but you have pity for somebody you consider to be inferior, don't you think?"

In Antibes I had a room at the little Hotel Royal, where Graham Greene had once stayed, which is only a short walk to his apartment. I made fun of the room to him: there was no space at all because of a huge spongy bed which felt like a mountain of damp American bread. He was very fond of the hotel, however, and said he had been quite happy there. Then, suddenly, he told a very small sad story, as a person might suddenly hand you a snapshot or an old letter for no discernible reason. It happened years ago: Mr. Greene was checking out of the Hotel Royal to make a plane. The bill was not ready. He began to fuss. Mademoiselle Koepel, a beguiling French woman who still runs the front desk and manages to conceal the fact she is overworked, was too slow for him that day. Mr. Greene lost his temper and spoke so sharply to her that at the airport he called to tell her how sorry he was. He remembers it all. It is not just the small cruelties of other people that cause him pain.

Extracted from Gloria Emerson, "Graham Greene: Our Man in Antibes," *Rolling Stone*, 9 March 1978, 45–49.

Notes
1. A. J. Liebling, "A Talkative Something-or-Other," *New Yorker*, 7 April 1956, 136–42.
2. See note 2 on pp. 217–18 of the Israel Shenker excerpt, "Graham Greene at Sixty-six."
3. In 1968, he admitted to Christopher Burstall that *The Power and the Glory* was his "best" book "by a long shot." See "Graham Greene Takes the Orient Express," *Listener*, 21 November 1968, 672–74.
4. Presumably Father Leopoldo Duran with whom Greene traveled periodically in Spain.
5. See *The Honorary Consul* (383–87) for Father Rivas's understanding of God.
6. Arthur Calder-Marshall, "The Works of Graham Greene," *Horizon* 1, no. 5 (May 1940): 367–75.
7. Greene describes the "Great Spectacular" of the signing in *Getting to Know the General*, 120–25.
8. "How could they tell that for a writer as much as for a priest there is no such thing as success." *Collected Essays*, 463.

Graham Greene's Other Island

Pierre Joannon

PIERRE JOANNON: *Your first visit to Ireland was in 1923, just after the Civil War. What were your impressions?*

GRAHAM GREENE: It seems very distant now. I went with a cousin and we walked from Dublin to Waterford. The impression remains of broken bridges all the way along the route. It was a week after De Valera[1] had issued his order to dump arms. We didn't find any enmity except in one town where people threw a few stones at us on the road and in a pub where the owner pretended that there was no food, although we could notice people eating eggs and bacon. That was all.

As a young undergraduate, I had no introduction whatsoever.[2] We knew nobody. We did stop at the house of, I think it was, the poet Katharine Tynan on our way down. She was living quite contentedly in a rather big house but she was boycotted by the local people who claimed that there was a ghost in her drive. They didn't wish to offend her by giving any other reason.

But of course it is very dim in my memory now. I wrote an article on my first impressions of Dublin in a paper called *The Saturday Westminster* which was a very good weekly paper of the period: I suppose it was one of the first things that I ever got published.[3]

PJ: *You went to Northern Ireland in 1977 to see the present troubles for yourself. Again, what were your impressions?*

GG: I was horrified. It was to me a situation far worse than the one I experienced during the London Blitz. How people could go on living under that tension is something I found really extraordinary.

I saw people from various stratas. I met the Protestant Bishop of Londonderry. I spent a long day with Gerry Fitt[4] whom I admire extremely. I met a senior member of the Alliance Party,[5] an Irish poet, some students and scholars, businessmen, etc. . . .

PJ: *As a stranger, did you have the feeling that you were personally in danger?*

GG: Well, I felt uneasy because I was an English Catholic with little sympathy for the Provisional I.R.A. Also, as you know, I had been in the Secret Service during the war and people wrongly say that one never leaves the Secret Service. Last but not least, I was lent a government car by the then Labour Government because I had asked for facilities to see the situation for myself. I had a protestant driver who didn't encourage me to take risks: he too remarked that I would probably be taken for a C.I.D. [Criminal Investigation Department] man. He would drive me a little way into the Falls area, then he would stop the car and say he had better not go any further because after this point it would be difficult to turn if there was any trouble.

PJ: *Being a Catholic yourself, and furthermore an English catholic (I do not say a Catholic writer as I hate this label just as much as you do), do you feel a particular responsibility or a particular interest as far as the Irish problem is concerned? Do you see it in the light of the "religious war" so often referred to in the popular press?*

GG: Well, I certainly feel a personal interest as an Englishman and as a Catholic, and I always have.

I had a romantic feeling for the Old I.R.A. as a boy and for Ireland's struggle for independence. But I think the position today is very different: I can't see any real link between the Provos [Provisional I.R.A.] and the Old I.R.A. I can see no links with a man like Michael Collins[6] who was a hero in my youth. I can see no links with the idealism of a man like Erskine Childers.[7]

In Belfast the easiest way of getting about is to hire a taxi, though you don't take a taxi for yourself, you rather "join" a taxi in which you find yourself with four or five people and possibly a chicken, and pay only your share of the price. Well, I was warned not to take a taxi, because all the taxis were owned by the Provos (I suppose that is why the authorities lent me a car). Most of the big self-service stores were also owned by the Provos. Many small shopkeepers, including Catholics, had been kneecapped because they had refused to pay protection money. It seemed to me that the new Provo I.R.A. was closer to the Chicago gangsters than to the idealism of men like Erskine Childers and my friend Ernie O'Malley.

Furthermore, it can be said that the Old I.R.A. had a mandate from the people. In the General Election of December 1918, out of 105 candidates returned for Ireland, 73 were Republicans. Actually the Provos have no such mandate. They despise the ballot because the electors do

not favour them. And I don't think that the election of
Bobby Sands[8] in the Fermanagh-South Tyrone by-election
invalidates this argument. The result was exaggerated by
the emotional effects of his hunger strike and the deliberately false assumption that to elect him was the only way to
save his life. One wonders what would have happened if
the S.D.L.P.[9] had run a candidate. To offer a choice only
between a Catholic Provo and a hard-line Protestant was
unfair to the Catholic population. And there may have been
also a good deal of terror at work in the figures: in a situation like that, one would have been afraid to abstain from
voting, and who can say that there was no intimidation at
the polling station?

Now, to answer to the last part of your question "How
far is there a religious element in the situation?" my opinion is that religion is being used as a mean of propaganda
or the description of a social condition. The U.D.A. and
the Provos are not engaged in a religious war. It is a war of
political power and what goes with political power: money.

PJ: *Is this statement of yours* [Mr. Maudling[10] or his successor will sit down over the coffee and the sandwiches
with representatives of Eire and Stormont,[11] of the I.R.A.
and the Provisional I.R.A., to discuss with no preordained
conditions changes in the constitution and in the borders
of Ulster. Why not now rather than later?] *still valid after
ten years or would you say that you have changed your mind?*

GG: I feel the situation was very different when I was
writing. I don't think I would say now that it would end
inevitably around a Conference table. I think like Conor
Cruise O'Brien[12] that a redrawing of the Border should be
considered but I don't think the Republic particularly want
that, do they? Also I do not think that Britain should leave

Northern Ireland precipitately. I do think that the troops are necessary there for the time being. My opinion has rather altered since Maudling's time, I must say, with the course of events and the increase of atrocities and terrorism. At the time when I wrote that letter, terrorism was not so extreme and I think there was a certain idealism left which I no longer believe in on either side. The Provos are not even supported by their countrymen in Eire with whom they say they share the same spiritual Republican faith.

PJ: *In* Doctor Fischer of Geneva, *your hero is tempted to commit suicide. Among the various means to kill himself, he contemplates starvation and quotes the example of Terence McSwiney, the Lord Mayor of Cork,*[13] *adding: "after all, starvation might perhaps be the proper answer, a clean and discreet and private way out." How about the hunger strike as a much publicized and public way out? As a Catholic and a man with a vast experience of—and should I say sympathy for—political dissent all over the world, what is your opinion on the hunger strike for political motives, and especially on the systematic campaign of hunger strike which caused the death of Bobby Sands and his companions in 1981?*

GG: As a Catholic, I don't agree with one of the condemnations of the Catholic Church regarding these hunger strikes. I don't think that a hunger strike is what used to be called a mortal sin. Theologically, suicide was regarded as a mortal sin because it was an expression of despair and I think theologically the Cardinal is perfectly correct in not condemning it. What I think is very condemnable is to allow hooded men in uniforms to fire with guns at a funeral. I would like to see it made a condition of a hunger strike being buried properly in a cemetery that no armed men should be on the scene. But I am not against hunger striking as such. I don't object to it as a method of protest, I only object to the cause in this case. There is another point. What is the psychological condition of the hunger striker as he approaches death? Who are by his bedside? If he wishes to change his mind towards the end, what are the pressures on him to continue? Is he master of himself or is he a puppet?

Terence McSwiney was fighting a good fight, Bobby Sands wasn't. For a young English boy of that period the sacrifice of the Lord Mayor of Cork was part of a very romantic revolution against imperialist England.

PJ: *You rightly recall that a large sector of British public opinion was very hostile to the government during the Black and Tans war,*[14] *which is apparently not the case with the present troubles in Northern Ireland.*

GG: Yes, the opposition was very strong in the twenties. Indeed, it was the protest of the English conscience which forced the government to withdraw the Black and Tans. As far as I am concerned, I suppose I always had a sympathy with attacks on British colonialism. There is a very fine poem by Wilfrid Scawen Blunt[15] who was not an Irishman though he espoused the Irish cause in the 1880s and went to prison in Ireland for his opinions, called "The Wind and the Whirlwind" which I always found very attractive, especially these lines about the defeat of the Egyptian leader by the British troops.[16]

> I care not if you fled. What men call courage
> Is the least noble thing of which they boast.

and then it goes on:

> Oh I would rather fly with the first craven
> Who flung his arms away in your good cause,

Than head the hottest charge by England vaunted
In all the record of her unjust wars!

PJ: *What is the historical or political figure that you admire
most in the Ireland of today or in the last sixty years or so? As
for the character whom you hate most, I suspect that it is the
Reverend Paisley which you describe to Marie-Francoise
Allain, in a fine book of interviews entitled* L'Autre et son
double *(Belfond, 1981), as the "abominable Paisley."*[17]
Abominable in what sense: like Pinkie in Brighton Rock
*who, according to the priest, might be saved at the last
minute, or rather like Papa Doc or Hitler, hopeless cases for
which you recommend the most radical treatment: murder?*

GG: In a way, Hitler seems to me such an obvious mad-
man that perhaps he wins mercy in the end. Paisley is not
mad. I could play you one of his sermons which I taped
while I was in Belfast. He talks about himself as the
Reverend Dr. Paisley, head of a branch of the Presbyterian
Church which he has invented himself. I think he is an
abominable man. A protestant bishop told me a story
about him. He was a young curate in Belfast at the time.
News came to his ears that there was likely to be an attack
on a Catholic area by Orangemen, and with a large number of Protestant clergy he formed a human barrier at the
entrance of the Falls with linked arms. Then suddenly a lot
of drunken Orangemen with sticks appeared with the
intention of marching in. They were faced by their own
Protestant clergy and that made them hesitate. Finally they
began to break up into little groups and the danger passed.
After the danger was over, a tall figure in a mackintosh
arrived at the back and said "Come, follow me fellows, this
is not the way to deal with the Catholics" and marched
them away. Of course, it was Ian Paisley. This is a story I

like. Some less amusing. For instance, it is difficult to forget that in June 1966, long before the actual troubles
began, four young Catholic barmen were riddled with bul-
lets at the Watson's Bar in Malvern Street in the Protestant
Shankill area. These sectarian murders were perpetrated
by members of the Ulster Volunteer Force, a body publicly
associated with Paisley. One of the murderers said at his
trial: "I am sorry I ever heard tell of that man Paisley or
decided to follow him."

PJ: *You have set many novels in troubled lands: Mexico in*
The Power and the Glory; *Haiti in* The Comedians;
Vietnam in The Quiet American; *Cuba in* Our Man in
Havana, *etc. . . But Ireland never inspired you. Why?*

GG: I don't know. Maybe because I have never spent
enough time in Ireland. And maybe because Ireland was
on my doorstep. It's like somebody who lives in a city, a
visitor comes, and he begins to see his city for the first
time. One doesn't know the things on one's doorstep.
Which is one of the reasons why I went to Belfast. It was
absurd: I had been in Malaya during the Emergency, in
Kenya during the Mau Mau rebellion, in Vietnam during
the French war, and I had not even taken a look at what
was going on next door. But it wouldn't be enough to take
a look, I would have to stay a long time to write a book.

PJ: *Ireland is too close. Maybe this is why the "Irish ques-*
tion" was and still is so largely ignored or misunderstood by
the English people. Would you agree?

GG: As far as politics are concerned, that is perhaps
true. But not as far as literature is concerned. Irish writers probably had a better audience in England than in
Southern Ireland, partly due to the censorship there.
Incidentally, four of my books were banned in Ireland:

The Heart of the Matter; The End of the Affair; England Made Me; and *The Quiet American.* But in each case, the appeal was successful. Anyhow, I suspect that James Joyce, Elizabeth Bowen, Yeats, Shaw, Flann O'Brien even, probably had their biggest audience in England. So the English do read about Ireland. They are not so ignorant.

PJ: *Fair enough, but in your works, and especially in your essays you seldom mention Irish authors or Irish literature as a possible source of influence or even interest. Is it by inadvertence or are you totally cut off from the Irish stream of culture?*

GG: It is purely accidental. My essays are based on reviews and the books I reviewed were the choice of the editor. I never reviewed poetry and therefore I have never written about Yeats whom I consider with Hardy as the two greatest poets of my lifetime. Joyce I always admired for his short stories. Elizabeth Bowen also, and Flann O'Brien: I claim to have been with Joyce one of the two writers who wrote about his [Flann O'Brien's] first book *At Swim Two Birds* at some length. Twenty one years later, I was much honoured to open a book of his, because I always bought his books, and find a dedication in it. It was *The Hard Life* and the dedication runs thus: "I honourably present to Graham Greene whose own forms of gloom I admire, this masterpiece." No, the Irish culture has always meant a great deal to me. There are innumerable poets I admire even going back to James Clarence Mangan.[18] And one of my favourite novelists now is Brian Moore who has settled in America but who comes from Northern Ireland.[19] Perhaps his best work was done when he was writing about Northern Ireland. Another Irish writer has been a life-long friend of mine, Sean O'Faolain,[20] whom I saw when I went to Dublin after Belfast. We went on a pilgrimage to the Martello Tower of Joyce together. As far as painting is concerned, I am a great admirer of Jack B. Yeats and the proud possessor of two of his later works. I am also very fond of another less known Irish painter, Roderic O'Conor who was a friend of Gauguin. He was with him in Brittany and Gauguin invited him to go with him to the South Seas. But he didn't go and continued to work in Paris where he had a studio. I have got one of his pictures which I like very much, a woman combing her hair in front of a mirror, which is very near to Bonnard. . . .

Pierre Joannon, "Graham Greene's Other Island," *Etudes Irlandaises*, 6 December 1981, 157–69.

Notes

1. Eamon De Valera (1882–1975), frontline fighter in the Easter Rising of 1916, became leader of the Fianna Fáil party and served as prime minister of Ireland in 1937. He was president of Ireland from 1959 to 1973.
2. This statement contradicts an earlier one in a letter to his mother dated 9 June 1923: "I've got an introduction to a Free State senator, also I've got at one of the big Sinn Fein Johnnies through the Irish Nationalist here. Moira O'Neill is putting me up." Sherry, *The Life of Graham Greene, Vol. 1*, 134.
3. *Weekly Westminster Gazette*, 25 August 1923.
4. Gerry Fitt (1926–), Northern Irish politician and M.P. for a Belfast constituency. He was a "moderate" who advocated more cooperation with the British and founded the Social Democratic and Labour Party (SDLP). He was elevated to the peerage in 1983.
5. A nonsectarian party that came into being in the early 1970s.
6. Michael Collins (1890–1922), a leading I. R. A. man from Cork, took part in the negotiations that led to the Anglo-Irish agreement of 1921. He was assassinated by the antitreaty faction of the I.R.A. the following year.
7. Erskine Childers (1870–1922), London-born writer of Anglo-Irish parentage and an advocate of Irish independence, fought with the republicans against the new Irish Free State government until he was captured, court-martialed, and executed. *The Riddle of the Sands* appeared in 1903.

8. Bobby Sands (1954–81), Northern Irish nationalist, was elected M.P. while serving a prison sentence. He went on a hunger strike in 1981 when the authorities refused to consider him a political prisoner and died in Hillsborough, Co. Down.

9. Social Democratic Labour Party.

10. Sir Reginald Maudling (1917–79), Home Secretary in Edward Heath's cabinet, was responsible for conceding the policy of internment in Northern Ireland. Greene had questioned his method of "deep interrogation" in a letter to the *Times* dated 26 November 1971. Sir Reginald resigned as Home Secretary in 1972.

11. Seat of Parliament in Northern Ireland.

12. Conor Cruise O'Brien, "Donat O'Donnell" RIA and RSL (1917–), writer, professor, political columnist, and one-time Minister of Posts and Telegraphs (1973–77) in the Republic of Ireland, a member of the Senate (1977–79), and editor-in-chief of the *Observer* (1979–81).

13. Terence McSwiney (1879–1920) went on a hunger strike when he was arrested in August 1920 and died seventy days later.

14. British troops noted for their brutality in suppressing the Irish Nationalist movement in the first two decades of this century.

15. Wilfrid Scawen Blunt (1840–1922), English poet and traveler with strong anti-imperialist views.

16. In all probability, a reference to Ahmad Urabi Pasha (1839–1911) who was defeated by the British at Tel el Kebir in 1882 when they occupied Egypt.

17. Marie-Françoise Allain, *L'Autre et son double. Entretiens* (Paris: Pierre Belfond, 1981), 151. (Guido Waldman's translation, *The Other Man*, omits the epithet.)

18. James Clarence Mangan (1803–49), prolific Irish writer, died in abject poverty. His best known poem is perhaps "Dark Rosaleen."

19. Brian Moore (1921–), Irish-born Canadian novelist, is now a resident of the U. S.

20. Sean O'Faolain (1900–91), Irish critic and short story writer, served, at one time, in the I.R.A.

God and Literature and So Forth . . .

Anthony Burgess

Greene is on the fourth floor. His balcony overlooks the cramped shipping (like teeth so close set you couldn't twang dental floss between them). In summer the noise of motor traffic is as loud for him as for me. The days of authorial seclusion, Maugham and the Villa Mauresque,[1] are long over. Writers live in small flats and hope to have a daily help. The best décor in the world, which you can't get in London or Paris, is marine sunlight. Greene looks well in it. Seventy-five years old, he is lean, straight, active. The blue eyes are startling, especially in all this light. We are to talk about his work, especially his new novella, *Doctor Fischer of Geneva.*

ANTHONY BURGESS: *Graham, you've practised all the literary forms—verse, drama, the novel, the short story, the essay, even biography. I wonder if you ever wanted to practise any other art.*

GRAHAM GREENE: I'm tone-deaf. I can't draw or paint. I've worked in the cinema, of course—as critic, scriptwriter, even in the cutting-room—that was when I was a co-producer. All my novels have been filmed, with one exception —*It's a Battlefield.* Ironically, that was the one book I wrote with the intention of adaptation to the screen.

AB: Doctor Fischer *cries out to be filmed doesn't it? It's short, so no director is going to want to cut it. There's a fine scenic background—winter Switzerland—and a climax, an elaborate dinner-party in the snow with great bonfires, which you must have seen as film even while you were writing it.*

GG: Well, yes, the preliminaries to filming it are already under way. I suppose you could say that, just as landscape painting was behind Sir Walter Scott, film is behind or before me. It's the great visual art of our day, and it's bound to influence the novelist.

AB: *With all except one of your novels filmed, and several short stories, you're exemplary as the filmable novelist. How many of the films do you find satisfactory—I mean, as saying in dialogue and image directly what you've already said to the reader's imagination?*

GG: *The Third Man* certainly works, but of course I wrote that as a film —having first done a kind of literary treatment which reads well enough as a story in its own right. I saw *The Third Man* again recently in Paris. There's a whole new generation discovering it. Yes, it still works. *The Fallen Idol,* too. I'm not happy about a good number of the others. Endings get changed. *Travels with My Aunt* stops before the story I wrote really gets started.[2]

When *The Heart of the Matter* was filmed we weren't allowed to show a suicide on the screen. That ruined the whole point —self-elected damnation on the part of Scobie. Seeing a preview of *The Human Factor* just recently,[3] I was disappointed that so much of the book just couldn't find a correlative in cinematic images.

AB: *Without having seen it, I'd say right away that it wasn't possible to deal with Buller, the boxer dog, who needs the devices of literary description to turn him into a character.*

GG: Both Kim Philby and Harold Acton said that they liked Buller better than anyone.

AB: *No wonder. Buller licks his testicles with the juicy noise of an alderman drinking soup. He leaves trails of spittle on the bed like a bonbon. You can't film the phraseology. I'd say also that you can't translate that bit about the alderman into another language. We make literature out of our own traditions as well as our own language. Which brings me to the Graham Greene style, which is wholly a matter of words. What is it that's peculiarly Greeneish in the way you use words?*

GG: I started off with the desire to use language experimentally. Then I saw that the right way was the way of simplicity. Straight sentences, no involutions, no ambiguities. Not much description, description isn't my line. Get on with the story. Present the outside world economically and exactly.

AB: *You're a strongly visual writer. I mean, I see things clearly when I read your work. I don't feel that the vision has to be fulfilled in cinema adaptation—which is what people usually mean when they talk about "visual possibilities" in a story. The cinema images are redundant. It's all in the book.*

GG: You think that? I think there are solidities—I mean I try to be accurate. Then someone comes along and says that boxers don't salivate like Buller. Or (it was you who said this) there are no carrots in Lancashire hotpot. Or there isn't an ABC on the Strand.

⌇

AB: *. . . I approach your books in two ways. I swallow a new Greene novel whole, with great speed. Then I slow down for a second reading and taste it. Then three months later go back to it for the various aftertastes I've missed.*

GG: I'm happy to think that I'm read that way. The more I think of it, the more I worry about this division of literature into the great because hard to read, the not so great—or certainly the ignorable by scholars—because of the desire to divert, be readable, keep it plain. You don't find Conan Doyle dealt with at length in the literary histories. Yet he was a great writer. He created several great characters—

AB: *Eliot admired him but didn't think him worthy of a critical essay—not like Wilkie Collins.[4] And yet Eliot lifted a whole chunk of* The Musgrave Ritual—

GG: Where?

AB: *In* Murder in the Cathedral. *You remember—"Whose was it?"—"His who is gone."—"Who shall have it?"—"He who will come."—"What shall be the month?" And so on. In the Sherlock Holmes story we have "Whose was it?"—"He who is gone."—"Who shall have it?"—"He who will come."—"What was the month?" Almost identical.*

GG: Something ought to be done about this double standard. I admire writers like Stanley Weyman. Victor Pritchett had the nerve to write about Rider Haggard after reading only two of his books. Haggard has to be read entire. H. G. Wells too. I've been seeking out the novels of the so-called middle period in old bookshops and I find them remarkable. There's also Bulwer Lytton. His *Pelham* deals with an illicit love affair in a thoroughly contemporary way.[5]

AB: *Why not write a book, or certainly an essay, on the literary snobbism which prefers symbols and ambiguities to the straight art of story-telling?*

GG: I leave that to you.

AB: *In the same way, Eliot admired* My Fair Lady *but wouldn't take it with the right literary seriousness. Otherwise he wouldn't have accepted lines like "I'd be equally as willing for a dentist to be drilling than to ever let a woman in my life." Only Auden took Lorenz Hart seriously.[6]*

GG: He wrote songs with Richard Rodgers, didn't he? I met Rodgers and Hammerstein when they were doing a stage adaptation of *The Heart of the Matter.*[7]

AB: *Not a musical, for God's sake.*

GG: No, a very bad straight adaptation. I may not be musical but I've written popular songs. I like to put them in my novels, as you know.[8] Now some of them have been set to music. They're broadcasting three of them on French radio.

AB: *Write the book of a musical and I'll do the music.*

GG: Oh, I had this idea of a musical in which a band of girls steal chasubles and croziers and then get themselves up as bishops before the Archbishop of Melbourne falls in love with Canterbury. There's a good telephone song there—"Cantuar calling Melbourne."

AB: *Do it, please. Auden who took Hart seriously, was responsible for the lines*

Is this a milieu where I must
How grahamgreeneish! How infra dig!
Snatch from the bottle in my bag
An analeptic swig?[9]

He's referring to a college where he's going to give a lecture, and there may be nothing to drink. Why should the analeptic swig be grahamgreeneish?

GG: I don't think he means my drinking habits. I can take alcohol—a couple of Scotches or dry martinis and a bottle of wine a day. My liver was vaccinated by my undergraduate thirst.

No, grahamgreeneish seems to refer to a particular kind of fictional character I've created—white men going to seed in outlandish places. Unshaven, guilt-ridden, on the bottle. One word I seem to be associated with is seedy—

characters I mean, not myself. It's not a happy term, a bit vague. There are such people. But they seem to have become, in their transference to my fiction, symbols of something of mankind after the fall, perhaps.

AB: *Would it be right to say that your novels were the first fiction in English to present evil as something palpable—not a theological abstraction but an entity symbolised in glass-rings on the brothel table, joyless sex, dental caries (Mexico in* The Power and the Glory*), hopeless and empty men in exile?*

GG: Evil's in Hitler, not in dental caries. I see we're getting on to myself as a Catholic novelist. I'm not that: I'm a novelist who happens to be a Catholic. The theme of human beings lonely without God is a legitimate fictional subject. To want to deal with the theme doesn't make me a theologian. Superficial readers say that I'm fascinated by damnation. But nobody in my books is damned—not even Pinkie in *Brighton Rock*. Scobie in *The Heart of the Matter* tries to damn himself, but the possibility of his salvation is left open. The priest's final words are that nobody, not even the Church, knows enough about divine love and judgment to be sure that anyone's in hell.

AB: *Last time we met you said you no longer believe in hell. And then Pope John Paul II, before going off for the summer to Castel Gondolfo, reaffirmed the doctrine. You've got to believe in hell as you've got to believe in the resurrection of the body.*

GG: I've no difficulty in accepting the idea of the transfigured flesh. As for hell, God's love goes on getting in the way of God's justice. Purgatory I begin to understand more and more—progressive purification, the divine vision getting nearer and nearer.

AB: *I'm a cradle Catholic—ridiculous phrase; who invented it?—and you're a convert. Do you see much difference between the two kinds of believers?*

GG: Very little. Since Pope John converts and cradle Catholics—ridiculous phrase; who invented it?[10]—have had to grow accustomed equally to a new kind of Church. Converts can be rigorous, of course. Evelyn Waugh showed great theological rigour when attacking some of my earlier work.

AB: *I admired him greatly, but he scared me. I wanted to visit him but never dared. The daughter of his I met in America said he was approachable, no monster. I remain scared even of his shade. If he had a son I suppose I'd be scared of him too.*

GG: He has sons.

AB: *I never knew that. What do you think of the present state of the novel in English?*

GG: Beryl Bainbridge is very good, Muriel Spark too, of course. I used to read Frank Tuohy. And William Golding. R. K. Narayan I still love.[11]

AB: *Don't you find the British novel parochial?*

GG: There was a time, in the nineteenth century of course, when it could be both parochial and universal. Not now perhaps. I don't read much American fiction. Bellow? I liked *Henderson the Rain King*—a remarkable picture of Africa for a man who'd never been there. John Updike, no. The Southerners, no. Faulkner is very convoluted. Patrick White? I liked *Voss*.[12]

AB: *Both Bellow and White got the Nobel Prize. When are you going to get it?*

GG: Yes, I was asked that question by a Swedish journalist. How would you like the Nobel Prize? I said I look forward to getting a bigger prize than that.

AB: *Which one?*

GG: Death. Let's go and eat lunch . . .

Extracted from Anthony Burgess, "God and Literature and So Forth
. . . " *Observer*, 16 March 1980, 33, 35.

Notes
1. Somerset Maugham (1874–1965) settled in his home, Villa
   Mauresque, at Cape Ferrat near Nice in 1928.
2. *Travels with My Aunt* (MGM, 1972). Produced by Robert Fryer
   and James Cresson. Directed by George Cukor. Screenplay by
   Jay Presson Allen and Hugh Wheeler. Starring Maggie Smith,
   Alec McCowen, and Lou Gossett.
3. *The Human Factor* (Rank Organization, 1979). Produced and
   directed by Otto Preminger. Screenplay by Tom Stoppard.
   Starring Nicol Williamson, Richard Attenborough, Derek
   Jacobi, Iman, and Sir John Gielgud.
4. William Wilkie Collins (1824–89), Victorian novelist, author of
   The Woman in White (1860) and *The Moonstone* (1868), one of
   the first novels that deal with the detection of crime.
5. Edward George Bulwer Lytton (1803–73), first Baron Lytton, is
   a versatile Victorian writer whose early novel, *Pelham*, appeared
   in 1828.
6. Lorenz Hart (1895–1943), American song lyricist, collaborated
   with Richard Rodgers for twenty-five years.
7. See note 1 on pp. 101–2 of the Robert Ostermann excerpt,
   "Interview with Graham Greene."
8. Greene was very much interested in popular songs. In *A Gun for
   Sale*, the song "It's Just Kew for You, But for Me It's Paradise"
   haunts Raven and his girl. Greene had hoped that another popular song "It Was Just a Way of Talking" in *The Confidential
   Agent* would be put to music but it was left out of the film version
   of the novel. "I can see myself as a writer of popular songs,"
   Greene once said to his friend Ronald de Couves Matthews. "I
   have a few good ones in *My Girl in Gaiters* . . . What I secretly
   wish for is the ability one day to write a musical comedy." *Mon
   Ami Graham Greene*, 188.
9. "On the Circuit," *Collected Poems of W. H. Auden*, ed. Edward
   Mendelson (New York: Random House, 1976), 549. See note 2
   on p. 127 of the Philip Toynbee excerpt, "Graham Greene on
   'The Job of the Writer.' "

10. Both are saying "ridiculous phrase" tongue in cheek because both know that Anthony Burgess used it referring to Greene in a symposium. See Philip French, "Man of Mystery: The Enigma of Graham Greene," *Listener*, 4 October 1979, 441–43. Greene had also used the term in connection with Burgess in a letter to the *Tablet* dated 12 April 1975 in which he defends himself against the charge of Jansenism. The Greene/Burgess relationship seemed to have been vague and uneasy and apparently ended by mid-1989. See Anthony Burgess's personal memoir of Greene in the *Daily Telegraph*, 4 April 1991, 19.

11. Beryl [Margaret] Bainbridge (1934–), English novelist and short story writer and author of *A Weekend with Claude* (1967, 1981) and *Another Part of the Wood* (1968, 1979).

    Muriel Spark, OBE, Scottish-born novelist whom Greene seems to have admired for he chooses her to guard the entrance to his "Pantheon." See p. 137 of the George Adam excerpt, "A Pantheon of Contemporary Writers."

    Frank Tuohy (1925–), FRSL, is an English novelist whose works are characterized by a strong sense of social and physical realism.

    R[asijuran] K[rishnaswami] Narayan (1907–), Indian novelist, sets most of his novels in the fictional kingdom of "Malgudi." His first novel is *Swami and Friends* (London: Hamish Hamilton, 1935).

12. Victor Martindale Patrick White (1912–90), English-born, Australian novelist and Nobel Prize winner (1973). *Voss* was published in 1957 (New York: Viking Press).

The Paradox of Greene's Universe

Marie-Françoise Allain

MARIE-FRANÇOISE ALLAIN: *. . . You say you have "betrayed a great many things" in the course of your life (I think you are alluding to your sentimental life) . . .*

GRAHAM GREENE: Yes, I'm sure I've been a bad husband and a fickle lover!

MFA: *That is what I was going to ask you: how can you admit that and yet show such stability as a writer?*

GG: I suppose one can work very hard to accomplish a certain task—writing—and that as a result one can't be a very diligent husband or lover.

Perhaps writers are fickle by temperament, because the individual who finishes a novel bears little resemblance to the one who began it. One lives so long with one's characters that they tend to influence one. For instance, my last bout of depression, my worst, I think, coincided with the gestation of *A Burnt-Out Case*. I can find reasons for this in my private life, but also in my two-year cohabitation with the deeply depressive Querry, with whom I never in fact identified myself.

The fact is, one is changed by one's own books. The writer plays God until his creatures escape him and, in their turn, they mould him.

MFA: *So you think you are very different from the man who wrote* The Power and the Glory?

GG: Oh definitely. I'm much older. Life changes us a little more each day, doesn't it? I'm not the man I was two years ago. One's eroded. Time nibbles at us bit by bit, stone after stone.

MFA: *But do you recognise yourself in your books?*

GG: No, I never revert to them, never give them a thought, unless I'm compelled to, as now.

The critics, too, ought to be a little more inclined to forget what one has written previously, but they always expect one to remain absolutely constant. I suppose it's easier for them to decree that I'm a "one-book man" than to recognize that change happens. This is why *Travels with My Aunt* was poorly received in England, while I consider it one of my best books. I expect similar reasons to lie behind the general refusal to grasp the importance of fantasy in my books. No one's ever questioned me about it or really commented on it. When *A Sense of Reality* came out, the title, which was meant to be ironical, was taken at face value. It seemed to me rather amusing to apply the word "reality" to a book which was so remote from it. I served up quite a new dish—but nobody noticed.

The intrusion of dreams and fantasy into my other books has been overlooked in the same way. Few critics remarked on the dragon scene in *The Human Factor*, or the fable told to the young woman by Querry.

MFA: *Do you think that writing has helped to strengthen your faith?*

GG: No, I shouldn't say so. My books only reflect faith or lack of faith, with every possible nuance in between. I don't see why people insist on labelling me a Catholic writer. I'm simply a Catholic who happens to write.

MFA: . . . *And the Church has recognised herself in your novels, even to the extent of condemning* The Power and the Glory *because you had broken certain rules in introducing "paradoxical and extraordinary situations." So Catholicism provides you with points of reference, though even these rules might be there only to be broken, would you not say?*

GG: I've never willingly used these points of reference. There does exist a pattern in the carpet constituted by Catholicism, but one has to stand back in order to make it out. A great deal of time has elapsed between the various novels you've mentioned. Before *Brighton Rock* I wrote a whole series of books quite unconnected with religion. Lately I've drawn away from the subject again even though theology does make a fresh appearance in *The Honorary Consul* in the person of the guerrilla priest. I'm thinking also of *The Quiet American* in which suddenly, at the end, the journalist Fowler is sorry for Pyle's death and expresses a wish to turn towards something or someone to discharge his sense of guilt. In most of my novels one can find a religious influence.

But I refute the term "Catholic writer." Cardinal Newman, whose books influenced me a great deal after my conversion, denied the existence of a "Catholic" literature. He recognised only the possibility of a religious dimension superior to the literary dimension, and he wrote that books ought to deal first with what he called, in the vocabulary of the day, "the tragic destiny of man in his fallen state." I agree with him. It is the "human factor" that interests me, not apologetics.[1]

I think, actually, that the whole argument in *The Power and the Glory* was deeply rooted in me from childhood precisely on account of the human factor. I remember members of my family coming back from their holidays in Spain, sometimes, terribly shocked because in some little village they had come across a priest living with his housekeeper, or keeping a mistress, and so on. I found their indignation exaggerated because, even though I wasn't a believer, I saw no reason why a man should not be different from his function, that he could be an excellent priest while remaining a sinner. I learnt to analyze the paradox of Grace more subtly after my conversion, from reading St. Thomas Aquinas, St. Francois de Sales, Fr. D'Arcy and Fr. Martindale (both English theologians) —but the paradox was an integral part of my universe.

MFA: *Is that why you concede to people condemned by human justice the possibility of being saved "between the stirrup and the ground"?*

GG: Yes, God's justice is not like that of a judge. It is a mathematical justice. (One talks of a just line.) It is very different from human justice with the distortions which witnesses, legal considerations, etc. can give to an ordinary judgement. God's justice derives from total knowledge. This is the reason why I don't believe in hell: if God exists—I'm convinced He does—He is omniscient; if He is omniscient, I can't bring myself to imagine that a creature conceived by Him can be so evil as to merit eternal punishment. His grace must intervene at some point.[2]

MFA: *Would you allow a chance to such individuals as Papa Doc, Hitler and their like?*

GG: I'd favour the death penalty in their case, but the death penalty—even an eternal death penalty—is not hell.

MFA: *In your novels you are content to substitute yourself for God!*

GG: All writers, even the worst, are led into assuming a role vaguely comparable to God's, for they create characters over whom they exercise almost total control. I should add, though, that a writer is even more like a double agent than he is like God: he condemns and sustains his characters by turns. Their relationship is so ambiguous that even the characters come to elude his control—as with Scobie in *The Heart of the Matter*—one doesn't know whom to blame.

MFA: *You are a believer even though you say that you are only "keeping a foot in the door." In your opinion, does faith give an additional dimension to writing?*

GG: Human beings are more important to believers than they are to atheists. If one tells oneself that a man is no more than a superior animal, that each individual has before him a maximum of eighty years of life, then man is indeed of little importance. I think that the flatness of E. M. Forster's characters, and Virginia Woolf's or Sartre's, for example, compared with the astonishing vitality of Bloom in Joyce's *Ulysses*, or of Balzac's Père Goriot, or of David Copperfield, derives from the absence of the religious dimension in the former. Mauriac's characters are equally endowed with this strange substantiality. In *La Pharisienne*, when one of them—a very minor character—crosses a school yard, we have a sense of having seen him in flesh and blood, while Mrs. Dalloway doing her shopping leaves one indifferent. She moves out of our minds as easily as she moves out of Harrods.

Along the same lines I should say that very few good writers have emerged from the Communist world, with the exception of a Solzhenitsyn or Pasternak or a Sinyavsky, who have in fact retained their sense of the religious. The Welfare State has driven God off the stage, just like the devil, but it has failed so lamentably that I have the impression God is making a timid reappearance. History tends to prove that Faith is reborn from its embers. Would a Solzhenitsyn have existed if Communism had met with a more obvious success?

MFA: *That is the meaning of the question to which you have not replied: "Is it through evil that one comes to religion?"*

GG: When evil achieves such a degree of perfection as to wear supernatural trappings, then it can rekindle faith in the supernatural. But extreme goodness has the same power. I've experienced it in contact with extraordinary men who were endowed with it—Padre Pio, whom I've mentioned, and similarly a priest in Indo-China; the Japanese had tortured him—they had ripped off his nails. He lived in a little hut not far from Dien Bien Phu. I don't know what's become of him. He said mass with anyone who passed that way. I have no model of sanctity in mind but I believe that he was a saint.

MFA: *In your epigraph to* The Heart of the Matter *you quote Charles Péguy: "The sinner stands at the very heart of Christianity . . . No one is as competent in the matter of Christianity as the sinner. No one, except the saint." And concerning the paradoxes of Christianity you write in an essay: "The Christian inhabits a territory bordering on Good and Evil, and its bandit country."[3] Does Catholicism coincide so perfectly with human nature, as you see it?*

GG: That's what I used to think thirty-two years ago. I've not thought about it since.

MFA: *Well, this vision of a world caught between two fires, a vision which is different from the dichotomy pervading* The Man Within—*I was wondering whether it arose out of the influence of Catholicism.*

GG: *The Man Within* was a beginner's novel, but I was already a Catholic. All my books, except for that dreadful collection of verse published at Oxford, were written after my conversion. My way of grappling with human nature has little to do with Catholicism; it derives from my experience of life, from what I can observe. It would be no different if I were a Buddhist. For me, the sinner and the saint can meet; there is no discontinuity, no rupture. I believe in reversibility.

But the basic element I admire in Christianity is its sense of moral failure. That is its very foundation. For once you're conscious of personal failure, then perhaps in future you become a little less fallible. I know a poem by Thomas Hardy which illustrates this particular consciousness of failure. May I read you part of it?

"You taught not that which you set about,"
Said my own voice, talking to me,
"That the greatest of things is Charity . . . "
And the sticks burnt low and the fire went out
And my voice ceased talking to me.[4]

MFA: *Your own voice seems to give you little peace.*

GG: That's true; especially at night. That's when failure stares me in the face. I've written some bad books, but I've also failed in charity, compassion, and I've been cruel.

MFA: *Is this the tribute which a "spy of God," as you call yourself in one of your* Essays, *is bound to pay?*[5]

GG: Did I say that? I don't believe it!

MFA: *G. K. Chesterton, whom you so admire, and who is also a convert to Catholicism, did introduce into his books a God who plays the part of spy, or rather, of detective.*

GG: Not a God, Father Brown. They're not his best novels!

MFA: *Are you still hounded by God?*

GG: I hope so! I hope so! I'm not very conscious of His presence, but I hope that He is still dogging my footsteps. I also find myself thinking, not so much that He is pursuing me, but that certain extraordinary circumstances have had a beneficial effect on my life—I don't mean in terms of professional success or in terms of money, but in terms of happiness. My life has been radically transformed by events which happened for no logical reason.

I perceive, then, certain conducting threads in this labyrinth; I assume they're not put there on purpose, but they are wound off under the eye of some sovereign power watching man's free will functioning. This power has simultaneous knowledge of past and future. The same phenomenon is given man in John Dunne's *An Experiment with Time,* in which he claims that during sleep dreams draw their substance from the future as well as the past, that the sleeper is in a position overlooking both. The omniscient God does not obstruct the functioning of free will, but He knows the past and the future—He has set their wheels in motion.

MFA: *What is God like?*

GG: A mystery, an inexplicable force. That's why, when one prays one shouldn't, in my opinion, address oneself to this inexplicable and mysterious force but to His intermediary, Christ. I think there's an element of truth in the myth about man being created in His image. But it is easier to pray to Christ than to an abstract entity. Human love can be only a pale reflection of the emotion that God must feel for what He has created.

MFA: *As He appears in your novels, God is not as good as you are suggesting. Your literature is not that simple. It expresses conflicts between contradictory elements, between the hunter and his prey, loyalty and disloyalty. And yet nobody would dream of saying that you present a dichotomized universe, for these elements always have an obscure and disturbing way of merging. You, however, seem temperamentally poised on the dizzy edge of darkness rather than of light. Are you not fundamentally a Manichean who has never succumbed to his vice?*

GG: A Manichean[6] believes that the world is wholly in the hands of God . . . I mean of the devil.

MFA: *Your first slip—do you confuse God and the devil?*

GG: Well, listen: in *The Honorary Consul* I did suggest this idea, through the guerrilla priest, that God and the devil were actually one and the same person—God has a day-time and a night-time, but that He evolved, as Christ tended to prove, towards His day-time face—absolute goodness—thanks to each positive act of men. I thought I had invented a new theology for my dissident priest, so I was a little disappointed when my friend Fr. Duran told me that this was all perfectly compatible with Catholic doctrine.

MFA: *So you shuffle the cards in order to counteract an over-simplification.*

GG: On the contrary: I try to find simple explanations for complex phenomena.

MFA: *Then would you publicly defend Hans Küng and Edward Schillebeeckx, the "heretics" of the Catholic Church today?[7]*

GG: I would defend them as Christian theologians but not as Catholic theologians. I'm not in opposition to Rome. I know that in my books I've introduced characters—especially priests—who verged on heresy. (That's why *The Power and the Glory* was once condemned by the Holy Office.) But I've too often seen the absurdity, exemplified in the Anglican Church, of a bishop remaining a bishop even though he doesn't believe in the Resurrection, nor even the historical existence of Christ. There are certain points of reference which cannot be abandoned, otherwise one might as well go and become a Buddhist or a Hindu. I believe in the necessity of a minimum of dogmas, and I certainly believe in heresy, for it's heresy that creates dogmas. In this sense heresy has great value.

MFA: *So have Küng and Schillebeeckx!*

GG: Yes. They bring a new breath. I must admire Hans Küng, especially for his book *On Being a Christian.* Schillebeeckx is a great and very learned, very estimable theologian; but, as a barely practising Catholic, I find it very disagreeable when a historical event like the Crucifixion is turned into some wooly sort of symbol. The twentieth chapter of St. John's gospel can stand with the best of eyewitness reports, and I don't see why Fr. Schillebeeckx has to turn it into a symbolic sequence. If one considers oneself a Catholic, there is a certain number of facts which have to be accepted.

On the other hand if I were told that for some reason or other they had got it wrong about the Virgin Mary, or that the Trinity was no longer an article of faith, that would barely disturb my faith. The Trinity, for example, is nothing to me but a mathematical symbol for a mystery. One can talk about "the communion of saints"—though I'm not at all sure what it means. I believe in the existence of the saints. But the existence of the Trinity is to me of no importance: it illustrates an attempt to explain the inexplicable.

MFA: *So would you agree with "the new heretics" on a certain number of points?*

GG: I'm in favour of having these subjects aired, so long as one is not posing as a Catholic theologian but only as a Christian theologian. So long as differences between the

Churches exist, those differences ought to be upheld, otherwise one becomes as foggy as the Anglicans. Catholicism has to remain human. A man lived: Christ. He lived in history. Why turn him into a concept, fit only for a handful of visionaries?

This debate shows that the Church is still on the move, that we're a long way from the Inquisition. Hans Küng is free to teach. No one has been excommunicated, not even, at the other extreme, Msgr. Lefebvre.[8] I think that, all in all, this controversy has enabled me to discover an amusing paradox, almost a Chestertonian one: while Fr. Schillebeeckx's declarations were intended to make the unbelievable credible, they have had the opposite effect on me—they have suddenly revived in me a deep faith in the inexplicable, in the mystery of Christ's resurrection. And I don't think I'm alone in having reacted this way. Don't you think there's something like a small miracle of grace there for we who are semi-lapsed?

MFA: *Do you yourself regard faith as a disease or a blessing?*

GG: It would be a blessing if I were permanently conscious of it—which has never been the case. With age, though, doubt seems to gain the upper hand. It's my own fault. I've never been too much of a religious person. There was a time, long ago, when I might have considered myself a practising Catholic. I still often go to Sunday mass, but I no longer feel at home, for reasons of my own—besides, the mass has changed considerably. It's no longer said in Latin; and all my education after my conversion was bound up with the mass in Latin. Even at Chungking in China I was able to attend a service I understood. Since the change to the vernacular, when I travel, I can't follow the Catholic services; they're in a different tongue each time. Nor do I care for the freedom given to priests to introduce endless prayers—for the astronauts or what have you—as they do in Antibes.

MFA: *Do you go to Communion?*

GG: No, for I've broken the rules. They are rules I respect, so I haven't been to Communion now for nearly thirty years. The last time I went to Confession was at Phat Diem in Indo-China. I had been following the particularly murderous battles between the French paratroops and the Viet-Minh. The sight of so many corpses made me afraid. Fear drove me into the Cathedral, round which the whole Catholic population was seeking refuge. The inhabitants had set up a whole lot of market stalls under the walls—they thought they'd be safer there.

So I went to find a Belgian priest I knew to hear my confession to the sound of gunfire (it was ten years since I had last confessed). He told me to say one Our Father and one Hail Mary. He also gave me one of the *Tintin* books to read as I had nothing else to hand.

MFA: *What do you mean when you say you have "broken the rules"?*

GG: In my private life, my situation is not regular. If I went to Communion, I would have to confess and make promises. I prefer to excommunicate myself. That's why I said, at a conference in Paris with Mauriac, that I could only speak in the name of the "semi-lapsed," comparable in this respect with certain Communists who have reached the dangerous edge where faith wavers.

MFA: *The priest in* The Power and the Glory *also broke the rules, since he was father of a little girl, and he was a drunkard and fornicator, and yet . . .*

GG: But he could always say mass. He was never stripped of that right.

MFA: *While you, you are happy to torture yourself, are you not?*

GG: No, I became less depressive with age. I have, if you like, more doubts, but my faith has grown too. There's a difference between belief and faith.[9] If I don't believe in X or Y, faith intervenes, telling me that I'm wrong not to believe. Faith is above belief. One can say that it's a gift of God, while belief is not. Belief is founded on reason. On the whole I keep my faith while enduring long periods of disbelief. At such moments I shrug my shoulders and tell myself I'm wrong—as though a brilliant mathematician had come and told me that my solution of an equation was wrong. My faith remains in the background, but it remains.

MFA: *So you are happy . . .*

GG: Not very. Who is?

MFA: *Well then, at peace?*

GG: I'm just not bothered. I'll have it sorted out soon enough . . . or else I won't.

Extracted from Marie-Françoise Allain, *The Other Man: Conversations with Graham Greene*, trans. Guido Waldman (London: Bodley Head, 1983), 142–43, 159–65, 168–70, 172–73. *Editor's title.*

Notes

1. When in 1949, Marcel Moré asked him for his views on the "Catholic novelist," Greene could hardly comprehend the question for he saw no common ground between novel writing and apologetics: they were two different occupations. See Père Jouve and Marcel Moré, "Propos de table avec Graham Greene," *Dieu Vivant* 16 (1950): 127–37.

2. Greene's views do not seem to have changed very much. In an interview accorded to George Adam twenty years or so earlier, he expressed the same views in very much the same words. See p. 140 of the George Adam excerpt, "A Pantheon of Contemporary Writers."

3. Greene, "Paradoxes du Christianisme," *Essais Catholiques*, 44.

4. Thomas Hardy, "Surview," *Collected Poems* (London: Macmillan, 1952), 661. This is the last poem in Hardy's 1922 volume of poetry, *Late Lyrics and Earlier.*

5. In his address entitled "La civilisation chretienne: est-elle en peril?" (Grandes Conférences Catholiques, Brussels 1948, trans. Philip Stratford as "The Last Pope," *Graham Greene. Reflections*, ed. Judith Adamson), Greene refers to Catholic writers as ". . . we, the spies of God . . .," " 120.

6. For the Manichean tradition, see note 8 on p. 82 of the Jean Duché excerpt, "A 'Jansenist' Writer of Thrillers."

7. Hans Küng (1928–), Swiss professor and ordained priest and Edward Schillebeeckx (1914–), Belgian Dominican professor, were liberal theologians censured by the Roman Catholic Church and forbidden to teach for a period of time.

8. Archbishop Marcel Lefebvre is a French dissident traditionalist. He maintained his opposition to the new liturgy of the Catholic Church even after announcing his resignation in 1982.

9. Thomas A. Wassmer, S.J., affirms, from a theological viewpoint, that there can exist a "valid tension" between "theological faith and rational disbelief." See "Faith and Reason in Graham Greene," *Studies* 48 (summer 1959): 163–67, also published as "Reason and Faith as Seen by Graham Greene," *Drama Critique* 2 (November 1959): 126–30.

A Rare Occasion: Graham Greene on TV

Bernard Violet

BERNARD VIOLET: *Graham Greene, you have refused interviews with the B.B.C. and French T.V. for 20 years—why have you accepted today?*

GRAHAM GREENE: Perhaps I was a little seduced by you, Mr. Violet! I don't like the idea of appearing on T.V. I admit I think an author has to be a private person. One has known authors who have been spoilt by T.V. and have become "comedians." I can't explain why you managed to persuade me, but you did! On this occasion *only*. It doesn't mean that I shall ever appear again.[1]

BV: *You are a famous writer but the man behind your books is little known to the public. Who are you, Graham Greene?*

GG: I am my books.

BV: *In the* Dictionary of Authors *your name appears between the French writer Julien Green . . .*

GG: I know him . . .

BV: *. . . and Robert Greene, another Englishman.*

GG: I don't know him.

BV: *He died in 1592 . . .*

GG: Oh yes, yes — the Elizabethan. Yes I know him — his work!

BV: *All one can read about Graham Greene is "Born in 1904. English . . ." Isn't that a rather short biography?*

GG: Oh I think it's sufficient. It gives my age! *(laughs)*

BV: *Is age important to you?*

GG: I think it becomes important as one grows older because one sees the approach of the "wall" in front of one and one sometimes wonders whether it's worthwhile trying to write another book because one may never finish it.

BV: *Do you often think of the "wall" as you put it?*

GG: Yes, but not with fear.

BV: *You're English, not British, I believe?*

GG: In a way, because I'm a quarter Scotch.

BV: *When I talked to Burgess and said he was an English writer, he said, "No—a BRITISH writer!"*

GG: I don't like the word British. I call myself English, but the fact remains that I am a quarter Scottish.

BV: *You converted to Catholicism in 1927.[2] You were 23 at the time. Do you remember why you changed your religion at that tender age?*

GG: It was not at all an emotional affair. I was engaged to be married to a Catholic. I was an atheist and I thought it would be useful to the marriage if I could understand a little of what she believed and so without pretending that I was going to be a Catholic, I took instruction from a priest. I was working at the time in the City of Nottingham as a journalist — learning to be a journalist and I had my instructions on the tops of buses and all sorts of places and I found myself convinced intellectually that probably Catholicism was *nearer* the truth than other faiths.

BV: *It wasn't just to oppose the Protestant faith in England?*

GG: No, not at all. And I felt no emotional attachment to Catholicism until I went to Mexico during the Persecution there and that gave me a sense of sympathy for the persecuted, which gave an emotional attachment to my faith.

BV: *You were also war correspondent. You have been round the world and finally ended up on the Côte d'Azur. Is this part of the world the ultimate for an English writer?*

GG: No, not necessarily. But I've known le Côte, I've known Antibes since 1948 I would think. I came first to Antibes because a great friend of mine, Alexander Korda, the film producer, had a boat in the harbour and we used to go off in the boat together. Then the years passed and I used to rent a flat for some months of the year near the ramparts of Antibes and the time came when I caught a very bad pneumonia in Moscow and my doctor advised me to spend the winters out of England and so Antibes was the natural place for me to go and I have become very attached to Antibes.

BV: *How do you explain the reason for so many English writers coming to this part of the world—like Burgess, Somerset Maugham?*

GG: Burgess was mainly in Italy I think. It's only fairly recently he's come to Monte Carlo. I hardly regard Monte Carlo as part of France. But Somerset Maugham, yes, was on Cap Ferrat. But my reasons were purely personal and they ceased to be health because my health is good, but the first reason for settling here was health.

BV: *Do you still advise your compatriots not to settle on the Côte D'Azur as we can see in your book J'accuse?*

GG: I would make an exception for Antibes. My attachment to Antibes remains. There are other parts of the Côte d'Azur about which I am less happy, as you probably know.

BV: *What attracts you especially about Antibes?*

GG: I have many friends among the merchants, the restaurant owners, among people in general and I've always found the Antibois extremely generous and kind. For example, during the 1968 troubles I was in Italy and came back to Antibes. The banks were closed. I had no money and I found everybody willing to lend me money, to give me credit and a spirit of friendship which I appreciate.

BV: *Now about your book* Monsignor Quixote. *There is an obvious link with Cervantes'* Don Quixote. *Since when have you been interested in him—from your childhood?*

GG: No. Curiously enough I'm not very fond of the book! I find long passages of it very boring *indeed.*

BV: *But it's the character of Don Quixote himself that really interests you, isn't it?*

GG: Yes, *le personnage* more than the book, but the idea came to me because I was in the habit of making motor trips in Spain with a friend of mine—a priest, who was also a Professor of literature in Madrid[3]—and during the course of our journeys the idea came of a book and over five years, I think, we've every year made a trip—except this year when I have been rather preoccupied—and the book was about three years in the making.

BV: *There seems to be many similarities between your character, Monsignor Quixote, and Cervantes' Don Quixote.*

GG: I don't think he is quite the same. I think Don Quixote, as we call him in English, was a far more aggressive character than the Monsignor and he was more sure of himself. I've drawn a character one of whose characteristics is *doubt.* He even doubts certain aspects of his faith while Don Quixote has no doubts at all, so I took him only as a starting point and there are certain parallels—the guardia civile taking the place of the windmills, with a gunman replacing the galley slaves. But I don't wish to be tied to the character of Don Quixote.

BV: *Your character is not as strong as Don Quixote and is perhaps more endearing because of his human qualities and weaknesses, don't you think?*

GG: Yes, I think in the same way Sancho is not like Cervantes' Sancho. He's a more intelligent man—and less earthy.

BV: *There seems to be great understanding and even affection between the two main characters of your book, Monsignor Quixote and the communist mayor.*

GG: Yes, because they discover in their conversations that they are both of them people who have certain doubts. The Mayor prefers orthodox communism to Eurocommunism, but at the same time, you feel that he has a doubt at the back of his mind. Just as there is a doubt always at the back of Monsignor Quixote's mind.

BV: *Isn't it a caricature of the Church's hierarchy?*

GG: Yes—the hierarchy in communism also. The Politbureau against the Curia.

BV: *What finally appears to frighten you most are the governing powers who think people should be led with an iron hand. You seem in favour of disorder?*

GG: Well, I suppose I would perhaps reluctantly call myself an anarchist, but an anarchist following in the steps of an English writer called Herbert Read who was a poet and philosopher—and an anarchy meaning that power should be exercised as near to the people as possible. Regions should have more power but the central government—the power of central government should be reduced.

BV: *You say that doubt puts an end to the freedom of action. Should man have doubts?*

GG: Yes. Yes.

BV: *But you don't attach much importance to doubt.*

GG: To me, it's a human quality. A dogma, I don't like, I don't care for dogma. For example, I make a little fun of a dogma—the Trinity— because it seems to me the dogma of the Trinity is an attempt by a rather clumsy mathematician to describe a mystery.

BV: *Would you like to describe how Monsignor Quixote describes the Trinity to the Mayor?*

GG: Oh, yes, with the bottles of wine. But he makes a mistake. He compares the Trinity with the two and half bottles of wine they have drunk because they are the same substance, they came into existence at the same time, but he realises he has made a mistake in putting only a half-bottle for the Holy Ghost because the Holy Ghost should have been an equally full large bottle—so they have to drink a bit more to make the heresy correct!

BV: *Would you say that the two main characters of your book represent two forms of intelligence—Intellect and Emotion?*

GG: I don't know. You've put a question I can't answer because I haven't seen it in that light. I think that is for a critic to say. The author often doesn't know his own book.

BV: *Do you think you have written a pessimistic book?*

GG: No, not pessimistic, I don't think. But in all my books there is always a measure of hope introduced. You had a philosopher—Gabriel Marcel—a Catholic positivist . . .

BV: *Christian existentialist . . .*

GG: Christian existentialist—and he once wrote a little thing about me in which he said that I was an existentialist because I had reduced hope to its smallest proportions—but the hope is there always.

BV: *Why do you feel nearer to a philosopher like Gabriel Marcel than Sartre for example?*

GG: I'm not a philosopher and frankly I'm not able to read Gabriel Marcel with any understanding—the only thing in existentialism that I understand a little bit is its relationship with Kierkegaard, but I'm not a theologian or a philosopher and it's beyond me.

BV: *But there are a lot of rather metaphysical reflections in your books aren't there?*

GG: Only superficial I think.

BV: *As you don't believe in religion or any political ideology—what can save mankind in your opinion?*

GG: Oh, but I *do believe* in religion. What I distinguish is between faith and belief. One may have less belief as one grows older but one's faith can say "Yes, but you are wrong." Belief is rational, faith is irrational and one can still continue to have an irrational faith when one's belief weakens.

BV: *But one needs to be rather sceptical?*

GG: Well, that involves a certain scepticism about aspects of Christianity or I would rather say, certain aspects of Catholicism.

BV: *I referred earlier to Sartre's notion of commitment. In your books we can see that man not only doubts but also has to choose. He can never stay neutral.*

GG: That's true I think. In *The Quiet American*, for example, the journalist there believes that he's not committed and he prefers to call himself a reporter rather than a correspondent, but at the end he finds himself committed to some extent in Vietnam—and I find in my own life—I find myself committed.

I've spent a lot of time recently in Central America—in Panama—I've visited Nicaragua—I've found myself committed with the Sandanistas. I certainly at the beginning found myself committed to the Fidelistas in Cuba but I admit that my commitments don't always endure and one may find oneself committed to something one had not at one period approved of. So that my allegiances are a little bit fluid.

BV: *You have committed yourself on the Côte d'Azur as well. . .*

GG: Yes.

BV: *Are these commitments the logical sequence of your commitments elsewhere—as in South America?*

GG: Yes, I find myself frequently engaged . . . Perhaps it's sentimental, but I find myself frequently engaged on the side of the victims and the victims may be the victims of communism or fascism but one finds oneself engaged.

BV: *If you wrote* The Third Man *today would it still have the same ending? Would the hero choose duty before affection?*

GG: That was a film, you know, more than a story. I liked the film but the story as I wrote it was the treatment of the film and then I wrote the screenplay afterwards and I regard the finished product as a film—the character there was a slightly infantile character—he had never grown out of his adolescence. His admiration for Lime was a very adolescent one. I don't consider him a typical character in my books.

BV: *Faced with such a situation yourself, which would you choose, duty or affection?*

GG: I think it would be duty and sometimes it would be "affection." But it depends on the circumstances so much.

BV: *You were once called a Manicheist, but you're not, are you?*

GG: Not at all, no, because Manicheism believes that there are good and evil equally balanced and that the world is in the hands of Evil[4] which I don't believe at all. Nor am I a Jansenist as my friend Burgess always accuses me of being, because as you know the Jansenists have a crucifix where Christ's arms are raised above his head to show that he died for the elect.[5] I don't believe that in the least, and in none of my books does that idea come and I have no belief whatever in Hell.

BV: *But the elect in your books are marginals like Pinky saved through sin . . .*

GG: Not Pinky. A doubt is raised in the reader's mind at the end of what his fate will be, but I don't think there is any definite salvation promised to Pinky. But all the same I was then experimenting. I was trying to picture somebody so evil that one *could* picture him condemned to Hell and I failed even there to imagine such a thing, because I do not believe in hell.

BV: *In almost all your books there is a sinner—the sinner who believes in his salvation through his own sincerity.*

GG: It would take me hours to find the answer to that question. But why—you've spoken quite correctly about my work—but then why do you regard me as a pessimist?

BV: *Well, sceptical if you prefer . . . Do you think poverty and ugliness are the basis of grace and salvation?*

GG: I think very likely they are . . . Christ said that the rich man who went to heaven was like a camel passing through the eye of a needle. I think the more comfortable you are, the more successful you are the less grace you probably have.

BV: *Do you feel yourself closer to Monsignor Quixote than to the drunken priest of* The Power and the Glory?

GG: Yes. I think I feel closer to Monsignor Quixote. The priest in *The Power and the Glory* was a little too orthodox for my taste.

BV: *But you said once that of all your works* The Power and the Glory *had given you the most satisfaction.*

GG: Yes, years ago, but now I prefer other books and one changes. I prefer for instance *The Honorary Consul.*

BV: *Is the Graham Greene of today a wise man?*

GG: Not at all! Not at all!

But one changes and books belong to one's past and one is no longer the author who wrote *The Power and the Glory.* Now I'm simply the author who wrote *Monsignor Quixote.* But in two years time I'll be the author perhaps who wrote some other book.

BV: *Between Good and Evil, is man really master of his fate?*

GG: No he's preyed on, as it were, by his environment, his inheritance. I think free will is there, but a very limited free will. If you are born in a slum, a great deal of your free will has vanished. If you are born of alcoholic parents some of your free will has vanished. No man has complete free will. If you're rich and very successful, your free will is limited by your success.

BV: *For Burgess, evil is necessary as it allows a choice between good and evil. Do you think evil exists?*

GG: Yes, certainly. It is part of the human predicament. It can take various forms. Evil can be a lack of generosity. Evil can be cruelty—there are many forms of evil.

BV: *Does evil corrupt through the mistrust it creates?*

GG: Yes.

BV: *What do you mean by quoting Shakespeare's words: "There is nothing either good or bad, but thinking makes it so."*

GG: Well, I had Monsignor in mind when I put that line in and I can't analyse myself why I thought it was suitable. It seemed to me suitable and I don't know why. There are these curious mysteries in writing you know, you do something and you feel it's right but you don't know why.

BV: *Creation goes beyond the creator?*

GG: Yes, and the character, the life of the character takes possession of the writer and he does something which a writer never imagined he would do.

BV: *You are being compared to François Mauriac. Do you feel close to him?*

GG: Yes. And we were great friends I'm glad to say. In the last years of his life. I was a publisher just after the war for three years and I published a collected edition of his books which helped the friendship! And I also intrigued to get him an honorary degree at Oxford. But I liked him enormously. I liked the fact that he was "méchant" his tongue was "méchant." He was amusing and I think, probably, unlike me, a Jansenist.

BV: *You don't seem to like many writers, especially English writers. Somerset Maugham, for instance . . .*

GG: No—but there are writers whom I *do* admire very much in English and among people of my generation. I was both a great friend and great admirer of Evelyn Waugh and there are several younger writers today whom I admire in England.

BV: *Who?*

GG: (Well, probably) I don't know if they are translated into French. There's a woman Beryl Bainbridge. There's an Irish, Northern Irish writer who now lives in America, who's called Brian Moore. There's Muriel Spark who now lives in Italy . . . There are a number of writers.

BV: *And in France?*

GG: Well, I'm very ignorant about the contemporary novel in France. It's a matter of laziness. It takes me longer to read a French book than it does an English book. I like the early Julien Green very much.

BV: *Is it the troubled Christian in him you like?*

GG: Perhaps! Perhaps! (laughs).

BV: *Who else?*

GG: Well . . . there's Bernanos, but I read him in translation.

BV: *What about South American writers? Marquez, for example?*

GG: I like Marquez very much. We are great friends and have even worked together. No, not on a novel . . . but to secure the liberation of hostages in San Salvador.

BV: *What do you think of contemporary literature in general? Is it alive and powerful?*

GG: Yes. I think literature is like the beam from a lighthouse . . . it moves from one area of experience to another. I think Marquez deserves the Nobel Prize. At this time, the beam of the lighthouse is locked on Latin America. It was focused once on France, especially at the time of Mauriac, Cocteau and Sartre. But literature is alive and well.

BV: *Do you think the world has changed over the past half century?*

GG: Yes. I believe the world has deteriorated considerably since the last war as a result of terrorism, dictatorship, especially the military dictatorships in Latin America. I often ask myself whether the world has been infected by Hitler. His death did not put an end to terrorism; it has introduced terrorism into the bloodstream of Europe. Would the Red Brigade have existed if there were no Hitler? He has taught the world cruelty.

BV: *Are the massacres in the Palestinian camps of Sabra and Chatila*[6] *the logical outcome of Hitler's legacy?*

GG: Yes. The situation would have been different if Hitler had not existed. There would have been no PLO and I'm convinced that Palestine would have settled its problems if there were no Hitler.

BV: *You condemn American imperialism in* The Quiet American. *Do you think America has become more democratic since?*

GG: No. I believe America is like a paralyzed giant, especially with its present president. It shocks me to see Reagan providing aid to the military junta of San Salvador. When you think of the three raped and murdered nuns, three American nuns: that should have been enough reason to stop United States aid—just as Carter did once. Today, the situation in Nicaragua is serious: the old Somoza guard remains a menace to Nicaragua; so are the incursions along the Honduran border. Children have been killed as they taught peasants to read and write. I can't understand Reagan's position when he complains that Nicaragua buys too many weapons. They need these weapons to defend themselves against the military regime of Honduras and the followers of Somoza.

BV: *What do you think of the Soviet behaviour . . . in Afghanistan, for example?*

GG: I do not like that invasion at all . . . but it shocked me less than the invasion of Czechoslovakia. In Afghanistan, there was a bloodthirsty and Stalinist tyrant Amin—bad publicity for the communists—and that was perhaps some excuse for their intrusion. But I think the Soviets have discovered how difficult it is to occupy that country—just as the English did in the nineteenth century.

BV: *What is your opinion of the war in the Falkland Islands?*[7]

GG: To me it's a silly war which shouldn't have taken place. I think the first fault lay in the British Foreign Office who had given the impression that we wished to get rid of the Falklands. The second fault was Argentina's, by their invasion of Southern Georgia, which had never been Argentinian and had never been Spanish. But when they decided to attack I think we were right to reply and I hoped that the one good which might come out of it, and it may still come out it, would be the fall of the military junta in Argentina.

But the curious thing was an Argentinian journalist wrote to me before we landed in the Falkland Islands asking what I thought about the situation and I wrote back to her saying: *"The difference between your country and mine is that you will not be able to publish my letter while I can publish anything that you care to write"*. . . . And then I went on to say much as I have said now—the first fault is ours— but the one good thing that would come out of it would be the fall of the military junta . . . . To my surprise, it was printed, during the invasion of the Falkland Islands, by the *Clarion*, which is the biggest newspaper in Buenos Aires.

BV: *How would you analyse the present situation in the world? Is it leading to a catastrophe?*

GG: I think there would have been a catastrophe probably if a "catastrophe" now didn't mean a nuclear war. One wonders—I wonder—I'm no economist—how we're going to get out of the economic situation? We got out of the economic situation in the thirties because there was a war. Now how do we get out *without* a war? How do we get out of the economic situation—and a war would mean probably nuclear weapons in the end.

BV: *Do you think the world might go mad?*

GG: Well, there I'm optimistic.

BV: *Is your optimism inspired from hope in the youth of today?*

GG: I don't know—I don't know enough young people to answer that but I would not like to be young at this period of history.

BV: *Isn't today's youth rather disillusioned?*

GG: Yes. I think they have every right to mistrust their elders.

BV: *What was Graham Greene like as a young man?*

GG: Well, in the 20's of course it was a period of the hunger marchers and the early 30's—Stephen Spender has a poem with the line "We who live under the shadow of a war, what can we do that matters?" So that in a sense I have experienced a little of what the young experience today, because all through the 30's one knew that the war was coming, and now the young probably *fear* that war is coming. I'm, as I say, more optimistic because I think that common sense will save the world.

BV: *Do you think that the arrival of Socialism in France can give new hope to the youth of today?*

GG: I hope so . . .

BV: *What do you as a writer and man expect of life now?*

GG: I wait for . . . peace.

BV: *Do you think it will come?*

GG: Perhaps . . .

BV: *Are you optimistic or pessimistic about the future?*

GG: I'm thinking about personal peace, not world peace. I'm optimistic about world peace but less so for personal peace.

BV: *What troubles you?*

GG: Many things are difficult these days.

BV: *On the Côte d'Azur? In your private life?*

GG: In my private life. I'm optimistic on the whole for the world.

BV: *Do you think love can save humanity?*

GG: Common sense, I think, may save humanity.

Bernard Violet, "Le terrorisme est une conséquence de l'Hitlerisme: Un entretien avec Graham Greene," *Les Nouvelles Littéraires*, 9 December 1982, 24–26. *Editor's title.*

Notes

1. This is indeed a rare occasion when Greene allowed two takes of the interview to be telecast by the French FR3 Côte d'Azur and the German ARD (November 1982). For a man who is so much involved with film and theater, Greene's continued resistance to television coverage seems almost irrational. He has continually avoided all dealings with TV. When he consented to appear before the British Film Institute in 1970, his conditions were: "No TV or radio coverage; no interviews; no word to the press where he would be staying." (Philip Oakes, "Graham Greene," *Sunday Times*, 1 March 1970, 58). He "flatly refused" Christopher Burstall's request that he appear in a film but allowed "a long conversation which might form the basis of a film." He was "afraid of playing a part on the screen" and he would then "cease to be a writer [he'd] become a comedian." See Christopher Burstall, "Graham Green Takes the Orient Express," *Listener*, 21 November 1968, 672–74, 676–77. John Heilpern notes in 1975 that Greene shares with Samuel Beckett the "unique distinction among famous men" that he has never appeared on television. He did admit to Sydney Edwards, however, that though he has always refused television interviews in the West, he gave a T.V. interview in Budapest in 1975(?) but requested that it *not* be shown in the West. (Sydney Edwards, "A Rare Interview in News of the Arts," *Evening Standard*, 28 November 1975, 24.) The Hungarians obliged. As late as January 1987, Greene, amused by the idea of the documentary, *The Other Graham Greene*, accepted to cooperate in its production provided that such cooperation did not entail his appearance on the screen; otherwise he would "have had to refuse" Nigel Finch's request.
2. Greene's conversion to Catholicism took place in 1926 not 1927.
3. Father Leopoldo Duran, S.J.
4. See note 8 on p. 82 of the Jean Duché excerpt, "A 'Jansenist' Writer of Thrillers."
5. Though it is most difficult to define Jansenism accurately, the image of the crucified Christ that Greene describes is consistent

with the Jansenist principle that denies the freedom of the will and the possibility of resisting Divine Grace.

6. On 16 September 1982, Christian militia, allowed by the Israeli occupying forces to enter these two Palestinian refugee camps in West Beirut, slaughtered some 600 people, including women and children.

7. See note 18 on pp. 427–28 of the Maria Couto excerpt, "The Solitude of the Writer and Political Involvement."

Travels with "The Complete Hero"

Auberon Waugh

Even while he was writing his new novel, *Monsignor Quixote* . . . Graham Greene was gloomy about its reception. It would annoy Catholics and Marxists, he said, and nobody else would be remotely interested in it. When, having read the book, I told him I did not think it would annoy Catholics much — in fact it was almost impossible to think of anything which would annoy Catholics nowadays — he looked even gloomier. "The book starts with a joke about the Trinity.[1] You don't feel they might think it goes too far?" he asked hopefully.

To annoy his fellow-Catholics might almost be an essential part of the practice of his faith, a solemn Christian duty. As he gets older, Graham Greene seems to become more and more Catholic, although he denies this hotly. "I believe less, and accept more, through obedience. For instance," he added wistfully, "I could easily do without the virgin birth. But my faith tells me I am wrong." Smugness and certainty are the greatest enemies of religion, he believes, a curious attitude for a convert to Roman Catholicism. Doubt is an essential ingredient of any faith, whether Catholic or Marxist.

At 77 he looks extraordinarily well on this diet of doubt. There is a natural sweetness of nature, a modesty and friendliness about the man which make all who know him well fiercely proud of their friendship. In my own case his benevolence is transferred. He knew and loved my father, and will believe no ill of the son.

The friendship between Graham Greene and Evelyn Waugh was a strange and rather beautiful thing. In elevated or conceited moments I imagine I understand exactly those qualities in each which appealed to the other. Waugh was a sucker for certainties; Greene is a sucker for doubts. What they shared, I think, was a certain honesty, a recklessness, and a keen awareness of everybody else's absurdity. At any rate, it was enough to bind them together with hoops of steel. The happy result, from my own point of view, was that I inherited a hoop or two.

There is something bland and beautiful in his trust. Conversation jumps disconcertingly from whether the Pope is trying to commit suicide with his programme of world travel to the effects of opium on sexual performance, or from malicious rumours about his own sex life to the politics of South America—all discussed with total honesty and without a trace of self-consciousness.

"Do you think the Pope is seeking an end? He would be the first Pope to have committed suicide. I feel that is very interesting. His visit to El Salvador could easily be part of a self-destructive urge. I can't think of any other reason for going there at the present time."

He speaks in a speculative, tentative voice. Everything is open to discussion. Nothing is likely to shock him. Friends will be relieved to hear that Graham Greene has no desire to be involved in El Salvador.

He is not a remotely political person himself, despite being obsessed by political struggles. He has lived in Antibes for 16 years, dividing his time between a modest two-roomed flat overlooking the harbour and a more daunting one in Paris in the Boulevard Malesherbes where he keeps most of his books. It is crammed from floor to ceiling with them and, although he seldom spends more than eight weeks a year in Paris, he does miss his books.

There can be no question that he is fully committed to the struggle,[2] now in its third year. When I visited him he would normally have been in Paris to escape the heat and the crowds of summer, but after an attempted break-in at his flat in Antibes he had decided to sit it out alone. Another reason he could not leave was that his opponents have a way of serving writs on him in his absence, with the result that several judgments have gone against him unopposed.

There was something rather sad about the thought of this immensely distinguished elderly man, living alone in his two-room flat with a loaded pistol close at hand[3] (he enjoys fantasies about a shoot-out with Daniel Guy, whom he once counted as a friend).

Before meeting him again, I was prepared to believe that old age had affected his judgment. As everyone knows, he once played Russian roulette and his restlessness took him to many of the world's trouble spots, inspecting bloated corpses floating in the African sunshine and other unpleasant reminders. Was there also not an element of exhibitionism in the campaign, even childishness? Where was the gentleness, the deep understanding of twisted, malevolent natures which led one critic to suggest that "compassion" was not the right word for his attitude to sin so much as "complicity"?[4]

A few hours in his company were enough to convince me that his powers had not slipped in the least. The gentleness is still there, and all the high intelligence. There is nothing pathetic about his existence—he has plenty of friends, does not seem to be lonely or even bored, and escapes most of the squalor of bachelor existence by having no kitchen and eating out in one of three excellent local restaurants. In fact, he has little appetite for food now, despite his large frame, and more often than not does not eat in the evening, taking a dry Martini or two before early bed. By day he writes at his desk in the drawing room with a view of the harbour.

As his handwriting is more or less illegible, his correspondence with the outside world is carried out through his sister[5] who lives in Sussex, to whom he dictates letters over the telephone, which are then typed on ready-signed sheets of writing paper with the Antibes address. Living alone, he has no protection against the telephone and his chief anxiety seemed to be that the English newspapers would discover his new telephone number, recently changed with enormous difficulty.

Nor is it true that the strain of epic battle—still being conducted in a white heat of fury at the brutality and mismanagement of lawyers, the apparent venality of police and local government—has stopped him writing. *Monsignor Quixote* is a product of these years: a touching, funny, some might say deeply dotty study of friendship and conflicting faiths. It arose from four trips with his friend and spiritual mentor Father Leopoldo Duran, who is Professor of English Literature at Madrid University.

"It is not my opinion that Marx was a holy man. That was a whim of the Monsignor. I find Marx an old bore," he explained disarmingly. He also finds Cervantes' *Don Quixote* on which the novel is partly based, pretty boring.

Among his latest book's main themes—the need for doubt, the unimportance of the distinction between fact and fiction, the overriding validity of jokes—its political or ideological content is the least important. Monsignor Quixote is a Catholic despite the Curia, the Communist Mayor is a Communist despite the Politburo; they are both survivors. Neither takes to a revisionist version of his faith: both faith and doubt must be fundamental.

Greene is sceptical about popular charismatic religion, and was rather annoyed when a miraculous breathing statue of the Virgin Mary which he was taken to see in Assisi did actually appear to breathe. "The local Communist mayor had just spoken out against this superstitious credulity and, do you know, he was struck dead that day. Rather impressive really.

"The crowd just sat around eating sandwiches, but we decided to do the thing properly, lying on our backs for the best view. It certainly gave every sign of breathing."

He still hopes that the Holy Shroud of Turin will prove to be genuine, but only because it will annoy so many people. . . .

The main argument of *Monsignor Quixote* might have appeared at any time in his writing, but the form is puzzling. In addition to the skeleton of Don Quixote there are distinct undertones of Giovanino Guareschi's *Don Camillo*,[6] the twee Italian parish priest who also has a sort of teasing affection for his Communist mayor. A little inquiry revealed that this was not an accident.

But why should our greatest and our best writer of English take as his models a nauseating low-brow Italian sentimentalist and a Spaniard he finds boring? The answer lies, perhaps, in a compulsive spirit of self-mockery which has surfaced from time to time in Graham Greene ever since anybody started to take him seriously—and probably even before. "I didn't think *Don Camillo* was as bad as all that," he said mildly, when I put this view to him.

He is serious in his campaign against the corruption and injustice of officialdom in the south of France. It is not just a means of escape from boredom. His generous and chivalric spirit is outraged; above all, his most intimate loyalties and affections are touched. But he cannot help, also, seeing something slightly ridiculous in the spectacle of a 77-year-old troubadour, all saddled up and ready to carry his lance against the dragons to defend his lady's honour.

"No, I am not going to leave Antibes. I have never even thought of it," he says defiantly. They may not be windmills which he is fighting, but he is aware that others will think so, and half of him rejoices in the absurdity of it, while the other half knows that his cause is just. Perhaps that is a definition of the Complete Hero. I hope he never wearies.

Excerpted from Auberon Waugh, "Travels with 'The Complete Hero,' " *Telegraph Sunday Magazine*, 12 September 1982, 30–33.

Notes

1. Chap. 1 concludes with Father Quixote's bishop attributing the promotion to the rank of monsignor to the "strange stirring of the Holy Spirit." But it is the monsignor's attempt to explain the Trinity in terms of three bottles of wine ("Same substance. Same birth. They're inseparable. Whoever partakes of one partakes of all three" [p.42]), which some readers may find humorous in its simplicity, ingeniousness, or offensiveness.

2. The struggle with the municipal establishment of Nice resulted from Greene's inquiries into the criminal background of Daniel Guy who was married to Martine Cloetta, the daughter of a couple whom he had befriended in the French Cameroons in 1959 and

who now lived in Antibes. Greene believed that Nice had become the privileged haunt of the most powerful criminal milieu in the south of France and had permeated local government and the judiciary, too. *J'Accuse* (London: Bodley Head, 1982) sets out Greene's accusations against the high level corruption in Nice. The pamphlet was suppressed by the French courts and Greene was fined some $4,000 for defamation. (It should be noted that Martine's mother, Yvonne Cloetta, was Greene's "girlfriend" and companion for over thirty years until his death in 1991. On his deathbed, Greene asked Cloetta to prepare his dream diary for publication. For an interesting account on the influence of certain women on Greene, including Yvonne Cloetta, see Alex Kershaw, "An End of the Affairs," *Guardian Weekend*, 31 October 1992, 6–10.)

3. Greene, whose attention to accuracy is "scrupulous," resented such misrepresentation and noted to Norman Lebrecht (see p. 389 of the Lebrecht excerpt, "Commitment to Central America and a Passion for Religion") that he did not even have a gun license! On the other hand, Jon Swain notes that Greene "continues to carry a CS gas canister in his pocket for protection." (*Sunday Times*, 7 March 1982, 8).

4. Greene's sense of "transcendent" evil, noted Walter Allen in his early perceptive analysis of the novels, was "real, experienced along the nerves and in the blood" (Walter Allen, "The Novels of Graham Greene," *Penguin New Writing* 18 [July–September 1943]: 148–60) and, whereas Sean O'Faolain argued that Greene's interest in evil and ugliness was originally instinctive or emotional, "Donat O'Donnell" (pseudonym of Conor Cruise O'Brien) criticized Greene for believing "emotionally in evil" (*Chimera*, 1947, 18–30). But as a humanist, Greene's interest in evil lay in its effect on the human heart, on the "sin-sodden minor-public-school men" of the novels rather than on its "fundamentally theological" aspect. His portrayal of the sinner may have been a shade disturbing for conservative Catholics in the forties, but it drew an accolade from no less a person than Father C. C. Martindale when he wrote: "The author leads us to look into the sinner's eyes with, precisely, the eyes of Christ" (*Tablet*, 26 June 1948, 402). By exercising the reader's sympathy for the sinner, Greene restored to the novel not only man's due proportions as a

being "worthy to be fought over by Satan and God" (W. Peters, "The Concern of Graham Greene," *Month*, November 1953, 281–90) but has also cultivated a profound respect for the mysterious transforming powers of Grace.

5. Elizabeth Dennys.

6. Giovanni Guareschi (1908–68), Italian journalist and writer. The humor and humanity of his stories about a parish priest and a communist mayor in *The Little World of Don Camillo* (1950) made him famous.

A Conversation with Graham Greene

Karel Kyncl

KAREL KYNCL: *In Prague it's rumoured that you have forbidden publication of your works in Czechoslovakia in protest against the Soviet invasion of the country in 1968. Is this true?*
GRAHAM GREENE: No, it isn't true. What I imagine happened is that they didn't much care for my visit in 1969 because it was after that that the publications stopped. But I never, never asked not to be published. With the Russians it did happen and perhaps they took my refusal of the Russians as being an example that they should follow. During the Daniel and Sinyavsky imprisonment I asked them to cease publishing.[1] And the Russians in their curious way are quite scrupulous, and they followed my instructions when I said I didn't wish any further books to be published. Now they are publishing again because I said "as long as Daniel and Sinyavsky are in prison," and so in the last few years they have started publishing again.

KK: *So even in this respect Czechoslovakia is more Soviet than the Soviet Union?*

GG: Yes, and I think that you are the only one of the Communist countries which doesn't publish me. Even the

Chinese have begun and Yugoslavia has always done so, Rumania does so, Bulgaria has just begun, I think.

～～

KK: *In January 1969, a young philosophy student, Jan Palach, publicly set fire to himself in the centre of Prague. His death was a terrifying protest against the Soviet occupation and marked the beginning of the disintegration of human values in Czechoslovakia. Your view of this act, expressed in our television interview in 1969, displeased the authorities very much. What is your opinion today of Palach's death?*

GG: The same as when you asked me the question all those years ago. That speaking as a Catholic I don't regard this as a suicide. I regard it as a very courageous act which you can compare in war to a man who, knowing he will be killed, goes up against a machine-gun post with a grenade, alone. That nobody would regard as suicide, and I don't regard Palach's deed as suicide.

KK: *I remember that then your attitude surprised me, and I am still surprised today. It seems to contradict religious, and particularly Catholic, views of voluntary death. Or am I wrong?*

GG: Yes, I think you are. I think that the Catholics are more flexible in their theology than moral theologians would lead you to believe. I wrote a play about suicide, my first play which was called *The Living Room*, about a girl who in despair about a love affair kills herself, and the attitude of the priest is very much like my attitude to Palach, and nobody in the Church objected to that play.

KK: *Jan Palach has become an Orwellian non-person in Czechoslovakia. His remains were secretly transferred from a Prague cemetery to the country and his name is taboo for historians and the media. People under the age of 30 have probably never heard of him.*

GG: Well, he's a temporary non-person I would have said, because history will change and one day the history books will once again change, and perhaps when the history books change and he becomes a person again it will be all the more dramatic and effective to the young because they knew nothing about it.[2]

KK: *I was once unshakably convinced that Communism is the best and most rational solution to all the problems of mankind. Only gradually did I reach the conclusion that I had been terribly wrong. Now I mainly feel a great distaste and distrust for ideological concepts which claim to have an all-embracing recipe. But is this enough?*

GG: I think that the mere fact that you are doubtful about your own attitude is a very healthy one, because I think that doubt is the best quality in human beings. That's really the subject of the last book I wrote, *Monsignor Quixote*. I've never, except for four weeks at the age of 19, I've never been a member of the CP . . . but I have lingering hope that in certain areas of the world, under certain conditions, there will be a kind of Communism which is acceptable. For example, I don't consider the Sandanista government in Nicaragua as Communist, and I was shocked by the Pope's visit there. I know many members of the government in Nicaragua and I visited it twice, last time in January 1983, and I think it's a very valuable thing that there are two priests actually in the government. The Minister of Culture is an old poet who would not have any great influence, but the Foreign Minister D'Escoto is a Marino father; and not actually in the government but in charge of health and education is a Jesuit priest; and I've taken a completely opposite view to the Pope in that I think he was completely misled by his Polish experiences where the Russians tried to introduce a national Catholic Church in Poland, but the circumstances were so completely different. Nicaragua emerged with a government out of a civil war of which its priests were a part, and I think that it will be perhaps more Socialist than Communist.

KK: *But what about the political prisoners in Nicaragua, for example, and the way they are treated?*

GG: There are certainly several thousand National Guardsmen in prison in Nicaragua. No one was executed at the end of the civil war, but I don't think there are any, apart from the National Guard—I don't know, I rather question your statement. Perhaps Mrs. Jeane Kirkpatrick is behind this.[3] I've just written a letter to the *Times* because there's an interview with her in the *Times* today in which it says she has documentary evidence for the brutal treatment of the Miskito Indians. Well, Borge, Minister of the Interior, said that he felt they had made a mistake and behaved stupidly with the Miskito Indians in not explaining sufficiently to them why they were being removed to camps in another part of the country. But I spoke to an American nun, a sister, working with the poor in Nicaragua, who had been there for 10 years—so she had experienced Somoza, experienced the civil war, and she visited the Miskito Indians in their new camps outside the war zone and she said categorically they are well fed, well housed, and well looked after.[4]

KK: *What is your opinion of these two extreme reactions to inhuman social conditions? On the one hand, there are those who decide to adjust for the sake of survival. And on the other hand, there are those who risk imprisonment for the sake of their opinions—not deeds! and thereby risk losing months or years of their own life as well as endangering their loved ones.*

GG: That's a very, very difficult question because that really goes to the conscience of that particular individual, and I wouldn't say he was wrong to conform under those circumstances or wrong to go to prison — it's such an individual decision.

GG: I don't think it is necessarily a writer's job to set himself up as a kind of defender of human rights. I think his job is to write the idea that comes into his head which deals with human characters, in certain conditions, but not to have messages.

KK: *The trouble is the messages are there!*

GG: Well, people can dig one out perhaps, but I think the only message that I would wish to convey is fallibility. Doubts.

KK: *Don't you also face the same dilemma as your readers? You too must reach individual, personal, partial answers. A writer can suggest a few alternative solutions or leave this or that problem completely open, but as a private person you take a stand.*

GG: I think the writer doesn't lose his right as a human being to speak on political subjects — it's only that I wouldn't wish to be a political writer.

KK: *Men cannot only doubt.*

In 1972, a number of writers and intellectuals in Western Europe formed a committee for the defence of about a hundred Czechoslovak citizens, arrested and sentenced for having allegedly 'damaged the process of consolidation' in the country. I was one of the hundred, hermetically isolated from the outside world.

KK: *Our inability to tell whether or why something does or does not happen in a Communist country is to a large extent linked to the peculiar psychology of the Communist system. So you understand this psychology and these reactions?*

GG: No, I am sure I don't, but I think that perhaps one of the causes of this difference between authoritarianism, like the South American dictators, and Communism, is that Communism has the ambition still to be a world-wide type of society, and therefore they are sensitive to bad propaganda, whilst the authoritarian state is a nationalistic state, they have no such desire. Argentina didn't wish to govern the whole of South America and therefore they were more cruel in a sense and more violent in their methods because they didn't mind bad propaganda.

KK: *How do you explain, for example, that a few months after the invasion of Czechoslovakia the Soviet Union submitted to the United Nations a draft resolution condemning in the harshest possible terms the use of force in international relations and extolling national sovereignty? (To be followed by Afghanistan and Poland.)[5] And how do you explain the fact that Communist officials apparently do not find it absurd that all the barbed-wire obstacles, Berlin Walls, and minefields are on their side of the border? Although, if one extrapolates from Marx, they should be on the other side to keep the oppressed classes of the West from a mass exodus to the East?*

GG: I agree, but then again you could add, it's not exactly Marxist nor is it Leninist, is it? Communism has moved away from Marx and from Lenin . . .

I admit I had certain hopes when Andropov[6] came to power, because one felt that there might be less ideology and more realism. Whether that might still happen — I still have a certain hope.

KK: *What do you think of man, of people . . . Have we got a chance in this deranged world?*

GG: Well, that's a very horrible question to answer. I think the development of the imagination is one of the most important things — through sensible education and through ability to stimulate the imagination. It's difficult for an imaginative man to be cruel without feeling shame at cruelty.

Extracted from Karel Kyncl, "A Conversation with Graham Greene," *Index on Censorship* 13, no. 3 (1984): 2–5.

Notes

1. In June 1967, the BBC televised a "factual construction" of the Moscow trial of Andrei Sinyavsky and Yuli Daniel, the two Russian writers who were severely punished and imprisoned for publishing their work in the West. The program, which was called *The First Freedom*, drew attention to the dissident movement in Moscow. Both Sinyavsky, who published in the West under the pseudonym Abram Tertz, and his friend Daniel (1925–88), another underground writer, were arrested in 1965 and sentenced to work in labor camps for having published works allegedly slandering the Soviet Union. Larisa Daniel's appeal to world opinion on behalf of the two writers appeared in the *Times*, 13 January 1968, 8. Greene's attempt to turn over the royalties of his books in the Soviet Union to the wives of Sinyavsky and Daniel received a "cold response" from the Union of Writers in Moscow as did his request to the editor of the *Literary Gazette* (Moscow). See Greene's statement recorded in the minutes of the PEN meeting in 1968 (*Encounter*, June 1968, 62). In a letter to the *Times* (4 September 1967) protesting the failure of justice at the time of the Daniel-Sinyavsky trial, Greene also wrote: "If I had to choose between life in the Soviet Union and life in the United States of America, I would certainly choose the Soviet Union . . ." Many correspondents seized upon this remark and seemed to forget that the main intent of the letter was the unjust imprisonment of Daniel and Sinyavsky by the Soviet authorities. (See also his letter to the *Times*, 9 September 1967). Quoted out of context, the remark becomes both sensational and provocative.

2. Greene's words in 1984 are rather prophetic. Five years later, in the fall of 1989, the history books did change and Jan Palach remains a hero to people of Czech or Slovak origins.

3. Jeane J. Kirkpatrick (1926–) was the U. S. Ambassador to the United Nations. A leading article in the *Times* (10 April 1984) carried her comments on the situation in Latin America, among other things. She was also profiled in the *Sunday Times* (8 April 1984). Greene's response is in the form of a letter to the editor and is dated 13 April 1984.

4. Some 10,000 Miskito Indians living along the Coco River were relocated to enable the Sandanista government to defend itself against incursions from Honduras. Greene expresses the same sentiment in very much the same words in a letter to the editor to the *Spectator*, 21 April 1984.

5. Soviet troops invaded Afghanistan in December 1979, and martial law was imposed in Poland in December 1981 following the encouragement and "advice" of Moscow.

6. Yuri Vladimirovich Andropov (1914–84), member of the Politburo and head of the KGB, succeeded Leonid Brezhnev in November 1982 as general secretary. He was generally regarded as a "liberal" in the West.

Greene's Jests

John Sutro

On the occasion of Graham Greene's 80th birthday I am attempting to summarise some aspects of a friendship which, starting through our mutual friend Mario Soldati[1] in Rome 1947, has flourished over the years in London, Paris and Antibes. There were also journeys to Amsterdam (I remember a visit to a bordello from which we fled as the girls looked so unsightly), Berlin before the Wall where we were able to enter East Berlin with few formalities, and perhaps a trip to Copenhagen.

I shall begin with the account of a bizarre jest we concocted together, which Graham himself has described. However, since he was in Kenya during the first month of its existence, I had the task of holding the fort alone. I refer to the Anglo-Texan Society founded in August 1953 with Graham as President and myself as Vice-President.

It all started when Graham and I travelled up to Edinburgh to see his play *The Living Room* performed there. We stayed at the Caledonian Hotel. After dinner we were in the lounge having drinks. Sitting in a corner of the large room, looking rather forlorn, were two girls, one very attractive, the other less so. Graham thought it would be fun to invite them to join us and wrote a note which he asked a waiter to give them. By mistake the invitation was handed to an elderly lady who was not amused. Next time the note reached the right destination and the girls came over to our table. Graham clearly showed his preference for the prettier one, leaving me with the other. The girls were from the state of Texas. We had a delightful evening. Next day we saw them again. As we had become friends Graham suggested they should join us in his box at the theatre that night. They accepted with pleasure and enjoyed the performance. I must say those Texan girls really enlivened our stay in Edinburgh and taught us quite a lot about Texas.

We returned to London on the Edinburgh express, spending a considerable time in the restaurant car having lunch and in the afternoon imbibing quantities of Black Velvet. After a while Graham, who must have been brooding over Texan maidens, said, slurring his words: "Let's found an Anglo-Texan Society." I agreed whole-heartedly. Next step was a letter to the *Times*[2] from the two of us announcing the Society's foundation and inviting all those interested to get in touch. The *Times* published the letter but neither of us saw it since Graham had left London for Nairobi whilst my wife and I had gone off to Paris where Gillian's[3] mother had lent us her flat. Hardly had we arrived when the telephone rang: it was a London news agency intrigued by the letter and wanting to know more about the project. Taken by surprise I answered as coherently as possible.

On our return to London, I found over 60 letters awaiting me, some from very eminent people including Sir Hartley Shawcross M.P., Attorney-General, Sir Alfred

Blossom M.P., Mr. Samuel Guinness the banker, and many others, all warmly approving the plan and wishing to join. Nothing could stop the Anglo-Texan Society going from strength to strength. Clearly Graham's name on our letter had caused the furore. I had no choice but to pursue as the Society had somehow launched itself of its own volition. Writing paper was ordered. A second announcement[4] appeared in the *Times:* "The Society has by now been inaugurated. The officers include Mr. Samuel Guinness and Sir Alfred Blossom M.P." Graham remained President whilst I became Chairman.

The most spectacular event in the Society's history was a gigantic reception held at Denham Film Studios, at that time the headquarters of the United States Air Force. Graham could not attend the party as he was in Vietnam. As well as members of the Anglo-Texan Society and their guests, 1,500 Texans were present. The American Air Force provided three barbecues of prime beef. London buses were roped in to transport passengers from Piccadilly Circus to Denham. The Society had supplied dozens of barrels of draught cider to wash down the prime beef. The Governor of Texas commissioned the United States Ambassador to London, Mr. Winthrop Aldrich, to act as Texas Ambassador for the day, and Mr. Aldrich in person handed me the Texan flag.

The Society prospered; many cocktail parties and dinners took place, members kindly lending their homes for these functions. In particular I recollect a dinner party at the House of Lords given by courtesy of Lord Blossom (as he became), a cocktail party at which the Duke of Edinburgh was present which Graham's elder brother Raymond presented Graham to the Duke saying, "Sir, may I introduce my baby brother?" A very special occasion was a dinner given by Mr. Samuel Guinness at his house in honour of Mr. Neiman Marcus, head of the famous store in Dallas renowned for its luxury goods of the highest quality, no expense spared for providing nothing but the best. Gillian, who sat beside him at dinner, found Mr. Marcus rather melancholic and not easy to draw into conversation.[5]

Before embarking on the tale of our other fantasy I would like to go back to earlier days. There was a droll evening in Paris when after dinner Graham said, "Why don't we go and see a blue film?" and asked Gillian if she had any ideas on the subject. Gillian said, "The best thing would be to ask a taxi driver. They know Paris by heart." We found a cab and got it. Gillian, who is bilingual, said to the man, *"Où peut on voir un film porno?"* Gillian was wrong. The driver knew nothing about blue films. Graham proposed going to Fouquet's where a friend of his often went to have a drink at the bar and who might help. Graham and I went in. No luck, the friend was not there. When we were back in the taxi Gillian said, "While you were away the driver suggested, *'Emmenez-les au Sexy et on partage.'* ('Take them to the Sexy and we'll share.') "He thinks I'm a tart with two Brits in tow," Gillian added with a certain amusement. Graham said, "I hope you accepted." "I refused," Gillian replied. "Let's go to the Sexy," Graham said. On arrival Gillian dashed into the place, leaving the taxi driver to collect his full commission for bringing clients to the *boîte de nuit*.[6] The evening was to prove rather expensive. Tepid champagne, a ghastly show, tourists galore. Alas no blue film.

A favourite haunt of Graham's was in the Rue de Douai which he frequented under an assumed name (later on the madame discovered his true identity). One night Graham took us there with his sister Elizabeth. The four of us were ushered into a bedroom containing a huge bed, chairs, and behind a screen the usual sanitary equipment. Champagne was brought in. Then two girls appeared, both dark-haired, far from slim and not very young. They stripped and performed on the bed while we watched. I was a bit embarrassed, the others took it in their stride. More champagne arrived; the girls got down to work with renewed zeal. After a while they suggested Elizabeth and I should depart leaving Gillian and Graham to participate in a *partie carrée*.[7] "We could have lots of fun," the girls said. The offer was politely declined and we went home, a rather tipsy quartet. In retrospect the sight of us fully clad sitting solemnly around the couch on which women with nothing on were cavorting must have been hilarious.

Graham is very generous with gifts, taking much trouble to find something unusual which would give pleasure. Aware of our passion for collecting owls (he put them into *The Human Factor* and also named a little Christmas book *A Wedding among the Owls*, an extract from the novel), one day he returned from Brighton bearing in triumph a splendid antique owl in carved wood containing two ivory clothes brushes engraved with S. Gillian's proudest possession is a gold pencil engraved with the words "G from G," also a small kinky silver and glass boot, owl tumblers from Paris for her birthday—but the list is too long to go on with. Of course he gave us all his books when they came out, inscribed with witty and affectionate phrases. But what we value above all is the book of stories he dedicated to us, *A Sense of Reality*. That touched us deeply.[8]

During one of his first edition searches in England with his brother Hugh he unearthed a copy of my uncle's *Mollentrave on Women*, a comedy by Alfred Sutro performed in 1905, which Graham found very diverting. He greatly admires Oscar Wilde's *The Importance of Being Earnest*, judging it the finest English comedy since Wycherley's *The Country Wife*. Of Bernard Shaw he once said, "A genius but a bore," which after reading my set of 32 volumes I feel contains more than a grain of truth.

Now for the John Gordon Society, an absurd affair which ultimately made Vladimir Nabokov famous. For Christmas 1955 Graham was asked by the *Sunday Times*, as were other distinguished writers, to give his choice of the three best books of the year. He slipped in Nabokov's *Lolita*, one of those green-covered volumes of the Traveller's Companion series "not to be sold in the USA or UK" and eagerly purchased by book-lovers because of their doubtful moral contents. In fact the works were of a high literary quality. After publication of Graham's choice, not a murmur from the London press about *Lolita* until one bright journalist on the *Sunday Express* got hold of a copy which he gave to read to his Editor-in-Chief Mr. John Gordon. From that moment the uproar commenced. Ian Gilmour and his *Spectator* were to play an important part in the foundation of the Society when John Gordon in the *Sunday Express* started off his campaign denouncing Graham and the *Sunday Times* for recommending to the public what he considered was a pornographic book.[9] After reading John Gordon's condemnation of *Lolita* and its sponsors Graham took up the cudgels together with the *Spectator*.[10] Then came the idea of forming the John Gordon Society "against pornography," inspired by Graham, tongue in cheek—another chance to use his genius for practical jokes. We were all amused and excited, Ian Gilmour and I staunchly supporting the plan, Ian letting Graham reply to John Gordon in the *Spectator*. On Tuesday, 6 March 1956, a private meeting was held at

6.30 p.m. at Albany to discuss the formation of a society provisionally called the John Gordon Society. The host was Graham. The minutes of the meeting give a list of the names, which include Mr. A. S. Frere (Heinemann), Mr. Ian Gilmour, Mr. Peter Brook, Lord Kinross, Venetia Murray (*Picture Post*), Lady Bridget Parsons, Baroness Budberg, Mr. Angus Wilson representing Stephen Spender, Mr. T. O'Keefe (Hutchinson's), Lady Juliet Duff, Professor A. J. Ayer, Mr. Christopher Chataway (Independent Television News), Mr. Janes (*Spectator*), Mr. David Farrer (Martin Secker & Warburg), Miss Helen Winick (*Books & Careers*), Mr. Christopher Isherwood, etc. About 60 people were present . . .

The farce continued: Letters poured in from everywhere, either enquiring about or applying to join the John Gordon Society. Many were sent to a fictitious secretary, "Miss Christine Thompson" at 32 Westbourne Terrace. My office was deluged with correspondence, cables to POGO LONDON and stamped addressed envelopes were strewn around like autumn leaves.

On 5 May 1956, John Gordon wrote a most courteous letter to Miss Thompson, thanking the Society for its invitation. He was looking forward ardently to a meeting with us all, so he was delighted to take the opportunity we offered. But he thought we should change the subject on which we wished him to speak. We had proposed "The necessity of censorship." As he was opposed to censorship, he could hardly make a speech defending it. He proposed, instead, that we make the subject "Pornography," which was the original, and he presumed still the main, interest of our Society. He suggested that instead of a lecture we make the function a debate. He suggested that our distinguished

President, Mr. Graham Greene, should undertake to defend pornography in books and newspapers while he would oppose it. As the subject was of wide public interest and, he was sure we would agree, of considerable importance to the community, he thought attendance at the debate should not be restricted to members of the Society but should be open to all who wished to participate.

On 23 May 1956, another letter to Miss Thompson was sent by Mr. John Gordon. He wanted to know where we proposed to hold the meeting. If space was limited he would be happy, as he had said before, to provide us with adequate accommodation. He was sure we would agree that it would be a pity to spoil the evening by limiting the audience. Of course we should invite the press. The more publicity we got the better. After all the real object was publicity. As for the subject to be discussed, he thought we need not worry about any possible differences of opinion between our President and himself regarding what pornography was. He felt sure that they both knew exactly what it was.

On the day, we all arrived early at the Horseshoe Hotel feeling rather worried that perhaps Mr. John Gordon might not come. Our backs to the door, we never heard it open when, also before time, a tall figure slipped in. Everything about him was grey, hair, face and suit. "Am I in the right room for the John Gordon Society dinner?" he asked. "Yes," we said. "I am John Gordon." After some small talk, we took our places at the table. Antonia Pakenham and her fiancé Hugh Fraser were also present. Gillian sat next to John Gordon. . . .

I will close the random recollections with a comical occurrence from the Côte d'Azur, when Graham and I were lunching at the Restaurant Félix in Antibes. Graham met us at Antibes station; he seemed well and relaxed, so we walked across Antibes, avoiding mad dogs and motor cycles. At Félix, Graham's usual table was reserved for us. Graham hurried off to buy the *Times*, and we settled down. On his return, dry martinis were ordered, we consumed roast beef, potato purée, and had a pleasant talk. Graham had just been on a visit to Panama, also Nicaragua and Cuba. "Fidel," he said, "was skinnier than last time and in very good form." The restaurant was not very full: three people at the table behind us, one man in a corner by the window.

While we were having coffee the solitary luncher got up to leave, suddenly stopping in front of our table. He said to me, "Has anyone told you you look exactly like Alfred Hitchcock?" It transpired that the stranger lived at Vence where he ran an art gallery. He asked us for our names. I gave my name, Graham said "Greene," upon which the stranger replied, "An easy name to remember," oblivious of the fact that sitting in front of the table was one of the finest writers in the world.

Extracted from John Sutro, "Greene's Jests," *Spectator*, 29 September 1984, 16–19.

Notes

1. In 1954, Mario Soldati, Italian novelist and filmmaker, directed *The Stranger's Hand*, whose story Greene had supplied. Greene also worked as co-producer with John Stafford and Peter Moon.
2. Letter to the editor, *Times*, 22 August 1953, 7.
3. Gillian is John Sutro's wife.
4. Letter to the editor, *Times*, 23 December 1953, 7.
5. In "A Thorn on the Yellow Rose" (*Daily Telegraph Magazine*, 22 November 1974, 59–60), Greene gives his own version of how the idea first occurred. He also says that he "unburdened [his]

guilty conscience" to Mr. Marcus on that occasion and resigned from the presidency on 1 April 1955.

6. French for nightclub.

7. French for foursome.

8. *A Sense of Reality* (1963) includes four stories: "Under the Garden," "A Visit to Morin," "Dream of a Strange Land," and "A Discovery in the Woods" and is dedicated to "John and Gillian Sutro."

9. Under "Current Events" (*Sunday Express*, 29 January 1956, 6), John Gordon condemned *Lolita*—which he had read at Greene's recommendation—as "sheer unrestrained pornography" and found the book wholly devoted to the central character's "exhaustive, uninhibited and utterly disgusting description of his pursuits and successes" with the "nymphets." Three weeks later (*Sunday Express*, 18 February 1956, 6), he turned on Greene and advised him to see a psychiatrist for his "odd views," accused Sutro of "playing Sancho to Quixote Greene," and denounced the *Spectator* for throwing its "protective mantle over pornography as well as homosexuality." He then challenged the *Spectator* to serialize the novel.

10. In his letter to the editor (*Spectator*, 10 February 1956, 182), co-signed by John Sutro, Greene suggested the formation of a society "to represent the ideals of Mr. Gordon in active form." In his article "The John Gordon Society" (*Spectator*, 9 March 1956, 309), Greene announced that the society had held its inaugural meeting and completed the election of its officers. The issue aroused a certain amount of controversy in the form of letters to the editor—an average of three a week from 17 February 1956 until 23 March 1956 when, finally, the editor of the *Spectator* pronounced the correspondence closed regarding the Society and its activities. Interesting to note that on the pages of the *Sunday Express*, John Gordon proclaimed the "proud honour" of having the Society named after him (26 February 1956, 6), expressed his willingness to debate (4 March 1956, 6), and announced with "pride and joy" that the Society Graham Greene had founded "in repentance" had come through "the travail of birth" (11 March 1956, 6).

Commitment to Central America
and a Passion for Religion

Norman Lebrecht

Greene's sensitivity about his latest encounter with Castro, his description of it as "a mission" and his recent decision to change the subtitle of the book[1] to "The Story of an Involvement" reveal a commitment to the affairs of Central America that runs deeper than any cause he has championed since he supported Vietnam's independence in the 1950s. He has made himself expertly aware of the factional divisions of El Salvador, the literacy campaign in Nicaragua and the latest military manoeuvres in Honduras.

"I've never found myself very politically moved in England," he reflects. "I have only voted once in my life. It was soon after the war when I cast a protest vote for the Communist in the constituency of Westminster. (He hastens to add: "That was a joke.") I find myself getting involved in politics that are really a matter of life and death, as they were in the Far East and are in Central America. Where children's lives depend on it. If *Getting to Know the General* comes out, I want it to appear before the U.S. presidential elections. I feel strongly about Reagan's

policy in Central America. The United States is upholding
the people who murdered Archbishop Romero in San
Salvador and are responsible for thousands of other innocent deaths. America is supporting them out of an absurd
anti-Commie obsession. I don't think the Salvador rebels
are getting more than a trickle of arms from Nicaragua.
Their small-arms are American-supplied. They get them
by killing their enemies in the National Guard and taking
their weapons.

"As for Nicaragua, it is far better off under the present
government than under Somoza.[2] There are Marxists in
the government, true, but there are also Catholic priests. I
propose to dedicate the book to friends of Omar Torrijos,
including the Sandinistas and the El Salvador freedom
fighters. It may have some nuisance value during the
election."

Greene's affair with the region began in 1976 with a
telegram from Brigadier-General Torrijos, inviting him to
Panama. "I don't know to this day why he asked me. I
don't think he had yet read anything of mine, although he
was an avid reader and it was through him that I met
Gabriel Garcia Marquez. Omar hated to be called
"General." He had come to power with a fellow-colonel
who was of the right, but soon put him on a plane to
Miami. We became real friends. Each year the telephone
would ring and I would be told that an air ticket was waiting for me. Chu Chu was a man Torrijos trusted more
than his own chief of staff. He was interested in photog-
raphy and one day went to a camp where Torrijos kept his
800 "Wild Pigs," trained in guerrilla warfare. He was so
impressed by them that he applied to join. The officer
said: 'You're too old.' Torrijos happened to be in the camp
that day and heard about the professor who wanted to be
a fighter. He said: 'Let the old fool try.' So he did, and he

passed. They wanted to make him an officer, but he refused. So he joined Torrijos's security guard."

Torrijos had been training guerrillas for war with the United States. Talks aimed at giving Panama control of the Canal Zone had stalled and American troops in the zone had killed young Panamanian demonstrators. "Omar said, 'If the students go into the zone again I'll have one alternative: to shut them up or go with them. And I won't shut them up.' He had a dream of confrontation. But he liked President Carter, and accepted the eventual treaty as second best. Carter had been told by the Pentagon that he would need 100,000 troops to defend the canal." Greene attended the signing of the Panama Treaty in Washington as an honorary member of the Panamanian delegation. As a private British citizen his visits to the U.S. are restricted on account of his supposed Communist sympathies.[3]

"Before the last U.S. elections Omar said: 'Of course I want Carter to win. But it will be more fun if Reagan does.' He felt Reagan was capable of renouncing the treaty. If he had done, Omar would have fought. He said, 'We can hold Panama City for 24 hours. We can hold out in the jungle and mountains for two years. And long before that, the American people will have been revolted by the whole business.' For the first time since the U.S. Civil War 40,000 American civilians in the Zone would be in the firing line." Torrijos died when his private plane crashed in the mountains in August 1981. Greene's book, intended as his epitaph may also become his post-mortem. "At first I accepted the official report of his death. The weather was very stormy, and I saw no reason to think that the Americans had any desire to kill him. I can see that the Salvadoran military would. But Chu Chu has always believed that Omar was killed. He now says there is new evidence. If there is, one would have to publish it."

Torrijos involved Greene in many of the hemisphere's hotspots. He acted, together with Garcia Marquez, as a go-between in securing the release of two British bankers kidnapped by rebels in El Salvador in 1979. A subsequent attempt to free the South African ambassador failed when the hostage died in captivity of natural causes.

Torrijos sent Greene to meet George Price, the embattled Prime Minister of Belize,[4] protected from Guatemalan hostility by a garrison of British troops. "Price wanted to be a priest, but had to leave the seminary when his father died leaving a large family to support. He still behaves like a priest: rises at 5.30, hears mass every day and leads a celibate life. Torrijos, who did not have much in the way of religion, was a great friend of Price—who is not a military man at all—which demonstrated for me the extent of his human sympathies."

Greene supports the British presence in Belize. He also endorses Britain's other regional venture in the Falklands, "a silly war but a necessary one." He admires Mrs. Thatcher for her integrity. "I would certainly have voted for her in 1979, because the honesty of the Labour leaders had not been very high. I still believe in her honesty, but I don't like her policy.

"Today I would vote SDP. I consider myself a social democrat, not a Marxist. I don't like the extreme left slant in the Labour Party. Mind you, I approve very much of what Kinnock[5] said in Washington about Central America. I wrote as much to the *Times*, but they didn't publish my letter."

For the past 18 years he has followed British events largely through the *Times* which he buys daily in Antibes. He returns to London four or five times a year to see his family and publishers. On his latest visit, unusually, he overcame a natural shyness to give his first public speech for 15 years. His advertised presence at the Best Novels of Our Time campaign attracted an unseemly scramble of literati eager to sit beside an immortal, and a battery of newsmen straining to catch his every word.

He does not like journalists: "they get things wrong." [6] To make his point, he picks up the *Times* report of his Best Novels speech and snorts at its confident assertion that he "seldom leaves his home in the South of France." On the contrary, in addition to visits to Britain and Central America, he keeps a flat in Paris for regular use and goes to Switzerland periodically to see his daughter and friends. The price of preserving his privacy, it seems, has been to create a legend of Greene the recluse.

His own attention to accuracy is scrupulous and he tolerates nothing less in others. "When Auberon Waugh, who is a friend,[7] wrote a full page on me in the *Sunday Telegraph*, I counted ten errors of fact. He said, for example, that I have a revolver under my bed—which is untrue, and could have got me into trouble. I don't even have a licence. And if my enemies thought I was armed, they would shoot first. My friend Chu Chu says a revolver is an aggressive weapon; it is no use in self-defence."

He granted this interview as a favour to his paperback publishers, Penguin, allowing them to choose the writer but stipulating rigid time limits. In the event, once human contact was established, Greene proved to be forthcoming and flexible, resisting very few questions and extending our time together by two hours, yet revealing of himself only what he wanted to reveal.

We met at The Ritz, where he stays in London, and began talking in the car on the way to have his photograph taken by Lord Snowdon.[8] "He last took my picture on the day I left England in 1966. He made me look very wistful; on the contrary, it was one of few occasions when

I was cheerful." In Kensington we stop to browse at a second-hand bookshop part-owned by Greene's younger
brother, Hugh, former director-general of the BBC.
Greene takes a keen interest in the business ("we all chip
in with review copies, but we get a fair price") and recalls
his own fantasy, woven while on air-raid duty in the Blitz,
of opening a quiet bookshop.

At lunchtime we descend to one of the pubs around St.
James's frequented by Greene and his wartime MI6 colleagues. If "Greene Land" were other than an imaginary
territory invented by critics, the warren of streets and alleys
south of Piccadilly could serve as its capital. Greene is envi-
ably at ease in these surroundings, a tall, patrician figure in
a tweed coat and striped suit who passes unnoticed in the
throng of minor civil servants and business clerks in a fusty
public bar. He speaks softly, in an educated but unexagger-
ated accent, his diction enriched by a glottal "r" and an
endearingly slurred "th." He says "fru" for through, "fings"
for things. He laughs breathily and often.

He lunches on two long, thin sausages and a pint of bitter, English delicacies unobtainable in the South of
France. He is irritated by any suggestion that his
Englishness or familiarity with England may have been
impaired by self-exile. "One critic reviewing *The Human
Factor* said I was out of date because a man in the book
was buttoning up his flies when crossing the inn yard at
the King's Arms at Berkhamsted. Well I've still got flies; I
hate zips. I'm still wearing the four suits I bought more
than 20 years ago, and I'm sure the poor man in the book
couldn't afford better."[9]

He saves the suits for his travels. At home, he dresses in
summer clothes. A further concession to the Mediterranean
climate is to dilute his whisky in soda, though he does not

usually drink till the evening, with a day's writing behind him. "If I'm working, I have toast and tea in the morning, then write until I have my bath and get dressed. I generally lunch out and in the evening heat up a snack (a nice man from the *Guardian* wrote that my flat doesn't have a kitchen:[10] what nonsense!). After dinner, with half a bottle of wine and an aperitif, I do revision. My ear is better at that time to catch the sound of a sentence." He is unmusical in any tonal sense. He does not listen at home to records, nor watch television, except for news programmes.

This monastic, dedicated and apparently placid old age is lived, however, amid an intrusively hostile environment. Two years ago Greene published a bi-lingual pamphlet, *J'Accuse: The Dark Side of Nice*, about, amongst other things, the divorce of a property developer, Daniel Guy, and his wife Martine, a friend of Greene's. Like all his books it received worldwide distribution. Copies were quickly confiscated by the French authorities on the grounds that the book "intruded into the private life of Daniel Guy." It is still on sale in neighbouring Monte Carlo.

Martine Guy[11] now lives in Switzerland. Greene describes her as "my greatest friend; I have known her since she was a child of six." Every night, lying in bed, he prays for her children. "It is the only thing I pray for. I ask that the situation get solved quickly, quickly, quickly. Then I am ready to be off."

This nocturnal submission is Greene's central act of devotion as a "semi-practising" Catholic. He goes to mass regularly but does not take communion, "because I have broken the rules." He considers himself a Catholic agnostic. Yet his passion for religion is undimmed and his name appears frequently in the Catholic press contesting one or other aspect of doctrine. "Many Catholics would prefer me to have left the religion altogether," he sighs. Some of his books have been banned by the Holy See, but *Monsignor Quixote*, a travelogue-cum-dialogue between a priest and a Communist that Greene firmly expected to inflame the faithful, has been blessed instead with universal acclaim.

His isolation beside the Mediterranean does not preclude close relations with his family. He continues writing, he asserts, with a trace of irony, to support them. "I've got two grandchildren at an expensive age. One is at engineering college, the other apprenticed to an architect. I help my son and daughter. I have a wife to help, too, quite a lot of responsibilities."

Occasionally the family debt is repaid in literary coin. It was at his daughter's Christmas table at Jongny that he conceived the sinister plot of *Doctor Fischer of Geneva or The Bomb Party*. The evil doctor has become the latest of Greene's creations to be made into a film. It is one of few that he has personally sanctioned after rejecting several scripts. Ultimately he approved a treatment by the producer, Richard Broke. "He visited us on set in Switzerland for two or three days last winter," says Broke, "and even came out for the icy night filming on the lake. We wondered for a while whether we could persuade him to play a cameo role." Greene may have been tempted to act but on this occasion did not fall. His only film appearance, in François Truffaut's *La Nuit Américaine*, was made without the director's knowledge.

He stubbornly refuses to appear on television, resisting even the subtle blandishments of his younger brother when head of the BBC. But his love of the movies survives from his 1930s era as a film critic, and he flushed with

pleasure when I reported Richard Broke's unsolicited tes-
timonial: "He's not just a novelist: he's a working film
man." At the request of his sister, Elizabeth Dennys, he
has selected 17 films for the forthcoming Brighton
Festival, the only ones bearing his name that he likes.
They include four for which he wrote screenplays himself:
Brighton Rock, Our Man in Havana, The Fallen Idol and, most
famously, *The Third Man.*

Quite unexpectedly, he has just been confronted with
another film treatment he wrote 40 years ago entitled *The
Tenth Man* and set in wartime France. Even more surprisingly, he intends to publish it unchanged as a novel early
next year.

"When the war was over and I left government service,
I wasn't confident of being able to support the family on
writing. I had done very little writing during the war. So
I sold myself to MGM on a slave contract under which
they owned everything I did. Then recently I got a letter
from someone I don't know in America saying, do you
know that a story of yours called *The Tenth Man* is to be
published? I made enquiries and found that MGM had
discovered it in their archives and owned all the literary
rights, the film rights and everything else.

"I didn't take it seriously at first, because as far as I
remembered it was something I had jotted down on two
sheets of notepaper. When it reached me, I saw it was
rather longer than *The Third Man.* It is a short novel.
Initially I was planning to use all kinds of blackmail to
stop it being published, disowning it in the press and so
on. Then to my disquiet, I found it was really rather good,
in fact rather better than *The Third Man.* I have made only
tiny alterations, a word here and there. The trouble is, it's
not bad. Anthony Blond[12] got hold of it, but he has

behaved very well. He will publish it together with the Bodley Head, paying a royalty to MGM."

Greene is now keen to resume work on "an abandoned novel" of some 10,000 words that has been lying in the drawer for some time. "I rather like the beginning," he laughs.

He no longer expects this, or any of his published books, to win him the Nobel Prize that most English readers fervently believe he deserves. "Don't let's talk about it," he urges. "It's always the same story of poor Mr. Arthur [sic] Lundqvist[13] saying 'over my dead body.' I don't think I have ever met the man, although I used to go to Sweden quite a lot. I'm too old now, anyway. I don't expect it and I don't resent it. God knows what I would have done if I had ever got it. I wouldn't have liked to dress up in a white tie and tails to receive it."

As a poor substitute he has been made a Companion of Literature by the Royal Society of Literature. He will receive his scroll shortly before his 80th birthday, later this year, together with two other new Companions, Samuel Beckett and William Golding, both Nobel Laureates.[14] Greene will undoubtedly declare himself, without discernible irony, to be honoured in their company.

Extracted from Norman Lebrecht, "The Greene Factor," *Sunday Times*, 1 April 1984, 33–34. *Editor's title.*

Notes
1. Lebrecht is referring to *Getting to Know the General* (1984).
2. General Anastasio Somoza was ousted by the Sandanista National Liberation Front in 1979. The U. S. continued to support his followers, the Contras, well into 1988.
3. See note 3 on p. 112 of the Kenneth Tynan excerpt, "An Inner View of Graham Greene" and note 2 on pp. 217–18 of the Israel Shenker excerpt, "Graham Greene at Sixty-six."

4. George [Cradle] Price (1919–), leader of the People's United Party, became prime minister when Belize gained independence on 22 September 1981. He is an avid reader of Greene's novels.

5. Neil [Gordon] Kinnock (1942–), Welsh-born politician, was elected leader of the British Labour Party in 1983. He resigned as leader when Labour failed to get a majority in the 1992 election.

6. Greene's dislike for journalists is almost legendary and dates back to the fifties. An entry in his Congo Journal for 6 March 1959 reads: "Usual trouble with a journalist. Made an appointment for tomorrow evening when I shall be gone." (*In Search of a Character*, 90). The dislike for journalists seems to have grown more acute with time. Michael Mewshaw noted that Greene, like other novelists, had learned "the hard way to avoid idle conversation with journalists" and records Greene's words: "It's got so I hate to say who I am or what I believe." (See p. 258 of Mewshew excerpt.) In 1984, John Vinocur noted that not the "most affecting side" of Greene's personality shows when he speaks about "those who have somehow miscast what . . . [he] remembers doing or saying." *New York Times Magazine*, 3 March 1985, 36–39.

7. Auberon Waugh (1939–), eldest son of Evelyn Waugh, is an English journalist and novelist and currently editor of the *Literary Review*. The article in question appeared on 12 September 1982.

8. Anthony Armstrong-Jones Snowdon (1930–), versatile photojournalist was able to bring sympathy to photographic stories. He married Princess Margaret in 1960 (divorced 1978).

9. In *The Human Factor*, Colonel Daintry was sitting at the wheel of his car when "a man came across the yard from the outside lavatory, whistling a timeless tune, buttoning his flies in the security of the dark, and went into the bar." (270)

10. John Cunningham, "Plain Thoughts of an Englishman Abroad," *Guardian*, 19 December 1983, 11.

11. Martine's marriage to Daniel Guy and the events surrounding their subsequent divorce led to the publication of *J'accuse*.

12. Anthony Blond (1928–) is an English literary agent, publisher, and writer.

13. Artur Lundqvist is a member of the Swedish Academy, the body that awards the Nobel Prize for Literature. See Peter Lennon,

"Why Graham Greene Hasn't Won a Nobel Prize and Solzhenitsyn Has," *Book World* 28 (December 1980): 1–2, 6–7.

14. Also in preparation for his eightieth birthday, the *Times* asked prominent figures to pay their respects to Greene's genius. These were published on two consecutive days, 6 and 7 September 1984, and included tributes from Lord Gowrie, Minister of the Arts; A. J. Ayer, philosopher and author; Malcolm Muggeridge, author; Nicholas Last, professor of divinity; Keith Waterhouse, author and columnist; the Duke of Norfolk; Anthony Quinton, philosopher; and David Steel, leader of the Liberal Party.

Graham Greene: On the Short Story

Philippe Séjourné

The elderly, slightly parched face spoke of experience while the penetrating look and clear eyes denied he might be a man of the past. He had opened the door himself and there was warm benevolence in the kindly welcome, also the same diffidence I had heard on the phone: there is little I can say, I am not a specialist of the short story.

But the desire to be of some help and the call of truth soon led to frank acknowledgements and rich confidences: after a short conversation, Graham Greene offered to lay the stage with some preliminary remarks. Then, while the roar and hoot of traffic "that did not use to be there when I first moved in" occasionally burst in through the closed windows, we soon felt carried away by the challenge of words and the interplay of incessant query and dangerous defining . . . or self-defining.

When eventually I had to take leave, I had discovered underneath the writer who had labelled his numerous ventures in as as many titles, the sturdy man who had garnered this experience without bending under the load. Quite the reverse: erect, open to wit and humour, his mind alert to taunting questions or quick at the definite response, now visibly and painfully aware of the wiles of the world, now willingly giving himself away with boyish laughter . . . eager as ever to hear the latest call that might reach him from near or far!

Being one of those for whom his work has proved one of the few lasting founding stones on which life is built, it was something of a miracle I found the words he spoke and the silent ones of his hands and eyes and light summer furniture . . . so closely resembling those he had written:

For this mainly, thank you Mr. Greene!

Because of the obvious sincerity which I did not want to lose and in spite of a few imperfections inevitable in the natural flow of conversation, the text of Graham Greene's interview has been preserved practically word for word:

GRAHAM GREENE: As far as short stories are concerned, I've only written a few, one volume called *Twenty-One Stories,* and two small volumes of short stories. I don't feel at home in the short story, partly because as a novelist, some of the charm of writing a novel is that you don't know everything which is going to happen. I generally know the beginning and I generally know the end; but all kinds of things as may happen in the middle which I had not expected . . . The short story being a much shorter piece I have not found the method of surprising myself in the short story and therefore, reviving my interest. And therefore, my short stories have played a very small part in my life: my own short stories. The short story has one advantage, I think, which Chekhov used a great deal is the open end, that one is not left with an anecdote. And the novel, I think people would be disappointed with the novel having worked through perhaps three hundred pages if the novel had an open end. The novel has to have a closed end, I think. But perhaps, I don't know what my difficulties in the short stories . . . where they arise. I have written a few which I like but to me it's a difficult technique.

PHILIPPE SÉJOURNÉ: *Well thank you for this introduction which already provides some necessary clues as to your general attitude to the short story. Now, I would like to raise a question about what you wrote in the introduction to your* Nineteen Stories *in 1947: "I present these tales merely as the by-products of a novelist's career." This seems to be in accord with what you have just said . . .*

GG: Yes, yes.

PS: *But what you wrote then, was it just about yourself? Or do you believe that novelists in general find short stories mere adjuncts to their main work?*

GG: No, I don't think, I was talking only about myself, although I think an example of a writer who really abandoned the novel was V. S. Pritchett. I think he found the short story was more important to have and more tractable than the novel, although I like very much one of his early novels. I think it was called *Dead Men Leading* or *Dead Man Leading.*[1] But he seems to have almost given up the novel. But on the other hand, we have a very good short story writer in England, an Irishman, William Trevor,[2] and he has written as many novels as short stories, so that he seems to be an adept with both. And of course, one has the great example of James Joyce. I think "The Dead" is one of the finest short stories, not only in the English language, but in literature.

PS: *Now, I thought you might have changed your point of view a little although from what you have just said you probably have not, however. In the Introduction to your* Collected Stories, *you still speak of the short story as a form of escape, but you also write: "I believe I have never written anything better than 'The Destructors,' 'A Chance for Mr. Lever,' 'Under the Garden' and 'Cheap in August'. . ."*

GG: Yes, that's quite true.

PS: *Is that as far as your short stories are concerned? Nothing better than any other short story or considering the whole of your production?*

GG: I don't think so. I would still say that it applies to my short stories. Those were the ones perhaps I preferred. But I would hesitate, I think, to say that they were better than what I consider my best novels. But I think these were the short stories, certain short stories in which I feel I did succeed. To some extent "Under the Garden" did have an open end, which I found the most difficult thing to achieve.

PS: *What did you find so good about them? What were the qualities you enjoyed in these short stories?*

GG: Well, first of all, readability, I think, which I don't always find among some of your critics (laughter).

PS: *Well, personally I find those very good indeed but they are quite a few besides I like as much.*

GG: Yes.

PS: *I am thinking in* Twenty-One Stories *of "The Innocent"* . . .

GG: Yes, I think I can say that's good, it's a little bit anecdotal, isn't it? And perhaps, I have an unfair prejudice against the anecdote. The anecdote is too closed, perhaps.

PS: *Would you say the same about "The Jubilee"?*

GG: I'd say about the same thing. There again, I think it's quite a good anecdote, and I'd put it in the same class as one called . . .

PS: *Also, I thought that "Under the Garden" is excellent but also "Dream of a Strange Land" which I find disconcerting . . .*

GG: Yes, I like that.

PS: *. . . and "The Discovery in the Woods."*

GG: Oh yes! My attempt at science-fiction (laughter). The only science-fiction I have written.

PS: *I found something biblical about it. Weren't you rewriting the story of Noah's Ark and that sort of thing?*

GG: Well, I am beginning to forget the story now. I've forgotten how the story ends.

PS: *They find the big ship stranded . . .*

GG: They find the big ship stranded. How does it end?

PS: *. . . and they say they're sorry there are no longer any giants now. The little girl says that . . .*

GG: Oh yes! Because, the dead old giants. Yes. Yes. I dare say Noah's Ark was somewhere in my mind.

PS: *And how do you like these . . .*

GG: One thing that might be of interest on the short story, is that at least two short stories have been dreams, that I've had at night. "Dream of a Strange Land" was really a dream. The only thing which was not in the dream was the revolver shot at the end, and curiously enough, one called "The Root of All Evil" which was a funny story, was simply a reproduction of a dream I had had at night. In fact, I woke laughing (laughter).

PS: *More generally would you say that the short story serves a purpose of its own? Is there a need in our world for the short story? Does it help to give a better, a more complete picture of the world?*

GG: I suppose somebody who has written as Chekhov did a whole oeuvre in the form of the short story certainly serves a purpose of getting a whole picture of the world. One volume of short stories . . . I find myself—although I admire Trevor's short stories, I admire Pritchett's short stories—I come to read a volume of short stories with hesitation and reluctance. I don't want to change my mood every thirty pages. I like to feel myself taken into something of length, where I am going to stay with the characters over a long period. I find it disconcerting like reading an anthology of poetry. I prefer to read the works of a poet rather than a few poems by this poet and a few others by another poet. I find the change disconcerting. But that's a purely personal attitude. I'm sure that many people prefer the short story to the novel, probably, for the very reason that I find them disconcerting.

PS: *But when you're about to write something, how do you feel that it is going to be a novel or a short story? Is it because it is a particular theme, does it seem to you that this theme has to be worked out in a short story?*

GG: Yes, and . . . I don't know. Perhaps I'm eccentric in this. I know the number of words before I begin to write: not fairly roughly, but rather accurately. For example in the novel *The Human Factor*, I decided would be around a hundred and ten thousand words. And it turned out to be around I think a hundred and eleven thousand, three hundred and something. I have this habit of believing in some sort of computer in the brain that I mark every hundred words as I write with a little cross and keep count of the number of words written all the way through the book. And the same with the short story. And so I imagine that when an idea comes to me, I can feel this will be four thousand words, two thousand words or ninety-five thousand words.

PS: *I read somewhere that you said you wrote about three hundred words every day . . .*

GG: That's what . . . It used to be five hundred. I'm lazier. It's the minimum I set myself. It may be three hundred and fifty five. And the three hundred is marked, but it's to give myself the necessary energy to, at any rate, do something every day.

PS: *But if you write a short story, don't you try to write the whole short story in one go?*

GG: No. I can't do that. It's too long.

PS: *Now, because of its dimensions, do you feel that one of the weaknesses of the short story is that it has to deal with something extraordinary? Because it is going to be so short, that it has to be more violent, to deal with some extraordinary event, extraordinary character, or an extraordinary set of circumstances?*

GG: I don't think it does necessarily. I wouldn't say that Chekhov dealt much with violence, or even . . . some of his stories may deal with extraordinary circumstances, but I wouldn't have thought it was a characteristic of Chekhov. I don't think it would be a characteristic of Pritchett. Or even of Joyce . . .

PS: *. . . but maybe of some of your own stories?*

GG: Some of my own stories, certainly. But then, my novels have often dealt with violence too.

PS: *I am thinking of some extraordinary events, for instance, the man who brings back the body of his little son in a plane . . . in "The Overnight Bag". . .*

GG: Oh, there is nothing in his bag. He is not really bringing a child back in his bag. It's his imagination.

PS: *"The Shocking Accident" is rather extraordinary, too, the pig falling from a balcony . . .*

GG: This was based on a reality. There was an accident of that kind in Naples once (laughter), where a pig was being fattened on a balcony.

PS: *You seem to have borrowed occasionally from incidents you have actually seen on the street?*

GG: Yes, and overheard in a restaurant.

PS: *How much truth is there in for instance "May We Borrow your Husband"? How much did you retain from an overheard conversation?*

GG: I changed the venue. I was staying in a hotel at Cap Ferrat and looking out of the window. I was watching a pair, a couple of homosexuals during a day, outside. And the idea came to me from that. I imagined the circumstances, I imagined afterwards certain circumstances, but it came to me from watching them. And then as I didn't know Cap Ferrat especially well, I changed the scene to Antibes.

PS: *And in "Chagrin in Three Parts".* . .

GG: The restaurant is Felix au Port, and there were a couple of lesbians whom I used to see dining there frequently and whom I regarded from a distance. There was no incident like in the story but they read the book later and spoke to me and were very pleased at thinking that they were the characters in the story (laughter).

PS: *I don't want to be indiscreet, but I'd like to ask you how you feel the differences in technique when you set about writing a short story or a novel? Do you feel you are confronted with a different world?*

GG: Yes, I feel that I'm confronted by something which is going to go very rapidly. And finish in a rather short space of time, say a week. And that in a way, I feel that one has got to be more concentrated, to get over the effect one wants rapidly, that there's a kind of time element pressing on one while for the novel I like to feel a whole period of time confronting me where I can change my mind, when a character can suddenly alter. There is a kind of feeling of leisure about writing a sentence while for the short story, I feel now "I've got to get this done."

PS: *Do you know from the start what the short story is going to be? The whole of it?*

GG: I think yes, and and that is what worries me about the short story. But as I say, I want to be refreshed by surprises.

I'm glad when a character behaves in a way I never meant him to behave. When a line of dialogue comes out of the blue and seems to have nothing to do with the story. And one obeys one's instinct and puts it in and then one hundred pages later, the reason for it appears. As if the unconscious is working all the time in a novel. And the short story seems to me more the conscious than the unconscious at work.

PS: *Would you say that novel writing is an obstacle to the writing of short stories? Are there not some kind of habits that may be in your way?*

GG: Well, certainly. I think I'd written (apart from childish things) a good many novels before I even attempted a short story. I would say that I had written three novels before . . . I think the first short story of mine (apart from a childish thing when I was sixteen) was one called "At the End of the Party" about two children. And that would have been published, I think, around the early 1930's.[3] And I would have published three novels before I did that, and written five.

PS: *In terms of technique of the short story, what importance do you give to the plot? Is it essential there should be a plot in a short story?*

GG: No, I would dislike to say that anything was an essential in writing, because it seems to limit one, and I don't think that one should feel that there are any limits. And, I mean, for example, there is a little anecdote short story of mine which one can hardly say to have a plot: when I am left alone in a railway carriage with a baby and his mother has gone to the lavatory. I mean there is no real plot in it. Still it could be called an anecdote I suppose, but it goes a little bit beyond an anecdote, in looking into the future of the child.

PS: . . . *Do you think humour or some form of comic is a good ingredient in the short story?*

GG: I certainly think it's a good ingredient to have a certain bit in a novel. But I'm not sure it's necessarily so in a short story.

PS: *Don't you think it could help the principle of revelation which is so . . .*

GG: Yes, I mean some short stories demand an element of humour, even sad stories, but I would not call it an essential.

PS: *Because, of course, humour is so important with you, I mean it's almost a philosophical sort of humour: the gap between what life is and what it might be . . .*

GG: Yes, yes.

PS: *But you don't think it's more obvious in your short stories?*

GG: I wouldn't have thought so. I should have thought that there are humorous short stories and non-humorous short stories. There is much less of a blend than there is in a novel.

PS: *Of course, there is a variety in your use of the comic, from a mild form of humour which you reveal for instance in "The Innocent," to the gross laughter of "The Overnight Bag" or "Alas Poor Maling" with his borborygms . . .*

GG: (Laughter.)

PS: *Now speaking about your characters in short stories, do you think thay can be approximately the same as the characters in a novel?*

GG: I don't think there is room to develop a character so much as in a novel, do you? And one of the things I like about the novel, and I think I've only brought it off once, is that the character can change, and is not the same at the end of the novel as he is at the beginning. I think I brought that off in *The Honorary Consul,* where the two principal characters have changed a good deal in the course of the story. But that there is hardly room to do in a short story. I think you've got to establish a character sufficiently vividly to the reader . . . and one has to simplify for that reason a bit.

PS: *Would you go so far as saying that some of them are mere pretexts or supports for the story, the story being the important element?*

GG: I'm afraid that's true probably. I don't think that that's a thing to be glad of.

PS: *I have a wonderful sentence by Alberto Moravia: "Characters in short stories are the products of lyrical intuitions, those in a novel are symbols."*

GG: Say that again, would you.

PS: *"Characters in short stories are the products of lyrical intuitions, those in a novel are symbols."*

GG: That's interesting. I don't . . . I'd rather think a lot about that. I think I can see the possibility of that being true (laughter).

PS: *When he speaks of a symbol, I think he explains afterwards that he means a symbol of a whole sociological background, and even philosophical . . .*

GG: In that case, yes, I think I would agree.

PS: *That would mean they are much richer, much more developed than . . .*

GG: Yes, yes. He's put it very succinctly, and when you put things succinctly, you have to think a lot before you accept it. But I think he is right. Yes.

PS: *Would you agree, again speaking of characters, that in short stories the external forces, such as destiny or circumstances or even the definition of the short story with its limitations, may play too great a role at the expense of a natural development of characters?*

GG: I'd say yes. I think that's fair. But one begins to . . . look always for exceptions.

PS: *But the fact that these external circumstances are so important in comparative weight in the short story . . .*

GG: Yes, yes.

PS: *. . . is it not the reason why so many weak people are introduced, or inexperienced, passive people, of course the misfits we were speaking about, or in particular children . . . You introduce many children in your stories.*

GG: I also do, I think, quite a lot in the novels. It's not only in the short story.

PS: *But in the short stories, they are sometimes central characters, which I don't think they are in your novels.*

GG: In "The End of the Party," certainly they are central, "The Innocent," yes. They play a big part in *The Comedians,* in *The Human Factor.* I think even in *Our Man in Havana.* After all children are I don't know what in the population of the world, what percentage of the world are children. They play a large part in life (laughter). It's rather like when one is accused of introducing Catholic characters. One has to admit in England, at any rate, one in ten people is Catholic. And it would be remarkable if you had books which didn't have at least one Catholic character . . . I mean, I'm accused of introducing too often Catholic characters but the answer in England is that ten per cent of the population is Catholic, so it would be really odd if a Catholic did not figure in a good many novels, even if the writer is not a Catholic.

PS: *About* The Honorary Consul, *you have just said again that it's one of your favourites because the central character is different at the end of the novel. Is this not an indirect condemnation of the short story because there is no time for a character to change?*

GG: I don't think it is a criticism of the short story. It means that the short story is a different form of art. Just as the novel can't include poetry, the short story can't include, can't deal with certain things.

PS: *Well, I'll come to my concluding question. I hope I have not been too long . . .*

GG: (Laughter). Not a bit.

PS: *If you had to give advice to a young writer, what would you tell him makes a good story?*

GG: Oh, my goodness.

PS: *Or the reverse question: what are the main causes of failure? Is it because one is too ambitious, wants to put too many things into a short story, or fails because of lack of technique, lack of simplicity . . .*

GG: Bad style.

PS: *Or because he does not respect what I'd call the unities, a short story having to be limited in place, in time, in the number of people introduced?*

GG: Well I can imagine . . . I don't know. Because . . . You speak about unities there, unity. I can imagine suddenly that somebody would produce a brilliant short story in which the first two pages took place in Hong Kong, the next two pages in San Francisco, and ended up in Buenos Aires. I can imagine it being done. I don't like the idea of any rules. And the use of the word "essential." I think that Joyce broke all the rules that were possible to break. My only advice would be to say: "Get ahead with it, and let us see it when it is done" (laughter). But I would hesitate to give him any advice.

PS: *You said that you much preferred reading a novel than a series of short stories. Would you think it is a good idea, a sort of remedy for that, to write a collection centering on one subject, more or less what you have done in your comedies of sexual life for instance?*

GG: Yes, yes. That makes it slightly approach nearer to the novel, perhaps. But of course, I mean, all these things are exceptions. I've read, and reread continuously Chekhov, for instance, Turgeniev [sic]. I don't hesitate to read a volume of short stories by Pritchett or by Trevor.

PS: *Because of the unity you find there?*

GG: The unity there; the author provides the unity. But I'm afraid I'm unadventurous, and I don't feel a strong inclination to read a book of short stories by an author whom I don't know, or a new author. It's a very unfair prejudice of course which publishers also have.

PS: *Would you go as far as foretell the end of the short story like some people today think that the novel has little more to say?*

GG: No. I think they've said the story or the novel has nothing more to say ever since Homer.

PS: *Would you agree with and can you explain the fact that the short story is much more popular in English-speaking countries than in France?*

GG: Is it, yes. You don't have . . . Since Maupassant, who have been your great short story writers?

PS: *Not many . . .*

GG: No, it is quite true.

PS: *There are one or two today . . .*

GG: And yet, there is very little encouragement to people, to new writers to write short stories in England. They have very few papers now. There were more in the early days of this century, more magazines who took short stories, than there are now. I can only think for the moment of one magazine which has a fairly limited circulation, perhaps two that take short stories in England, which is a handicap, when you also have a handicap of a publisher who is unwilling to risk money on a volume of short stories, unless by an author who he believes will write novels.

PS: *But you don't think there is anything special in the French mentality that is an obstacle to writing short stories . . .*

GG: Now you can tell me that better than I can (laughter).

PS: *But you've lived in France so long!*

GG: But you've lived in France a great deal longer . . .

PS: *Well, thank you very much indeed!*

[In the course of the conversation that followed, the problem of adapting the short story to the television was raised:]

PS: *Did you have any short stories made into films? And were you satisfied with the result?*

GG: Yes, television in England did a series called *Shades of Greene* in which they produced eighteen stories in thirteen installments. And for the first time on the whole I was thoroughly satisfied with the films. There were only four that I thought very badly done. They were very faithful to the subjects and the plots and the characters and some were outstandingly good and one which I would have thought would have been the most difficult was perhaps the best: *Under the Garden.* They tried to sell the series to France incidentally, but were told that the stories were too intellectual. These films were too intellectual. I don't know what was meant by that (light laughter).

PS: *But you were not satisfied with your novels made into films? Do you see any reason for that?*

GG: Yes, the novel is more difficult to make into a film. I've had experience with script writing for films. A novel is too long to make even a long film. It has to be cut drastically. And often what is cut seems unimportant and yet in cutting something which seems inessential, the character becomes flat and faded.

Extracted from Philippe Séjourné, "Graham Greene: On the Short Story," *Cahiers de la Nouvelle* 4 (1985): 11–24.

Notes

1. *Dead Man Leading* (London: Chatto and Windus; New York: Macmillan, 1937).
2. William Trevor [Cox] (1928–), member of the Irish Academy of Letters, resides in Devon, England. Among his novels are *The Old Boys* (1964) and *The Boarding House* (1965). He is best remembered, however, as a short-story writer. His *Collected Stories* appeared in 1992.
3. "The End of the Party," *London Mercury*, January 1932, 238–44, and included in *Nineteen Stories* and *Twenty-One Stories*.

The Solitude of the Writer and Political Involvement

Maria Couto

MARIA COUTO: *My analysis of your work rests on the premise that you were moved by Socialist ideals in the 1930s, that your politics has developed but has not changed. Did you belong to any political party?*

GRAHAM GREENE: I would be inclined to agree with that. I did belong to a party for a short time. I joined the ILP, the Independent Labour Party around 1933 which was on the left of the Labour party and have always been on the Left,[1] but I did not have much time to be fully involved and soon resigned. As for Catholicism, I haven't liked all that Vatican II did, but it was a breath of air, anyway. Since I am critical, I am suspect from the Catholic and from the Socialist point of view; I cannot be wholeheartedly a Socialist according to a fixed Marxist standpoint or a Catholic by those who wish to extend the dogma of Papal infallibility.

MC: *When this point of comparison between your work and Orwell's was made at a recent discussion,[2] Stephen Spender had this to say:*

I don't think one can think of Greene as political in quite the same way as Orwell. Orwell had great political insights into the class system, and realised that everything in England really is class. I think he became rather hypnotised by this. The other thing he understood quite well was the possibility of an authoritarian kind of society controlling absolutely everything including the thought processes of the people who belong to that society.

GG: Well, I never went the whole hog like Auden, Spender, Caudwell.³ They joined the Communist Party. I joined it for a matter of weeks as an undergraduate with my friend Claud Cockburn as a joke though he later became a serious Communist.⁴ It is natural for some of those like Spender to be a little suspicious to find me getting closer and closer to positions they have abandoned. Their God failed. I suppose I am suspect because I have never involved myself in the ideology of politics. My ambiguity makes me suspect to the literary and to the Catholic establishment.

Cockburn saw much more of Spain than Orwell, Spender or Auden. He was a remarkable man and my friend at Berkhamsted and at Oxford but I didn't see much of him for the last thirty years before he died. He was the only real Communist. He had a position as *Times* correspondent in Washington which he gave up on principle. For the others it was only a temporary romantic attachment, never really serious. How anyone can take Spender seriously to this day I can't imagine. Auden yes, Spender no.⁵

I was not part of any group. I am not alienated, nor an "outsider" as is sometimes claimed. I like to work alone, in solitude, or at best in the company of one person who is close and with whom one can discuss and talk. Writing needs solitude.[6] I could never function as writers do in France where they meet as groups and discuss each other's work. That would be the end. That's one of the reasons why I could not be with Auden, Spender and Cecil Day Lewis. Working in a group can be incestuous and one would feel the need to compromise, I think. I'd rather be with a group of businessmen than with writers. At least I'd learn something.

MC: *Would you like to talk about the 1930s?*

GG: For me it was the period of the Hunger Marches and the General Strike.[7] It wasn't like the demonstrations now when on the whole the standard of living has risen a great deal. The hunger marchers were really hungry. I have been accused of betrayal because during the General Strike I had a certain loyalty to my paper, the *Times*, and did not join the strike. If we'd stopped, Churchill's would have been the only voice to be heard, no independent voice at all, only the official one. Not only had the *Times* to fight the strikers, it had to fight off Churchill as well. He was trying to launch his own paper, *The British Gazette*, with the support of the extreme right and a moderate voice was essential.

MC: *Do you know you have sometimes been referred to as right-wing? Is it to do with your trip to Germany?*

GG: That was during the Weimar Republic but how could it be called right-wing when the Weimar Republic was, if anything, to the left? Yes, I see that Bergonzi calls me right-wing and in a later chapter illustrates the influence of Auden on my work which I do not suppose he thinks is right-wing.[8] Very strange. I went with Claud Cockburn to the Weimar Republic in our undergraduate days; it seemed a romantic adventure and there was no hint of Nazism then; Hitler had not appeared on the scene.[9]

It was the fact that I did not join the strike which made the pseudo-left regard me as right-wing but Orwell came to my defence writing that I might prove to be the first Catholic writer in English to be a fellow-traveller. Later on with Franco, the fact that I was a Catholic did not help. Orwell was inclined to think that Catholics would necessarily support Franco, for example, which I never did. I did not support the Republican side either because there were things they did I didn't like any more than I could bear Franco. I couldn't take the romantic view of them as others did. The primary guilt was Franco's, but I couldn't feel wholeheartedly for the Republic although I could feel wholeheartedly against Franco and for the Basque Republic.

MC: *In Orwell's letters there are references to you as part of the group around* The Criterion.

GG: I never read it, nor was I part of any group. Orwell hated *The Heart of the Matter* for some reason. I don't care for it myself.[10]

MC: *There was an article on Anthony Blunt[11] that said intellectuals of his generation were drawn towards Communism as a reaction to the materialism of the United States and its popular culture that was sweeping over England. Would you agree?*

GG: No. I think it was a reaction to the crisis in England; the Hunger Marches, real poverty, real hunger. The hunger marchers then were quite different from the trade-union rioters now. They were really people who had not had enough to eat and I think it was that that turned us all to the left. Burgess, Maclean, Philby[12] were all at

Cambridge about the same time and then the authorities began to wonder whether there might have been similar characters in Oxford in the twenties. I once received a questionnaire with a list of names of Oxford characters — I knew several of them. I've often wondered that I haven't been suspected myself.

I think Philby genuinely believed in Communism. In the SIS during the war we were a little group dealing with Iberia with Kim Philby at the head of our operation and he was much the most efficient man in the British Secret Service. Oh yes, I did admire him — he did his job extremely well. As for Communism, he was recruited by the Communists at the time of Hunger Marches and I'm sure he didn't commit treason for money. He lived out his belief and I admire him for that.

Philby's Communism had nothing to do with reactions against the policies of the United States which didn't seem such a danger as they seem today. Their policy in Central America is certainly driving me now to be more friendly towards Communism than I would otherwise be. They've driven Castro to choose Communism and are pushing the Sandanistas towards Communism.[13] What's ugly about the United States — not the American people but the occupants of the White House — is their desire to have the whole of the American continent under their control right down to Chile.

MC: *When you wrote* Getting to Know the General *some reviewers suggested you like dictators. In my book I've called them father-figures—Ho Chi Minh, Castro, Torrijos.*

GG: It's exaggerating a bit to call me an admirer of Ho Chi Minh; the original essay I wrote is not entirely in his praise; it is called "A Man as Pure as Lucifer" which is hardly complimentary. Castro has done a great deal for his country and there are undoubtedly enormous improvements there since the fall of Batista in education, in health. If authoritarianism has raised its ugly head it is not ugly in the sense of authoritarianism in San Salvador or Videla's[14] in Argentina, or Pinochet's[15] in Chile. But the United States are responsible for Castro moving further and further to the left. He's got no alternative; he's got to live and the people have got to live. Every overture he makes to the United States is rejected.

I was shocked when he supported the Russian invasion of Czechoslovakia because a few days before he had made a speech in which he had said that each country must make its own way to socialism. And then I met the Italian ambassador to Havana who told me that Castro had no alternative: there was a whole *équipe* ready with Dorticos, then the President, to move against him if he said a word against Russia. I had always thought Dorticos a figurehead and the real power was with Castro but apparently Dorticos was the head of the group ready to take over and then we would have had a Communism more extreme than Castro's.

MC: *In your recent interview with the* Sunday Times[16] *you spoke of Castro and Mrs. Thatcher with the same sort of admiration.*

GG: Did I say I admire her? Well, not all that much. Perhaps I said what is true, that is that I would have voted for her in the first election because we had had two Labour Prime Ministers in whom honesty was not a very strong point. On the whole a woman is more honest than a man, I think. But I wouldn't vote for her now. I felt that she might do some good when she came in after the long spell of Wilson and Callaghan but I certainly don't think she's admirable in all she does.[17]

MC: *Did you comment at all during the Falklands war?[18]*

GG: I wrote in an Argentinian paper that it was a stupid war and that the only good that could come out of it was the fall of the military junta. I think that Mrs. Thatcher ought to come much more willingly forwards to talk because it would help the new democratic Government. You know what Churchill said, "Jaw-jaw is better than war-war." The war itself was a brilliant exercise, a very interesting one from NATO's point of view and I don't see how it could have been avoided under the circumstances but we were partly responsible for the circumstances. At the same time it was difficult to come to serious talks with a Government where 30,000 people have disappeared;[19] so authoritarian that it was perhaps not possible to have reasonable talks with them.

GG: I regard myself as European, but Europe, like Communism, is being created by the United States. It created Communism in Nicaragua and Latin America and European reactions to America now are forming a Europe closer to Communism. What one would like to see is a reform of Communism in Russia rather on the lines which seemed to be happening in Czechoslovakia. This would minimise the antagonism between Europe and Russia. And maybe then we would have a neutral Europe which could stand up against and modify the imperialism of the United States.

MC: *How do you react to the suggestion that you romanticise the left?*

GG: Maybe I do. But I don't think I romanticise the Communists. I have a certain sympathy and there's a link between Communism and Catholicism, the Curia and the Politburo. But there's not much of the real Communism left; it's becoming a State Capitalism. In any case I'd

rather romanticise the Left than romanticise the Right as
Evelyn Waugh did.

MC: *Do you agree that there is an element of Jansenism in
your work?*

GG: Those who say I am a Jansenist have not read theology. Anthony Burgess who is a born Catholic accuses
me of Jansenism.[20] Born Catholics are not strong on theology. I don't believe in such a thing as hell, for example.
I have a hope that there is something beyond death certainly, but not hell. François Mauriac could be accused of
Jansenism; I admire him, but he went too far and in that
sense my work is not Catholic at all. I'm exactly the opposite of the Jansenist. I believe in "between the stirrup and
the ground."[21]

Gabriel Marcel, the French philosopher, and also a
Catholic, claimed that I was an existentialist. I don't know
what existentialism is except as a picture of life as it is but
he claimed I was a Catholic existentialist and that I'd
reduced hope to its smallest possible size. Original sin does
not mean anything much to me any more than the Trinity
does. The Church seems to me to be an attempt that was
needed, perhaps, long ago, to explain a mystery. Once you
try to explain a mystery you get things tabulated. But I
certainly believe there is good and evil in the world.

I am sympathetic to a religious belief but I can't wholeheartedly be a Catholic, or wholeheartedly a Christian. As
I get older and older I lose more and more my belief in
God. I have always liked the Biblical saying "Lord I
believe. Help my unbelief."[22] I try to believe and what
remains of my faith says that I'm wrong not to believe. I
make a distinction between faith and belief.[23] Faith is irrational and belief is rational. I would describe myself as a

Catholic agnostic, not an atheist, and I feel a link with Catholicism. I feel no link with Anglicanism at all. When I became a Catholic and had to take another name, I took Thomas, after the doubter.

Christian Marxism? I don't know much about Marxism. In South America today we certainly see Christianity as it always should have been—with the Church actively involved in the struggle for justice. The Pope made a big mistake attacking the presence of priests in the Nicaraguan Government and he behaved badly there. He'd been wrongly advised, probably by Cardinal Ratzinger.[24]

MC: *I'm amused when you say that you don't know what Liberation Theology means.*

GG: I am not a theologian. If it means that the priests are allowed to play their part in politics in defence of the poor then I'm all for it.

MC: *Don't you think Liberation Theology suggests the overlap between Marxism and Catholicism?*

GG: Yes. We've got the same structures in the sense that you can compare the Curia and the Politburo; both are bad. And I think the church today is concerned with poverty. Perhaps as the church becomes more concerned with poverty and human rights the Marxists become less concerned with poverty and there's nothing to show they are concerned with human rights. I find that the most interesting comments on my books have come from Catholics and Communists and there is a parallel between the rather hesitant doubts of some of my Communist friends and my own doubts.

MC: *How much was Father Rivas modelled on Camillo Torres?*

GG: Not at all. Camillo Torres was a young man who found himself in a particular position but Rivas was a much older man and I had to invent a theology for him. My friend, Father Duran, says it is perfectly acceptable by the Catholic Church. Rivas was affected by certain things in Paraguay and by the fact that the head of the Church sat down to dinner with General Stroessner. Things went too far when a priest, Camillo Torres, actually carried a rifle in Colombia, shooting and killing. That's a job for the layman. I don't say it is wrong to kill. But I don't agree that priests should not take part in political situations as intolerable as Somoza's.

I visited the Jesuits in Paraguay. They were under strict surveillance, and their telephones were being tapped. The Archbishop of Santiago in Chile made a very good stand against Pinochet from the beginning, and he supported Allende. I went to a curious service in the Cathedral in the middle year of Allende's government; it was on the National day. The Archbishop presided, a Methodist and a Jewish rabbi said prayers, a Jesuit preached the sermon, the whole Government attended as also the Chinese from the embassy. A good ecumenical service, I thought. Quite recently his successor has been condemning Pinochet in the most outspoken terms and unlike Archbishop Romero in Salvador, he has managed to survive. The Church in Panama is practically non-existent and in Cuba it was always only skin-deep; it was an upper-class religion and didn't have its roots in the people as in Nicaragua. Voodoo is the real peasant religion in Cuba; I've attended two Voodoo ceremonies, in Cuba and Haiti.[25]

MC: *Have you consciously tried to subvert the adventure form?*

GG: Yes, oh yes, I wanted my novels to be in a sense adventure stories too. I have always liked adventure stories and I was consciously reacting against the Bloomsbury group.[26] I did not like Forster's book on the novel: "Oh yes, I suppose we have to have a story."[27] He was very superior in his attitude to the story. And so I felt let's go back to story-telling. I think there was also a certain pride in having R. L. Stevenson as my mother's cousin.

MC: *How much did the theatre and film influence you?*

GG: Film certainly. The Victorian novelists were influenced by painting; their descriptive scenes were static because they were thinking in terms of pictures. I belong to the age of the cinema. I have tried to make my descriptions with a moving, hand-held camera.

MC: *You've said in an interview: "I try to restrict myself to homeground if I can, English backgrounds, London whenever possible. I've always made that a rule."*[28]

GG: That interview was given quite a while ago[29] and I have gone out of England for my subjects more often than not. But I always try to have an English character. . . .

. . . I've often been asked what draws me to these places and the only answer I can think of is that politics out there are not an alternation of political parties but a matter of life and death. I am interested in such politics and I write about such politics.

MC: *You have commented on political developments all over the world. Why have you not written about India?*

GG: I think India rather frightened me by its size. I have enjoyed myself very much during two weeks in Goa,[30] but to write about India in a novel I would have had to live there over a considerable period of time and I think I was daunted by the problems. I am probably wrong, but I've always felt that Communism was in the end perhaps the only thing that could work in a country so divided—how was it going to rise from that extreme poverty? I know things have changed a lot but the poverty is still there. But then one has seen the failure of Marxism in Africa.

MC: *To get back to Africa, I find your writing has compassion and a great sense of involvement but your criticism of the Creole is not justified because the Creole in many ways has combined two cultures and has identified himself with national aspirations. By Creole do you mean Western-educated, or does it have connotations of colour?*

GG: Not of colour. I've used the word in the sense used in West Africa of Africans who have lived for some generations in the West and have then returned to Africa as they did to Liberia and Sierra Leone from America. It does not apply to people who have not left their country and still belong to a tribal society.

My first encounter with the Creole was in Liberia and I did not like what I saw. He had taken control of a tribal country and was not very nice to his fellow-countrymen, even, in the case of Krus, selling them into slavery. I did not find this a serious factor in Sierra Leone among the educated class and when I wrote against Creoles I was writing mainly about Liberia.

MC: *Would you agree that your involvement with the world began with* Journey Without Maps?

GG: If you live at all you become involved. My first political book was *It's a Battlefield,* a little before *Journey Without Maps.* It is the only book in which I have worked consciously with a cinematic technique, so it has never been filmed.

MC: *Conrad and James are the ones you acknowledge as masters. Is there any philosopher or writer apart from these who has been a formative influence?*

GG: Conrad and James I would say are the serious influences though Conrad was a bad influence and I had to stop reading him for more than twenty years. I have read two of Chardin's books, and Hans Küng on infallibility is very good. I have a great admiration for Kierkegaard. As a Catholic I'd say Newman was the important influence on me; he was dead against infallibility and he was a magnificent writer of English. I specially like his *Essay on the Development of Christian Doctrine.* He argues against a too-dogmatic church and demonstrates the evolution of ideas.

Travel did help me understand and appreciate other religious traditions but I don't think I was ever a thorough Catholic. I accepted Catholicism as an intellectual likelihood, that it was perhaps nearer the truth than other religions. I wanted to understand what my future wife believed in, but I wasn't prepared for that reason to become a Catholic. I went for instruction to understand, and then decided that perhaps Catholicism might be nearer the truth than other faiths. I had no emotional attachment to Catholicism till I went to Mexico and saw the faith of the peasants during the persecution there.

Extracted from Maria Couto, *Graham Greene: On the Frontier, Politics and Religion in the Novels* (New York: St. Martin's Press, 1988), 206–21. *Editor's title.*

Notes

1. On 11 August 1933, Greene made the following entry in his diary: "Joined the ILP. My political progress has been rather curved." Sherry, *The Life of Graham Greene, Vol. 1,* 461.

2. *Author's note. Did You See?*, BBC 2, 10 January, 1984, when some of the programs on Orwell were discussed. Kenneth Tynan writes:

> Greene's Oxford years had proved to him that the best of English literature, from Shakespeare to James Joyce, had always been produced from the Christian standpoint. It infuriated him to hear men like Stephen Spender deploring the death of politically conscious novelists in England. Political novelists said Greene in the course of a public wrangle with Spender, aimed at an attainable objective, and once that objective had been gained, all passion died. Look, he exhorted his audience, at the later Russian cinema. Religious novelists on the other hand, could never gain their objective, and accordingly their care and passion never diminished. Greene has always preferred a sense of passionate inadequacy to a sense of fulfilment. (*Harper's Bazaar*, "An Inner View of Graham Greene," February 1953, 129 and 209).

3. It was almost fashionable in the "Red" or Marxist thirties for poets and writers to join the Communist Party. Auden, Spender, and Cecil Day-Lewis, among others, did: Auden joined in 1932 but left in disgust in 1939 after the Nazi-Soviet Pact and Spender's Marxism evaporated or was modified by World War II. Philosopher "Christopher Caudwell" [Christopher St. John Sprigg, (1907–37)] died fighting in Spain. Most of his works were published posthumously.

4. Both Graham Greene and Claud Cockburn joined the Communist Party in 1925. See Cockburn under List of Contributors.

5. Graham Greene, never a great admirer of Stephen Spender, is perhaps unnecessarily harsh in his judgment of Spender, but his endorsement of Auden is critically valid and justifiable.

6. Greene expressed the same sentiment twenty-five years earlier to George Adam, the *Figaro* correspondent. See p. 138 of the Adams excerpt, "A Pantheon of Contemporary Writers."

7. Trade unionists declared the General Strike in 1926. There was no violence.

8. Bernard Bergonzi, *Reading the Thirties: Text and Content* (London: Macmillan; University of Pittsburgh Press, 1978). In chap. 3, "Auden/Greene," Bergonzi stresses the "affinities" between the two writers and describes Auden's influence on Greene's prewar fictional prose.

9. The trip to the Ruhr Valley took place in the summer of 1924.

10. See George Orwell, "The Sanctified Sinner," *New Yorker*, 17 July 1948, 69–71, for his views on the novel.

11. Anthony Frederick Blunt (1907–83), British art historian and Surveyor of the Queen's Pictures, was also a Soviet spy who seems to have collaborated with Guy Burgess, Donald Maclean, and Kim Philby. His involvement in espionage was only made public in 1979 when his knighthood was annulled.

12. Donald Maclean (1913–83) and Guy Burgess (1910–63) were two British officials in the Foreign Office who had access to secret information and defected to the Soviet Union in 1951. They were presumably recruited during their undergraduate days at Cambridge. Kim Philby, recruited by Burgess in 1940 into the British Secret Service, had access to sensitive information that he transmitted to the USSR before his defection in 1963. See also Greene's introduction to Philby's *My Silent War*.

13. For the counterargument to Greene's "ideological attachment" to an anticapitalist system, see William Buckley, "Where Greene Went Astray in Nicaragua," and Norman Podhoretz' editorial comment, both in the *Sunday Telegraph*, 23 March 1986, 2 and 16.

14. Jorge Rafael Videla was head of the military junta that overthrew Evita Peron in 1976. He remained president until 1981.

15. Augusto Pinochet (1905–) overthrew the government of Salvadore Allende in September 1973. He ruled Chile until he was forced to relinquish power after the 1990 elections.

16. Interview with Norman Lebrecht, the *Sunday Times*, 1 April 1984. *Author's note.*

17. Norman Lebrecht reports that Greene "admires Mrs. Thatcher for her integrity," believes in her honesty but does not like her policy.

18. On 2 April 1982, Argentina ended seventeen years of talks with the U. K. when its troops landed on the Falkland Islands. Though a British fleet reached the vicinity within three weeks, the war

only ended with the surrender of the Argentinian garrison on 14 June. See also Greene's comments on pp. 353–54 of the Bernard Violet excerpt, "A Rare Occasion: Graham Greene on TV."

19. Human rights groups pressed continuously for a full investigation of the *desaparcidos*, especially after the proposed transition to democracy that followed the Falkland war and the claim that over 1,000 unidentified bodies were discovered in several cemeteries.

20. Anthony Burgess writes: "It is sometimes said that Greene's Catholicism is not strictly orthodox, that he adheres to the Jansenist heresy. If this means that he broods more on man's unborn depravity than on his ability to be regenerated, this is true: he is more interested in presenting evil than good." *The Novel Now* (London: Faber and Faber, 1971), 61. See also his "Religion and the Arts: The Manicheans," *Times Literary Supplement*, 3 March 1966, 153–54.

21. When in *Brighton Rock* Rose expresses her fear of dying suddenly, Pinkie says: "You know what they say— 'Between the stirrup and the ground, he something sought and something found.' " (110).

22. The Gospel of St. Mark, 9:24.

23. Thirty years earlier, Greene had clearly implied this distinction in his short story, "A Visit to Morin." See also Father Thomas A. Wassmer's affirmation of the "valid tension" between the two, from a theological viewpoint, in "Faith and Reason in Graham Greene," *Studies* 48 (summer 1959): 163–67.

24. Joseph Cardinal Ratzinger is prefect of the Congregation for the Doctrine of the Faith, Rome. *Author's note.*

25. Voodoo is an active faith based on the worship of sun, water, and other natural forces, closely associated with black magic and blood sacrifices, derived from Africa, especially Dahomey, as well as Catholic ritual elements.

26. See note 2 on p. 262 of the Michael Mewshaw excerpt, "Graham Greene in Antibes."

27. Greene is referring to E. M. Forster's 1927 classic book *Aspects of the Novel* in which Forster admits in chap. 2, "a little sadly . . . Yes—oh dear yes—the novel tells a story."

28. Interview with J. Maclaren-Ross, *Memoirs of the Forties* (Alan Ross, 1965). *Author's note.*

29. This interview took place in 1938 when Greene was living at 14 North Side, Clapham Common, London.
30. In 1963, Greene visited Goa as a correspondent for the *Sunday Times*.

"I'm An Angry Old Man, You See"

John Mortimer

"Do you still dream stories?" A number of plots, I knew, had wandered, unbidden, into Graham Greene's unconscious mind and been trapped with a pencil at his bedside in the moment of waking.

"I have an enormous index of dreams. I put down the names of all the people in them. Khrushchev, for instance."[1]

"Tell me."

"Well, I dreamt I was having dinner with Khrushchev, at some official banquet, and he looked down at my plate with horror and said, 'You're eating meat, on a *Friday?*' "

It was a dream, I thought, which told a lot about Graham Greene's favourite meeting place, the point at which doubting Catholics and sceptical communists, no longer totally convinced by the faiths to which they feel bound by loyalty, join hands in some kind of mutual understanding. I might have pursued the thought but there were more vital matters to discuss.

"The most important thing is, what will you have to drink? A vodka and tonic? I think, yes, I think perhaps I'll have a dry martini. This is the little cocktail shaker I had made at Asprey's[2] to take to the Vietnam war."

The silver shaker, large enough, perhaps, to carry two drinks to a battlefield, is the only real sign of luxury in Mr. Greene's small home in an Antibes apartment block. It is true that his windows look out over the boats in the sun-lit port, but the overflowing books are piled on the floor, the bamboo furniture is extremely simple and the cover on his smallish double bed is a patterned, revolutionary towel, presented to him by the guerrillas in El Salvador. It must be about 40 years since he owned a motor car.

"I've always had girlfriends that could drive and had cars. Three of them in succession. That's useful. You know, I've been with my present girlfriend 26 years, for longer than most marriages.[3] Shall we get this over and then we can walk down to the port for lunch? I told Félix you were com-ing. I showed him your picture on the front of the *Spectator*."

"I suppose I ought to ask you about the state of the world. I mean, is this the worst time you can remember?" He has lived for 81 years to be undoubtedly the best nov-elist now living, and probably among the greatest of this century. He has made the Nobel Prize look foolish by not having been awarded it. He has seen more wars and rev-olutions than most of us can remember having read about and he has flown thousands of miles and spent hours in the company of presidents and prime ministers in pursuit of a life-long love affair with Spanish America. He is tall, thin, stooping, energetic and talks endlessly, a man with grey, curiously transparent eyes, small dark pupils and what look to be arthritic fingers. This year he plans to visit Russia in search of experiences and Capri in search of another novel. It is impossible to think of him as old.

"The worst time? You mean the horrible state that Reagan's got us into? Well, it's certainly the most dangerous for many years, and that's entirely due to Reagan. I think the attack on Libya⁴ was absurd and unjustifiable. I mean, they talk about self-defence and all because of the death of one American soldier! Reagan's behaviour in Nicaragua? He's certainly caused the deaths of more innocent women and children than Gaddafi could ever be blamed for. But I suppose Reagan's hand is forced, to some extent, by his constituency. The only bright spot I can see is that I have every confidence in Gorbachev. He seems to have a great deal of common sense. I remember what a KGB man said—they're the least conservative, you know, and they get sent abroad—anyway he said, 'There's no hope of change as long as the old men are there.' Gorbachev's one of the young men and I don't think he prays so much to the Holy Figure of Karl Marx."

"Have you heard from Kim Philby lately?" I knew that the Great Defector had occasionally supplied Mr. Greene with news of political feelings in Russia.

"Not for years. And then he was complaining that it was difficult to read Henry James."

"Why was that?"

"I think he started at the wrong end, with *The Golden Bowl*, and, of course, Philby's an old man now."

"We were talking about Nicaragua. You've been there lately?"

"Three times in the last few years. You know, it's really not communist. The President's a doubtful Marxist and the ministers of foreign affairs and education are both priests.⁵ Can you imagine communists leaving education in the hands of a Jesuit priest? I went down to Leon, the second city, with the minister of the interior who is a Marxist, but an agreeable friend, and we walked through the crowds at the Feast of the Immaculate Conception.⁶ The minister had no guards and all the houses were lit with statues of the Virgin and people were calling out, 'To whom do we owe our happiness? Maria Immaculata!' and handing out bon-bons. The conservative and liberal posters were all still up on the walls. Do you know that 75 per cent of the people voted in the Nicaraguan election? That's 25 per cent more than vote for an American president. Well, if that's communism all I can say is that communism is improving enormously and we all ought to encourage the improvement."

"So why's Reagan so afraid of the Nicaraguan government?"

"You know what my brother was in danger of after an operation for a cataract? Channel vision! Isn't that what they call it? You can only see in an extremely narrow line. You can't see round the sides of any problem. Reagan's got channel vision."

"And you think Contra terrorism in Nicaragua is worse than Libyan terrorism?"

"I heard from an American Sister, a Californian, and she described the body of a young Nicaraguan churchman murdered by the Contras. His eyes had been gouged out and the skin taken off his legs and he'd been castrated. I wrote to the *Times* and told them the story and I said that I hoped that the leaders of the West meeting in Tokyo[7] wouldn't condemn selective terrorism. They wrote back that they found my letter interesting and distressing but they couldn't print it! Well, if they found it interesting and distressing why *didn't* they print it?"

Mr. Greene lay back against the printed banana leaves on his armchair cushions. He was laughing at the absurdity of the *Times*'s reply and his eyes were wide open in surprise at the callousness of the world. When he talks, his 'r's make a slightly guttural click at the back of his throat.

"They used to talk about angry young men,"[8] he was still smiling, "but I'm an angry old man, you see."

"You seem to be more sympathetic to South American Marxists than to the British Labour Party."

"I liked Gaitskell. I can't say I cared for Wilson or Callaghan.[9] I've got nothing against Mr. Kinnock."

"And Mrs. Thatcher?"

"At least she's got courage, and that's quite rare in a Prime Minister."

"But you've always had a special feeling for Latin America."

"Oh, always. And then I was attracted by the way people suffered there for their beliefs. First in Mexico at the time of the religious persecution, then in Salvador. You know when Romero was murdered by men armed by Reagan when he was celebrating Mass?[10] He was the first bishop to be murdered while celebrating Mass since Thomas à Becket."

"If I could just ask you about God . . . "

"Oh yes. I suppose so." I knew his dislike of being thought of as a "Catholic novelist."

"Is He responsible for the mess we're in? I mean did He invent the nuclear bomb?"

"Or Reagan? No. I wouldn't hold God guilty for either. I think we've been responsible for ourselves, ever since the apple got eaten. Mind you, I'm not entirely sure what God is. I suppose you could describe me as a Catholic agnostic."

"What's God like? Is he a judge?"

"I've no idea."

"Do you go to Mass?"

"Oh yes; but I hate the new Mass. I always stand at the back and try to miss the sermon."

"What are you thinking, when you're in church?"

"I look at that beggar kneeling there and I pray that I could have as much faith as that. But on the whole I think there's a sporting chance that God exists." He was prepared to take the great gamble.

"Why?"

"I'm sure Christ was historically true. And the Resurrection is so vividly described in the Gospels. It's such a wonderful piece of reporting[11] that I'm inclined to believe it. And if it happened God must exist. And then I remember going to the south of Italy to see Padre Pio, a little stocky priest who'd received the stigmata. Some monsignor at the Vatican said, 'You're going to see our Holy Fraud?' But when I got there I saw Pio forever pulling down his sleeves to hide the marks on his hands; they were about the size of two-shilling pieces. You're not allowed to wear gloves when you're celebrating, you see, so he just pulled down his sleeves. He said a very long Mass, but to me it seemed to pass in about five minutes. Padre Pio took over the pain of a young man who was dying of cancer of the testicles. This boy died without pain, but the priest was sometimes racked with it at the altar. It was thought to be a miracle, but when he was given money Padre Pio wanted it spent on a modern hospital."[12]

"But you have doubts?"

"Of course. When you're received into the Catholic Church they give you another name, just in case your Anglican baptism didn't work. So I chose the name of Thomas. I liked two things about Thomas, one was that he was the doubter and the other was that, at the end, he said, 'Let's go up to Jerusalem and die with Him.' "[13]

"Do you go to confession?"

"Once a year. My friend the priest from Madrid comes to say Mass in this room and then I confess. It usually takes about three minutes."

"You've written about your infidelities and various love affairs during your marriage. Are those sins that you confess and feel guilt about?"

"I feel guilt, of course, if I have hurt other people . . . . "

"But they're not sins in relation to God?"

"I don't feel that."

"Why a *Catholic* agnostic?"

"I suppose because, if there is a God, the Catholics probably come nearest to getting Him right."

"But what about this pope?"[14]

"Wrong about all sorts of things. When one of the ministers in Nicaragua knelt in front of him he wagged his finger disapprovingly and wouldn't stop. But I think he may be changing his views on liberation theology."

"Who was the best pope?"

"Undoubtedly John. You know Khrushchev sent him a telegram on his 80th birthday?"

"You've written a lot in *The Lost Childhood* about Henry James's awareness of the power of evil. There are the wicked servants, for instance, in *The Turn of the Screw*.

"What does evil mean to you?"

"I suppose Hitler was evil. I can't feel that Reagan's intelligent enough to be evil. Are there evil characters in my books? I'm not sure. Perhaps there's always a question mark over them."

"Do you believe in the Devil?"

"I'm an agnostic about him too. But I can't believe there's a Devil and not a God."

"Your Catholicism's always been on the side of the poor and the oppressed . . . "

"Well, I hope so. But . . . " Mr. Greene looked doubtfully at the bamboo furniture, and, perhaps, even more doubtfully at the small cocktail-shaker made for Vietnam. "Here I am in a very nice apartment."

～⌒

. . . I asked him to look back to the days when his first novels weren't selling and he was struggling to support a family. "What would you have done if you hadn't become a famous writer?"

"I'd've kept a second-hand bookshop."[15] Graham Greene looked round at his boyhood treasures, the great adventure stories in their gilt bindings, tales of Rupert of Hentzau and Alan Quatermain and Eric Brighteyes. "I think I'd've been quite happy doing that. Is that enough questions? Good! Now we can go down to the restaurant."

As we walked past the boats and through the archway in the wall by the old port he said, "You know what I did with my Spanish royalties on *Monsignor Quixote?* I gave half to the Trappist monastery at Osera[16] and half to the Salvador guerrillas. I don't see why you shouldn't publish that."

～⌒

"So you're going to do another novel?"

"I'm going to try. I started it ten years ago and stopped. Then I went on with it five years ago and stopped. Now I daren't even look at my notes until I get to Anacapri and start working. There's some sort of magic there, I don't know what it is."

"You believe in supernatural influences?"

"I suppose I'm an agnostic about magic as well. But I always work far more quickly there."

"What do you do, to get yourself started?"

"I always read a book by Henry James. That gets me in the mood and makes me feel it's worthwhile struggling."

"Do you read Conrad still?"

"Not much. I'm not sure he wasn't a bad influence on me. But I'm very fond of *Heart of Darkness.*"

"And Robert Louis Stevenson?"

"Oh well, of course. I have a sort of family pride in him. He was my mother's first cousin. When I was a child I played on Stevenson's bagatelle board. I once knew a couple of pages of Stevenson almost by heart, it was so wonderfully written. It was a description of action, which is much harder to do than streams of consciousness. And do you know, he didn't use a single adverb! No one jumped quickly or walked stealthily. Of course, if you get the verbs right you don't need adverbs at all."

"You've never liked adverbs, have you?"

"No." He was no longer smiling and spoke with the chilling disapproval he had reserved for President Reagan. "I think adverbs are absolutely bloody."

We had walked back to the flat for a last calvados and now it was time for the taxi to Nice Airport.

"What's been the happiest time of your life?"

"Impossible to tell. It's been such a mixture."

"You seem remarkably happy now."

"Old age is never a very happy period."

"At least you don't have to worry whether you will succeed as a novelist."

"That's true." He smiled, seeming a little tired now. "You don't have to worry about success, or radiation. I'll come down in the lift with you," he said when the taxi arrived. "It'll give us a little more time to talk."

In the lift I said, "I hope it goes well with the novel."

"I thought of a name for a character the other day. 'Quigley.' I like that name very much. I shall cling to Quigley."[17]

Extracted from John Mortimer, "I'm an Angry Old Man, You See," *Spectator*, 14 June 1986, 9–12.

Notes

1. This diary of dreams was begun in 1965 and ended in 1989. See also his comments to his niece Louise Dennys in the excerpt "The Greene Factor" on pp. 275–76.

2. Asprey and Co., Ltd., is a London-based firm that designs and supplies the Royal family with silverware and ornate objets d'art.

3. Yvonne Cloetta. For an account of the women who influenced Greene's life, see Alex Kershaw, "An End of the Affairs," *Guardian Weekend*, 31 October 1992, 6–10.

4. In mid-April 1986, the United States Air Force launched a massive air strike against Libya ostensibly to preempt production for chemical warfare.

5. The president of Nicaragua then was Daniel Ortega. The minister for foreign affairs was Father Miguel D'Escoto and the minister of culture was Father Ernesto Cardenal (admonished by Pope John Paul II). Tomás Borge Martinez was the minister of the interior.

6. Greene narrated the same episode in a letter to the editor, *Spectator*, 21 April 1984, 17.

7. This is a reference to the meeting of the leaders of the western industrial countries which was held in Tokyo 21 May 1986.

8. "The Angry Young Men" or the Chelsea set is a label that gained widespread currency in the late fifties from writers such as John Osborne, Kingsley Amis, John Wain, and John Braine, whose works expressed anger and rebellion very much like the American "Beat Generation" or beatniks in the years following World War II. In an earlier interview, Greene had dismissed them as a "school" but admitted their individual worth.

9. Hugh Todd Gaitskell (1906–63), British politician elected leader of the Labour Party in December 1955.

   Sir [James] Harold Wilson (1916–) succeeded Hugh Gaitskell as leader of the Labour Party in 1963 and became prime minister in 1964. He resigned as Labour leader in 1976.

   [Leonard] James Callaghan (1912–) was elected prime minister on Harold Wilson's resignation in 1976, but he resigned as leader of the Opposition in 1980.

10. Oscar Arnulfo Romero y Galdamez (1917–80) was shot on 14 March 1980, while saying mass in a small chapel in San Salvador.

Thomas à Becket (1118–70), Archbishop of Canterbury, was murdered after Henry II impetuously voiced his wish to be rid of him. He was canonized as an English martyr and his tomb became a shrine for pilgrims that Chaucer described in his prologue to the *Canterbury Tales*. The tale of his murder was dramatized by T. S. Eliot in *Murder in the Cathedral* (1935).

11. Greene is probably referring to the narrative as given in the Gospel of St. John, 20.

12. See also Greene's comments on this issue to John Heilpern, "On the Dangerous Edge," on pp. 243–54.

13. When Jesus announced his plan to go to the dead Lazarus, it was Thomas who suggested that all the apostles go too "that we might die with him." John 11:16.

14. Pope John Paul II. ·

15. ". . . For more than thirty years my happiest dreams have been of second-hand bookshops," Greene writes in his introduction to David Low's *With All Faults* (Tehran: Amate Press, 1973). But his affection for second-hand bookshops is not confined to dreams; Greene's love for book-hunting amounted almost to a passion. "Second-hand booksellers," he writes, "are among the most friendly and the most eccentric of all the characters I have known. If I had not been a writer, theirs would have been the profession I would most happily have chosen. There is the musty smell of books, and there is the sense of the treasure-hunt." Quoted in *Reflections*, sel. and intro. Judith Adamson (Toronto: Lester and Orpen Dennys, 1990), 285.

16. In Galicia, northwest Spain.

17. Mr. Quigly was the gentleman whom the Captain had arranged to meet Jim Baxter when he arrived in Panama. Greene's description of him is almost Dickensian. "His trousers were like a second skin. He was narrow as well—narrow shoulders, narrow hips—even his eyes were close together. He was like a character in a serial newspaper." *The Captain and the Enemy*, 111.

Getting to Know Graham Greene

Jay Parini

Greene, at 84, is almost boyish in appearance. He is tall and slender, with leathery well-tanned skin. His hair is silvery white, brushed neatly to one side. His eyes dart about impishly as he talks over a bottle of Bordeaux in the little restaurant, Les Plaisirs de la Vie, where he normally takes his lunch. We sit outside, with a lovely view of the old harbor, which is crammed with sailing yachts. Greene seems voluble and relaxed, speaking in the crisp accent typical of "public school" boys or Oxford dons in the 1920s. He radiates the self-confidence and good cheer of the successful writer who has been everywhere and met everybody and remains unfazed.

JAY PARINI: *It's rather intimidating to begin an interview with Graham Greene, who has written such scathing things about journalists. I'm thinking of your portraits of Mabel Warren in* Stamboul Train *or Minty in* England Made Me.

GRAHAM GREENE: Even worse, there was Parkinson in *A Burnt-Out Case.* He pursued Querry, the famous architect, into the jungle, looking for copy. I, however, manage to fend off most pursuers. In your case, I somehow failed.[1]

JP: *Can we get right down to it and talk about influences on your work?*

GG: It would be self-dramatizing to claim Henry James or Conrad—both very great influences. But I prefer to mention Rider Haggard, Stanley Weyman, or Anthony Hope, who wrote *The Prisoner of Zenda* . . . authors whom I read as a boy and often reread.[2] Or Captain Gilson, from whom I stole a scene in *England Made Me.* I'm also fond of a character, Raffles, in the novels of E. W. Hornung.[3]

JP: *What about E. M. Forster?*

GG: I always resented him, the way in which he dismissed the idea of the story—as in *Aspects of the Novel,* where he says, resentfully, "Oh, yes, there has to be a story!"[4]

JP: *He thought of plot as a coat rack upon which language somehow got itself hung.*

GG: That's it. But I'm a storyteller. It was a reaction, perhaps, against the fashion.

JP: *Did you reject Modernism altogether?*

GG: No. I greatly admired T. S. Eliot and Ezra Pound.

JP: *But those are poets. What about James Joyce—a novelist who, like you, wrote a lot about Catholics?*

GG: Joyce wrote the best short story in the English language, "The Dead." I admire *Dubliners* and *Portrait of the Artist.* But I tried to reread *Ulysses* a few years ago and found it hard work.

JP: *What did you dislike about the Modernist fiction?*

GG: Stream of consciousness. I got tired of it very quickly.[5]

JP: *In other words, Virginia Woolf bored you to death?*

GG: No, I like *To the Lighthouse.* But I just didn't want to be a disciple of the Bloomsbury group.

JP: *Conrad was clearly an important influence.*

GG: A disastrous influence. I had to stop reading him quite early in my career.

JP: *Yet* A Burnt-Out Case, *published in 1961, was a very Conradian novel. I'm thinking of the Congo setting, the intense symbolism, and so forth.*

GG: Indeed. When I went to the Congo, I took with me only a few books. One of them was Conrad's *Heart of Darkness* — one of my favorites. Now that I'm in no danger of being influenced by him, I can appreciate him.

JP: *I recall that Evelyn Waugh accused you of basing the hero of* A Burnt-Out Case, Querry, *on yourself. Was he right?*

GG: Absolutely not! Waugh was terribly shocked by the book as a whole. He thought I was dismissing Catholicism. We had a correspondence about it, and he quoted Robert Browning's poem about Wordsworth: "Just for a handful of silver he left us . . . . "[6]

JP: *Which of your friends at Oxford were writers who later became well known?*

GG: Claud Cockburn and Peter Quennell.[7]

JP: *Was Cockburn [father of Alexander Cockburn, the journalist] a good writer?*

GG: I liked his novels very much. And he was a brilliant reporter. He founded a paper called *The Week* — an early version of *Private Eye.* I liked his autobiographical books, too.

JP: *And Quennell?*

GG: He came up to Oxford a year after me. We'd been at school together. But he aligned himself with a group of aesthetes,[8] and our friendship cooled. We remain friends, however, to this day.

JP: *Were you a maverick at Oxford?*

GG: Not really, though I had a period of heavy drinking. I was drunk all day for over a term and attended no lectures. I was in love with my sister's governess, who was engaged to marry a man who lived in the Azores. I got drunk every day after breakfast and stayed drunk till bedtime. But that passed.

JP: *You had nothing to do with the Waugh crowd—the Bright Young Things, as they were called?*

GG: Harold Acton's clique. No. Though Claud was on the fringe, and Peter Quennell joined them. They both pretended they were homosexuals for a while, just to fit in. Acton, of course, was the genuine article. I edited a student paper for a brief while, and I published some of Acton's poetry. It was good, but he didn't continue as a poet.

JP: *Your first book was* Babbling April, *a collection of poems. Why did you abandon poetry?*

GG: I didn't. I continued, rather secretly, to write poems. I still do.

JP: *You've always said that Robert Browning has been a major influence on your life and writing.*

GG: Yes—but Tennyson's a blind spot. He's too melodic. I frequently use poems as epigraphs—as in Browning's epigraph to *Getting to Know the General,* my book about Torrijos.[9]

~~~

JP: *How do you regard the Sandanistas?*

GG: I like Daniel Ortega and his wife very much. And Tomás Borge. The funny thing is that everybody in Nicaragua is a poet! Ernesto Cardenal, of course, is an important poet, as well as a party leader. It's all quite astonishing. I went across the border in 1979 for the first time and went up into the mountains, where the Sandanistas worked with the peasants by day and educated them by night. The literacy rate, you know, has gone shooting up in Nicaragua.

JP: *What do you think of the U. S. role in that region?*

GG: The Church has been very good. The bishops have been anti-*contra* all along. But I think Reagan is a fool as well as a monster. He's done great damage to America as a whole. His support of death squads in El Salvador is especially horrific.

JP: *Have you been to El Salvador?*

GG: I was asked to visit the rebels, but I couldn't risk it. I'm known as a supporter of the anti-government forces, and I would never have made it from the airport to rebel-held territory. I gave half my Spanish-language royalties from *Monsignor Quixote*, my last novel before this new one, to the Sandinistas. The Salvadorans, knowing my sympathies, would have been lying in wait.

JP: *Do you see any hope for democracy in El Salvador?*

GG: I can only say that I hope Reagan's successor cuts off aid to the Duarte government.

JP: *And Honduras?*

GG: An American stronghold, but very unwise. The Hondurans have begun to resent the U. S. presence. Have you read Noam Chomsky's *Turning the Tide?* It's a very fine book about the region.[10] You know, I hadn't realized until then that the extent of American dominance in that region goes all the way back to Abraham Lincoln!

JP: *What will happen in Central America? Will the Arias plan work?*[11]

GG: I'm optimistic. The talks are still going on, though I'm sorry Miguel Obando y Bravo, the bishop, has turned against the Sandinistas. He once wrote, in effect, an encyclical letter justifying their revolt against Somoza. That was a courageous act, since he might easily have wound up like Archbishop Romero, who was murdered in El Salvador.

JP: *It has been said that there is religious persecution in Nicaragua.*

GG: I know, but that's absurd. There are priests in the cabinet! There's a Jesuit in charge of health and education. Nicaragua is a terribly open society. I remember walking through vast crowds in Managua with Tomás Borge, the Sandinista leader and theologian, and he had only one bodyguard with him. He was perfectly safe. And the Church is everywhere. There's a statue of the Virgin in every house in the country.

JP: *Perhaps one can see the acting out of liberation theology in Nicaragua.*

GG: I think so. Tomás Borge, for instance, is both a prominent theologian and a Marxist.[12]

JP: *I would think that liberation theology should interest you, since it represents a coming together of the two main strands of your writing—the socialist and the Catholic. This, after all, is the subject of* Monsignor Quixote, *which is really an extended dialogue between opposing visions.*

GG: I suppose so. I had to make a speech in the Kremlin last year — Gorbachev had invited me — and I said more or less that. I pleaded for cooperation between Catholics and Communists. In effect, *The Power and the Glory,* my novel set in Mexico, could be seen as a forerunner of liberation theology.

JP: *What do you think of Gorbachev?*

GG: I have great hope for him. I was relieved when the last congress took place. He's an honest man going a very difficult road. His speech at the Kremlin affair I attended was a long one—an hour—but it had humor in it, was modest, there were no polemics . . . tremendous common sense. It will be terribly important for the United States and the Soviet Union to cooperate, you know. They'll have to strike and crush anyone — Israel, Libya, Pakistan — who dares to attempt a nuclear exchange.

JP: *How do you react to the Soviet invasion of Afghanistan?*

GG: Remember, it was not Gorbachev's doing. Even Andropov, before him—a former head of the KGB—was against it. What Americans conveniently forget is that the former government in Afghanistan had just murdered the American Ambassador there.

JP: *Africa has always fascinated you. What do you think of the recent chaos there—as in Mozambique, where the group called Renamo has murdered 100,000 people?*

GG: I often think that ordinary Africans were better off under most colonial regimes.

JP: *Are you nostalgic for colonialism?*

GG: Indeed not! But in places I knew well—say, Sierra Leone—colonialism was really more like paternalism. White men could not own land, and tribal laws were supported. The only thing they did not uphold was the death penalty. The district commissioners I knew were a very idealistic group who worked closely with tribal chiefs. Kenya, of course, was another matter. White men could own land there, and they became repressive.

JP: *Since your earliest days as a novelist, in the 1930s, you've been an obsessive traveler, prowling the globe like a hunted man. What have you been looking for?*

GG: The chief enemy of my life is boredom. Travel is a way of escape, a flight from boredom.

JP: *Why did you adopt Panama in recent years?*

GG: I've always been fascinated with the region; then—quite unexpectedly—I got a telegram from General Torrijos inviting me to Panama for the winter as his guest. I don't to this day know why. That was in 1971. I think his great friend Gabriel García Márquez suggested it.[13]

JP: *Did you know García Márquez?*

GG: Not then. I got to know him later. Anyway, a ticket to Panama would arrive every year, and I would accept it. I went each winter, except 1979, when I had to have a cancer operation. In 1981, I was packed to leave the next day when news came of the general's death in a plane crash. I had lost a very dear and close friend.

JP: *You saw him frequently when you were in Panama?*

GG: All the time. He liked to have somebody there when he had lunch. The Americans said he was an alcoholic, but he drank away the weekends, like all Panamanians. During the week, he was sober.

JP: *Can you tell anything about the origins of* The Captain and the Enemy?

GG: I started it more than fifteen years ago, then abandoned it for a long time. It gave me a great deal of trouble.

JP: *It strikes me as an anthology of your previous books, combining the satirical bent of* Our Man in Havana *with the thriller aspects of* This [sic] Gun for Sale *and the very domestic, English aspects of* Travels with My Aunt. *It seems, in part, like an autobiography, too.*

GG: That's right. The school in the novel is not unlike Berkhamsted, which I attended and where my father was headmaster.

～

JP: *Do you identify with certain characters?*

GG: Not usually.

JP: *I understand that Norman Sherry[14] has been writing your biography.*

GG: He's been working on it for eleven years and has only got to 1939. And it's already more than 200,000 words long! He won't finish till the next century, I should think. The poor chap has had bad luck. He caught dysentery in the same place in Mexico where I did.

JP: *In the postscript to your* Collected Essays, *you say that success for the artist, as for the priest, is an illusion. Can you elaborate?*

GG: Success for a priest would be sainthood. Success for a writer would be to be a great writer—like James or

Conrad. There are few great writers. I'm a small boy compared to them.

JP: *You often mention Henry James as an influence. I don't understand.*

GG: I've learned a good deal from James. Not his style. He taught me that a scene must have only one point of view. I try for a firm point of view. That's the beginning of craft.

JP: *Are you a "popular" writer?*

GG: Not really, though I've occasionally sold well . . .

JP: *Was your experience with the film industry a good one?*

GG: I enjoyed working on films, especially with Carol Reed, who was a very good director. The first one I did was *The Fallen Idol,* based on a short story of mine. We then made *The Third Man,* which was a great success. Later, we made *Our Man in Havana,* which failed in most ways. Most of my novels have made poor films, for various reasons. Elizabeth Taylor ruined *The Comedians,* my story about Haiti. She insisted on choosing her own clothes, which was a mistake. What's unusual is that virtually all of my novels have been filmed.

JP: *Do you still see many films?*

GG: I used to be a film critic for the *Spectator,* before the war. I saw a lot of films then. But I've lost interest.

JP: *But films have influenced your writing?*

GG: Very much so. The Victorian novelists were influenced by painters. What I found dull in Trollope—even Dickens—were the long descriptions of natural scenery. I took the moving camera as a technique and used cutting in a cinematic way.

JP: *You've also written half a dozen plays for the stage. But—if I'm not mistaken—these have been relative failures.*

GG: What! *The Living Room* ran for ten months in London. *The Complaisant Lover* ran for a year. *The Return of*

A. J. Raffles had a deliberately limited run by contract with the Royal Shakespeare Company, but it was done very well. The truth is that I always thought of myself as a playwright. I have a new play on hand just now, though I haven't found the right producer. It's called *The House of Reputation*, a story of two rival brothers in a central European city.[15]

JP: *Will you ever do another screenplay?*

GG: No. I'm too old and tired.

JP: *Looking back over your novels, which ones do you consider your best?*

GG: *The Power and the Glory, Monsignor Quixote, The Honorary Consul,* and *Travels With My Aunt.*

JP: *I see you've chosen two books of high spirit—comedies, really—and two rather dark works. You seem to oscillate between these types of books.*

GG: I'm a manic-depressive by nature.

JP: *In a clinical sense?*

GG: Just temperamentally. I have periods when I'm more or less manic and times when I'm depressed. But I live more on a plateau in old age. I'm less depressed now, more manic.

JP: *Could you reflect on the American phase of the war in Vietnam?*

GG: It was a fatal mistake for Kennedy to get involved in Vietnam. The Geneva Accords called for free elections. Had they been allowed, Ho Chi Minh would have been elected by the whole country and you would have had a kind of Yugoslavia in Southeast Asia dominated by neither Russia nor China.

JP: *Your novel about Vietnam,* The Quiet American, *which you wrote in 1955, was strangely prophetic, wasn't it?*

That is, it foreshadows American involvement in that country—with disastrous results.

GG: Yes. It was extremely unpopular in the United States when it first appeared.

JP: *How did you react to the Vietnamese invasion of Cambodia after the U.S. withdrawal? As you can imagine, there was a lot of "I told you so" going around.*

GG: I'm sympathetic with the Vietnamese. Pol Pot[16] was a tyrant, supported by China. He killed millions, of course. It was a warranted invasion. The Vietnamese intend, I believe, to pull out. But Pol Pot is very much alive.

JP: *Are you a Marxist or a Communist?*

GG: I'm not an economist. If I had to find a phrase, I'd say I was a social democrat.

JP: *Are you working on anything right now?*

GG: I'm doing a little book about epitaphs, nothing serious. Apart from that, I have no plans.

Extracted from Jay Parini, "Getting to Know Graham Greene," *Interview* 18 (1988): 70–73.

Notes

1. Greene's dislike for journalists has become legendary. See note 6 on p. 395 of the Norman Lebrecht excerpt, "Commitment to Central America and a Passion for Religion."

2. Sir Rider Haggard (1856–1925) was mostly remembered for his novels of African adventure. Greene notes his "discovery" of Haggard in *A Sort of Life* (51), but, two decades earlier, in his 1951 review of a biography of Haggard—written by Haggard's daughter—Greene acknowledges the "enchantment" that the adventure novelist had exercised over him.

   Anthony Hope, pseudonym for Sir Anthony Hope Hawkins (1863–1933), English novelist chiefly remembered for the creation of the romantic domain of Ruritania as a setting for novels such as *The Prisoner of Zenda* and *Rupert of Hentzau.*

Stanley [John] Weyman (1825–1928) was a lawyer and author of historical novels, such as *Gentleman of France* (1893).

3. E. W. Hornung (1866–1921), Arthur Conan Doyle's brother-in-law, best remembered for his creation of A. J. Raffles, the gentleman burglar, who made his first appearance in *The Amateur Cracksman* (1899).

4. See note 27 on p. 428 of the Maria Couto excerpt, "The Solitude of the Writer and Political Involvement."

5. Though Greene almost always wields a psychological scalpel, his "consanguinity" with the stream of consciousness is largely limited to his early novels.

6. This is the opening line of Browning's "The Lost Leader." Evelyn Waugh had refused to review *A Burnt-Out Case* for the *Daily Mail* because he disapproved of the moral implications of the novel — a revival, in fact, of the dispute over Scobie in *The Heart of the Matter* that took place in public in the pages of the *Tablet* (June–July 1948). This time the discussion remained private and, according to Christopher Sykes, "No bones were broken, and the friendship in no way faltered." *Evelyn Waugh: A Biography* (Boston: Little, Brown, and Co., 1975), 432.

7. For information on Claud Cockburn and Peter Quennell, see notes in the list of Contributors.

8. For the "aesthetes," see note 4 on p. 47 of the A. L. Rowse excerpt, "Graham Greene: Perverse Genius."

9. The epigraph to *Getting to Know the General* is not from Browning but from Tennyson ("Audley Court," lines 70–71). All Greene's novels, with the exception of *The Confidential Agent* and *Travels with My Aunt*, have epigraphs. He often uses epigraphs to sum up a conflict or underline a theme. See "The Significance of Epigraphs in Graham Greene's Work," *Journal of English Studies* (Pradesh, India) 10, vol. 1 (1978): 633–48.

10. [Avril] Noam Chomsky (1928–) is an American linguist and political activist who began a revolution in linguistics with his *Syntactic Structures* (The Hague: Mouton, 1957). His critiques of American foreign policy began with his outspoken opposition to American military involvement in Vietnam with *American Power and the New Mandarins* (London: Chatto and Windus; New York: Pantheon Books, 1968) and have continued in seven

or eight volumes. *Turning the Tide* (Boston: South End Press) appeared in 1985.

11. On 18 August 1987, in Guatemala City, the presidents of El Salvador, Guatemala, Honduras, and Nicaragua agreed to a plan proposed by Oscar Arias Sanchez, the president of Costa Rica. The accord proposed a ceasefire, effective 7 November, to implement the reforms in the Arias plan that included, among other items, the restoration of the freedom of the press and political association, a general amnesty, and internationally-observed elections.

12. Tomás Borge was the Minister of the Interior then.

13. The opening paragraph of Part I of *Getting to Know the General* refers to the winter of 1976 as the time when Greene received the telegram inviting him to visit Panama.

14. Norman Sherry, FRSL, professor of literature, Trinity University, San Antonio, Texas.

15. To date, this play has not been performed nor has it been published.

16. Pol Pot was named premier of Cambodia after the March 1976 elections. In 1977, the Communist Party of Kampuchea was officially recognized as the country's governing body.

Why I Am Still a Catholic

John Cornwell

The apartment was tiny, modest; his living room floodlit with Mediterranean sun from the sliding balcony window. There was just room for a cane sofa with cushions, and a matching armchair; a table covered with a simple cloth served as a desk. There were bookshelves with rows of Nelson and Oxford Classics, and other books, well-worn, but meticulously displayed, among them the distinctive covers of the works of Hans Küng. There were several pictures on the walls, exclusively, I judged, of sentimental value.

It might have been the temporary lodging of a celibate schoolmaster, or a priest; the brownish striped wallpaper seemed institutional; not one item betrayed the wealth, the distinction, or even the good taste of its occupant—except perhaps those books.

Traffic roared in the street below. The sound of aircraft indicated the proximity of the flight path to Cannes.

"I normally keep this open, but I'll shut it for your machine," said Greene, pulling the window to.

Then he sat down immediately on the cane sofa and faced me, hunched, as if a trifle apprehensive; there was a hint of the confessional about the proceedings.

"Why," I asked, "here?" I nodded towards the forest of masts in Antibes harbour. "Were there tax advantages?"

He began to laugh breathily.

"No, no. I came to live here so as to be near to the woman I love. I have a girlfriend, a friendship of 30 years. She lives close by. We see each other most other days. She is married, to a Swiss husband; but he is . . . *complaisant.* All parties are in agreement. My friend and I usually have lunch together; spend the afternoon together."

Since we had sat down the years had somehow vanished from him. His skin seemed to glow with health. His hearing was clearly impeccable; his eye-sight penetrating.

"You are perhaps the most famous Catholic layman alive . . .," I began. "But what sort of a Catholic are you? Do you go to church? Do you go to confession? Do you even *believe?*"

"I call myself now a Catholic *agnostic*," he snapped. There was no petulance; but his lips seemed to implode with the emphatic force of the words.

"I go to Mass usually on a Sunday," he went on. "I've got a great friend, a priest from Spain, Fr. Leopoldo Duran, who has permission from his bishop to say the Mass in Latin and say it anywhere, so if he comes here he says it at that table. And if I'm travelling with him, he'll say Mass in the hotel room . . . although only on a Sunday. And to please Fr. Duran I make a confession now—of about two minutes; although I've nothing much to confess at the age of 85; and I take the host then, because that pleases him. There's plenty in my past to confess, which would take a long time, but there's nothing in my present because of age. And lack of belief is not something to confess. One's sorry, but one wishes one could believe. And I pray at night . . . that a miracle should be done and that I *should* believe."

"Did you ever relish confession?" I asked. "In the days when you *had* something to tell?"

"Not much . . . "

"You became a convert to Catholicism more than 60 years ago . . . . "

"A *sort* of convert," he corrected me promptly. "The woman I wanted to marry at that time was a Catholic and a very practising Catholic against the will of her mother, and I thought I should at least understand what she believed in even if I didn't believe in it myself. Therefore I took instructions from a Fr. Trollope and then became convinced that at any rate this might be nearer the truth than the other religions of the world."

"The path to Catholicism is often a quest for greater certainty, a clearer authority. Were you also looking for something like that?"

"I was much more interested in the theological *arguments*. I read a good deal of theology during that period: I thought that the arguments for Catholicism were more convincing than those of other religions."[1]

"Which theological arguments influenced you?"

"Newman, Von Hügel, Unamuno.[2] And I liked Frank Morrison's book *Who Moved the Stone?* I liked Unamuno's spirituality; and especially his book on Cervantes. I enjoyed reading that more than Don Quixote itself. I also love Unamuno's *The Tragic Sense of Life*."

"But what do you believe now? I'm wondering how a Greene catechism might read?"

He was looking at me directly, warily.

"You say you take the host to please Fr. Duran. But do you *believe* in communion?—the Real Presence in the Eucharist?"

"I believe in it as a commemoration of what I think happened at the Last Supper. A *commemoration.* Not necessarily to be taken literally."

Every word was precisely enunciated. He was looking at me defiantly, I thought.

"There are places in Africa," he went on, "where there is no idea even of *bread* in our sense, and no means to make or acquire it. How can one be too literal, too dogmatic, about the way in which the Eucharist is understood?"

"You talk about having had plenty to confess in your own past life. But did you actually believe in sin in a theological sense?"

"I've always rather disliked the word sin," he said promptly. "It's got a kind of professional, dogmatic ring about it. Crime, I don't mind the word crime, but the word sin has got a kind of priestly tone. I believe that one does something *wrong* . . . and it may be a little wrong and it may be a big wrong. I never liked that strict division of mortal sin and venial sin in the Catholic Church. And then again, it depends on the consequences; some apparent little wrongs can cause more pain than apparent big wrongs. It depends on the circumstances and human relations."

"Your characters are often trapped between their weaknesses and their consciences. Do you think that temptation, a sense of guilt, adds to the spice of life?"

"No. I'd rather be without it."

"And what about Satan? Do you believe in the devil, or in demons?"

Greene smiled wanly. "No. I don't think so."

"Do you believe in angels?"

A chuckle. "No, I *don't* really."

"Do you believe in hell?"

"I don't believe in hell. I never have believed in hell. I think it's contradictory. They say that God is mercy . . . so it's contradictory. I think there may be *nullity,* and for others something that is conscious. But I don't believe in hell and I feel that purgatory may happen in *this* life, not in a future life."

"By nullity you mean annihilation?"

"Yes. Hell is suffering; but nullity is not suffering.

"And who deserves this nullity?"

"People like Hitler . . . he would be wiped out."

"And what about yourself? Are you optimistic about your own survival beyond death?"

"Well, I would love to believe in it. And there is a mystery somehow. And one would like to let it be more than this world."

"Do you fear death?"

"No, and especially now . . . . I'd like it to come quickly. What I fear is lingering illness. I had cancer of the intestine ten years ago. I assumed that that would be that, so I wrote a number of letters and tried to arrange things in a nice way as far as I could without mentioning why. But I don't feel any fear of death."

"And what about heaven?"

"I couldn't conceive what heaven could be. If it exists it's an entity I can't visualise in any way. My idea of heaven would be that it would be something active, rather than happiness with people one had loved, a form of activity in which we could influence life on earth . . . perhaps one's prayers in that state could influence somebody on earth."

He paused for almost half a minute before adding: "I think that an inactive heaven is rather a sense of boredom."

"It's difficult to imagine," I ventured, "any kind of human existence without one's body and personal memories . . . . "

"Yes," he intervened swiftly, "and if one had that one would want to make use of it."

"I suppose one's ideas about heaven depend on one's notion of God. How do you think about God?"

He fell silent. For a moment his eyes looked strangely shifty, haunted.

"Do you contemplate God in a pure, disembodied way?" I asked.

"I'm afraid I don't," he said flatly.

"You think of God as Christ?"

"Yes, more . . . yes, that's closer to it."

"It sounds as if belief is a struggle for you."

He sat musing for a while. "What keeps me to . . . it's not strong enough to be called belief . . . is St. John's gospel, it's almost a reportage, it might have been done by a good journalist, where the beloved disciple is running with Peter because they've heard that the rock has been rolled away from the tomb, and describing how John manages to beat Peter in the race . . . and it just seems to me to be first-hand reportage, and I can't help believing it . . . . I know that St. Mark is supposed to be the earliest gospel, but there's just the possibility of St. John's gospel having been written by a very old man, who never calls himself by name, or say 'I,' but does describe this almost funny race, which strikes me as true."

"Don't you think there's a rational basis for a belief in God? Or the after-life?"

Greene looked down for a brief moment into his lap, unsmilingly. Then he began to chuckle breathily with raised shoulders. "That reminds me of Freddie Ayer," he said, "you know, the atheistic philosopher.[3] He always said that given just half an hour he would convince me that there was absolutely *nothing.*"

"Did you ever take him up on that?"

"No. It would have bored me," he said with some feeling. "Anyway, I've never really been able to understand logical positivism."[4]

Then, after a pause. "Professor Ayer began to hedge a little towards the end. He claimed to have died for four minutes in the Fulham Road hospital. But I didn't find his near-death experience all that convincing. What puzzled me was how did he know whether he had seen his great bright light *after* his heart had stopped rather than *before* his heart had stopped? In any case, after the heart stops a certain consciousness surely remains in the brain."

I said: "Do you really think that God intervenes in the affairs of man in miraculous, or mystical ways?"

Greene smiled wryly and hunched his shoulders. "Well . . . I don't know. I feel it's a mystery. There is a mystery. There is something inexplicable in human life. And it's important because people are not going to believe in all the explanations given by the Church. . . . Curiously, I carry a photograph of Padre Pio in my wallet."

Greene took a well-worn wallet from his trouser pocket and fished out two small photographs. They were slightly dog-eared; sepia. As he handed them to me I detected a faint air of self-consciousness; as if, English gentleman that he was, he had been caught out in a gesture of Romish extravagance.

One depicted Padre Pio in his habit, smiling. The other showed him gazing adoringly at the host during Mass.

"Why do you keep them in your wallet like that?" I asked.

"I don't know. I just put them in, and I've never taken them out."

"When you visited Padre Pio were you looking for something at that time?"

"I may have been. During those years I was more or less attached to a woman who had great faith, and that may have influenced me to try and strengthen my own."

"And Padre Pio seems to have given you that desired stimulus. . ."

"Well, at any rate, it introduced a *doubt* in my *disbelief*." Greene laughed gently, an air of self-mockery.

He went on: "Padre Pio had asked for a hospital to be built, which seemed to me a remarkable request for a man who could heal people miraculously. He had a doctor friend who had come there to look after the hospital project, and that is where I stayed. It was through this doctor that I was invited to go for a personal interview in the monastery. And I refused because I said I didn't wish to change my life."

"You thought he might have made a saint of you?"

"No . . . but I might have lost the person I loved."

He looked up, almost a glance of mischief. Then his face became earnest.

"Padre Pio had strange powers. There was one famous case I knew of: a boy of about 16 who was in great pain with cancer. The mother went to see Padre Pio and he told her that he would take the pain on himself. The boy's pain immediately departed and during that period I heard from my friend who often visited there that at intervals during the Mass Padre Pio looked as if he was convulsed with agony. The boy eventually died, but without pain. These were stories by people who knew him and were on the spot."

"If you hadn't had your mysterious experience with Padre Pio you might possibly have lost your faith?"

"I don't think my belief is very strong; but, yes, perhaps I would have lost it altogether . . . . "

"Do you have a veneration for any other saint?"

"No." He looked at me directly again. "But I've always had a certain sympathy for Thomas the Doubter."

"Your faith, then, is tenuous."

"One is attracted to the *Faith*," he said with a wry smile. "Believing is the problem."

~

"Do you ever wonder what it might have been like to be a monk?"

"I'm afraid I like women far too much for that." He rocked to and fro a little with mirth.

"When James Joyce portrayed the struggle between the vocations of priest and writer in *Portrait of the Artist*, he argued that the writer was pitched in rivalry against God — that the writer's instinctive attitude was 'Non serviam.'"

"I do not know that the writer is *against* God. But the writer in a sense is a little God working by instinct; for example, I've found that the beginning of a book is very sticky and I generally know roughly the beginning and roughly the end; I know nothing about the middle, and I sometimes put in something that makes no sense whatever, it doesn't seem to help the character or action or anything else. And then perhaps a year later, as I'm approaching the end, the reason for it appears as if without knowing, by instinct, that this particular thing would be needed 150 pages along."

"Is this being *guided* by God, or being God-*like*?"

"God-*like*," Greene chuckled. "It's this ability to control the past, present and future . . . . " He paused for a moment, his eyes alert as if striving for a recollection. He went on: "Once in the midst of *A Burnt-Out Case* I was completely blocked and I didn't know how to go on, and on my way through Rome I had a dream which was not my own dream, it was the dream of my character; and the next day I put it into the manuscript and I became unblocked: the book went on . . . . Somehow there's a parallel there with the mystery of individual free will and predestination."[5]

"You will always be remembered as a *Catholic* writer. Do you like that idea?"

"I always claim *not* to be a Catholic writer. They only *discovered* that I was a Catholic after I wrote *Brighton Rock.* I'm a writer who happens to be a Catholic. Not a Catholic writer. And that's what Paul VI meant when he told me that my books would always offend some Catholics, and that I shouldn't pay any attention."

"Do you think that becoming a Catholic made you a better writer?"

"I think I was in revolt against the Bloomsbury School, E. M. Forster, Virginia Woolf, and I thought that one of the things that gave reality to characters was the importance of human beings with a future world: it made the characters far more important . . . . I found a certain flatness in the Bloomsbury circle of writers. There was something missing."

~~~~~

"A lot of things have changed in the Catholic Church since you became a convert in 1927. Do you find the Church today more, or less, to your liking?"

"I'm very uncomfortable with the Church's teaching on contraception. I think that contraception is vital for human life. And instead of that, through the Church's teaching, you have an increase in abortions which one is reluctant to see; but overpopulation in Africa and all round the world I think that contraception and planned birth is a necessity. In any case, it was quite clear that the majority of bishops under Paul VI were in favour of contraception, but he ignored it and went his own way; even though he made it clear it was his own way and it could be changed. So I'm very uncomfortable with the present Pope, who wants to enforce the old rules."

"One of your characters in *The Power and the Glory* says that the faithful should be loyal to the Church they have — rather than some ideal of a Church that does not exist."[6]

"I've always been very keen on Newman, because he believed in the development of Christian doctrine, that the Church can change. It's not stuck in a rut — this is *true* and that's *untrue*."

He paused for a moment. His face seemed to cloud over. "Don't you find," he continued, "that the Roman Curia reminds you a little bit of the *Politburo?*" He mused for a while, before adding, with a little sigh, "But even the Politburo is changing."

"You once said that your relationship to the Church was that of a member of the Foreign Legion fighting for a city from which you were in exile. Does one go into exile in the desert — join the Foreign Legion — because it's impossible to live up to the high ideals of the imperial capital?"

"Ideals can be good or bad, and what I feel is that the Church at the moment is enforcing bad ideals. I think humanity demands control of birth. I wouldn't call the Church's attitude there an ideal, I would call it an ideology. . .

"In *The Power and the Glory* you depicted courageous priests who faced death rather than abandon their calling. Does it depress you to see so many priests nowadays abandoning their ministries?"

"It does not depress me. I accept it as a fact, and I tend to put the blame on those who are now in authority in the Church." Greene leant forward, staring at the floor intently. "When I was with the Gurkhas in Malaya," he continued, "I met an army chaplain; after dinner I found myself alone with him. I brought up the subject, and he said: 'We're losing more people from the Church with this contraception thing than anything else.' And he said that in the confessional directly somebody started confessing about contraception he would change the subject at once and ask — 'Have you done anything against charity?' That seemed to be a reasonable attitude in a priest."

Greene was now staring at me challengingly. There was a hint of combat.

"Don't you believe," I asked, "that the Catholic Church is entitled to put forward arguments from natural law?"

"Well, I think it's an *un*-natural law," he countered emphatically. "Sex is not only a question of pleasure. They run down *love*, and call it *pleasure*."

"Did you ever confess the 'sin' of contraception yourself?"

"No . . . I don't think I ever confessed that," he said guardedly.

"But did you practise it during the days when it was universally regarded in the Church as a mortal sin?"

"I used to try and *manage* it," he said, a cautious note in his voice. "Because my wife was very much afraid. Her mother had made her afraid of childbirth, and at the same time I didn't want her conscience to be upset. I tried to manage things skilfully . . . but a child did come in the end."

"You've been very outspoken in politics. Have you used your position as a leading Catholic writer to affect the opinion of church leaders on birth control?"

"I had lunch alone with Cardinal John Heenan, at the time of Vatican II. And a friend of mine, Archbishop David Mathew, said, 'For goodness sake don't bring up contraception!' But I *did*. And I told the cardinal that I knew two Catholic girls who'd had abortions, but which they would not have had if they had been practising contraception. We talked quite a bit, and he seemed to become much more moderate in the course of our conversation. And I think I did influence him."

"From what you say, you're against abortion."

"Yes. At any rate, I'd like to see them reduce the legal number of weeks even further."

"Is there any way out of the contraception dilemma for the Church?"

"I think it could all be solved by a better Pope . . . . "

"So where has this Pope gone wrong?"

"I don't think this Pope has doubt," went on Greene. "I don't think he doubts his own infallibility." He paused, shoulders hunched. "He reminds me a bit of Reagan, you know, John Paul II. He's always on television, isn't he? He's a good actor. And he wanted to be an actor when he was young. He needs a big crowd, or a camera crew. Gorbachev, on the other hand, reminds me much more of John XXIII."

"John Paul lacks doubt, you say, and yet you pray to *believe*."

"In a curious way I've always believed that doubt was a more important thing for human beings. It's *human* to *doubt*. We're now entering a period where Marxism is being doubted by Marxists. I mean, he's no longer infallible,

Marx. And the Pope is no longer infallible. And I think it's a great value, those two aspects. Isn't it lack of doubt that gives rise to fanaticism? We're seeing in Russia doubt raising its head, and we're seeing Catholics rejecting unyielding dogma . . . . In this sense Communism and Christianity are coming closer together; but unfortunately the present Pope is attempting to re-establish infallibility."

"Marxism nevertheless sees human nature as perfectible by social and political change alone. Isn't that a problem for Christians?"

"Don't you think that Marxists are now realising that it's *not* perfectible by *any* means?"

"Yet as a Christian," I said, "you would say that human nature is perfectible through redemption."

"I don't believe in perfectibility *any* way, on *either* side. We can improve conditions, but I don't think we can expect a perfect world. I think that Marxism began to have its own theory of infallibility, and now it's losing it."

"Is it possible to be *right*-wing and a good Christian?"

"It would be perhaps difficult." Greene chuckled to himself. "And difficult also for the complete Marxist to be a Christian."

"Have you involved yourself with liberation theology?"

" . . . Intellectually I like the *idea* of liberation theology—the option for the poor, and their base communities, the determination to spend time in trying to improve their situation, their *morale* rather than their *morals*."

"You've always inclined to the Left, but isn't there nevertheless something fundamentally conservative about the very *notion* of original sin?"

"I've always disliked the phrase original sin. I would rather say that human beings were born with certain *tendencies* for which they were not responsible. And there may be something reactionary about the current leadership of the Church, perhaps, but I don't think that applies to the Church as a whole—the priests and the people. That's the interesting thing about Archbishop Romero: he was regarded before he was made bishop as a reactionary, but immediately he was consecrated he started to attack the military and death squads; and his final sermon was an appeal to the troops to disobey orders rather than to kill. He was the only archbishop since Becket to be killed saying Mass. But he has had very little appreciation or praise in Rome."

"Since you converted to Catholicism, the Church has become more ecumenical; are you strongly ecumenical?"

"I'm *fairly* . . .," a short laugh, "ecumenical, yes. I think I have reservations. I don't think we can expect to be ecumenical with Muslims and Buddhists, and this, that and the other. . . . Or even the Jewish faith. But I'm ecumenical in the Christian communities . . ."

"You said that you were originally attracted by Catholicism because it seemed closer to the truth than any other religion. Did you feel that it was closer to the truth than any other Christian denomination?"

"Yes, I think I felt that."

"And do you still feel it?"

"But I think that it's had worse faults than some of the others. The evil side has been very evident in history. I mean Torquemada,[7] and some of the popes. I wouldn't call the present situation evil, but I would have liked to have a John XXIV."

"Have you ever in your life attempted to convert another person to Catholicism?"

"I tried to *prevent* somebody I was very fond of. I did my best to prevent her, somebody I knew who was *tempted* to become a Catholic. And I . . ." Greene had stopped, to laugh to himself. ". . . I managed to persuade her not to."

"Some people might think that a bit mean."

"Well, I didn't think she'd be really happier for it. She was just temporarily influenced, *too* influenced, perhaps . . . . "

"You have remained loyal to the Catholic Church in a public sort of way. You separated from your wife, for example, and you never divorced. But you've had long-term intimate relationships with other women."

"I have had close relationships with women for quite long periods: 12 years, 11 years, 3 years . . . 30 years!" A short laugh. "They were not one-night stands, as it were. I've *had* one-night stands of course. But my friendships were relationships of a certain depth, and one kept friendship afterwards."

"You see nothing morally wrong with having mistresses?"

"It depends on the three people's point of view, if they're happy that way. Were I living with a wife I wouldn't like to have a mistress in secret, but I think it depends on the happiness of all three people."

"So you feel that your various relationships following your marriage were okay because the various parties were happy with the situation."

"I don't know that my wife was *happy* with the situation. But we got legally separated, and she made a dolls' house museum which occupied a lot of her time . . . she became an authority on dolls' houses. She also has a very nice house of her own."

"You don't believe in divorce?"

"Well, *she* wouldn't have believed in divorce. And it doesn't seem necessary."

"What about an official Church annulment? Would you have considered obtaining one?"

"I think it's part of the church bureaucracy . . . . One trick they can play nowadays is to claim that they were practising birth control from the beginning . . . ." His voice trailed with a faint air of disapproval.

"How devout are you nowadays as a Catholic, in a personal way? Do you pray? Do you say an occasional 'Our Father'?"

"If you go off in an aeroplane and something begins to go wrong, you don't say an 'Our Father,' you say a 'Hail Mary.' Most people do, I think. And yet even the feminists seem to be running down the stature of Mary in the Church. I automatically say a 'Hail Mary' when the plane leaves the ground. I've only had two crash-landings in my life, and I'm not afraid of aeroplanes, but I do it almost automatically."

"Do you believe in the power of prayer?"

"I *hope* that it does something." He looked tense for a moment, chortled a little to himself. "And I *do* pray . . . in some detail, at night. Generally *for* people."

"Formal prayers?"

"I say a 'Hail Mary.' And then I specify . . . things."

"Do you spend long praying?"

"No, five minutes perhaps."

"Do you pray the psalms?"

"The psalms *bore* me. And the Old Testament . . . . I made fun of it in my last book. Specially Ezekiel.[8] I like one or two hymns, quite minor poetry as it were. 'Abide With Me' I like."

"Devotion to Mary is often a stumbling block to non-Catholic Christians. Do you subscribe to a special devotion to her?"

"I don't care for *Mariolatry* very much . . . ."

"Do you ever fear," I said provocatively, "the 'eye of the needle'?—You must be very rich." Looking around me at the modesty of his apartment I realised that my question was even more ironic than I had intended.

"I've given it all away," said Greene simply. "I'm paid a salary by a fund in Switzerland. There was a time when I had a wife and two children, and I was down to my last £20."

He was giving his snuffled laugh again. "When I realised that I was doomed to go on living forever, I felt I should let my children enjoy my money now rather than wait for it. They both have very nice houses."

"How much property do you own yourself?"

"Apart from this place I have a flat in Paris—a friend of mine lives there at present. I have a house in Anacapri, which is usually occupied: I bought that with the money I made on *The Third Man*."

"At 85, you must think of death rather often."

Greene laughed again. "I had an uncle who died at the age of 92, falling out of a tree . . . he was trying to cut away a dead branch."

"What, in the final analysis," I said, "does your religion mean to you?"

Greene looked at me directly, wonderingly. He was raising his glass delicately to his lips. He seemed at that moment ageless; there was an impression about him of extraordinary tolerance, ripeness.

"I think . . . it's a *mystery*," he said slowly and with some feeling. "It's a mystery which can't be destroyed . . . even by the *Church* . . . . A certain *mystery*."

Then he sipped his cocktail with immense relish.

Extracted from John Cornwell, "Why I Am Still a Catholic," *Tablet*, 23 September 1989, 1085–89.

Notes

1. Cf. his statement to Joachim Fest on the same topic: "The arguments . . . convinced me that Catholicism perhaps came closer to the truth than did *my lack of belief.*" Joachim Fest, "Graham Greene at Eighty: Musings on Writing, Religion, and Politics," *World Press Review,* December 1984, 31–32. (My italics).

2. Baron Friedrich von Hügel (1852–1925) Austrian-born English theologian was founder of the London Society for the Study of Religion and author of *The Mystical Element in Religion* and *The Reality of God.*

   Miguel de Unamuno (1864–1936) was a Spanish philosopher and writer, the author of *The Life of Don Quixote and Sancho,* and a volume of religious poetry.

3. Sir Alfred Jules Ayer (1910–89), English philosopher and professor of philosophy at Oxford (1947–59), was the author of *Language, Truth, and Logic* (London: Gollancz, 1936) that aroused much hostility by reducing the significance of moral and religious discourse.

4. Positivism, the philosophical system originated by the French philosopher and social theorist Auguste Comte (1798–1857), maintained that knowledge is restricted to phenomena and that such knowledge is relative, not absolute. Logical positivism is a twentieth century development, of Viennese origin, much concerned with determining whether or not statements are meaningful and insisting on the distinctive nature of logical and mathematical truth to the exclusion of "transcendent" knowledge.

5. For Greene's fascination with dreams, see note 2 on p. 18 of the Claud Cockburn excerpt, "An Early and Incipient Fascination with Dreams."

6. When the wife is worried about her son for having spoken to Padre José, the husband says: "This is a small town. And there's no use pretending. We have been abandoned here. We must get along as best as we can. As for the Church—the Church is Padre José and the whisky priest—I don't know of any other. If we don't like the Church, well, we must leave it." *The Power and the Glory,* 28.

7. Tomas de Torquemada (1420–98), Spanish Dominican priest and first inquisitor-general of Spain who displayed pitiless cruelty in discharging his duties. He is largely responsible for the expulsion of Jews from Spain, and his name is generally associated with the horrors of the Inquisition.

8. In Greene's last novel, Liza persists on Sunday Bible readings so "Jim" embarrasses her by reading from Ezekiel 5:1–4 and 23: 17–19. *The Captain and the Enemy,* 69–70.

Epilogue

Graham Greene's wanderlust and interest in world affairs, especially in socialism with a human face, never seems to have diminished with age. Between 1986 and 1989, for example, he visited the then USSR three times and, in his speech before Mikhail Gorbachev in 1987 at the Kremlin, he disclosed his "dream" for cooperation between Roman Catholics and communists and for the occasion when there would be an ambassador of the Soviet Union "giving good advice at the Vatican." One of his last public appearances was in Dublin in November 1989 when he was invited to present book awards to John Banville and Vincent McDonnell.

When Greene was not obsessively traveling to the world's troubled spots or searching for authentic material for his novels, he resided and worked in his sparsely furnished, modest, two-room apartment on the fourth floor of a building overlooking the harbor in Antibes, the only town on the Côte d'Azur, he once wrote, where he "could have borne to live." He spent much less time in his Paris apartment or his house in Anacapri. It was in Antibes where he adhered to his routine of writing 300 words per day before turning to his daily activities and his letter writing. It was also in Antibes where he wrote *May We Borrow Your Husband?*, a collection of short stories set in the Côte, and all the works that followed.

Greene feared senility and old age even more than he feared death. He once indicated that he would rather die in a plane crash. But it was not to be. After living in Antibes for more than twenty-five years, Greene was forced to leave the city he loved best for Switzerland because of ill health. In a moving handwritten letter to Pierre Merli, the mayor of Antibes, Greene regretfully announced on 7 March 1991 his decision to change his residence from Antibes to be close to the hospital and the physician treating him. Even then, he retained his apartment, though there must have been little doubt in his mind that he would ever return to it.

Greene's career as reporter, publisher, biographer, writer of children's books, critic, dramatist, and novelist came to an end on 3 April 1991 when he died at the age of eighty-six in Vevey, Switzerland. His life-long study of humankind's evil, combined with his accomplished story-telling skills and his desire to address topical issues of the times, makes him one of this century's great writers, managing both to combine entertainment with seriousness. His use of the popular form of the thriller as a vehicle for serious thought often disconcerted critics and frustrated any attempt at pigeonholing him as a novelist. By extending the boundaries of the English novel to include religious, social, and political dimensions, and by breaking the confines of provincialism, Graham Greene has achieved international fame and gained the recognition and respect of his confrères. But it is not just his legacy as novelist that continues to intrigue, entertain, and provoke; the "enigma" of Graham Greene continues to tease the reader. Any frontal assault to know the man only from his works is fruitless and fraught with hazard; but the few interviews he gave, people's recollections of him, and his letters to the press shed much needed light for, in the words of David Pryce-Jones, "Graham Greene is his own most complex creation."[1]

Notes
1. David Pryce-Jones, "Graham Greene: The Novelist as Enigma," *Now*, 27 February 1981, 32.

Supplementary Reading List

Allain, Marie-Françoise. "Entretien. Graham Greene: le danger m'interesse moins qu'autrefois." *Nouvelles Littéraires*, 28 August 1980, 19.

Allen, Walter. *As I Walked Down New Grub Street: Memories of a Writing Life*. London: Heinemann, 1981; Chicago: University of Chicago Press, 1982.

Amis, Martin. "Graham Greene at Eighty." *Observer*, 23 September 1984, 7.

Barrat, R. "Graham Greenes Bekehrung." *Neues Abendland* (Augsburg) 4, no. 22 (1949): 338–39.

Boyle, Raymond M. "Man of Controversy." *Grail* 35 (July 1952): 1–7.

Bryden, Ronald. "Graham Greene Discusses the Collected Edition of his Novels." *Listener*, 23 April 1970, 544–45.

Burgess, Anthony. "Graham Greene: 'Mes personnages sont des miteux . . . pas moi!'" *Le Point* 399 (12 May 1980): 174–75.

_____. "A Talk With Graham Greene." *Saturday Review*, May 1982, 44–47.

Burstall, Christopher. "Graham Greene Takes the Orient Express." *Listener*, 21 November 1968, 672–74, 676–77.

Catholic Profiles: Series 1. Introduction by Michael de la Bedoyère. London: Paternoster Publications, 1945.

Cendre, Anne. "Graham Greene: 'Non, je n'écrirai pas de memoires . . . Ce serait indiscret!'" *Le Soir*, 1–2 January 1974, 7.

Charles-Roux, Père J. M. "Un Souvenir de Graham Greene." *Adam International Review* 46, nos. 446–48 (1984): 23–25.

Church, Richard. "Graham Greene." In *British Authors: A Twentieth-Century Gallery with 58 Portraits.* British Council Series. London: Longmans, Green, and Co., 1943.

Coffey, Raymond R. "Winning His Lifelong Battle against Boredom." *Washington Post*, 4 April 1976, K1 and K3.

Cunningham, John. "Plain Thoughts of an Englishman Abroad." *Guardian*, 19 December 1983, 11.

Edwards, Sydney. "A Rare Interview in News of the Arts." *Evening Standard*, 28 November 1975, 24.

Fallowell, Duncan. "An Interview with the Man Who Never Gives Interviews." *It*, September 1983, 41–42, 48, 54.

Fest, Joachim. "Graham Greene at Eighty: Musings on Writing, Religion, and Politics." *World Press Review*, December 1984, 31–32.

French, Philip. "Man of Mystery: The Enigma of Graham Greene." *Listener*, 4 October 1979, 441–43.

Garric, Alain. "Greene à Antibes: L'aventure en hiver." *Libération*, 18 December 1984, 24–25.

Gilliatt, Penelope. "Profiles: The Dangerous Edge." *New Yorker*, 26 March 1979, 43–44, 47–50.

"Graham Greene." *Plays and Players* 6, no. 10 (1959): 5.

Greene, Sir Hugh. "Childhood with Graham." *Adam International Review* 46, nos. 446–48 (1984): 8–14.

"Greeneland Aboriginal." *New Statesman*, 13 January 1961, 44–45.

[Grindea, Miron]. "A la recherche de Graham Greene." *Adam International Review* 46, nos. 446–48 (1984): 4–7.

Harwood, Ronald. "Time and the Novelist—Graham Greene Interviewed." *Listener*, 4 December 1975, 747 and 749.

Igoe, W. J. "Living Writers—7: Graham Greene." *John O'London's*, 6 July 1961, 24–25.

Jerrold, Douglas. "Graham Greene, Pleasure-Hater." *Picture Post*, 15 March 1952, 51–53.

Jouve, Père, and Marcel Moré. "Propos de table avec Graham Greene." *Dieu Vivant* 16 (1950): 127–37.

Joannon, Pierre. "Graham Greene Breaks the Silence." *Speak Up,* 12 March 1988, 30–33.

Kershaw, Alex. "An End of the Affairs." *Guardian Weekend,* 31 October 1992, 6–10.

Lambert, J. W. "Knowing the Worst." *Adam International Review* 46, nos. 446–48 (1984): 17–19.

Leblanc, Alain. "Graham Greene: 'A 78 ans, je me leve toujours avec le même enthousiasme.'" *Paris-Match* (1982): 32.

Lemoyne, James. "Looking Back—and Ahead." *Los Angeles Times,* 25 September 1980, sec. 5, p. 17.

Lewin, David. "Greene: The Power of His Glory." *Los Angeles Times,* 24 June 1979, 43.

Mayne, Richard. "Collected Guilt." *Listener,* 2 April 1970, 455–56.

"Men Who Fascinate Women." *Look,* 6 September 1955, 43.

Meyer, Michael. "Greene Test." *Listener,* 3 January 1980, 10.

Mortimer, John. "The Master Is Still Learning." *Critic* 39, no. 1 (1980): 4–6.

Moutet, Anne-Elizabeth. "Graham Greene, Still Seeing Red." *Sunday Telegraph,* 10 May 1987, 15.

Naipaul, V. S. "Graham Greene." *Daily Telegraph Magazine,* 8 March 1968, 28–32.

Newcombe, Jack. "Greene, 'The Funny Writer,' on Comedy." *Life,* 23 January 1970, 10.

"A New Honor and a New Novel." *Life,* 4 February 1966, 43–44.

Nicholson, Jenny. "Graham Greene: A Third Man of Real Life." *Picture Post,* 14 August 1954, 18–19.

Oakes, Philip. "Graham Greene." *Sunday Times,* 1 March 1970, 58.

Parinaud, André. "La leçon de vengeance de Graham Greene." *Arts,* 25 April 1956, 1, 6.

Peyrefitte, Alain. "Graham Greene: Un agent secret dans les mystères de l'âme." *Figaro Littéraire,* 15 April 1991, 8.

"Profile: Graham Greene." *Observer,* 27 November 1949, 2.

Pryce-Jones, David. "Graham Greene: The Novelist as Enigma." *Now,* 27 February 1981, 32, 34, 36.

R[aman], A. S. "Chiaroscuro." *The Illustrated Weekly of India,* 19 January 1964, 20–21.

Reinhardt, Max. "Publishing Graham Greene." *Adam International Review* 46, nos. 446–48 (1984): 25–26.

Rosenblum, Mort. "Graham Greene at Seventy-seven: No 'Final Words.'" *St. Louis Post-Dispatch,* 12 September 1982, sec. 3L.

Sabov, Aleksandr. "Grèm Grin: 'Mir gluboko, neuznavaemo izmenilsia . . . ' " *Literaturnaia Gazeta* 38 (17 September 1986): 15. (In Russian).

Schmidthues, K. G. "Graham Greene." *Die neue Heimat* (Berlin) 4 (1959): 429–33.

Servadio, Gaia. "Another Shade of Greene." *Evening Standard,* 9 January 1978, 17.

Shuttleworth, Martin, and Simon Raven. "The Art of Fiction III: Graham Greene." *Paris Review* 1 (autumn 1953): 25–41.

Shuttleworth, Katherine. "Graham Greene." *Book-of-the-Month Club News,* June 1948, 6–7.

Solomon, Petre. "A Sort of Friendship." *Adam International Review* 46, nos. 446–48 (1984): 33–36.

Todd, Olivier. "Graham Greene: 'Je ne crois pas à l'enfer et au diable.'" *Le Point* 968 (8 April 1991): 92–94.

Valerie, Odette. "Graham Greene reconnait aujourd'hui: 'J'ai choisi la France a cause de ses grands vins.' " *Paris Match,* 30 June 1978, 42.

Vinocur, John. "The Soul-Searching Continues for Graham Greene." *New York Times Magazine,* 3 March 1985, 36–39.

Wardle, Irving. "Graham Greene." *Plays and Players* 12, no. 1 (1964): 7.

Wastberg, Per. "The Empire of Imagination." *Adam International Review* 46, nos. 446–48 (1984): 29.

Waugh, Auberon. "Profile: Graham Greene." *Daily Mirror,* 22 May 1968, 18.

Wiseman, Thomas. "Graham Greene Tries His Hand at Shaw." *Evening Standard,* 24 August 1956, 6.

Yuenger, James. "It's Not Easy Being Greene, says Graham." *Chicago Tribune,* 25 March 1976, sec. 3, pp. 1 and 2.

Young, Gavin. "Pink Gin and Panama." *Observer,* 12 March 1978, 37.

Chronological Listing of Greene's Works

~~~~~

Novels

The Man Within. London: Heinemann; New York: Doubleday, 1929.

The Name of Action. London: Heinemann, 1930; New York: Doubleday, 1931.

Rumour at Nightfall. London: Heinemann, 1931; New York: Doubleday, 1932.

Stamboul Train. London: Heinemann, 1932; (U.S. title): *Orient Express.* New York: Doubleday, 1933.

It's a Battlefield. London: Heinemann, 1934. New York: Doubleday, 1934.

England Made Me. London: Heinemann; New York: Doubleday, 1935.

A Gun For Sale. London: Heinemann; (U.S. title): *This Gun for Hire.* New York: Doubleday, 1936.

Brighton Rock. London: Heinemann; New York: Viking Press, 1938.

The Confidential Agent. London: Heinemann; New York: Viking Press, 1939.

The Power and the Glory. London: Heinemann; (U.S. title): *The Labyrinthine Ways.* New York: Viking Press, 1940.

The Ministry of Fear. London: Heinemann; New York: Viking Press, 1943.

The Heart of the Matter. London: Heinemann; New York: Viking Press, 1948.

The End of the Affair. London: Heinemann; New York: Viking Press, 1951.

Loser Takes All. London: Heinemann, 1955; New York: Viking Press, 1957.

The Quiet American. London: Heinemann, 1955; New York: Viking Press, 1956.

Our Man in Havana. London: Heinemann; New York: Viking Press, 1958.

A Burnt-Out Case. London: Heinemann; New York: Viking Press, 1961.

The Comedians. London: Bodley Head; New York: Viking Press, 1966.

Travels with My Aunt. London: Bodley Head; New York: Viking Press, 1969.

The Honorary Consul. London: Bodley Head; New York: Simon and Schuster, 1973.

The Human Factor. London: Bodley Head; New York: Simon and Schuster, 1978.

Doctor Fischer of Geneva or The Bomb Party. London: Bodley Head; New York: Simon and Schuster, 1980.

Monsignor Quixote. London: Bodley Head; Toronto: Lester and Orpen Dennys; New York: Simon and Schuster, 1982.

The Captain and the Enemy. London: Bodley Head; Toronto: Lester and Orpen Dennys; New York: Viking Press, 1988.

Other Works

Autobiographies

A Sort of Life. London: Bodley Head; New York: Simon and Schuster, 1971.

Ways of Escape. London: Bodley Head; Toronto: Lester and Orpen Dennys; New York: Simon and Schuster, 1980.

Biographies

Lord Rochester's Monkey. London: Bodley Head; New York: Viking Press, 1974.

An Impossible Woman: The Memories of Dottoressa Moor of Capri. Edited and with an Epilogue by Graham Greene. London: Bodley Head; New York: Viking Press, 1975.

Children's books

The Bear Fell Free. London: Grayson and Grayson, 1935.

The Little Train. London: Eyre and Spottiswoode, 1946; New York: Lothrop, Lee, and Shepard, 1958.

The Little Fire Engine. London: Eyre and Spottiswoode, 1950; (U.S. title): *The Little Red Fire Engine.* New York: Lothrop, Lee, and Shepard, 1953.

The Little Horse Bus. London: Max Parrish, 1952; New York: Lothrop, Lee, and Shepard, 1954.

The Little Steamroller. London: Max Parrish, 1953; (U.S. title): *The Little Steamroller: A Story of Adventure, Mystery, and Detection.* New York: Lothrop, Lee, and Shepard, 1955.

Essays

The Old School. ed. London: Jonathan Cape, 1934.

British Dramatists. London: Collins, 1942.

The Lost Childhood and Other Essays. London: Eyre and Spottiswoode, 1951; New York: Viking Press, 1952.

Essais Catholiques. Trans. Marcelle Sibon. Paris: Editions du Seuil, 1953.

Collected Essays. London: Bodley Head; New York: Viking Press, 1969.

J'accuse: The Dark Side of Nice. London: Bodley Head, 1982.

Film criticism

The Pleasure Dome. London: Secker and Warburg; (U.S. title): *Graham Greene on Film.* New York: Simon and Schuster, 1972.

Film treatments

The Third Man and The Fallen Idol. London: Heinemann; (U.S. title): *The Third Man.* New York: Viking Press, 1950.

The Tenth Man. London: Bodley Head and Anthony Blond; Toronto: Lester and Orpen Dennys; New York: Simon and Schuster, 1985.

Miscellaneous anthologies

The Spy's Bedside Book. Eds. Graham Greene and Hugh Greene. London: Rupert Hart-Davis, 1957.

Yours etc.: Letters to the Press, 1945–89. Ed. Christopher Hawtree. London: Reinhardt Books, 1989.

Reflections. Sel. and intro. Judith Adamson. London: Reinhardt Books in association with Viking Press, 1990.

A World of My Own: A Dream Diary. Ed. Yvonne Cloeta. London: Reinhardt Books; Toronto: Alfred A. Knopf Canada, 1992.

Plays

The Living Room. London: Heinemann, 1953; New York: Viking Press, 1954.

The Potting Shed. New York: Viking Press, 1957; London: Heinemann, 1958.

The Complaisant Lover. London: Heinemann, 1959; New York: Viking Press, 1961.

Carving a Statue. London: Bodley Head, 1964.

The Return of A. J. Raffles. London: Bodley Head, 1975; New York: Simon and Schuster, 1976.

The Great Jowett. London: Bodley Head, 1981. (First broadcast: 6 May 1939, BBC).

Yes and No. London: Bodley Head, 1983.

For Whom the Bell Chimes. London: Bodley Head, 1983.

Collected Plays. Harmondsworth, England: Penguin Books, 1985.

Poetry

Babbling April. Oxford: Basil Blackwell, 1925.

Short stories

The Basement Room and Other Stories. London: Cresset Press, 1935.

Nineteen Stories. London: Heinemann, 1947; New York: Viking Press, 1949.

Twenty-One Stories. London: Heinemann, 1954; New York: Viking Press, 1962.

A Sense of Reality. London: Bodley Head; New York: Viking Press, 1963.

May We Borrow Your Husband? and Other Comedies of the Sexual Life. London: Bodley Head; New York: Viking Press, 1967.

Collected Stories. London: Bodley Head, 1972; New York: Viking Press, 1973.

The Last Word and Other Stories. London: Reinhardt Books; Toronto: Lester and Orpen Dennys; New York: Viking Press, 1990.

Travel

Journey Without Maps. London: Heinemann; New York: Doubleday, 1936.

The Lawless Roads. London: Longmans; (U.S. title): *Another Mexico.* New York: Viking Press, 1939.

In Search of a Character: Two African Journals. London: Bodley Head; New York: Viking Press, 1961.

Getting to Know the General: The Story of an Involvement. London: Bodley Head; Toronto: Lester and Orpen Dennys; New York: Simon and Schuster, 1984.

The Collected Edition of the works (Heinemann and Bodley Head), revised, approved, and introduced by Greene himself, is the definitive edition. The introductions, at once guarded and revealing, have been incorporated into *Ways of Escape.* The forerunner of *The Collected Edition* was *The Uniform Edition* (1949–60), which discontinued after the publication of *The Quiet American.* The same text is used for the *Library Edition* (1959–61). The standard paperback for Greene's works is carried by Penguin Books, which published its first Greene novel, *It's a Battlefield*, in 1940. Paperbacks are also available in the U.S. through Viking's Compass Books and Bantam Books.

Contributors

MARIE-FRANÇOISE ALLAIN is a journalist who teaches courses in American political fiction at the University of Vincennes, Paris. She is the daughter of French Resistance fighter Yves Allain.

H[ERBERT]. E[RNEST]. BATES (1905–74) is the author of twenty-four novels and twenty volumes of short stories and is best remembered by *The Modern Short Story*, perhaps the first of its kind in English on the genre. During the war years, he wrote under the pseudonym "Flying Officer X."

ANTHONY BURGESS (1917–93), was a prolific English novelist whose works are often noted for their black comedy and quasi-religious views. He was also a literary critic.

CLAUD COCKBURN (1904–81), author and journalist noted for his sympathy for the working classes, was Graham Greene's contemporary at Berkhamsted and Oxford. He was the *Times* correspondent in the U.S., then founded the *Week*, took part in the Spanish Civil War (on the Republican side), and became the diplomatic correspondent for the *Daily Worker* until he moved to Ireland in 1947. *I, Claud* . . . is taken from his three autobiographical volumes.

MARIA COUTO, teaches English literature in India and is a freelance writer on film and literature.

NIGEL [FORBES] DENNIS, English novelist, playwright, and critic. He was also staff book reviewer for *Time* and the *Sunday Telegraph*, drama critic for *Encounter* and, for three years, its joint editor.

LOUISE DENNYS, publisher and author, now resident of Toronto, is also Graham Greene's niece.

JEAN DUCHÉ is a French writer well versed in law and literature whose works range from *I Said to My Wife* to the five-volume *History of the World.*

ELIZABETH EASTON was an associate editor at the Book-of-the-Month Club.

GLORIA EMERSON is an American writer and correspondent who covered the Vietnam War from 1970–72.

BARBARA GREENE, Countess Strachwitz, is Graham Greene's first cousin and accompanied him on his trip to Liberia in January 1935.

ALEX JOHN HAMILTON, editor, novelist, and short story writer, is also a columnist and feature writer for the *Guardian,* radio critic for the *Listener,* and a frequent contributor to various magazines.

PIERRE JOANNON was a friend of Graham Greene and is presently editor of *Etudes Irlandaises* and honorary consul for Ireland in the south of France.

FRANK KERMODE, professor of English, King's College, Cambridge, was professor at Manchester University when this interview was conducted. He is one of England's leading critics and is the author of numerous works on critical theory.

KAREL KYNCL is a former Czechoslovak journalist and is now living in England. (Greene had appealed to the Czech authorities in a letter to the *Times* [15 February 1973] to release Kyncl who had been imprisoned for speaking out in October 1970 at the Union of Journalists.)

J[ACK]. W[ALTER]. LAMBERT was assistant literary and arts editor for the *Sunday Times* between 1962 and 1976 and served as associate editor and chief reviewer from 1976 to 1981. He has written on the theater in Britain and has served as member and chairman of various committees associated with the theater.

NORMAN LEBRECHT, freelance writer and music correspondent for the *Sunday Times,* is the author of eight books on musical subjects, among them *Mahler Remembered* (Norton, 1987) and *The Companion to 20th Century Music* (Simon and Schuster, 1993).

DAME ROSE MACAULAY (1881–1958) was an English novelist and author of several travel books. She also published studies on E. M. Forster and John Milton and three volumes of verse. She was a firm believer in the Church of England and expressed her moral and religious views in her writings.

J[ULIAN]. MACLAREN-ROSS (1913–1964) was a freelance writer, author of one novel, a collection of short stories, two memoirs, and numerous articles.

MICHAEL MEWSHAW, American professor, literary critic, and journalist, is the author of several novels and volumes of short stories.

JOHN MORTIMER, English playwright and author, is a regular contributor to periodicals and has written film scripts and television plays, including five in the *Rumpole* series.

MALCOLM [THOMAS] MUGGERIDGE (1903–90), English journalist, critic, and novelist, turned to journalism and writing in 1930 when he joined the liberal *Guardian.* His varied career as a journalist took him to the conservative *Daily Telegraph* in 1946 and to *Punch*, where he was editor from 1953 to 1957. He then joined the BBC and contributed many documentary programs on social, political, moral, and religious issues to *Panorama*, the current affairs television show.

ROBERT OSTERMANN is a World War II veteran who studied philosophy at University College, Cork, Ireland, and entered the Roman Catholic Church in 1947.

JAY PARINI is an American poet and novelist who teaches English at Middlebury College.

GENE D. PHILLIPS, S.J., is a consultant of the National Catholic Office of Motion Pictures in New York, an associate of the National Center for Film Study, and professor of English at Loyola University of Chicago.

OTTO PREMINGER (1906–86), Austrian-born producer and director, emigrated to the United States in October 1935, where he became a naturalized citizen in 1943. His last film, *The Human Factor*, was released in 1979.

SIR V[ICTOR]. S[AWDON]. PRITCHETT, novelist and critic, was also a director of the *New Statesman* and *Nation* and very much interested in travel, especially to Spain.

PETER QUENNELL, biographer, historian, editor, and critic was a contemporary of Graham Greene at Berkhamsted School and at Balliol, Oxford. A freelance writer and former book critic for the *Daily Mail*, he has also edited *Cornhill Magazine* (1944–51) and then coedited *History Today* (1951–79). Most notable among his critical and biographical works are his studies on Byron and Pope.

KATHLEEN RAINE achieved distinction as a poet in the fifties and, later, for her work on William Blake.

CECIL [ERIC MORNINGTON] ROBERTS (1892–1976) was literary editor of the *Liverpool Times* before he became editor of the *Nottingham Journal* (1920–25). He was the author of numerous publications, including travel books, novels, and poems.

CHARLES J. ROLO (1916–82), editor, writer, and columnist, edited *The World of Aldous Huxley* and is the author of *Wingate's Raiders* and *Radio Goes to War*. He also contributed regularly to the *Atlantic*.

A[LFRED]. L[ESLIE]. ROWSE, Fellow of All Soul's College, Oxford, was renowned for his studies of the Elizabethan period and for his controversial views on the dating of Shakespeare's sonnets. He was one of the six undergraduates who took part in the "Oxford Poets' Symposium" on the BBC in 1925.

PHILIPPE SÉJOURNÉ is professor emeritus at Université d'Angers, France.

ISRAEL SHENKER was a reporter for the *New York Times*.

JOHN SUTRO (1903–85), English producer and scriptwriter, was once director of Denham Studios, England.

PHILIP TOYNBEE (1916–81), literary journalist and critic, was also an English novelist noted for his interest in form and technique, especially for his experiments of infusing poetry into the novel.

MARTIN TUCKER is professor of English, Long Island University, in New York.

KENNETH TYNAN (1927–80) was an English drama critic for the *Spectator* and later for the *Observer*. He became literary manager of the National Theatre in 1963.

[ARTHUR] EVELYN [ST. JOHN] WAUGH (1903–66), hailed by Greene as the "greatest novelist of my generation," traveled widely in the thirties before establishing himself as one of England's leading comic novelists. After he was received into the Roman Catholic Church in 1930, the Catholic message became more steadily pronounced in his works. Though he had met Greene during his Oxford days and was acquainted with him and his works in the thirties, the two only became close friends in the postwar years. Their admiration of each other's novels was, on the whole, mutual and genuine.

AUBERON [ALEXANDER] WAUGH, Evelyn Waugh's eldest child, is a novelist and a journalist who has contributed widely to the *New Statesman* and the *Spectator,* among others. He is currently editor of the *Literary Review.*

Editor's note. Diligent research has failed to uncover biographical information for the following names:

GEORGE ADAM.

MADELEINE CHAPSAL.

RONALD DE COUVES MATTHEWS.

JEANINE DELPECH.

JOHN HEILPERN.

DAVID LEWIN.

RICHARD MCLAUGHLIN.

ROY PERROT.

S.V.V.

BERNARD VIOLET.

Index